STAGING CHRIST'S PASSION IN
EIGHTEENTH-CENTURY NAHUA MEXICO

STAGING CHRIST'S PASSION IN EIGHTEENTH-CENTURY NAHUA MEXICO

Louise M. Burkhart

UNIVERSITY PRESS OF COLORADO
Denver

© 2023 by University Press of Colorado

Published by University Press of Colorado
1624 Market Street, Suite 226
PMB 39883
Denver, Colorado 80202

Institute for Mesoamerican Studies
Arts and Sciences
233 University of Albany, SUNY
1400 Washington Avenue
Albany, NY 12222

The University Press of Colorado is a proud member of
the Association of University Presses.

The University Press of Colorado is a cooperative publishing enterprise supported, in part, by Adams State University, Colorado State University, Fort Lewis College, Metropolitan State University of Denver, University of Alaska Fairbanks, University of Colorado, University of Denver, University of Northern Colorado, University of Wyoming, Utah State University, and Western Colorado University.

ISBN: 978-1-64642-449-8 (hardcover)
ISBN: 978-1-64642-450-4 (paperback)
ISBN: 978-1-64642-451-1 (ebook)
https://doi.org/10.5876/9781646424511

Cataloging-in-Publication data for this title is available online at the Library of Congress.

Cover photograph by the author.

Contents

Illustrations

Foreword

MATTHEW RESTALL

How many millions of people on our planet have heard of the Nahuas, and how are the Nahuas perceived? Within Mexico, where millions of Nahuatl speakers still live, the answer is too complicated to address here. Outside Mexico, the diaspora of Nahuatl speakers is extensive but scattered; and the number of people with any knowledge of the Nahuas, past and present, is uncertain but probably low. However, if we narrow the term to "Aztecs," it is likely that such a number would be high and equally likely that the perception of the Aztecs by those many millions would be overwhelmingly negative.

The foundation of that global prejudice was laid with a comprehensive conviction by Spanish conquistadors and settlers, friars and priests, in the sixteenth century—then built on by Europeans on both sides of the Atlantic for centuries to follow. Its purpose was, initially and specifically, to justify colonization and conversion. Then, more broadly and largely unwittingly, it both supported and stemmed from the enterprise of European imperialism worldwide.

That colonialist monolith—call it neo-colonialist and racist too, if you will—is something that Nahuas have had to suffer and endure for centuries. Consequently, it is something that scholars of the Nahuas have been chipping away at for generations. Some have tried sledgehammers, others the tools of master masons, but the effort has been multidisciplinary—involving scholars not only in Mexico itself but in universities across the world, from Canada to Poland to Australia.

https://doi.org/10.5876/9781646424511.c000a

Since the publication of her first book in 1989, the seminal *The Slippery Earth: Nahua-Christian Moral Dialogue in Sixteenth-Century Mexico*, Professor Louise Burkhart has played a major role in that collective effort. Across a dozen volumes and numerous articles, working at the intersection of religious studies, the study of literature and theater, and the ethnohistory of the Nahuas in colonial Mexico—not just working at that intersection but *forging* it as a full-fledged sub-field—Burkhart has transformed our understanding of the Nahuas, their culture, and their experience of and contributions to colonial Mexican life. In doing so, she has provided us and future generations with beautifully sharp tools with which to keep chipping away at that monolithic image of the Aztecs as the *bêtes noires* of the Indigenous Americas.

Staging Christ's Passion is the latest such tool in two ways: it is her most recent study, but it is also the one that draws her keen eye forward in time to the eighteenth century. As is made very clear in the pages that follow, the foundation stone of this monograph is both one play and six, written in Nahuatl in eighteenth-century Mexico and translated by Burkhart into English. She presents us with what she calls "a composite translation" of the Nahuatl Passion play, but only after a full-length monograph that explores the intertextual history of the six plays, how they were developed by Nahuas from one original long-lost version, and why they became controversial. (A digital publication project—passionplaysofeighteenthcenturymexico .omeka.net—acts as a wonderfully rich sibling to this book, offering transcriptions and translations of the Nahuatl plays along with a growing body of relevant documents.)

Amid the many insights contained in the chapters and notes to the book, I am struck in particular by several of them. First, these Passion plays were written very much for local audiences. Like most works of art created throughout human history, we might expect them to have a short shelf life, to be—in the grand scheme of things—ephemeral. But unlike Christ in these Nahuatl versions of the Passion, all of which end with his crucifixion, these works of art have been resurrected. For, as their resurrector asserts, they "deserve a place on a global stage."

Second, these plays are not the result or product of conversion efforts by Spanish mendicants and clergy, a process so long conceived as one in which Nahuas and other Indigenous parishioners in the Americas played passive roles. As Burkhart has been reminding us for decades, Nahuas made the choices that resulted in these texts—and the complex set of beliefs and pious practices they reflected. These Passion plays were not tools of proselytization; Nahuas chose to create and enact them as expressions of *their* faith, *their* religion, *their* community worldview. The underlying story here is as much about the evolutionary persistence of Nahua culture (its "survivance") as it is about Christianity's diffusion.

It is easy to imagine that a Christ suffering torture and slow execution appealed to Indigenous peoples suffering the yoke of colonial rule, especially when we consider that Nahua actors playing Jesus thereby turned Jesus into a Nahua. But that assumption runs the risk of imposing on Nahua culture a melancholic stereotype. In fact, the Christ of the Nahuas was a benevolent patron, whose role was to protect and save his devotees, not to bring them sorrow. There is grim violence in the tale being told, to be sure. But in the end, even if this theatrical Jesus perished, the Nahua actor who played him went home to his family, "bruised and bloodied" but alive.

Alive as a link in the chain of community and culture that permitted these plays to survive in the Nahua literary underground, emerge eventually in print, and then appear online, where this century's Nahuatl speakers can read how their ancestors performed the Passion of *their* Christ.

Acknowledgments

Without two consecutive years of research leave, this book would have been a more modest production and its completion much delayed. I am grateful to the National Endowment for the Humanities (NEH), an independent federal agency, for the fellowship I held in 2019–2020, and to the Kislak Foundation and the John W. Kluge Center, Library of Congress, for appointing me to the Jay I. Kislak Chair for the Study of the History and Cultures of the Early Americas for 2020–2021. I also wish to acknowledge the NEH Scholarly Editions and Scholarly Translations grant that supports the Passion Plays of Eighteenth-Century Mexico digital publication project. This book depends on the transcription and translation work I did for that project; the archive of texts posted there supports further exploration of these plays and their context by readers of this book. I have also benefited from the work my co-PI on that project, Daniel Mosquera, carried out on the Spanish-language plays and related Mexican Inquisition documents. I also thank project personnel Nadia Marín-Guadarrama for her photographs of the Amacuitlapilco and Axochiapan plays and Abelardo de la Cruz de la Cruz for his insights into Nahuatl terminology in the plays.

My first translation endeavors with Nahuatl Passion plays were part of a decade-long collaboration with Barry D. Sell, so I thank him for working with me on the two Passion plays we published in *Nahuatl Theater: Nahua Christianity in Performance*. And I remain indebted to Raul Macuil Martínez for bringing the Passion play from San Simón Tlatlauhquitepec to Barry and me for that project, as it is a vital component of the corpus discussed in this book. John Frederick Schwaller has been a stalwart supporter of my research from the very beginning, and I thank him here for his many insights into the Passion story and its Mexican manifestations, especially as relates to the Stations of the Cross, the subject of his most recent book. I presented aspects of this research to the Northeastern Group of Nahuatl Scholars on multiple occasions. For their helpful comments I thank the group as a whole, especially John Sullivan, Justyna Olko, Gordon Whittaker, Agnieszka Brylak, and Julia Madajckak. The most gratifying aspect of my career has been my connection with the community of scholars of colonial Nahuatl in the United States, Mexico, and Europe; my work builds on that of more people than I can name here.

I thank Walter E. Little, publications director for the Institute for Mesoamerican Studies, University at Albany, State University of New York, for recommending this book for our series with the University Press of Colorado. At the Press, I thank Director Darrin Pratt, Acquisitions Editor Allegra Martschenko, Assistant Director Laura Furney, Production Manager Daniel Pratt, and my copyeditor, Cheryl Carnahan, for supporting the publication and assisting in its completion. Two anonymous readers for the Press offered useful comments that have strengthened the book's content.

Many volumes have been written on the Passion of Christ, and much more could be written just about the Nahuatl plays that are my topic here. I am honored to have this opportunity to bring some aspects of these Indigenous Mexican treatments of the Passion to a wider audience. The *macehualtin* who reset the story in their colonial *altepetl* developed insights and innovations that deserve a place on a global stage.

STAGING CHRIST'S PASSION IN
EIGHTEENTH-CENTURY NAHUA MEXICO

Introduction

This book tells the story of, and the story told by, six Passion play manuscripts from colonial Mexico. Scripted in the Nahuatl language, a lingua franca of both the Aztec Empire and the viceroyalty of New Spain, the plays enact events in Jesus Christ's life leading up to Easter, though no play stages his resurrection. Instead, they track his movements, and those of his friends and enemies, from Palm Sunday through to his death on the cross. They close either while the actor still hangs on the cross or once he is taken down and carried away. Five plays are complete; of the sixth, about two-fifths of the original text survives.

The story of Jesus's self-sacrifice and his triumph over death is Christianity's core mythos, but people of different times and places construe it in different ways. The formal evangelization program that transferred this story to Mexico began in 1524, only three years after the twin island cities Tlatelolco and Tenochtitlan fell to the Indigenous-Spanish alliance that ended Mexica imperial rule. Indigenous people, whether allies or enemies of the Spaniards, soon faced the political necessity of conforming—at least to a minimal and publicly observable extent—to an alien faith entrenched in Western European society and culture of the later medieval and early Renaissance eras. In this faith, Jesus's bodily suffering had become a focus for fervent devotion, and this fixation formed part of what Indigenous Mexicans encountered as they learned about Christianity.

https://doi.org/10.5876/9781646424511.c000b

Nahuas and other Indigenous people confronted these new stories with the baggage not of European religious trends and disputes but of their own long history, as they simultaneously made the social, political, and economic accommodations necessitated by colonial rule. Indigenous Passion performances arose as one outcome of these confrontations and accommodations and would turn out to be a particularly fraught one in the eighteenth century. Church leaders, who never deigned to find Indigenous Christian practice fully acceptable, cast their opprobrium first on Passion plays performed in Nahuatl and then, as well, on Spanish plays that mimicked them but lacked even the justification that had kept Nahuatl Christian theater alive until then: the notion that the ever-benighted Indigenous population needed such visible models to ensure even minimal compliance with the Church. These Spanish plays drew the attention of the Mexican Inquisition's office in Chalco, southeast of Mexico City. Inquisitors investigated. The four Spanish scripts they collected and the reports they wrote, all housed in the Inquisition branch (volume 1072, file 10) at the Archivo General de la Nación in Mexico City, have assisted in my own exploration here.

Pressured to Christianize, Indigenous people acquired new practices and beliefs, replaced some, and altered or retained others, hiding them when necessary;[1] colonial religion cannot be parceled into Christian and pre-Columbian components. The story of Jesus Christ was Indigenized throughout Mesoamerica, assimilated especially to the powerful and life-giving role of the sun in Indigenous mythos and to calendrical rituals of world or seasonal renewal. Today, many communities, whether they still speak Indigenous languages or have shifted to Spanish at some point in their history, act out or otherwise commemorate Passion-related events during the Lenten and Holy Week seasons. A Jesus identity has been claimed, at times, not just by actors but by leaders of Indigenous resistance movements.[2] While I include occasional examples, to attempt to survey such practices and appropriations either historically or ethnographically is beyond the scope of this book. However, by detailing what members of one major language group were doing with this story during the eighteenth, and likely the seventeenth, centuries, near the heart of Spain's empire, I provide both a portrait of one of the more elaborate Indigenous Passion adaptations and a basis for comparison across space and time.

I have been working with Nahuatl Christian texts since 1982 and never cease to find in them beautiful, creative expressions of their subject material, accommodated to Nahuatl language and often to Nahua cultural conventions and colonial circumstances. At the same time, these texts are artifacts of colonialism, of the process by which Christian evangelizers colonized the Nahuatl language itself, obliging its words to take on meanings and associations they did not previously have and inventing new words as necessary. Even though this process had limited success, Christianized usages percolated through the language and became part of everyday speech. William F. Hanks (2010), describing the impact of evangelization on the Yucatec Maya language, labels this a process of *reducción*, analogous to the way Indigenous communities were "reduced": that is, obliged to consolidate their dispersed members and relocate to places that would facilitate colonial oversight. Doctrinal formulas, internalized through rote memorization and repetition, spread beyond church-related usage. For example, petitions to colonial officials used terms that echoed the Passion of Christ or a penitent sinner's appeal for mercy (114, 316).

Nahuas learned to speak and write in the "reduced" Nahuatl that emerged from the unequal and complicated relationship between evangelizing friars and their Indigenous students and coauthors.[3] But mastery of this language contributed not only to mere survival under colonial rulers who insisted upon the acceptance of Christianity. Literature that Nahuas authored or coauthored, circulated, and recopied for their own uses supported their *survivance*—their active, engaged commitment to maintaining communal identity in the face of European domination.[4] For them, survivance strategies included making Christian stories and festivals their own, selecting and altering them, and even projecting them into their past. Theater became a means, in Jonathan Truitt's (2018, 109–110) words, to "own the tools" that connected Nahuas most closely and personally with the Catholic sacred as they conceived it. The fact that their most inventive techniques for the transculturation of Christianity met regularly with censorship and denigration is one of the many tragedies of colonial rule.

By devoting a book to these six Passion play manuscripts, I aim to place the beautifully written and creatively staged Nahuatl Passion play in front of many audiences that did not witness these performances in their own time and place. In the ongoing, 900-year history of Passion plays, the way Indigenous Mexicans adapted and enacted the story—working from the violent, patriarchal, and anti-Jewish material that was fed to them—merits attention from historical, anthropological, and artistic perspectives. Indeed, coming as it does from a colonized people, passed along and performed by Native Americans in their own language, this devotional practice carries a historical and global relevance beyond that of any single European tradition. It recontextualizes the Gospel accounts, and the accretions medieval Europeans layered upon them, within the religious practice of Indigenous Mexicans living, precariously, under Spanish rule.

Nahuas chose to enact this play; it was not forced on them. With it they transformed their communities into temporary Jerusalems, their townspeople not just into Christ, Mary, and other saintly figures but into the villains of the piece: Jews and Romans who commit violence and leave death in their wake. While the show demonstrated compliance with the evangelization project Spain deployed to justify its destructive imperial enterprise—declaring, in effect, "look what good Christians we are"—it also blew an emotional whirlwind across its actors and audience, a disequilibrating ordeal of physical abuse and gory suffering, vicious hatred and transcendent love, incompetent leadership and unfaithful friends, heavenly visitations and vile mockeries, laid out across a Palm Sunday afternoon. Actors layered foreign identities onto their bodies in a manner not alien to the way, in pre-Columbian rituals, people were turned into localized embodiments of gods by being dressed in their regalia and then sometimes dispatched through ritualized killing.[5] Jesus dies in the play—but the actor went home alive, albeit bruised and bloodied. Nevertheless, the play was a cathartic experience, perhaps, for audience and actors and a ritual of chaotic destruction and cleansing renewal, set at the dawn of spring. The plays lay a strong Indigenous claim to Christianity's core narrative. Once they met attempts at suppression, they shifted even more from an expression of compliance into an assertion of ownership.

While this volume is aimed at readers of English interested in Indigenous or colonial Mexico, the history and anthropology of Christianity, comparative religion, Native American literature, or the history of theater, a companion website, *Passion Plays of Eighteenth-Century Mexico* (passionplaysofeighteenthcenturymexico.omeka .net), presents the six texts in paleographic and standardized Nahuatl transcriptions as well as English translations. The four Passion plays in Spanish collected by the Mexican Inquisition are presented on the website, translated into English by my colleague Daniel O. Mosquera. I cite these plays using their folio number in the Inquisition file; readers who wish to explore these plays further can consult Mosquera's editions directly. In addition, we are posting the reports and other documents from the Inquisition case and some related documents on the suppression of Indigenous popular theater, which have never been published in English.[6] Nadia Marín-Guadarrama has assisted with this transcription and translation work. Rebecca Dufendach designed and maintains the website. This digital project provides a textual archive that complements this book, and I encourage readers to also explore the original sources housed there. We continue to add to and update this website.

The digital project is also directed in part to contemporary speakers of Nahuatl, through standardized transcriptions and also accompanying essays composed in Huastecan Nahuatl by Nahua anthropologist and language teacher Abelardo de la Cruz de la Cruz. We aim to make the texts accessible to contemporary Nahuatl speakers who may wish to read the work of their forebears. To that end, my standardized transcriptions on the website employ the "enriched traditional" or "ACK" (after the eminent Nahuatl linguists J. Richard Andrews, R. Joe Campbell, and Frances Karttunen) orthography promoted by John Sullivan, Justyna Olko, and their Nahua collaborators through publications of the Zacatecas Institute for

Education and Ethnographic Research (IDIEZ) at the University of Zacatecas, Mexico, and the Revitalizing Endangered Languages Project at the University of Warsaw (see Olko and Sullivan 2014).

This transcription system works within the conventions of colonial written Nahuatl—in the interest of making the vast corpus of colonial documents more accessible to contemporary Nahuas—but regularizes spelling and also shows glottal stops (as the letter "h"), which most colonial writers did not include in their work. I use the standardized orthography in this book when I include excerpts from the Passion plays and from other Nahuatl texts (unless otherwise stated), regularizing the colonial writers' variable manners of inscription. I also add a glottal stop to Spanish loanwords that end in a vowel to reflect how they were adapted into Nahuatl—for example, *mesah* for *mesa* 'table' and *coronah* for *corona* 'crown.' Anyone interested in orthographic or dialectal variation among the plays can consult the paleographic transcriptions on the website.

FROM ONE PLAY TO SIX

This study draws on six Nahuatl scripts, but I have been referring to "the" Nahuatl Passion play. Are there six plays or one? Both. All six derive from one original Nahuatl composition. Whether this was adapted from a Spanish play or first composed in Nahuatl based on one or more narrative sources in Spanish, Latin, or Nahuatl I cannot say for sure, though it seems most likely that some as-yet-unidentified Spanish-language source was the direct or indirect model for the bulk of the text. This could have been a narrative, like the Spanish text on which the Nahuatl play *The Destruction of Jerusalem* was based, or a theatrical piece, like the one that was adapted—rather freely—for the play *Holy Wednesday* (Burkhart 2010, 75–77; Burkhart 1996). No Nahuatl source currently known to me is sufficiently cognate with the plays to be their direct model—with the exception of the farewell scene between Christ and Mary, for which I have identified a sixteenth-century predecessor. As I propose in chapter 3, this non-biblical scene could have been added to the Nahuatl play after its original composition.

This model Passion play could have come from the busy scriptorium at the Indigenous College of Santa Cruz in Tlatelolco, a center of Nahuatl-Christian text production from its founding in 1536 through the first decades of the seventeenth century. In 1606, the Franciscan friar Juan Bautista Viseo (1606, prologue) reported that he and his Tlatelolca colleague Agustín de la Fuente had three volumes of plays prepared for publication. These books never reached the press: ecclesiastical suspicion of the genre kept Nahuatl plays from ever being printed during the colonial era. The friar categorizes these volumes as dealing, respectively, with penitence, the

Articles of the Faith, and parables of the Gospels. There is no obvious place here for a full-scale Passion play, but the prolific drama production is notable nonetheless.

A documentable case of dissemination from Tlatelolco can be seen in an Epiphany play composed there for fray Juan Bautista in the early seventeenth century—or so it appears, from an inscription to that friar on the play manuscript that Francisco del Paso y Troncoso published in 1902; the manuscript's present-day whereabouts are unknown (Paso y Troncoso 1902; Horcasitas 1974, 281–327). In 1724 a Nahua man named Carlos de San Juan was paid to make a new copy of a cognate play, at the behest of local dignitaries, in the town of Metepec, 63 kilometers from Mexico City in what is now the State of México (Sell and Burkhart 2009, 122–123; Burkhart, de la Cruz, and Sullivan 2017, 93). Metepec's play had lost any recorded connection to its metropolitan model—yet over a hundred years later, it retained nearly identical speaking parts, as well as what by 1724 was an archaic register of Nahuatl.

The model Passion play could have followed this pattern, or it may have been written later in the seventeenth century or back in the sixteenth. The variations among the extant scripts suggest that copies had been circulating for some time before these versions were written down. Performance may not have been continuous: the play could have been revived at some point between its original composition and the eighteenth century. Whatever the case, the text moved geographically from a center of Nahua scholarship and education to hinterland communities. And it moved through time to an era when that florescence of scholarship had receded into the past and Indigenous people had, overall, declined even further in status under colonial rule. In the second half of the seventeenth century, Indigenous communities began to recover somewhat from the horrific demographic collapse caused by the first century of Spanish colonialism. However, they had grown increasingly impoverished. By the mid-eighteenth century, an "overwhelming majority" of Indigenous Mexicans subsisted in difficult economic straits (Sousa 2017, 305). Jesus Christ's afflictions, anti-elite messaging, and identification with the poor might have resonated more powerfully with these new audiences than with the educated noblemen who wrote, or co-wrote with a priest, the model play.

Like all colonial Nahuatl plays, the Passion scripts retain the grammar of early colonial Nahuatl (or Stage Two Nahuatl, in Karttunen and James Lockhart's 1976 classification). The most striking feature preserved in this archaic register is that Spanish loanwords are limited and are restricted to nouns: cross, Passion, crown, tunic, saint, and so on. The sole exceptions occur in the stage directions for one of the plays, where a borrowed verb (*pasearoa*, from *pasear* 'to stroll') and a borrowed conjunction (*hastah* 'until') each appear two times.[7] Stage directions, overall, use more noun loans as well; for example, the apostles are *apóstoles*, rather than Jesus's students (*itlamachtilhuan*), only in stage directions. But whether the model play was recently written, rediscovered, or in continuous transmission, the existing scripts speak to Indigenous practice before and around the mid-eighteenth century and are valuable as records of that era.

The six plays are, in some places, strikingly consistent and thus likely preserve the wording of their original model. Notable examples include two of the longest speeches: Judas's deliberative soliloquy and Christ's address to his students after the Last Supper. This consistency denotes a certain reverence for these extended speeches as worthy of nearly exact reproduction through time and space—even the words of traitorous Judas. But some shorter scenes too are remarkably consistent. Elsewhere, however, many variations in the spoken dialogue, characters, and staging make each of the six manuscripts a unique production. As new copies of the plays were commissioned, their writers clearly felt free to introduce changes. They add scenes and speeches based on other sources, streamline some material, expand on other material, and move scenes from one place to another within the story. They change the names of speakers and add or remove characters. They make different suggestions regarding props, costumes, and sets. They call for different music. They also respond to criticisms of the performance by, for example, removing or minimizing the mimicked consecration of the bread and wine in the Last Supper scene.

Hence, while we lack the original, model play, we have a set of individual versions that add up to a much larger whole. While we might consider the author(s) of the model play the Nahuatl Passion's actual *playwright(s)*, distinguishing them from later redactors whom I will refer to as *scriptwriters*, the latter group includes creative adaptors who were not mere copyists or who dictated their innovations to copyists. We can see hundreds of decisions meant to improve upon the material handed down by earlier redactors. Plays that are similar in some scenes can be quite distinct in others, but we can, to a limited extent, trace subgroups within the small corpus. Innovations made in one version may appear in others—sometimes so similar as to indicate the copying of a written text, sometimes an approximation that may have been inspired by attendance at another community's performance. In one case, a redactor combined into one play two separate versions circulating in his local district while adding additional scenes and his own touches. Although we cannot precisely reconstruct the model play, we can get a pretty good idea of its content and compare the different changes made to it.

Undoubtedly, many other versions of the play once circulated in the literary underground of Nahuatl literacy, kept and treasured, borrowed and copied, pawned and stolen,[8] bought and sold,[9] lost to time and wear. From the Inquisition case we know that now-lost Nahuatl Passions were performed in Xochitlán and Tepoztlán, now in the state of Morelos; in Huejotzingo, Puebla; and in Amecameca, in the State of México.[10] Some plays remain guarded in local archives and are not, or not yet, available to academics; I know of one such case in the State of México.[11] Given the history of suppression and confiscation, one can hardly blame their keepers for their reticence. But these six provide ample fodder for the present study, which can then provide context for any additional Nahuatl Passions that reach a wider audience.

One of the six scripts was revealed in the course of the Tlaxcalan anthropologist Luis Reyes García's explorations of local archives in his home state. This is the incomplete play, from San Simón Tlatlauhquitepec, Tlaxcala, published by Reyes García's student Raul Macuil Martínez in 2010 and, with Macuil Martínez's collaboration, by Barry D. Sell and me in 2009. The play is held in the Archivo de la Fiscalía, which allowed photographs to be made of the manuscript; however, it is not currently accessible to outside scholars. Its twelve surviving folios preserve the action of the play from a short time after Jesus's arrival in Jerusalem to just after his flagellation. The document hunt also turned up two small Passion fragments, one leaf of a play and two leaves of Christ's speeches, from another Tlaxcala community, Atlihuetzia, which Macuil Martínez published in 2016.[12] As small as these are, they provide more evidence of the original play's spread and variations.

The other five Passion play manuscripts, all complete, bear witness to processes of suppression and loss that moved Nahuatl texts from communities to outsiders and eventually, in some cases, to public collections. One was acquired by Daniel Garrison Brinton (1837–1899), an American surgeon who dabbled in the literatures of Native America. The script ended up, with his other papers, at the University of Pennsylvania; I will refer to it, for convenience, as the Penn Passion play (or simply "Penn" or "the Penn play").

This play, forty-five leaves in length, lacks any date or indication of its place of origin. Its copyist gave it this title in Spanish and Latin, foreshadowing some of the early events in the play: "The Passion of Our Lord Jesus Christ from when his majesty bade farewell to his most holy mother together with his apostles. As soon as he bade farewell, he left, bringing his disciples, for the city of Jerusalem, where they received him and they sang to him the *Hosanna son of David, blessed, who comes in the name of the lord, Hosanna in the highest*" (italicized text in Latin).[13] A list of dramatis personae follows, with a Spanish heading: "Those who go out [on stage] in the Passion are these."[14] This is the only such list a copyist included in his script.

Then, after Christ and Mary each take one turn at speech, the writer copied in the opening lines of a published set of chants derived from the Gospel of Matthew. The source is the Franciscan friar Juan Navarro's *Liber in quo quatuor passiones Christi Domini continentur*, printed at the order's Tlatelolco establishment in 1604 and thus easily available to the friars and the Native scholars (Carreño n.d.). Navarro presents a plainsong Passion account, with Latin text and musical notation, using

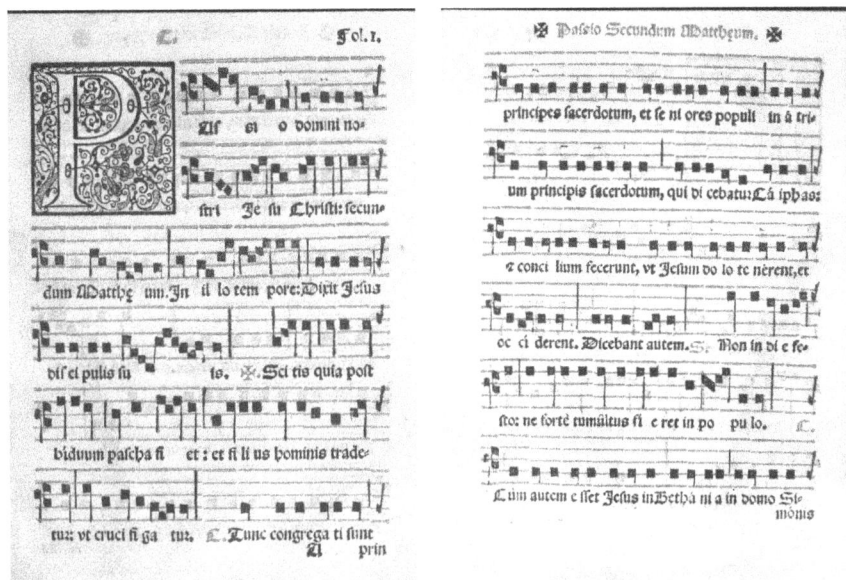

Figure 0.1. The beginning of the Passion According to Saint Matthew, in Juan Navarro, *Liber in quo quatuor passiones Christi Domini continentur* (Mexico City, 1604), folios 1r and 1v. Courtesy of the John Carter Brown Library, Brown University, Providence, RI.

excerpts from, in turn, each of the four Gospels (Matthew, Mark, Luke, and John).[15] The excerpt here in the Penn play corresponds to Matthew 26:1–5. The scriptwriter reproduces Navarro's words just as they appear in his book—apart from some misspellings of the Latin and one dropped phrase—and including the abbreviations "s" and "c" in red ink, indicating solo and chorus parts (Navarro 1604, 1r–1v; Penn Passion 1v–2r; see figures 0.1 and 0.2).

Having paused for this Latin interruption, the scriptwriter then restarts the Nahuatl play, replacing the initial two speeches with more expanded versions and continuing through Jesus's farewell to his mother, as prefaced by the initial title. It is not until the fourth leaf of the script that the passage from Matthew is reflected in the play. The "Hosanna" scene invoked in the title, from Matthew 21:9 and not part of Navarro's text, comes up a little later. The Spanish and Latin material frames and legitimates the play for observers who could not, or would not bother to, read the Nahuatl content.

Another play found its way to Princeton University, and I will call it the Princeton Passion play. The man who wrote out its fifty leaves gave it a similarly detailed heading, but in Nahuatl and Latin: "Here begins the precious and revered Passion of our lord Jesus Christ, the way he died for our sake, us sinners, as he came to save us. Here

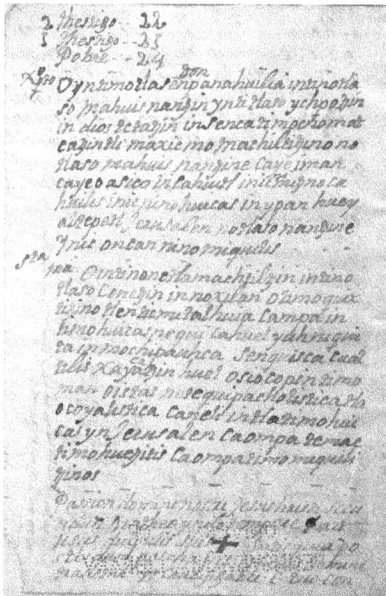

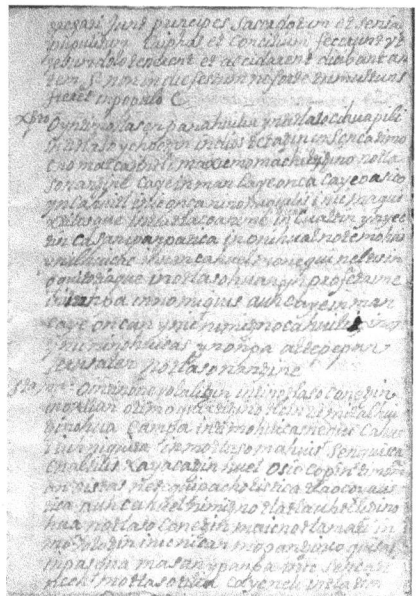

Figure 0.2. The University of Pennsylvania Passion Play, folios 1v and 2r. The end of the dramatis personae list appears at the top of 1v, followed by an initial exchange between Christ and Mary. The copied bit of Navarro follows, and then the play resumes with new opening speeches by Christ and Mary. The cross that precedes the word *scitis* in Navarro is particularly prominent three lines from the bottom on the first image. UPenn Ms. Coll. 700 item 200, Kislak Center for Rare Books, Manuscripts and Special Collections, University of Pennsylvania, Philadelphia.

it begins in the cemetery at the edge of the houses. Christ will come out, [with] all the apostles. The Jews will go in the lead. First, they will go inside. The Passion will begin. *The Passion of our lord Jesus Christ according to Matthew. Hosanna, son of David, King of Israel*" (italicized text in Latin).[16] Given the link we saw in the Penn play to Navarro's Saint Matthew Passion and the chants from Navarro's book that are cued later in the Princeton play, we can assume that the title refers to that work, not directly to the Gospel of Matthew or a model text based on that Gospel—as the play drew from many other sources as well. As in the Penn play, the copyist legitimates his work by relating the script to a Latin source. Also, as in the Penn play, the title highlights the "Hosanna" chant that will be sung early on in the action.

The cemetery setting envisioned here corresponds to a comment by the Dominican friar and Inquisition censor Francisco Larrea, who in 1768 prepared a twelve-page report for the Inquisition investigation. He says that ordinarily (*por lo regular*) the Passion plays, whether in Nahuatl or Spanish, are staged in cemeteries.[17]

He considers the graveyard settings appropriate because they are not as profane (*profanos*) as the public plazas or as respectable (*respectables*) as the church buildings.[18] This middle ground between the profane and the sacred was home to the actors' deceased relations, silent spectators at a show that itself ended in the deaths of Jesus and the two thieves.

Cemeteries witnessed other events as well. Until Archbishop Francisco Antonio Lorenzana banned these practices in 1769, religious confraternities conducted many of their meetings and ceremonies, often performed in memory of deceased members, in cemeteries (Larkin 2010, 151). Nahuas avidly joined these voluntary sodalities after the Franciscans introduced them, using them to organize both devotional and charitable acts (Webster 1997a, 1998; Richie 2011; Truitt 2018, chapter 4; Dierksmeier 2020). Many of these groups had Holy Week affiliations.

Someone other than the copyist of the script added a list of dramatis personae inside the front and back of the Princeton text's vellum cover. Other notes in what appears to be the same hand give us the names of one Señor don Bartolomé and one Gregorio Eusebio, the latter identified as the choirmaster (*m[aest]ro de capilla*), plus the date 1750. Given his religious leadership office, Gregorio Eusebio may have had charge of the performance, at least for that year. His name, consisting of two Spanish first names and no preceding "don," suggests he was of non-noble rank, though he could potentially have become a "don" if he continued to occupy high-profile public roles.[19] As for don Bartolomé, he was probably a local Nahua dignitary involved with the production, perhaps a leader of a religious confraternity or a member of the community's governing board. Below his name is written "dimas" in smaller letters. Dimas (also spelled Dismas) is the name assigned to the good thief crucified alongside Jesus (James 1924, 103–104). This character is simply *boen ladro* (for *buen ladrón* 'good thief') in the play itself, but this later annotator knew the name Dimas. Its association with don Bartolomé might indicate that this gentleman took the good thief's role himself. It was a small role but an arduous one, as don Bartolomé would have had to undergo a feigned crucifixion, leg breaking, and death.

A much later annotation tells us that the play was once in the possession of Father Canuto Flores, a Catholic priest from Tenancingo in the State of México, who had ethnographic and archaeological interests. Among his ecclesiastical postings in his home state were Chapa de Mota, in the north, where he was installed as parish priest in 1900 (Trinidad Basurto 1901, 226); Mexicaltzingo, where he died in 1946;[20] and apparently Tlalnepantla, since on the manuscript's inside back cover he wrote "Property of Presbyter Canuto Flores, Tlalnepantla, State of México."[21] So the play may well be from Tlalnepantla, or Father Flores may have acquired it elsewhere—though most likely within the State of México, given his position of authority in a number of its communities.

We can trace the remaining three plays to the suppression campaign to be discussed in chapter 1. In response to orders from the archbishop's office in 1757, a parish priest in what is now the state of Morelos dutifully collected six Passion plays from communities under his oversight. One of the six, now in the Archivo General de la Nación, bears this note on the first of its fifty-seven leaves: "Year of 1757. Reverend Father Curate [and] Minister fray Miguel de Torres remitted these six notebooks (*cuadernos*), and they are from his jurisdiction of Jonacatepec" (or Xonacatepec, as written in his day).²² For twenty-five years, this leaf had been a blank cover page. On the second leaf, an Indigenous copyist had filled the top half with Nahuatl script, recording first the date of his writing, "Today, Thursday the 11ᵗʰ of September of 1732," and then this précis for the play within: "Here begins the Passion that was done to our lord Jesus Christ as he entered the *altepetl* of Jerusalem on Palm Sunday. Here everything is shown, all the sufferings that happened to our lord Jesus Christ, by which he saved for us our life forces, our souls, we people of the world."²³ Below this the place name Amacuitlapilco appears twice, first on a pasted-on strip of paper reading "Del Pu[ebl]o D[e] Amacuitlapilco" and, below that, in the phrase "Amacuitlapilco De Xonacatepec," written in fray Miguel's hand. Amacuitlapilco lies just northwest of the town of Jonacatepec.²⁴

We can match fray Miguel's handwriting on this play to the inscription "Tepaltzinco De Xonacatepec" added to the beginning of an undated 116-page²⁵ Passion play, titled simply "It will begin on Passion Sunday of Palms."²⁶ This community, now called Tepalcingo, lies 10 kilometers from Jonacatepec. This play found its way to Tulane University. It was apparently still there when Arthur E. Gropp (1933, 282) wrote his catalog of manuscripts in the Department of Middle American Research. However, at some point it was removed. The Latin American Library retains a negative photostat of the original, which, fortunately, is very legible. Fernando Horcasitas published this play (1974, 335–419), as did Sell and I (Sell and Burkhart 2009, 160–241); it also appears in English in my book *Aztecs on Stage* (Burkhart 2011, 99–144). Some content in the Tepalcingo play varies enough from the other scripts to indicate use of another narrative or dramatic source, especially in Judas's interactions with the Jewish council and the chief priests' preceding deliberations (38–46 and a brief exchange at 68–69).

A third such note in fray Miguel's hand, "Axochiapan de Xonacatepec," is squeezed in above the Latin title of another play, "Passion of Our Lord Jesus Christ according to Matthew. In those days Jesus said to his disciples."²⁷ The original, with forty-five leaves, resides in the Archivo Histórico of the Biblioteca Nacional de Antropología e Historia in Mexico City, as manuscript volume 464; a photocopy is housed among the Fernando Horcasitas papers at the Latin American Library at Tulane University. Horcasitas (1974, 421–423) published a brief description of the text. Axochiapan lies 23 kilometers from Jonacatepec and just 16 kilometers from Tepalcingo. This play's Latin title is taken directly from the beginning of Navarro's Saint Matthew Passion (Navarro 1604, 1r), making this the third play to authorize itself by invoking that Latin source. This play also has the date 1732, on its final leaf.

With three of the six confiscated scripts known and intact, at least in facsimile, Jonacatepec's plays thus had a high survival rate, in contrast to however many other scripts were submitted to the archbishop's office—if other priests were indeed as cooperative as fray Miguel. However, if this priest had not written down the names of the towns, we would not know them. No Nahua wrote a place name on any of these scripts to claim it for his own locality or recorded his own role as reviser or copyist. The play transcends borders and localities, with scripts passing from place to place, radiating out from wherever the first version was composed and continuing to be passed along multiple lines of transmission. The Jonacatepec scripts could have been imported to those communities,[28] and manuscripts still in local archives may have been written elsewhere.

What did "passion" mean in Nahuatl? The title or précis inscribed on each of the five complete plays, whether in Nahuatl or Spanish, employs the Spanish loanword *passion* or *pasion*, which comes from the Latin noun *passiō* 'suffering,' which, in turn, derives from the verb *pati* 'to suffer.' But "passion" had a standard Nahuatl equivalent, seen above where the Amacuitlapilco play promises to reveal "all the sufferings that happened to our lord Jesus Christ" and appearing throughout the scripts themselves. This word, *tlaihiyohuiliztli*, can be translated as suffering or torments or something difficult to endure (in either singular or plural senses). The term is a deverbative noun based on the transitive verb *ihiyohuia* (Andrews 1975, 228). This verb contains the noun *ihiyotl* 'breath' plus the transitive suffix *-huia*, which means "to use or apply (the thing denoted by the source noun stem) in relation to s.o. or s.th." (358). The direct object prefix *tla-* denotes an unspecified thing or things. Hence *tla-ihiyo-huia* means "to apply breath to something." This has the extended sense of becoming fatigued or exhausted, a condition marked by intensified breathing.

Fray Alonso de Molina's 1571 (1992, pt. 2, 36v, 121v) dictionary defines *tla-ihiouia* as *padecer trabajos* 'to suffer or endure labors or hardship' and *tlaihiouiliztli* as *tormento, fatigo, o pena que se padece* 'torment, fatigue, or pain that one endures.' We get from breath to suffering to "passion"—but it is by extension, and it is more active than passive. Jesus applies his breath to things and wears himself out so much, through the hardships he undergoes, that he suffers pain and torment. The whole Passion story and each individual affliction are *tlaihiyohuiliztli*.

Molina's (1992, pt. 1, 93r) Spanish-to-Nahuatl vocabulary links three other nouns to the concept of *passion*: *cocoliztli* 'sickness,' *patzmiquiliztli*, and *nentlamatiliztli*. Both of these last two can be translated as "anguish," but *patzmiquiliztli* suggests a more graphic sensation of being pressed or squeezed (*patz-*) to death (*miquiliz-tli*), while *nentlamatiliztli* has more a sense of mental fretting or stewing, thinking useless thoughts, from *nen* 'in vain' or 'uselessly' and *tlamati* 'to think' or 'to know things.' Of these four choices, *tlaihiyohuiliztli* best fit the purpose.

Only three of the six plays bear dates: 1732, 1732, 1750. The Axochiapan play of 1732 borrows some of its content either from the extant, undated (but pre-1757) play from nearby Tepalcingo or a different copy of the same. All the plays share not only substantial content but also orthographic patterns, such as the use of the letter *s*, rather than *z* or *ç*, for the phoneme /s/—a displacement that begins in the later seventeenth century and thus serves as a diagnostic tool for dating (Lockhart 1992, 343).[29] As the plays are so similar, it seems best to date the whole corpus, tentatively, to approximately the first half of the eighteenth century, with the understanding that they are modeled on earlier manuscripts.

FROM SIX PLAYS TO ONE

For this volume, I have merged the six plays (published individually on the project website mentioned above) and the fragments from Atlihuetzia into a single, composite English version. This is not an attempt to reconstruct the original, model play, for I include elements that seem to have been added by later editors of the script. Rather, my intent is to pool contributions from the various people who created, passed on, altered, and embellished the play. I take the most extended or elaborate versions of each speech or scene, in order to represent the fullest development of the tradition, while omitting some variants in an effort to avoid redundancy or contradictions. I combine statements from different versions of the same speech if they add something rather than just repeat the same idea. Similarly, I include as many stage and set directions as are provided for any particular passage, opting for the more elaborate ones if a more inclusive composite would send actors in too many directions at once. Readers of this book thus have at hand, apart from these omissions, an expansive representation of the performance tradition without having to read the six different versions.

In this translation, I retain the original texts' usage of semantic parallelism, where two or more words or phrases with similar meanings are used instead of one. This is a distinctive feature of Nahuatl oratorical style[30] that theatrical speech helped maintain as part of a living oral practice. These pairings and triplings can make sentences seem a bit choppy and repetitive, with lots of commas, but I ask readers to see this as the poetic device that it is. Parallelisms add shades of meaning, highlight verbal acuity, and slow the pacing of a statement—allowing ideas to be delivered and received in a more deliberative fashion. This device was adapted to the introduction of foreign words, as a Spanish or Latin term could be paired with a Nahuatl term—sometimes a colonial neologism—that gave at least some sense of its meaning. Examples that occur in the play include *profetas* 'prophets' paired with the probable neologism *tlaachtopaihtoanimeh* 'those who say something first'; *cruz* 'cross' paired with the neologism *cuauhnepanolli* 'wooden crossed-over-itself thing' or, as I translate it, "crossed-wood device"; and *ánima* 'soul' paired with the neologism *teyoliya*. This instrumental form of the verb *yoli* 'to come to life' suggests something that enables one to live (Olko and Madajczak 2019); I translate it as "life force."

The reverential system, which adds honorific suffixes to nouns and additional prefixes and suffixes to verbs, is harder to convey in English. While at times I try to partially suggest this by using more formal language, much of this coding is lost in translation. As a general point, readers may note that reverential forms are used in reference to Jesus in the stage directions and in the speeches by his friends and supporters—and even by Pontius Pilate when persuaded of his innocence. The failure of Christ's enemies to use such forms coded disrespect into their every utterance. In contrast, the vocative form of address, another distinctive feature of Nahuatl, can be easily represented by an "O," as in "O my beloved mother."

In comparing the Nahuatl plays to the four Spanish-language plays in the Inquisition file, I find one striking difference to be the more dialogical character of the Nahuatl texts. That is, there is more respectful bowing and scraping as well as insults and informal chit-chat in the Nahuatl ones, more greetings and leave-takings, more expressions of gratitude, more acknowledgment of what other people have just said. Messengers quote the words of the person who dispatched them rather than simply conveying the information. Minor characters talk more, and there are more of them. Like the plays' frequent use of semantic parallelism and the reverential speech register, this expansive dialogue helps move the Christian story into a Nahua cultural and linguistic milieu. It calls to mind the strikingly oral, conversational mode of expression recorded in some earlier Nahuatl documents, such as the Bancroft Dialogues from approximately the 1570s (Karttunen and Lockhart 1987) or the short text from 1583 that Lockhart (1991, 66–74; 1992, 85–90) called "And Ana Wept." The pacing of the play allowed time for everyone to speak and for everything to be said. However, I want to note that the composite play has more of these short speeches than does any individual exemplar. Where scriptwriters may have lessened some of the original play's loquacity or, conversely, furnished their own characters with more turns at speech is difficult to say.

So that I can reference specific parts of the play, I have also imposed a somewhat arbitrary division into acts (indicated by upper-case Roman numerals), scenes (indicated by lower-case Roman numerals), and individual speeches and stage directions (indicated by Arabic numerals). Hence, II.iv.5 is the fifth speech or stage direction in the fourth scene of Act 2. These annotations run along the left margin of the text.

OPTIONS AND CHOICES

In chapter 1, I weave together historical developments on both sides of the Atlantic, shuttling back and forth through space and time to give readers a wider perspective on how the Nahuatl Passions came to exist and how they came to be controversial. Without the trend toward affective, contemplative Passion devotion that gripped Europe in the later Middle Ages, no Nahua men would have been put up on crosses. And without the mutual reinforcement of anti-Jewish hatred and Passion violence, Nahua actors would not have taken roles as vicious Jewish henchmen. Passion plays have been around for most of a millennium and have often, and inevitably, posed challenges to religious orthodoxy. The situation in Mexico, distinctive in some ways, fits into this larger historical pattern.

The subsequent chapters look comparatively at the six plays to map the range of available options and explore the choices made by the playwright(s) and the different scriptwriters as they set down their individual visions for the Passion performance. I also discuss the historical background of certain scenes or motifs, considering where they came from and how they may have seemed to Nahuas. As variations at the level of all individual speeches are too many to consider, I select larger issues where the variation either takes us into performance techniques, such as stage sets and music, or into decisions about how vital or controversial aspects of the story are to be told, which characters and episodes are to be included, and how they are meant to be perceived. I assume that variants closer to biblical or other Old World models also hew more closely to the original Nahuatl play, as its author(s) likely possessed a level of Christian education and access to written sources that the later scriptwriters did not.

Chapter 2 tracks the decisions scriptwriters and other show planners made about how to use onstage and offstage spaces, arrange and coordinate sets, and enliven the production with elements that vary across the corpus. These include the writing and reading of documents, the number and placement of angelic messengers, the pacing of certain scenes, the selection and placement of choral and instrumental music, and minor touches that add humor or realism. The chapter also considers the scale of the productions and the community investment they demanded.

Chapter 3 introduces the women of the Passion, exploring the extent and nature of their participation in the staged story and the variations among the scripts. The influence of European Passion literature, in which Mary's role as a fully human co-sufferer with her son helped many devotees relate emotionally to the story, can be seen in the plays. At the same time, the Nahuatl-speaking women are accorded enhanced respect and strength of character relative to European models, and their compassion and tears may bear different connotations.

Chapter 4 tackles the plays' most controversial scene, the staging of the Last Supper, to see how different scriptwriters reenacted the origin of the Eucharist and prototype for the Roman Catholic Mass. Some tread with caution, while others assert the right to have a Nahua Christ embodier bless and distribute the tortilla and wine. After-supper speeches by Jesus and Judas offer competing models for Nahuatl oratory. Judas's speech reveals his disordered state of mind but makes him a complex figure, not a cardboard villain.

Chapter 5 completes the discussion of gender by contrasting the women's bulwark of love and stability with the battering ram of male anger and violence that runs through the plays—especially after Jesus is arrested—and leaves a god dead on the cross. Each staging required decisions about how much violence would be acted out and how the characters would talk about it, a pained process as actors had to inflict and undergo these acts of destabilizing aggression. Readers are invited to read the composite play in full at any point in their encounter with this book or to refer to particular scenes and speeches in conjunction with my discussions of them.

Controversial Passions

THE SUFFERING CHRIST: EUROPE TO NEW SPAIN, 1000–1698

On March 9, 1698, the Indigenous leaders of Santiago Tlatelolco, the northern sector of Mexico City, requested permission to stage their annual Passion play, a type of performance that Spanish speakers called a *Nexcuitil* or *Nescuitil*. Palm Sunday that year fell on March 23, so only two weeks remained to prepare for a performance that would likely be staged on that day.[1] Much had to be done: rehearsals for actors and singers, putting up the stage and preparing sets, gathering props, securing a female donkey with a foal and possibly horses as well, and making sure that last year's costumes were in good shape and either commissioning any necessary repairs or replacements or arranging costume rentals. Vendors would want to stock up on refreshments and other goods to sell to the crowd of spectators.[2] The petition lists the Indigenous governor, Gabriel González, and fourteen other dignitaries. According to their entreaty, the Tlatelolca had performed their *paçion* since the founding of their church. The brief document is the first entry in a small file in Mexico's Archivo General de la Nación.[3]

The word *Nexcuitil* came from *neixcuitilli* 'something from which one takes an example.' Nahuas and Franciscan friars adopted this term in the sixteenth century to designate the theatrical productions that, beginning in the 1530s, presented Christian content written in Nahuatl and performed by Indigenous actors. Some plays told morality tales about sin and punishment. For these the word *neixcuitilli* was especially appropriate, paralleling the use of the Latin *exemplum* or Spanish

https://doi.org/10.5876/9781646424511.c001

ejemplo for short stories with moral lessons. Other plays enacted biblical narratives, stories of saints—including Mexico's Our Lady of Guadalupe—or Christian beliefs regarding the Antichrist and the Final Judgment.[4] The closest thing to a Passion play script known to survive from the sixteenth or seventeenth century is the play *Holy Wednesday*, from the 1590s, an extended treatment of one Holy Week scene: the farewell between Christ and Mary (Burkhart 1996; see chapter 3, this volume). Neither that play nor any of the six Passion play scripts uses the word *neixcuitilli* to describe its content.

Passion plays arose in Europe as part of a devotional orientation toward Jesus Christ's earthly life and suffering that began to emerge after the year 1000, when the expected millennium failed to materialize (Fulton 2003). Over the next few centuries, Christ's torment and death, along with Mary's own suffering, were probed in increasingly excruciating, even grotesque, detail. Maternal and filial suffering were intertwined, for the more graphic Christ's torments became, the more misery they provoked in his mother (Rubin 2009, 246). In turn, the crueler the literary or artistic depictions became, the stronger the emotional response they generated in devotees—at first nuns, monks, and friars but later laypeople as well—who sought to feel the pain Jesus and Mary had endured (Bestul 1996, 71–72). Seeking to walk in Jesus's final footsteps, pilgrims ventured to Jerusalem and trod the *Via Crucis*, or Way of the Cross. When such travel became too dangerous, devotees paced procession routes at imitation Jerusalems that sprang up in Europe or simply through the streets of their own communities (MacGregor 2000, 138–145), a practice eventually standardized and regularized in the Stations of the Cross devotion (Schwaller 2017, 123). This devotion prescribed a series of bodily movements conjoined with recitations in front of images, a performative sequence that devotees came to experience as "not merely an imaginary trip to Jerusalem but . . . an imaginary walk with Jesus in his final Passion" (Schwaller 2021, 25). Theater was an even more performative medium for rendering Jesus's last days and sufferings visible, accessible, and realistic—even if the goriest imagined torments had to be forgone by living actors.

European Passion plays could retell a long saga over several days, beginning with Adam and Eve's fall from grace and ending with Christ's resurrection or even later: a 1298 production in Friuli included stagings of Pentecost and the Last Judgment (Stern 1996, 93). Or they could focus on the events immediately preceding and surrounding his death on the cross. The earliest known Passion play was written in Latin at Montecassino, in southern Italy, early in the twelfth century (Sticca 1970, 47). Sandro Sticca sees this emerging genre as an outgrowth not of earlier, liturgical rites with dramatic trappings, such as the *Quem queritis?*, or "Whom do you seek?," of the Easter liturgy, or of poetic laments voicing the Virgin Mary's pain (*plancti Mariae*). It sprang, rather, from this new, Christocentric focus on Jesus's incarnation in human form and the physical torments he endured on earth (19, 42–43, 125). This early Latin dramatization, though it supplies plenty of detail on sets and gestures, stays very close to the accounts in the Bible—although, strikingly, its succinct crucifixion scene does not even mention Jesus's death (100, 105–106).

As vernacular-language play traditions developed, so did realism, emotive expression, and anguished elaborations on the Gospel accounts—in tandem with Passion literature and art more generally (Sticca 1970, 128). Passion plays were performed in Italian by the mid-thirteenth century, in French possibly by the late thirteenth century, and in German and English by the fourteenth century (54, 154, 157). Records for Spain are sparser. In the Catalan-speaking region, fragments of plays and records of performances date back to the fourteenth and fifteenth centuries, and a substantial extant script from the town of Cervera, dating to 1545 but incorporating material from 1534 and earlier, showcases sixteenth-century Catalan practice (Romeu i Figueras 1967, 104–105; Massip 1987; Stern 1996, 135–136; Duran i Sanpere and Duran 1984).

The earliest extant Passion play in Castilian was inscribed—in 599 lines of verse on blank pages in an account book—by Alonso del Campo, a chaplain of the Toledo cathedral, sometime between 1486 and his death in 1499 (Torroja Menéndez and Rivas Palá 1977, 77–79). About a quarter of this play reprises the poems "La pasión trobada" and "Las siete angustias de Nuestra Señora" by Diego de San Pedro, written around 1480; linguistic and metric archaisms in the work suggest that the compiler also drew on multiple earlier poetic texts going back as far as the late thirteenth or early fourteenth century (Pérez-Prieto 1997, 79; Blecua 1988, 82). Alberto Blecua (1988) concludes that del Campo copied the entire text—making errors typical of a copyist—from an earlier work, perhaps already assembled into dramatic form from diverse poetic pieces.

The Toledan play is striking for its lack of staged violence. Ronald E. Surtz (1992, 34, 37) surmises that del Campo preferred to have characters report on the crueler parts of the story, including the crucifixion, rather than stage them directly, such that his play alternates between direct enactment and evocative reporting. In light of Blecua's analysis, I consider this an effect of the play being cobbled together from an assemblage of poems composed for reading or recitation and not for the stage. As Castilian literature was richer in Passion poetry than in Passion plays, it may be that del Campo's draft is not the only play that simply turned earlier poetic treatments of the Passion into staged performances, without there necessarily being a formal script.

Passion-related theater in Spain often focused not on the events leading to Christ's death but on what happened afterward, especially his removal from the cross, burial, and resurrection (Shergold 1967, 26–34). Hence, for example, the two Passion plays by Lucas Fernández (1474–1541), though important in Spanish literature, take place after Christ's death and are not very comparable to the Mexican texts.[5] Religious confraternities sponsored dramatized "descent" and "resurrection" ceremonies; in the former, a statue with articulated arms would be removed from a cross and placed in a glass coffin or stage-set sepulcher by human actors (Webster 1998, 66–67).[6] Even with this rather stiff impersonator in the starring role, the performances, according to Susan Verdi Webster (67), "created a narrative quality and a strong sense of immediacy, and elicited profound emotional responses." But as for dramatizations that culminate in Christ's death, apart from the Cervera and Toledo plays I have found only one Spanish script from before the twentieth century, a play from Villasinta, León, dated 1856 but showing definite continuities with earlier literature (in Lozano Prieto 1985, 79–111).[7]

It is not known when full-scale Nahuatl Passion plays like the ones examined in this book began to be performed. The Nahua historian and longtime church steward don Domingo de San Antón Muñón Chimalpahin Quauhtlehuanitzin (1965, 291) reports that Coyoacan, on the lakeshore near Mexico City, staged its first Passion play in 1587. As Chimalpahin considered this notable, it may have been a new phenomenon, but this could have been a smaller-scale production. The Franciscan Agustín de Vetancurt (1971, pt. 4, 42), in his 1698 chronicle, describes *Neixcuitiles* of the Passion performed on Palm Sunday afternoons at San José de los Naturales, the principal Indigenous church in colonial Tenochtitlan. However, they do not seem to have been very elaborate. The actor who plays Christ, Vetancurt says, "takes communion with much devotion."[8] But the only scene the friar mentions is the lancing of Christ's side, and apparently an image, such as those used in descent ceremonies, substituted for Christ on the cross: he refers to *a* "holy Christ" (*vn Santo Christo*) and the placement of a bladder filled with red liquid (*licor de carmin*) on the wound (*la llaga*)—that is, the wound already carved or painted on the image's side. Nevertheless, the spectators filled the patio and surrounding rooftops, with many provoked to tears and tender emotions (*ternura*).

It is unlikely that even this more modest practice went back to the founding of Tlatelolco's original church structure, built between 1535 and 1543 (Kubler 1982, 587). Tlatelolco did, however, witness the first documented Christian theatrical production in Mexico, a dramatization of Judgment Day staged in 1531 or 1533.[9] By claiming such a primordial origin for their Passion, the Tlatelolca nobles added force to their petition—and indeed, the play may have been performed long enough to have taken on an aura of antiquity that made their claim feel factual.

They would not be the only ones to stake such claims. A late seventeenth- or early eighteenth-century Nahuatl primordial title from Cuernavaca presents the staging of the first Passion play as a foundational event in the community's early colonial history.[10] Primordial titles (community histories that staked claims to lands and noble privileges) often fictionalized early colonial history but in ways that offer insight into how the past was re-imagined and aligned with later concerns. The tradition or fiction that the Passion play was so foundational would serve as evidence that Christianity was firmly incorporated into public life at an early time. The passage takes a defensive stance that seems more appropriate to the later colonial era of its composition: the performance *in ahmo zan ahahuilli* 'was not just an amusement' but was done *ic tiquilnamiquizqueh in quenin omomiquilih toteotzin* 'so that we will remember how our (revered) deity died' (Horcasitas 1974, 335).

Tlatelolco had been the epicenter of Nahua-Christian scholarship. In 1536 the College of Santa Cruz was founded there, with Franciscan teachers, to educate an Indigenous intelligentsia. These classically educated Nahua noblemen engaged in decades of fruitful collaboration with Franciscan and other priests on linguistic and quasi-ethnographic projects as well as adaptations of Christian teachings into Nahuatl. Their work and that of other priests and Indigenous scholars yielded a vast corpus of published and unpublished writings pitched to all levels of Indigenous engagement with Christianity, from the basics of doctrine to songs and plays, sermons, esoteric treatises, and contemplative literature. The latter category included never-published Nahuatl adaptations of the *Imitatio Christi*, a text composed between 1424 and 1427, probably by Thomas à Kempis, a participant in the Christocentric *Devotio moderna* that arose in the Netherlands in the fourteenth century (Tavárez 2013; Marrow 1979, 20). *Devotio moderna* adherents in Spain published many editions and adaptations of Kempis's work in the sixteenth century, and it also apparently found receptive readers among Indigenous Mexicans (Tavárez 2013, 230–231).

Unpublished sermons on the Passion of Christ and devotional works dedicated specifically to that event number among the other Christ-related Nahuatl writings. Sermons for the different festivals of Holy Week retold the Passion story in much detail, sometimes with considerable dialogue. Their authors also explained what different elements in the story symbolized and what their listeners ought to think and feel in response. Dramatic productions allowed their audiences more latitude to interpret and react to the action in their own ways.

The most notable early Passion tract is the "Historia de la Pasión de Nuestro Señor Jesu Christo en lengua mexicana," which shares a manuscript volume in Mexico's Biblioteca Nacional with the famous song collection *Cantares mexicanos* and other texts, possibly dating to the sixteenth century but recopied in the seventeenth (in León-Portilla 1994, 192r–258v).[11] This account narrates the story in tremendous detail, extending over 127 folio-size pages and furnishing more than enough material for a playwright to select from and dramatize. However, it does not include all the events of the plays, and its style is more contemplative commentary than active dialogue, with much dwelling upon Christ's pain and bloodshed.

Shorter contemplative narratives can be found elsewhere in the Biblioteca Nacional Nahuatl collections. Among these number the twenty-folio "De la passion de noestro señor ie. xº" in the volume titled *Miscelánea sagrada*, and the thirty-one-folio "Passio domini nr̄i Jesu Christi" from 1617, in the volume *Sermones y ejemplos*, compiled by the Jesuit Horacio Carochi. A marginal note attributes the latter narrative to "Lorenzo," possibly the Nahua man of this name who taught in Jesuit schools for forty years and was accepted into the Jesuit order, but not until he was on his deathbed at age seventy (Pérez de Ribas 1645, 741–744).

Although their content bears only limited significance for this project, I also want to mention the fragments of a Passion narrative—mainly parts of a Last Supper account—that Abelardo Carrillo y Gariel (1949, vol. 1, 51–72) discovered, along with a pictorial tribute record and other papers, lining the chest cavity of a broken *pasta de caña* crucifix in Mexicaltzingo, in the State of México.[12] The people who made this statue, one of many such colonial crucifixes molded from maize leaves and an orchid-derived glue, literally incorporated the Passion story into their Cristo's body.

Also of considerable interest are the two Passion texts that comprise the bulk of a Nahuatl Christian copybook, or miscellaneous collection of devotional texts, housed in the Latin American Library at Tulane University.[13] The second text ends mid-word, and then there is a second copy of the two texts, incomplete at the beginning but extending beyond where the first copy of the second piece cuts off. The first piece is a narrative and contemplative treatment of the Jerusalem leaders' plot against Jesus, Judas's offer to betray him, and Christ's farewell to his mother. The second text, speaking instead in the voice of a teacher or preacher, offers a truncated farewell and an account of the Last Supper, foot washing, Jesus's after-supper preaching, the praying in the Garden of Gethsemane, and the arrest—not as a continuous narrative but interspersed with moral lessons. This copybook has a link to the Nahuatl Passion plays because the farewell scene in the first text—but no other part of the manuscript—tracks so closely with the fullest treatment of this event among the Nahuatl plays that some version of this text must have served as the scene's source (see figure 1.1).

Ranging widely in genre and subject matter, Christian texts in Nahuatl also range widely in how closely they hew to Christian orthodoxy, as opposed to putting forth innovative Indigenous interpretations. Mark Z. Christensen (2013, chapter 2) proposes a three-category classification ranging from relatively canonical, approved, published works with stated authors (though Indigenous coauthors are often left uncredited) meant for wide dissemination (Category One) to manuscript sources produced for local use with possibly some unorthodox content (Category Two) to Native-authored texts prepared with little or no priestly supervision and often

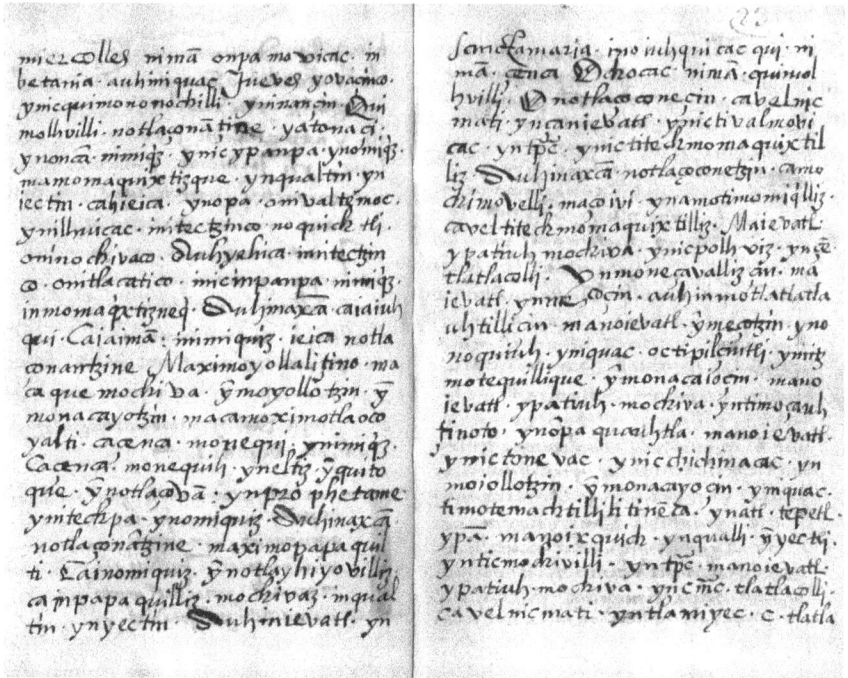

Figure 1.1. Part of the farewell between Christ and Mary in the sixteenth-century Tulane Passion text. *Pasión en lengua mexicana*, 22v–23r. Latin American Library, Tulane University, New Orleans, LA.

containing creative reworkings of Christian source material (Category 3). The Tulane copybook with the two Passion texts falls into this third category and shows that literate Nahuas were passing along and recopying Passion literature on their own initiative and for their own use—despite periodic attempts, by the Inquisition and other Church authorities, to restrict Indigenous people's access to unauthorized religious literature.

Nahuatl dramas can fall, depending on authorship and content, into either Category Two or Category Three (Christensen 2013, 89). Their public performance, in front of priests and other spectators, exercised some constraint over their content. The Passion plays might best be placed in Category Two. While unorthodox treatments do appear, for the most part the basic content is of Old World origin. However, it is recoded into Nahuatl language and Nahua formulas of prestige and social interaction. As succeeding chapters will detail, many subtle changes of content and emphasis archive ideas and intentions inserted by Indigenous redactors, sometimes at variance with canonical models. Even so, the strongest challenge to

Spanish and Catholic hegemony lies less in the Passion plays' written content than in their public staging by Indigenous claimants to the sacred story and its dramatis personae. And although never published, the plays transcended any single, local expression and reached a wider audience, in space and time, than perhaps any other Category Two creation.

Tlatelolco's Passion play could have been one of the plays that fray Juan Bautista and Agustín de la Fuente had put together by 1606 or, if not, then at least fostered by the same play-writing fervor. The contemplative *Devotio moderna* works adapted into Nahuatl in the same era, some by Bautista himself,[14] could have nurtured a desire to inscribe the story of Christ's self-sacrifice in a prolonged dramatic form. The publication of fray Juan Navarro's Passion chant book in 1604 may also have inspired an early seventeenth-century playwright, such that the extant plays' use of that work could date back to the original composition. In this same era, Tlatelolco's original church was being replaced by a new structure, completed in 1609 (Kubler 1982, 587). The Tlatelolca of 1698 could have been looking back to that event rather than the building of the first church as the setting for their first Passion play.

Indigenous people adopted from European practice another mode of collective, performative Holy Week observation: processions with images of the suffering Christ and sorrowing Virgin. Franciscan chronicler Gerónimo de Mendieta (1980, 436) provides a detailed eyewitness account of the 1595 Holy Thursday, Good Friday, and Easter morning processions in Mexico City, with their—in his reckoning—thousands of flagellants and hundreds of processional images. Chimalpahin (Lockhart, Schroeder, and Namala 2006) details a number of large-scale Holy Week and other processions he witnessed in the early seventeenth century. As in Spain, where the Seville processions are the most famous of these traditions, these street marches were sponsored and executed by religious confraternities. In the Baroque era, sculptural tableaux that were paraded through the streets in these processions promoted people's familiarity with events and personages of the Passion (Schwaller 2021, 77–79).

In the later sixteenth century, an Indigenous artist painted a procession on the church walls at Huejotzingo, just northwest of the city of Puebla. The murals, as analyzed by Webster (1997a, 1997b), depict a procession sponsored by a confraternity of the Holy Cross, one of the most popular such organizations in the colony. Robed confraternity members accompany an articulated statue of Christ as the Santo Entierro (holy burial) that, as seen in two paintings, had been mounted on a cross and then taken down by priests—a Franciscan in one painting and a Dominican in the other.[15] Artists painted similar series at other sixteenth-century churches, and the ceremonies were probably widespread as well (1997b, 78). Nahuas also carried out these "descent" ceremonies with statues that were then taken in procession at San

José de los Naturales and Tlatelolco (Lockhart, Schroeder, and Namala 2006, 219). Full-scale Passion plays could also culminate in processions,[16] and certainly many people who participated in Passion plays walked procession routes later in the week.

One processional mode of Passion devotion received a late seventeenth-century boost from fray Agustín de Vetancurt, the same Franciscan who wrote approvingly of the Passion performances at San José de los Naturales. Vetancurt (most likely in collaboration with one or more Native speakers) adapted into Nahuatl a popular Spanish guide to the *Via Crucis*, or Stations of the Cross, by the Spanish Franciscan Antonio de la Anunciación (Schwaller 2021, 62–65). Vetancurt's book was printed twice before 1700. No exemplars of either printing are known to survive. However, John Frederick Schwaller (2017, 121; 2021) identified a manuscript copy, with illustrations, that a Nahua man named Mateo, from San Juan Chicahuastla,[17] made in 1738. This manuscript shows that Vetancurt's work was employed by Nahuas at that time—very close to when some of the Passion plays were written—with at least this one copyist taking the trouble to reproduce it by hand, perhaps to compensate for an insufficient supply of the printed volume. The work presents a series of introductory admonitions plus an explanation and accompanying meditations, prayers, and canticles for each of the fourteen Stations of the Cross, devoting three or four pages to each station (Schwaller 2017, 124). It follows the standard sequence that characterized the practice from the seventeenth through twentieth centuries (Schwaller 2021, 20).[18] As listed by Schwaller (2017, 123), the stations are:

1. Christ condemned to death
2. Cross is laid upon him
3. His first fall
4. He meets His Blessed Mother
5. Simon of Cyrene is made to bear the cross
6. Christ's face is wiped by Veronica
7. His second fall
8. He meets the women of Jerusalem
9. His third fall
10. He is stripped of His garments
11. His crucifixion
12. His death on the Cross
13. His body is taken down from the Cross
14. He is laid in the tomb.

Every play starts its story well before this sequence, and no play stages each of these events. However, the plays stage most of them, and some people's understanding of the play may well have been informed by their experience with this parallel—and less controversial—devotion.

PASSION STAGES AS CONTESTED GROUND

Mateo from San Juan Chicahuastla made his copy of Vetancurt's book decades after its publication; we have no reason to suppose that the Stations of the Cross had become a contested practice in the interim. But let us return now to the Tlatelolca leaders whom we left awaiting the answer to their Passion play petition in 1698. Although Vetancurt's chronicle published that same year affirmed that live Passion performances remained useful "because the natives have no more understanding than [what] their eyes [see],"[19] even this condescending attitude no longer applied in Tlatelolco. For the answer the Tlatelolca nobles received to their petition was a resounding "no" from Archbishop Francisco Aguiar y Seijas y Ulloa. No Indian, he said, should impersonate Christ, and no others should strip the one who does or whip him bloody. No one should impersonate Saint Peter voicing his denial of Christ. No woman should impersonate the Virgin Mary.

Tlatelolco's own local priest, the Franciscan friar Miguel Camacho Villavicencio, penned a vehement denunciation of both Passion and Epiphany plays, inadvertently providing invaluable ethnographic details about the Tlatelolca tradition. He notes that the earliest evangelizers of Mexico, facing the challenges of language, may have seen fit to use live representations to educate their ignorant neophytes in the mysteries of the faith, but now almost everyone understands Spanish.

Fray Miguel goes on to malign the performances for promoting indecency and superstition. Women appear onstage. Actors—including all of the apostles in the previous year's production—are drunk. People greet the actor who plays Jesus with kisses and incense, as if he were really divine—or, in Nahuatl terms, was really a *teixiptlah*, or "localized embodiment," of a god (Bassett 2015). They do the same thing to the bread he blesses during the Last Supper scene. They soak handkerchiefs in his stage blood and use them in healing rites. Furthermore, too much money gets spent on the performances, which serve only to provide an afternoon's entertainment for the large crowd that assembles in Tlatelolco's main plaza—staying out so late that offensive things are sure to happen.

Fray Miguel and Archbishop Aguiar y Seijas y Ulloa are but two voices from a large chorus of men who disparaged and distrusted Indigenous Mexican Christianity or expressed the same disdain for Indigenous intelligence we see in fray Agustín. The structure of Spain's colonial enterprise demanded that Indigenous people occupy a low rung in the moral and social hierarchies. So even if they were not overtly worshipping beings whom Spaniards classified as demons or idols, they were practicing a suspect Christianity—superficial, more emotional than intellectual, larded with superstitions, carnal, excessive, indecent (Burkhart 1998). The archbishop pre-scribed more proper Passion observances: the people could carry images of Jesus and Mary in procession and have their priest explain everything for them. He might allow some representations of scenes, according to their customs, but only if they followed the archbishop's prescriptions—no Nahua Christ, no Nahua Mary. No control of the narrative. No embodiment of God in an Indigenous body.

It is not surprising that Passion plays were a lightning rod for ecclesiastical scru-tiny, whoever was performing them. Jody Enders (2008, 123) notes that Passion plays were controversial in Europe as well, "virtually since their inception." There is a fundamental contradiction, she observes, between faith and theater: faith demands a belief in intangible things that seem impossible, while theater makes things material and visible—its realism, in effect, makes faith seem superfluous (125). A Passion play, Enders elaborates (124, original emphasis), "manipulates veri-similitude in an artistic effort to make its audiences *believe* in its holy subject, all the while inviting them to suspend their *disbelief*—at least long enough to participate in its universe of *make-believe*. The problem for the faithful is that the dramatic sub-ject itself is *not* make-believe but Gospel truth." Theatrical performance, as Richard Schechner (1985, 6, 126) posits, always creates a liminal zone in which the actors are "not themselves"—since they are playing a role—but also "not not themselves," since they inevitably carry something of their own identity into the performance and may be personally affected by it. Add to this liminality the tension between the intangible sacred and its material mise-en-scène and the fact that we are dealing with the central Christian mystery of Christ's death in a (material) body and we might wonder why Church authorities tolerated these performances at all.

Theater also has a ludic quality—the sheer fun of dressing up and playing parts or watching others do so—that caused discomfort when applied to the Passion. Tlatelolco's fray Miguel complained that people laughed simply seeing the cos-tumed actors come out to perform. The famed Spanish humanist Juan Luis Vives, while writing his 1522 commentary on Augustine's *City of God*, sidetracked briefly to condemn the "great scandal of representing the Passion of Our Lord by actors."[20] These "ugly and dishonorable"[21] treatments of sacred matters are plagued by excess jollity among the players and spectators alike. People laugh at Judas. They laugh when the disciples run away from the soldiers at Christ's arrest, as do the fleeing actors themselves. People applaud when Peter cuts off Malchus's ear, laugh when the chambermaid challenges Peter, then boo when Peter responds by denying his affiliation with Jesus. Only the actor playing Christ maintains the serious demeanor appropriate to the context, expressing pain and sadness (Hervet 1584, bk. 8, 254).[22] It is unlikely that in Spain or New Spain, solemn Holy Week sermons, however vividly they described the long-ago events, provoked such outbursts—or so riveted their audiences. The Passion could be good entertainment, the plays kept alive by popular demand as well as the hope that the unschooled masses might at least learn something about Jesus's sacrifice.

Vives's discomfort was shared by other Spaniards. Indeed, Archbishop Aguiar y Seijas y Ulloa's proscription in some ways replayed what had happened in Seville a hundred years earlier, as documented by Webster (1998). Even the performances that used an articulated statue rather than a live Jesus actor, popular with confraternities throughout the sixteenth century, fell under ecclesiastical censure. The complaints began in 1511 under Archbishop Diego de Deza and culminated in definitive suppression in 1604 (42, 149–150). In response, Sevillanos made their processional images as theatrical as they could. Confraternities vied, over the seventeenth century, to commission the most elaborate *pasos de misterio*, portable Passion tableaux featuring multiple statues equipped with the appropriate props and placed in elaborate sets—constructions that still impress the city's many Holy Week visitors. These frozen moments of Passion plays were carried through the streets in narrative order (68–69). The *pasos* materialized the divine without any need for live actors and for the "excesses and improprieties" inevitably imputed to them (154–155).[23]

Despite all these similar worries in Europe, colonial critics of Indigenous Christianity were motivated by more than a concern with proper dogma, solemnity, or the age-old tension between theology and theater. Fear, too, lies behind their prohibitions and denunciations, the same fear that haunts all colonial endeavors: the fear of spoiling the illusion of authority and thus the ability to control—or at least appear to control—the people over whom they assert dominion but who outnumber them and resent their presence. This is the same fear that, in the sixteenth century, sent Spanish soldiers into the streets during Holy Week processions to ensure that the large gatherings of Indigenous people did not suddenly transform themselves into an army of anti-Spanish rebels. Rumors of such an uprising circulated every year (1572 letter from Viceroy Martín Enríquez in *Cartas de Indias* 1970, vol. 1, 283–284). Chronicling the excessive Spanish response to a rumored uprising of Black people in 1612, Chimalpahin says he and his fellow Indigenous observers "were not at all frightened by it but were just looking and listening, just marveling at how the Spaniards were being destroyed by their fear and didn't appear as such great warriors." He details the alleged plot and the brutal punishments and mutilations meted out against the purported rebels, expressing doubt that they were guilty of anything. Holy Week processions were banned that year (Lockhart, Schroeder, and Namala 2006, 212–227).

If processions with graven images posed such danger, the "make believe" reality that troupes of Indigenous actors, wearing the clothes and speaking in the voices of

Jesus and his followers, brought to life could be even more frightening. In the story of Jesus Christ, Jerusalem's Jewish and colonial Roman leaders fear the threat to their authority and social control posed by the roving rabble who acclaim a certain wonder-working teacher from Galilee. In the Nahuatl plays, these lowlifes and the man-god they love are all called *macehualtin*, the old Nahuatl term for the commoner class (singular *macehualli*). By 1600, this had become a generic word for Indigenous people, adopted by speakers of other Indigenous languages and also assimilated into Spanish, as *macehual(es)*.[24] So references that, in sixteenth-century writing, were intended to refer to the common people of Judea would later sound like references to Indigenous people, perhaps a distinct population from the Jews.[25] And Jesus is not just played by an Indigenous actor; in the plays he is himself a *macehualli* living under colonial rule. Because of this ethnic as well as class significance, I retain the words *macehualli* and *macehualtin* in my English translations. More than any other Christian narrative, the Passion spoke to the colonial condition itself, and Indigenous Christs challenged the priesthood's monopoly on the Christian sacred.

Archbishop Aguiar y Seijas y Ulloa's successor, don Juan de Ortega y Montañez, reaffirmed the former's decision in 1704 and obliged the curates of all Indigenous Mexico City parishes to confirm their acceptance of the ban.[26] While the 1698 and 1704 documents share a file in Mexico's national archive, a change occurred during that brief span of years that boded more ill for Indigenous religious freedom—as limited as it already was. In 1700 the French Bourbon dynasty replaced the Spanish Hapsburgs as rulers of Spain and its overseas dominions. The new king, Philip V, soon launched a century-long reform program intended to modernize and rationalize the oversight of the colonies.

Linked to the broader rationalizing trends of the European Enlightenment, the Bourbon Reforms stiffened the spines of Church officials already disposed to delegitimize Indigenous Christianity as backward, irrational, emotional, and dependent on spectacular outward display rather than solemn contemplation and reason. Reform-minded clergy, seeking to segregate spiritual divinity more rigidly from the material, aimed their ire not just at Indigenous practices of performative piety but, as Brian Larkin (2004, 494, 507–508) observes, at "ornate adornment of sacred space, lavish liturgical ritual, exuberant and oftentimes raucous feast-day celebrations, ostentatious funerary rites, excessive devotion to images and relics, and in general, the easy commingling of the sacred and profane common in Baroque Catholicism."[27] Passion plays, whether in Nahuatl or Spanish, were exuberant and raucous productions that intermingled sacred and profane as they retold a divine story in material form.

In 1757, Archbishop Manuel José Rubio y Salinas ordered that performances "of the Passion of Christ our Lord, which they commonly call *Nescuitiles*," be suspended throughout the archdiocese and that all scripts and other documents be submitted to his office for inspection (edict published in Ramos Smith et al. 1998, 259). Some communities did cease their performances, at least temporarily. However, as an unintended consequence, the decree inspired replacement performances in Spanish by so-called *gente de razón* 'people of reason'—that is, people of Spanish or mixed Spanish and Indigenous (mestizo) heritage.[28] But their religious expression would soon be constrained as well, for, as Serge Gruzinski (1989, 154) observes in his discussion of this case, "enlightened authorities took a dim view of all forms of Christianity that escaped their control." Unlike Indigenous *pasioneros*, these players fell under the jurisdiction of Mexico's Holy Office of the Inquisition, and in March of 1768, as rehearsals were under way, its Chalco office began an investigation.[29]

Inquisition commissary fray Antonio de Victoria headed up the early stages of the probe. His understanding was that after Rubio y Salinas's decree, "those who in the towns they call people of reason undertook to perform the Passion, and translating it from the Mexican language into our Castilian they perform it in some towns, with grave scandal, derision, and contempt."[30] The extant scripts in both languages do not indicate a direct translation from Nahuatl to Spanish, yet Victoria's impression that the Spanish ones replaced the abandoned Nahuatl ones may be correct. Horcasitas (1974, 428–430) suggests that Spanish-language theater had previously been an elite entertainment because Spaniards were an elite, but now the non-elite Spanish and mestizo population was large enough to support popular forms of theater, and the Nahua practices these people also enjoyed became a convenient model—in this case and perhaps in others as well.

Although not denounced for superstition or idolatry, the Spanish-language plays were considered just as indecent as the Nahuatl ones due to under-dressed Christs and, if anything, even more irreverent. Tlatelolca were amused by the sight of their costumed neighbors, but Spanish-speaking Judases seem to have worked especially hard for laughs, given that their clownish facial expressions and gestures became one of the Inquisitors' specific topics of inquiry. Victoria obtained his first script (or *cuaderno* 'notebook'; I will refer to it as Cuaderno 1)[31] from a Spanish man named Manuel de Avendaño, who turned in the anonymous "*comedia* whose title is Passio Domni Nostri Jesu Xpti" that he had purchased at a market. It seemed to Avendaño that the text contained things "against our holy faith."[32] Plays were later confiscated in the towns of Ozumba, Amecameca, and Tenango, along with some loose papers, including two versions of Pontius Pilate's death sentence (see chapter 2); these were bound into the case file with all the reports.[33]

In 1769, Archbishop Lorenzana banned "the *Nescuitiles*, live representations (*representaciones al vivo*) of the Passion of Christ our Redeemer," whether Indigenous-language plays or Spanish-language substitutes, along with certain "superstitious" (*supersticiosos*) dance traditions (edict in Ramos Smith et al. 1998, 262–264). Lorenzana accepts that live representations may have seemed suitable in the early effort to promulgate Christianity in "these realms" (*estos reynos*) given the "incapacity" (*incapacidad*) of their Native inhabitants, but two and a half centuries later there is no longer any justification for the "most grave sins, imponderable inconsistencies, mockeries, idle observances, irreverencies, superstitions, and other just causes"[34] that inspire his animus toward the tradition. We saw this same trope—what was acceptable back then is scandalous now—used by fray Miguel of Tlatelolco and can contrast it with the Indigenous attitude that what the ancestors did when they accepted Christianity and established their churches remained a model for the present. Larkin names Lorenzana as one of the three most avid promulgators of the Bourbon religious reforms; his insistence in this edict that Indigenous people can and must understand the faith through the word, and not through visual display, exemplifies the reformist outlook (Larkin 2010, 127, 137–139).

Although some copies of scripts were indeed confiscated—including at least half of my sample of Nahuatl plays—and some practices abandoned, official edicts and decrees that repeatedly speak out against the same practices may have been as performative as they were effective. They stock what Ann Laura Stoler (2010) calls the "colonial archive": documents that inscribe an illusion of colonial control but are more indicative of their authors' epistemological anxieties than of reality on the disputed ground of the colony. The proclamations of archbishops and Inquisitors show us the power of these popular Passions to kindle fear and loathing in the hearts of Spanish Church officials and the fraught political environment within which Indigenous people, as well as non-elite Spanish speakers, sought to practice their own versions of Christianity and celebrate its holy days as they saw fit. The devils and other abominations these churchmen saw so thinly veiled behind just about any Indigenous devotional practice lived, of course, only in their own imaginations. Even for Spanish and creole residents of Mexico City, the reforms preached by Lorenzana and his ilk had only limited and gradual impact (Larkin 2010).

Regardless of these edicts, various Passion performances continued on or were later revived or invented, in Spanish and Indigenous languages, up to the present day, the most famous example being the Passion of Iztapalapa in southern Mexico City, performed annually since 1843 (see Trexler 2003).[35] This colonialist attitude continued to characterize conflicts between the Catholic Church and Indigenous practice. For example, Reyes García documents how, during the fieldwork for his 1960 book, a priest interfered with Carnival and Holy Week activities in the Huastecan Nahua town of Ixcatepec (formerly Ichcatepec), viewing them as a work of the devil and an offense to God. Backed by a small minority of the population, the priest blocked performers playing "Jews" and "Pharisees" from enacting the arrest and jailing of Christ in the church atrium on Thursday and the lancing in the church on Friday, which would have been followed by a procession—all carried out using statues rather than a Jesus actor. The costumed performers were limited to dances that impinged less directly on the priest's sphere of control (Reyes García 1960, 51, 76–80).

Passion plays remain controversial in contemporary Europe and the United States, not for the reasons that troubled colonial churchmen but because the same devotional trends that gave rise to European Passion plays also nurtured anti-Jewish hatred. The plays, in turn, became "a key factor . . . in the demonization process and the tragic consequences that ensued" (Fischer 1996, 1). Such problematic productions may be long-standing practices, such as the play staged in Oberammergau, Germany, since 1634, which—at least until recent changes made by reformist director Christian Stückl—could be accurately characterized as "the best example of a Passion Play serving anti-Semitic purposes" (Rabbit Leon Klenicki, in Ashe, Rock, and Klenicki 1996, 12).[36] Or they may be more recent creations, like Mel Gibson's 2004 film, *The Passion of the Christ*.[37] Interfaith leaders have provided guidance on how contemporary Christian church or community groups can produce Passion plays that are free from damaging stereotypes and depict Jesus more realistically as a first-century practitioner of Judaism (Klenicki 1996).

The Nahuatl Passions were, however, heir to this long history of European hatred that Indigenous people inadvertently incorporated into their Christian literature as they adopted and adapted the texts provided to them. It could hardly have been otherwise, as both the Franciscan and Dominican orders—responsible for most of the initial evangelization of New Spain—brought a rabid anti-Semitism to America. Franciscans framed their own in terms of a militant millennialism dependent on converting Native Americans as substitutes for, or presumed descendants of, the Jews, whose prophesied conversion was to bring about the end of the world. Dominicans, frustrated by Jewish resistance to their preaching, pursued inquisitorial methods to seek out and punish any remaining traces of Judaism among people who had been forced to renounce their religion under fear of mob violence or expulsion (Davis 2013, 94–95).

As authors of later medieval Passion literature sought to meet their readers' desire for new and painful additions to the biblical Passion accounts, one strategy was to draw on the Hebrew Bible, taking passages that had previously been applied to Jesus in a metaphorical or prophetic sense and turning them into literal, narrative imagery (Marrow 1979, 203–204). For example, a reference to a winepress in Isaiah developed into the idea of Jesus being crushed by the weight of the cross, while allusions in Psalm 21 (22) to animals besetting the singer gave rise to brutish and doglike portrayals of Jerusalem's Jewish residents (Marrow 2008, 27–42; cf. Marrow

1979; Bestul 1996, 78). In this way, the Jewish people's own holy books were turned against them.

As the level of graphic violence in Passion depictions increased over time, so did the vilification and dehumanization of the men thought to have perpetrated these acts (Marrow 2008; Kupfer 2008a). This dehumanization manifests not just in violent behavior; the Jews in the story were depicted with physiognomy meant to incite repulsion, as in figure 1.2. In James H. Marrow's (2008, 52) view, it is probably impossible to retell the Passion story with an emphasis on its brutality without simultaneously provoking anti-Jewish sentiment. Thomas Bestul (1996, 69, 170) agrees that the increasingly graphic Passion tracts actively fueled hostility toward Jews. Their social and legal standing in Europe declined as Passion literature grew more violent, beginning in the later part of the eleventh century, and became especially precarious in the fourteenth, when they were widely blamed for the Black Death (75, 103–104). These accusations and those of ritual child murder and desecration of the communion host had in common the theme of bodily defilement, whether that was the physical body of Christ that so preoccupied Passion devotees or the social body of Christendom from which non-Christians were now excluded (79, 104–108).

Compared to devotees in other parts of Europe, late medieval Castilians who sought union with the divine were less fixated on graphic illustrations of Christ's torments (Robinson 2013). As book publishing expanded under Ferdinand and Isabella, however, illustrated Passion texts flourished. Such literature reflected and contributed to the anti-Jewish sentiment that culminated in the Great Expulsion of 1492 and persisted in the Spanish Inquisition's persecution of *conversos*, people from Jewish families who had accepted an at least nominal conversion as the price for remaining in Spain.[38] For sixteenth-century Spain, William A. Christian Jr. (1981, 192) documents fervent Passion devotions that coincided with frequent rumors that Jewish people were "whipping crucifixes or sacrificing children as if they were Jesus." Passion plays contributed to anti-Jewish hostility in their own way: Enders (2008, 125) notes that the verisimilitude of the plays made the Jews, who failed to believe what was rendered so real onstage, seem even more benighted. Attacks on Jews in Europe often coincided with Holy Week (Campbell 2008, 77; Kupfer 2008a, 10).

Until the Inquisition's anti-Jewish fervor cooled in the eighteenth century (Larkin 2010, 129), Nahuas occasionally witnessed persecutions of Jewish or allegedly Jewish residents of Mexico, such as the autos-da-fé of 1596, 1601, and 1603, which Chimalpahin chronicled (Lockhart, Schroeder, and Namala 2006, 59, 72–77). Indigenous people even participated in the procession for another large auto-da-fé, in 1649 (Gruzinski 1989, 85). Apart from enacting conformity with Christianity, they had no stake in perpetuating this hatred. But it was embedded

Figure 1.2. *Christ Carrying the Cross.* Veronica is at the lower left and Simon of Cyrene, face upturned, helps support the cross. Painting by Hieronymous Bosch or follower, 1510–1535. Museum of Fine Arts, Ghent. Courtesy of Wikimedia Commons.

in the model play, as in its European sources and in the early Nahuatl sermons that detailed the Passion. In the plays, Christ's vicious persecutors are repeatedly labeled Jews. References in the Gospels to the AD 70 destruction of Jerusalem—which Christians saw as divine vengeance for Christ's death[39]—are retained, as is the Jews' enduring acceptance of guilt expressed in Matthew 27:25. Chimalpahin himself illustrates how pervasive such discourse was when he says of Christ's death that the Jews put him on the cross and that his death was avenged by Jerusalem's destruction (Lockhart, Schroeder, and Namala 2006, 116).

In the Passion plays, two or three virtuous men appear among the leaders of Jerusalem, but viewers would hardly know that Jesus himself, along with his family and friends, was Jewish. With the term *Judiosmeh* (Spanish *Judíos* plus the Nahuatl plural suffix *-meh*) applied above all to a small band of characters who associate with the Jerusalem chief priests (see chapter 5), Nahuas could view not just Jesus and his friends but the bulk of Jerusalem's people as *macehualtin* like themselves rather than dehumanized villains. But the longer-term impact of this demonization of Jews can be seen in ethnographic accounts of Indigenous Mexican myth and ritual, where forces of darkness and enemies of the solar Christ appear under this designation, Ichcatepec's "Jews" and "Pharisees" just one case among many (e.g., Reyes García 1960; Taggart 1983; Bricker 1973; Gossen 1974).

Bestul (1996, 150–154) connects the increasing violence in Passion literature with an additional historical process that is a locus of controversy: the revival, during the twelfth and thirteenth centuries, of the Roman legal system, which led to an acceptance of torture as a means to extract confessions. Passion torments mirror some judicial torments: binding of hands, stretching of limbs (155). Bestul (157–158) argues that the exaggeration of Christ's torments did not turn people against judicial torture; rather, the grotesque depictions normalized torture as part of ordinary reality and—since the innocent Christ had been subjected to such treatment—even legitimized its use against Jews, heretics, criminals, and others to whom the Roman concept of legal infamy under which Jesus was crucified was now applied.

Early cases of torture and execution of Indigenous people for alleged religious crimes brewed a storm of controversy that left them, by order of King Philip II, exempt from persecution by the Holy Office of the Inquisition, once it was formally established in New Spain in 1571.[40] Even so, Inquisition proceedings sometimes called on Indigenous witnesses, and many people were aware of the Inquisition's actions against people accused of heretical or Jewish sympathies—as in the case of the autos-da-fé mentioned above. But apart from flogging, which became normalized in colonial Nahua life (see chapter 5), judicial torture—including that of Jesus—may have remained an alien and unaccepted practice associated with the worst excesses of colonial rule.

IN THE *ALTEPETL*

The Amacuitlapilco play's title, quoted in this volume's introduction, refers to Jerusalem as an *altepetl*, a usage repeated in all the plays. I retain this term in the English translations because it shows that Nahuas conceived of this (to them) mythical central place as analogous to their own corporate communities. The *altepetl* was the largest Indigenous political unit to survive the dissolution of the Aztec Empire and be incorporated into the Spanish imperial administrative structure. It was a type of ethnic state, given its political autonomy and the fact that Indigenous people identified more closely with their *altepetl* than with broader linguistic or cultural categories such as "Nahua." The word *altepetl* is an irregular combination of *atl* 'water' and *tepetl* 'hill' or 'mountain.' Water and defensible heights are good to have, but water and mountains were also animate entities embodying sacred forces; for example, the old rain gods stored water inside mountains. Though obliged to change their leadership structure from dynastic rulers to panels of elected men—offices nevertheless often dominated by the old noble families—the *altepetl* retained corporate ownership of land. They also maintained a non-hierarchical relationship among the separate residential areas within their boundaries, wherein the largest or most central population center shared authority with each of the smaller or outlying ones by rotating political offices among the components or having each represented on the *altepetl* council. Spanish administrators parsed these components into *cabeceras* and *sujetos*, head towns and subject towns, but on the ground they operated by Nahua terms. These three elements—local self-rule, land rights, and this non-hierarchical organization, termed "cellular" or "modular" by Lockhart (1992, 15–19)—were vital to the survival of corporate communities; within them, Indigenous people could continue to speak their own languages, run most of their own affairs, practice distinctive local cultures, and mount at least some defense against excessive tribute and labor requirements, land encroachment, abusive priests, and other colonial impositions.

Away from the few metropolitan educational institutions open to Indigenous students, the alphabetic literacy essential to the use of Passion play scripts was practiced and passed along within the *altepetl*. Every governing council, called by the Spanish loanword *cabildoh*, had to have an *escribanoh*, or notary. These men took down people's wills, recorded land transfers and *cabildoh* and court minutes, maintained tribute lists, wrote petitions, and penned a wide variety of other documents—playing a vital role in community affairs, including litigation (Haskett 1991, 110–111).[41] Administration of the local churches and chapels also required an *escribanoh*. Church affairs were in the hands of a *fiscal*, an administrator whose supervising priest might visit only on a rotating basis, leaving *fiscales* to exercise considerable local authority—especially in smaller *altepetl*. Only the *gobernador* 'governor,' head of the civil administration, held higher prestige (Truitt 2018, 50).

At least some of the men and boys who comprised church choirs learned to read and write and to score and read musical notation (Truitt 2018, 102). Doctrine teachers (*temachtihqueh*) taught the Roman Catholic catechism to children. So, every *altepetl* had at least some literate men,[42] especially among the nobility, but literacy did not permeate far within the population. Some actors could memorize their lines from a written script. The two-page fragment with some of Jesus's lines preserved in Atlihuetzia, Tlaxcala, presumably was part of a document prepared by or for a literate player of Jesus (Macuil Martínez 2016, 234). But many actors would need to be coached orally in their lines by people who could read or had memorized the words. The scripts, of course, record the intended text—subject to inspection by the local priest—not any ad-libbing that might have occurred in practice.

Most people in provincial eighteenth-century *altepetl*, especially those of non-noble heritage, received only a rudimentary education in formal Catholic teachings, limited to rote memorization and recitation of basic catechetical texts: the Our Father, Hail Mary, Apostles' Creed, Salve Regina, Fourteen Articles of Faith, Ten Commandments, and some other numbered lists. Priests who quizzed people on their knowledge of doctrine, as when administering confession or prior to marriage, or archbishops on tours of inspection were generally disappointed; often, people were allowed to answer "yes" or "no" rather than actually recite the texts they were supposed to have memorized as children and to employ in daily devotions.[43] If they had the Apostles' Creed down pat, they knew only this much of the Passion story: Jesus Christ "was tormented[44] for our sake by order of Pontius Pilate. He was made to stretch his arms on the cross. He died and he was buried."[45] The Articles of Faith said even less: "Jesus Christ was tormented for our sake. He died on the cross and he was buried."[46] A simplified, question-and-answer doctrine popular from the mid-seventeenth century on—a reflection, really, of priests' abandonment of more intensive catechetical education—says no more about Christ's last earthly days than does the Apostles' Creed (Burkhart 2014).

Pictorial catechisms gave similarly abbreviated statements using pictures, often bloody cords for "he was tormented," a bleeding figure on a cross, and a body bundled for burial.[47] Priests might tell more of the story, with appropriate Gospel readings and hymns, during Holy Week services. If the unpublished sermons composed in the sixteenth century, or similar ones, were in use in the eighteenth century, attentive Nahua parishioners could listen to detailed retellings of the story and become familiar over the years with these accounts of the events the play dramatized and how they were supposed to view them. However, the Indigenous-language fluency of priests and their dedication to presenting a sophisticated level of teaching to people they saw as crude and limited in their capacity had declined. Few people in the eighteenth century possessed the doctrinal knowledge of the Nahua scholars from a century or two earlier—men who were, of course, exceptional even in their own time.

The rosary devotion, though, was one avenue by which a basic recounting of the Passion events could become familiar to Nahuatl speakers who practiced this popular prayer cycle. Introduced by Dominican friars, the prayers were published in Nahuatl for the first time in 1565, by fray Domingo de la Anunciación. Jesus's five *tlamahuizolli tonehuizzo* 'painful marvels,' to be recounted on Mondays and Thursdays, each accompanied by one Our Father and ten Hail Marys, are: praying in the garden and sweating with blood, the flagellation, having the crown of thorns placed on his head, being sentenced to death and forced to carry the cross on his shoulder, and being nailed to the cross (Anunciación 1565, 77v–78v; transcribed and translated in Burkhart 2001, 125–126).

Visually, the Passion and its protagonists manifested themselves not just in pictorial catechisms or woodcuts in printed books, which may have reached only a limited number of users, but in the public works of art that everyone saw on the insides and outsides of their churches and chapels. Large figures of Christ on the cross hung in many churches, carved of wood or molded from lightweight *pasta de caña*. Paintings of the crucifixion, often with Mary, John, and Mary Magdalene in the scene, and sometimes other Passion events—the praying in the garden, the flagellation, Christ with Pontius Pilate, Christ on the way to Calvary, the descent from the cross—figure among the prodigious output of the sixteenth-century Indigenous mural painters.[48] Sixteenth-century sculptors carved Passion insignia—the crown of thorns, the nails, the lance, the sponge, and so on—onto large stone crosses erected, like depictions of a world tree or axis mundi, at the centers of the quadrilateral church patios (see figure 1.3). Later artists added new Passion-themed paintings and carved figures to the colonial churches.[49] Mateo of San Juan Chicahuastla, the Nahua man who made the copy of Vetancurt's *Via Crucis* book, included a series of his own original drawings: one for the title page and eight for individual stations, with an emphasis on Jesus and the cross, plus an additional drawing of a cross with flowers at the locations of the nails (see images and discussion in Schwaller 2017, 2021). Schwaller (2021, 191) suggests that his drawings of Christ could be based on the articulated statues used in Holy Week ceremonies, but they could also serve as models of or for Passion play staging (see figure 1.4).

Portable statues were carried in Holy Week processions, a popular practice that we saw condoned by Archbishop Aguiar y Seijas y Ulloa. Confraternities could commission and keep these statues, to be carried and accompanied by their marching members. In Tepalcingo, the home of one of the plays, an Indigenous confraternity had a miracle-working seventeenth-century statue of Jesús Nazareno, depicting Jesus fallen to his knees with the cross over his shoulder—statues of this type were particularly popular here in what is now Morelos (Taylor 2016, 205). When Spaniards sought to seize control of this confraternity and its Jesus, Indigenous people protested. The dispute continued, despite the intervention on the Spanish side of archbishops in 1724 and again in 1743. The Indigenous devotees asserted their rights over the statue again during and after the Mexican War of Independence; ultimately, the confraternity dissolved in the mid-nineteenth century (Reyes-Valerio 1960, 9–11; Taylor 2010, 196–199).

Many other images, of Mary as well as Christ, had stories of miraculous origin or miraculous activation—when a previously inactive image moved, wept, repaired itself, or showed other evidence of life. William B. Taylor found that most Mexican

Figure 1.3. Atrium cross, Tepeapulco, Hidalgo, with Passion insignia (originally placed in center of churchyard). Photo by the author.

shrines with miraculous images of Christ or Mary originated in the seventeenth century and flourished in the eighteenth. During this time, in the Valley of Mexico area, "as many as fifty-five Marian images and forty-seven images of Christ made news for working wonders" (Taylor 2016, 182; 2010, 25–30; cf. Taylor 2005). Jennifer Scheper Hughes (2010) traces one miraculous image of the crucified Christ from the sixteenth century to the present, framing her discussion as a "biography" because this Jesus is seen as a living community patron in Totolapan, Morelos. Totolapan's Christ has much company in his longevity: most of the colonial-era miraculous Christs still retain their wondrous reputations (Taylor 2016, 198). The eighteenth century saw more new shrines to Christ images than to Marian ones; even though the vast majority of these images showed Christ on the cross or in another phase of his passional agonies, these Christs were, like Mary, considered to be "santos"—not

Figure 1.4. Christ about to be nailed to the cross, in Mateo of San Juan Chicahuastla's redaction of Vetancurt's Nahuatl *Via Crucis*, f. 17. The figure on the left represents Calvary or Golgotha (Hill of the Skull), while other sketches represent a rope, hammer, three nails, and tongs for holding the nails (Schwaller 2021, 184, 186). Hatch marks on the body depict wounds from the flagellation. Image from the manuscript housed in the Copley Library at the University of San Diego, published courtesy of the Academy of American Franciscan History.

abstract figures but cherished community patrons—and were commonly described as "kind (*amable*) and most beautiful" (201, 218). This gentle perception extended to their actions: Taylor (2016, 218; 2010, 59) found Mexican Christ images to be associated primarily with local needs for protection and healing, similar to images of Mary, while in Spain Christs were linked to portents and plagues.

Ubiquitous Passion imagery kept certain scenes and personages in constant view, though often isolated from the larger Passion narrative to which they pertained. Meanwhile, the many stories of miraculous images fostered reverence and the ever-present possibility that a local image might reveal itself to be a particularly lively and involved local patron. Images also provided convenient models for costume and prop design and even sources of costume elements, which actors sometimes borrowed from church images to wear in the play. Fray Francisco Larrea, in his report for the Inquisition, defends this practice from its critics.[50] People borrow these vestments because they cannot afford to make good copies and so their performance "may turn out similar to the original Passion."[51] Far from disrespecting the images and accouterments, they, in their simplicity (*simpleza*), accord these material objects such excessive veneration that ministers are obliged to reprimand them. This is the old trope about peasants and other crude Christians identifying images too closely with the beings they represent, imposed upon a Mesoamerican view of materially embodied divinity to which this Dominican priest could grant no legitimacy.

Much church imagery resembled Europeans in coloring and facial features, but how validating an experience it was for Indigenous people in the eighteenth century to dress and see one another in these costumes and roles is difficult to say.[52] Indigenous people accepted Christian images as holy and meaningful in ways that may not be immediately obvious and in ways that many Spanish churchmen besides Larrea could neither understand nor effectively counteract (Taylor 2010, 23). It did not matter so much what they looked like. As noted above, crucifixes could look beautiful and kind to worshippers of multiple ethnicities. Hughes (2010, 7, 204) notes that the people of Totolapan do not see their miraculous Cristo as suffering, even though the statue represents Jesus in pain on the cross, and she criticizes the view—coming from liberation theology—that worshipping the crucified Christ somehow made people passive and resigned to poverty and suffering. Mexican images of Jesus show him suffering because that is how he was presented by the colonial evangelizers, not because Indigenous people freely chose a suffering Christ from a range of options (51). Suffering is not, then, the most salient feature of a Passion-related Christ image. He is a benevolent and protective patron, and people might extend these attributes to Jesus actors. When Indigenous people dressed up as Jesus and other Passion personages, the fact that the sacred beings had come to life in one's own *altepetl* may have been at least as significant as the fact that they now looked more like their local devotees.

We cannot presume to understand all the emotions Passion plays generated. Vetancurt observed tears shed at San José de los Naturales, and Larrea recalled seeing people weep while they watched the Passion play in Tepoztlán (55 kilometers from Jonacatepec), where he had seen the performance various times. Larrea assumed they were moved by repentance for their sins.[53] Here he voices the European view that tears shed over the Passion are physical evidence of internal sorrow for sins (Webster 1998, 177–178). The fact that people wept gives us a valuable insight into reactions to the plays, but they had not necessarily internalized fray Francisco's own moral concerns. Some may have simply felt sadness, or empathy for the characters, or distress at the violence and injustice acted out before their eyes. Some may have operated within the Indigenous "economy of weeping" Heather J. Allen (2015, 487–492) describes, in which people weep to elicit favors from gods or social superiors and weep again in gratitude when the favors are received. Kay Almere Read (2005) writes of how Mexica tears created positive, ethical, equilibrium-restoring effects in the external world, helping to keep cosmic and social orders functioning. With embodied saints and Jesus immanent onstage while chaos reigned, weeping observers may well have had concerns other than the state of their own souls.

Whether marked more by tears or by laughter, for nonliterate people in a provincial community, the Passion play was an amazingly rich storytelling and dramatic event. Compared to their simple catechisms, it was like jumping from a reading primer (which catechisms doubled as) to Shakespearean tragedy. They could learn much more about Christian Gospel and legend here than they were likely to get anywhere else and engage with it emotionally at a depth unlikely to occur during rote memorization and recital or passive listening. With casts of fifty or more, not counting musicians and extras plus other participants attending to various logistics and preparation, lots of people could take part in the artistic and bonding experience of being in a show. The fact that it was enjoyable to do so does not mean the sacred messages of the story were ignored or subverted.

A cross-dressing male youth could play a female role, as seems to have been the case in sixteenth-century practice, but fray Miguel of Tlatelolco makes it clear that by 1698, women had access to the stage and were playing female roles in Passion and Epiphany plays. Indigenous women had leadership opportunities within the religious confraternities that proliferated in colonial Mexico but few formal roles within the *altepetl* organization. Playing the Virgin Mary or another woman of the Passion story could be a significant public act of devotion and a source of prestige. Given the gender-based division of labor among Indigenous Mesoamericans, we can assume that women also typically made the cloth costumes for all the actors and prepared the food for the Last Supper (and any snacks for rehearsing actors). The tortilla that represented Christ's body—kissed and incensed according to fray Miguel—was patted out by a woman's hands.

In the introduction to this volume, I noted that the Princeton Passion names a choirmaster, Gregorio Eusebio, a likely director of the show (or at least of its music) and a possible actor, the nobleman don Bartolomé. We can add some other actors' names to this roster. When officers of the Mexican Inquisition investigated the Spanish-language productions that had aroused official ire, they visited a number of communities to ask questions. In early March 1770, a commissary of the Inquisition, don Juan Ignacio de Lardizábal, interrogated seven high-ranking Indigenous nobles—he uses the terms *indio cacique* and *india cacica*, applied by the Spanish to Indigenous rulers—in the *altepetl* of Huejotzingo. While they claimed to have no information about the scandalous plays put on by the "people of reason," they did share details of a defunct Nahuatl-language Passion play tradition. Even filtered through Lardizábal's legalistic Spanish, these Nahuas provide rare firsthand details.[54]

The first person interviewed was forty-year-old don Bernardo Peregrino, who had little information to offer but did recall that don Antonio de Guevara and the late Cristóbal Pérez played apostles and don Antonio's now-widowed sister played Mary. The sister, doña Gertrudis de Guevara, now forty-five years old, confirmed that she had acted as Mary. This was many years ago, she said, and the scripts they used were in Nahuatl (*mexicano*), as was the performance. Doña Lorenza Dorado, who gave her age as forty, stated that she had played Mary Magdalene but had not seen any Passion plays since she was a child. Lardizábal spoke next with don Antonio. The seventy-year-old reported that he used to play Jesus, his brother don Manuel played Peter, his sister doña Gertrudis played Mary, don Bernabel Bustamante—"who died inebriated" (*quien murio Ebrio*)—played Judas, and doña Lorenza Dorado played Veronica. This contradicts the latter's own statement, though she might have played Veronica and Mary Magdalene in different years or both with a change of costume.

In response to Lardizábal's questions about the *Disposicion comica* 'comic disposition' and other errors in the Spanish-language performances, don Antonio asserted that Huejotzingo's Passion had been performed in the church cemetery—the setting attested to by Larrea and the Princeton Passion—with permission from the priest, who reviewed the papers, "and that they did not do it in a mode of derision, or entertainment, but by custom and devotion to the Passion of Christ our lord."[55] Were this in Nahuatl rather than Spanish, he may well have used the same phrase, *ahmo zan ahahuilli* 'not just an amusement,' with which the Cuernavaca primordial title defended that *altepetl*'s Passion play. Furthermore, said don Antonio, "none of the performers were of those who in common usage are called *de razón*, because they all were Indians, although most of them were *caciques* and *principales*."[56]

Asked about the script, don Antonio recalled that they had obtained it from Amecameca, a Nahua community 60 kilometers away. His brother don Manuel, who gave his age as sixty-three, said they had given the papers to the late don Diego Álvarez to copy—making him the only named copyist of a Passion play—but don Manuel did not know where these papers were. When Lardizábal pursued the matter with don Diego's widow, fifty-year-old doña Josepha Cordero, she told him she formerly had in her keeping a handwritten book in quarto size "from where they took out the *papeles*"; the word *papel* here is ambiguous, as it could refer to papers or to roles in the play.[57] Two years ago, in financial distress, she had given this book to her nephew to pawn. However, he had lost it in a robbery. The twenty-seven-year-old nephew, Joseph Joachin Mexicano, confirmed his aunt's account, adding that the robbery occurred when he had gone to a religious festival, leaving his house unguarded. His efforts to recover the book and his other stolen property had been unsuccessful, but he promised to turn the book over to the authorities if he got it back.

Don Bernardo reported that the Passion play had been abandoned fifteen years earlier, on orders from the bishop. But the Guevara brothers told a different story. Don Antonio said the play was last performed thirty or forty years earlier, and don Manuel said it was more than thirty years; this time frame would correspond to the 1730s. The brothers agreed that the sudden, alcohol-related death of the Judas actor precipitated the play's demise. According to don Antonio, "It was ended because don Bernabel Bustamante, who played the role of Judas, having died *ahogado* (drowned or suffocated) by his own inebriation (as he has said), all his comrades were intimidated, and none of them wanted to take charge of that role, and that, and no other thing, was the motive for which from that time the said performances had ceased."[58] Don Antonio is asserting, with his emphatic "no other thing," that the decision was made by the locals, not forced on them by a bishop. Don Manuel confirmed that no one wanted the role after the sudden, drunken death of the man who played Judas. Whether it was the bishop or the booze that truly finished off Huejotzingo's Passion play, the story about the unfortunate don Bernabel's death suggests that playing this traitor's role was thought to carry some risk for the actor himself, whether it left him in a disordered, vulnerable state or subject to divine retribution.

Both don Antonio and don Manuel signed their names to their testimony—they were literate men who could have read their scripted lines. The fact that all the named actors held elite rank indicates that acting was a prestigious activity that could be dominated by an *altepetl*'s leading citizens, not something to be undertaken by ragtag roving players. The women may have been young girls when they performed, but don Antonio, by his reckoning, was in his thirties when he agreed to be stripped, flogged, beaten, mocked, and mounted on a cross. Far from bringing scandal upon his name, his acting may have been one method for accruing the prestige appropriate to a gentleman of his high rank. He is the only eighteenth-century Nahua Jesus we currently know by name.

A document in the Archivo de la Fiscalía in Atlihuetzia, Tlaxcala, home of the two play fragments, lists some other apparent Passion play participants.[59] Here it is the church officials of the community who recorded the Passion participants for posterity. Some were to provide props (lantern, white tunic) while others had roles: Domingo Ramos was Veronica, Dionisio Francisco was Reuben (Robeno), and other men were to play soldier roles (centurion, foot captain, standard bearer) and an unspecified woman. With both female roles here assigned to men, we can infer that cross-dressing for female characters remained a practice in at least some local traditions.

To the extent that we can identify *altepetl* where Nahuatl Passion plays were performed in the later colonial era, they fall into a rough arc passing from southwest
of Mexico City in the State of México (the unavailable script I was told of, if it
is from this time, and possibly the Princeton Passion, if it is from Mexicaltzingo
or Tenancingo), east and southeast through the state of Morelos (Jonacatepec,
Tepoztlán, Xochitlán, perhaps Cuernavaca), then northeast into the states of
Puebla (Huejotzingo) and Tlaxcala (Tlatlauhquitepec, Atlihuetzia) and the eastern
extension of the State of México (Amecameca, according to don Antonio, and the
Princeton play if it is from Tlalnepantla). The four Spanish-language plays are from
this latter area as well (see figure 1.5).

It may be that during the eighteenth century, after the archbishops suppressed
the Mexico City performances, the tradition flourished mainly in this provincial
hinterland. Above I noted the popularity of miraculous Christ images, and we
can plant this devotional mode quite firmly in the soil of the Passion-performing
provinces. Edward Osowski (2010, 27–28) labels the Chalco region a "Passion
of Christ devotion zone" for Indigenous Christianity, characterized by miracle-
working crosses and other Passion-related images, while devotions centered on
Mary enjoyed more popularity in Mexico City and its immediate environs. One
such miracle occurred in Tlayacapan in 1728, when a stone cross was perceived to
move in the pattern of the sign of the cross—a wonder accepted by authorities,
who granted the local Indigenous community permission to house the cross in a
new chapel (20–21). Of longer miraculous standing was the Santo Entierro at the
Sacromonte in Amecameca, a holy site representing the hill of Calvary and Christ's
cave tomb—likely a pre-Columbian sacred site adapted to this new purpose. The
Sacromonte shrine was ushered into existence by the local Indigenous ruler in the
sixteenth century, the first in what would become a regional array of Passion-related
sites (20; Osowski 2008).[60] This devotional focus would certainly have fostered the
performance of Passion plays, in Amecameca and throughout the region, and the
plays would have helped maintain interest in the local shrines. Cross-ethnic Passion
devotion then manifested itself in the Spanish plays gathered up by the Chalco
branch of the Inquisition, one of which was from Amecameca. Even if essentially
the same play was performed across the region, each *altepetl* could link the story
and personages to whatever local Passion shrine or image most meaningfully
embodied Jesus or his sorrowing mother: the Santo Entierro in Amecameca, the
Jesús Nazareno in Tepalcingo, and others.[61]

In addition to non-Indigenous Spanish speakers who watched and enjoyed the
performances, whether resident in the *altepetl* or visiting for the festival, the Nahuatl
Passions were surely seen and perhaps acted in by members of other Indigenous
language groups. Mazahua and Otomi speakers shared parts of these provinces

Figure 1.5. Map of the central area of Mexico, depicting communities mentioned in this study.

KEY:

★ extant Nahuatl play
▲ reported Nahuatl play
■ extant Spanish play

Drawn by Kendra Farstad.

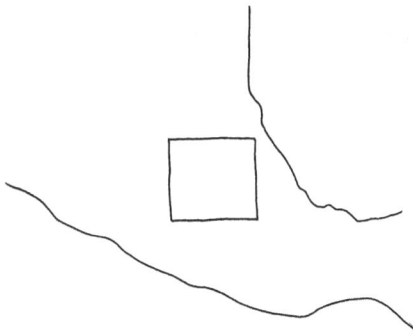

with Nahuas, living in their own or multi-ethnic communities and often speaking Nahuatl as a second language. A popular theatrical form, the Passion play was maintained by Indigenous religious leaders, like Gregorio Eusebio of the Princeton play, and tolerated—at least at some times and places—by Roman Catholic priests, who often had larger jurisdictions than they could oversee effectively. These Indigenous leaders and the *altepetl* residents who participated in the eighteenth-century performances knew not and cared not where the play originally came from or how far it had spread. It bore the authority conveyed by the written word, the archaic Nahuatl of their grandparents, and the sacred story it retold—a story inscribed into the landscape in miraculous shrines and images. Their concern was to make their show come off well, yielding blessings and prestige for their corporate community and its leaders, an engaging spectacle for visitors, profits for local commerce, and a chance for actors, musicians, set designers, and costumers to exhibit their talents.

2

Sets, Sights, Scribes, and Sounds

USING SPACE

Nahuatl theater did not skimp when it came to sets and special effects. Angels could be raised and lowered on platforms, souls could climb ladders from purgatory to heaven, Saint Michael could summon the dead from their graves, souls could suffer the flaming punishments of hell or purgatory, the Three Kings could ride horses to Jerusalem while the Star of Bethlehem led them along, Juan Diego could gather flowers for Our Lady of Guadalupe on the hill of Tepeyacac. Although Passion plays presented the unique challenge of safely raising three men on crosses, most of the staging was fairly straightforward.

Stage directions in the six scripts, though never as detailed as we might like, provide some information on how the plays were staged and how specific productions envisioned different uses of the performance space. The man who wrote out the Amacuitlapilco script is our most prolific consultant on matters of staging, but all the scriptwriters provide useful directions for their actors, sometimes differing from one production to another. I begin with what we can gather from the six scripts about the general range of practices. Variations in how specific scenes were staged will be covered in the next section.

Working outdoors, typically in cemeteries, the actors made use of a temporary stage, called a *tlapechtli* 'platform.' This had to be at least large enough to hold one or more tables with seating for thirteen or more people, possibly in a single row, so that the Last Supper, as well as meetings of the Jerusalem council, could be staged.

https://doi.org/10.5876/9781646424511.c002

It had to be sturdy enough for a convincingly menacing-looking group of soldiers to sneak across it and take Jesus into custody, falling down and standing up three times when they come face to face with their target.

Stage directions generally instruct actors to *hualquiza* 'come out' or 'come forth' when they enter the performance space, consistent with Spanish theater's usage of *salir* 'to leave' or 'to go out.' The Tepalcingo scriptwriter sometimes instructs actors to *hualcalaqui* 'enter hither,' but in general *calaqui* 'to enter' refers to exiting the stage, an action also indicated by *yauh* 'to go'—the latter consistent with Spanish plays, where actors *vanse* 'go.' *Calaqui* combines *calli* 'house' and *aqui* 'enter,' suggesting that actors leave the stage to go inside a building, whether a backstage space concealed from the audience by curtains or a more solid structure temporarily erected for the purpose. The fact that Spanish plays refer to the backstage or off-stage space as *dentro* 'inside' is somewhat analogous to the Nahuatl convention.

The offstage space did play the part of *calli* 'houses' in the Passion plays. A character might knock on a door set up there, from which one or more other actors emerge to speak with them, as when John and James come to the house where the Last Supper will be or John comes to summon Mary and the other women to Jerusalem to witness Christ's death. Judas might linger at the door to voice his grievances after his companions go inside. When the stage represents an indoor space, that same door could represent the way out of, say, the temple or the council meeting. In addition to this exit place, actors needed at least one other outlet, as sometimes they come from different directions or depart to different destinations. To conveniently move furniture and other large objects (such as representations of a garden and a jail) on and off the stage, an exit larger than a door frame was also required; alternatively, large props could be brought on from the sides of the platform. Sometimes actors are instructed to move to the edge of the stage (*tlapechtenco*), whether to separate themselves from the main action and perhaps speak to others from a distance or express private feelings or to declaim public proclamations from the different sides of the stage, with the audience standing in for the people of Jerusalem.

These large productions did not confine themselves to the platform. When Jesus comes to Jerusalem for his Palm Sunday entry, the stage is Jerusalem and Jesus and his party walk there from another spot (scenes I.ii and I.iii). His initial dialogues with his students and, if staged at this point in the play, farewell exchange with his mother could also occur at this offstage setting. Jesus then mounts the female donkey that some apostles (usually James and John) have obtained at his direction—from either the stage (if the donkey is to be taken from Jerusalem) or another offstage place, which in the Princeton play includes a small building housing the donkey (4v). He rides toward the stage, accompanied by his students and joined by children and other extras, waving fronds and flowers; figure 2.1 offers a

Figure 2.1. Christ rides into Jerusalem. Woodcut in Pedro de Gante, *Doctrina christiana en lengua mexicana*, Mexico City, 1553, f. 109r. Benson Latin American Collection, LLILAS Benson Latin American Studies and Collections, University of Texas at Austin.

sense of how the scene could be staged. The Amacuitlapilco script specifies that the apostles will be spread out as they walk (9r), requiring some degree of space. Jewish officials watch and comment from the stage. Jesus may dismount and begin to speak before getting up onto the stage to continue the action. The Princeton play (5r) calls for some kind of a gate or doorway (*puertah*), perhaps constructed at the edge of or adjacent to the stage,[1] through which the party enters the *altepetl* and through which the party heading for Calvary might also exit the stage, although this is not specified.[2]

Calvary, site of the crucifixion, is also separated from the main stage. This suits the geography of the actual Jerusalem, where this hill was outside the city walls. Placing the crucifixion off the stage served two purposes. The first is practical: raising the crosses holding Christ and the two thieves was a challenging and potentially dangerous endeavor. Being on solid ground in a spot where holes deep enough to give the crosses adequate support could be prepared in advance, with extra crew members carefully positioned to help lift the crosses and deploy ropes, would facilitate that scene. The second is theatrical: the *Via Crucis*, or Way of the Cross, could more realistically be re-created if there was a linear movement from the stage-set Jerusalem to the spot designated as Calvary. The several encounters that occur along the way could take place at different spots. Conceivably and depending on the distance, audience members could walk along with the actors to continue witnessing the action, transforming the space into more of a processional route, like those which many people would tread later during Holy Week. Hence two processions or procession-like movements frame the main action of the play: the Palm Sunday donkey-assisted entry and the removal to Calvary.

No Passion play requires trap doors or space beneath the stage to represent hell or purgatory, as do some other Nahuatl plays. Space above stage level is mentioned occasionally and could have been used more often than indicated. Jesus may ascend into the Garden of Gethsemane (located on the Mount of Olives or, according to some of the plays, Mount Zion). Pilate's house may have two levels so he can display Christ to the crowd from a balcony or other raised area (IV.iv.19). Calvary might be presented as the hill it originally was (Golgotha or Hill of the Skull, Tzontepec in Nahuatl), perhaps reusing scenery from the Mount of Olives (I.ii.32) or a Mount Zion set used as a backdrop for the Last Supper and Garden of Gethsemane scenes (V.i.15). Supports for the crosses might be hidden behind this raised area.

MAKING PLACES

The onstage space became different locations through set changes as well as the movements and dialogue of the actors. In several scenes, rows of men sit on benches or chairs, whether they are the leaders of Jerusalem meeting in council or Jesus and his students gathered to eat at the home of Simon the Pharisee or of their Last Supper host. Council meetings required mainly seating but also a table or two: an angry man occasionally whacks his hand on a table and the notary, when present, requires a writing desk. Much of the same furniture could be used in all these scenes. The

Last Supper table was laid with items needed for the meal. Though only Penn and Amacuitlapilco provide detailed lists (II.iii.25), all performances likely created the supper scene by laying a table with flowers, wine, tortillas and other foodstuffs, and tableware. Where the cleansing of the temple was staged (Axochiapan, Princeton, Tepalcingo; see chapter 5), tables might also be used to hold the merchants' wares, or they could be spread on the stage. Scriptwriters give no instructions for props or sets that would mark the space as a temple.

Also left largely up to the local directors is whether or how elaborately to represent the Garden of Gethsemane, when Christ goes there to pray after the Last Supper. Flowers, other plants, an imitation hillside, or walls that form an enclosure (*xochitepanco* 'flower wall-place' is the usual word for this locale) might be carried onto the stage. The Princeton play includes a stop at the Mount of Olives before the entry to Jerusalem: Jesus sits here while his students gather fronds and palm branches from this faux hill before walking on to Jerusalem. This set could easily have been reused when Christ goes to pray in the garden. Penn clearly calls for a garden space that Christ goes into, leaving his sleeping companions outside (20r), while Princeton has Christ descend from the garden to where the apostles doze (24v) and Amacuitlapilco's Christ leaves his companions at the edge of the stage while he goes in and out of the garden (29r). Other plays do not require Christ to move back and forth between his place of prayer and the spot where the apostles wait, but the space could be outfitted as a garden nonetheless. The angel who visits him there may appear high up, as he does in the Princeton Passion (25v), whether climbing to the top of a stage-set hill or revealing himself on a ladder or platform erected for the purpose. Figure 2.2 depicts how the scene might have been arranged in space, with the three apostles, Jesus, and the angel at different levels.

Every play features the Water Carrier whom Jesus knows will lead his messengers (again, usually James and John) to the house where he will observe Passover (II. iii.4). Wording in the Penn (9v) and Princeton (14r) plays genders Water Carrier as a young male. While his jug (*tzotzocolli*) indicates his errand, the water fetching can be staged more or less elaborately depending on whether a water source is provided. One is implied in the Penn play, where the script instructs Water Carrier to go take water (*concuiz in atl*, 9v). Princeton stagehands were to set up a *pilah* 'font' or 'trough' (from Spanish, 14r) where the actor could fill his jug. Amacuitlapilco (17v) sends him *in canin maniz atl* 'where water will be lying' in whatever sort of container might be chosen. This play's Water Carrier brings along a *xicalli* 'gourd vessel' inside the jug and uses it to fill the larger vessel gourdful by gourdful, the action pausing while this simple daily task is acted out. The delay justifies his subsequent concern that he is taking too long and may be chastised for dawdling. Time also passes because Water Carrier walks a long way before looking back and seeing

Figure 2.2. Christ prays in the Garden of Gethsemane while apostles sleep in the foreground, Peter holding his sword. Woodcut in Bernardino de Sahagún, *Psalmodia christiana*, 1583, 3v. Courtesy of the John Carter Brown Library, Brown University, Providence, RI.

John and James following. This detail suggests that the water source may have been set some distance from the stage, eliminating the need to move a large container of water onto the platform. This could be the case with Princeton's *pilah* as well.

Turning from water to fire, we find that Peter is always to be warming himself (*motohtonihtiyez* or *mozcotiyez*) outside the high priest Caiaphas's place when he utters his three denials of Christ (III.vi.1), a detail derived from the Gospel accounts. Stagehands thus must provide a real or simulated source of fire, but only Amacuitlapilco (35r) instructs them to bring in a *braseroh* 'brazier'—using the Spanish term even though braziers were also artifacts of Indigenous origin (*tlecaxitl*). Items of Old World and Indigenous origin, with their respective terminology, blend readily among the props, as they did in daily life. The term *tepozmacuahuitl* 'metal hand stick' for Peter's sword, in both the stage directions and Jesus's lines (III. ii.27, III.ii.29), is an exception to the generally easy inmixing of Spanish words. It is a deliberate archaism, invoking the obsidian-bladed *macuahuitl* 'hand sticks' that were the pre-Columbian Nahua warriors' most deadly weapons; scriptwriters could have chosen the loanword *espadah* 'sword,' or *cuchilloh* 'knife,' which Tepalcingo's scriptwriter does pair here with "metal hand-stick" (73).[3]

This archaism may function to Indigenize Peter and Jesus relative to the soldiers who are coming into the garden to carry out the arrest, a scene depicted in figure 2.3. Judas and the Jewish leaders always demand strong soldiers well armed with metal to carry out Christ's arrest, but the Penn Passion (21r) provisions them in the most detail, with a string of items described by Spanish words. They carry not just *hachas ihuan linternas* 'torches and lanterns,' which echo the lanterns and torches (*laternis et facibus*) of John 18:3. They also bear, in place of John's generic "weapons" or the swords and clubs of Matthew 26:47 (and Mark 14:43), *cadenas, sogah, lanzas, ihuan alabardas* 'chains, rope, lances, and halberds' (III.iii.1). Even though it is not unusual for the Nahuatl used in stage directions to be less conservative than the dialogue, this array is striking because words that could easily be rendered in Nahuatl, such as *ocotl* 'torch,' *tepozmecatl* 'chain,' and *mecatl* 'rope'—the latter two used frequently in the plays—are given in Spanish instead, yet all plays use "metal hand stick" for Peter's weapon. Since a lance is one of the implements of the Passion, its presence is not strange; indeed, one of these lances would probably be used to pop the bag of blood at Christ's side later in the play. But the halberds are a striking and menacing European addition to the arsenal.

After his arrest, Jesus is shuttled among a number of different locations that had to be represented separately and recognizably on the stage. In the Gospels, he spends Thursday night in Caiaphas's custody. Four of the plays provide a jail to house him during this interim, using the Nahuatl designation *teilpiloyan* 'place where people are tied up' or *teilpilcalli* 'house where people are tied up.' In the Princeton play

Figure 2.3. Judas leads the soldiers to arrest Christ; Peter cuts off Malchus's ear. Woodcut in Pedro de Gante, *Doctrina christiana en lengua mexicana*, Mexico City, 1553, f. 132v. Benson Latin American Collection, LLILAS Benson Latin American Studies and Collections, University of Texas at Austin.

(28v), he is taken inside a building (*calihtec*). It is unclear whether this is an onstage construction that is not given the label "jail" or if he is taken offstage and the audience simply hears the subsequent trumpeting and whistling of his captors. The Tlatlauhquitepec scriptwriter hustles him off to his various interrogators without an indoor interlude. Only Amacuitlapilco (35r) gives a hint about the jail stage set, and it is a bit cryptic: "Then they will take Christ to the jail. The jailhouse will appear in front of people, made in such a way that everyone will see the model, the sign."[4] This "model, sign" figure refers to positive moral examples—and certainly the play is intended to teach things—but it could be meant more literally here, as a model and representation of an actual jailhouse, like those overseen by *altepetl*

Figure 2.4. Christ is brought before Caiaphas. Woodcut in Pedro de Gante, *Doctrina christiana en lengua mexicana*, Mexico City, 1553, f. 136r. Benson Latin American Collection, LLILAS Benson Latin American Studies and Collections, University of Texas at Austin.

officials. But the scriptwriter clearly intended the inside of the jail to be visible to spectators. The Penn play stipulates that the detained Christ is to be tied to the trunk of an olive tree, a pointless gesture if no one could see him (see scene III.iv).[5]

When not jailed, Jesus is taken, in sequence, to Annas, to Caiaphas, to Pilate, to Herod, and then to Pilate once again—encounters that would resemble figure 2.4. The scripts correctly identify Herod as ruler of Galilee, but he appears to reside near Pilate in Jerusalem; since Holy Land geography is rather beside the point, no scriptwriter saw the need to explain, as John 23:7 does, that Herod happened to be visiting Jerusalem at the time. Occasionally, Christ is simply hauled *ixpan* 'in front of' or 'in the presence of' one of these potentates, but usually the scripts state that the man is at his residence (*ichan*). As *altepetl* leaders sometimes conducted official business at their homes (Sousa 2017, 248), for Christ to be taken to these different residences rather than to a central administrative structure would not have seemed odd. The door leading offstage could be deployed repeatedly to represent the different residences, with one actor leaving through the door and another then entering from it after Christ is yanked around the stage a bit, with the dialogue indicating who each man is supposed to be.

The Princeton play (26r) has a more elaborate setup. When Judas and the soldiers go to enact Christ's arrest, Annas, Caiaphas, Herod, and Pilate—the latter accompanied by Notary—are already instructed to be in their respective homes (*inchahchan*). They may each have a chair, as later both Herod and Pilate are to sit on one, and Notary would require his own chair and writing table. The Tlatlauhquitepec scriptwriter calls for a similar arrangement, with the four actors to take their places even earlier, right after Caiaphas orders Centurion to lead the soldiers to the arrest (6v). Apparently, Herod and Pilate come forth now, joining Annas and Caiaphas on the stage. Then *quinchahchantlalizqueh* 'they (Annas and Caiaphas?) will put them (Pilate and Herod?) in their respective homes.' After Judas then speaks of his satisfaction with his payment and leaves, they each greet them by name—again it is not clear who the "they" and the "them" are, but this exchange would let the audience know which actor plays Pilate and which Herod. These four "homes" might be arranged around the periphery of the stage, allowing the actors some space through which to proceed from one to the next. Meanwhile, the arrest, then the jailing and Peter's denial, then the mockery commanded by Herod, and then the flagellation could all take place center stage between the different interrogation scenes.

The Tepalcingo play (68–70) leaves Christ still kneeling in the garden (however it was represented) while the Jewish council comes in and sits down in another spot for a brief meeting, perhaps using furniture left on the stage from the Last Supper. They pay Judas his money, and then he leads the "strong soldiers" to arrest Christ. They need only walk across the stage. The split staging highlights the contrast between Jesus's vulnerable and prayerful pose and the plot unfolding against him.

The Amacuitlapilco scriptwriter envisioned another split-stage effect when Christ is held in jail overnight. The Jesus actor is onstage in the jail while the scene of Peter's denial (complete with brazier) plays out on another part of the stage. When the rooster crows and Peter realizes what he has done, he delivers his apology to Jesus face to face, going to kneel by his imprisoned teacher (36v). Peter speaks directly to him in the Tlatlauhquitepec play as well (10r), indicating that here too Christ has remained onstage—in this case, tied to a tree—while the denial scene and the preceding scene of John fetching the women have played out in his presence.

Whether he is kneeling in the garden, languishing in jail, or tied up to be whipped, scenes where action unfolds beside or around an immobilized Jesus emphasize how he remains the fulcrum of the plot even while he surrenders to his fate. Then, when he is in motion, from the arrest scene onward he is forced from place to place at the whim of others, sometimes (if not generally) in some circumnavigation or criss-crossing of the onstage space. Building on past experience and introducing new ideas, the scriptwriters paid attention not just to dialogue but to how different scenes could be most effectively and efficiently handled using the available stage techniques and spaces.

PERFORMING LITERACY

The Passion performances depended on written scripts, and each Nahuatl play includes performances of literacy itself: Notary and his writing desk are not static presences in their scenes. However, given that the corrupt notary was a stock character in Spanish Golden Age literature (Burns 2010, 14, 21–22), we might expect these characters not to be moral paragons, and that is indeed the case. In the morality play *The Merchant*, from 1687, we find a corrupt notary forging a document and, in exchange for a bribe, lying about a testament (Sell and Burkhart 2004, 252–257). In the 1724 Epiphany play *The Star Sign* and its earlier cognate *La adoración de los reyes*, Herod's notary acts like the notaries in the Passion plays, taking dictation and penning decrees directed at Christ's destruction (Sell and Burkhart 2009, 100–103; Horcasitas 1974, 310–313). But the Notary role is most prevalent in the Passion corpus.

The chief priests' decision to ban any offers of hospitality to Jesus and offer a reward for his betrayal gave scriptwriters their first opportunity to put writing on display. Informing the populace is the job of Notary, Town Crier, or both (II. ii.1–11). The Tepalcingo (37–38) and Penn (8v) plays use no documents in this scene: Caiaphas orders Town Crier to make the proclamation and he does so. The Tlatlauhquitepec scriptwriter opted to have Annas hand Notary a written document for him and Town Crier to announce, but in the other plays Notary does the writing and Town Crier does the proclaiming. The Amacuitlapilco stage directions make this very clear: Notary writes down the order, then shows it to the others and lays it on their conference table. Then Annas gives it to Town Crier, who reads it to the audience from three sides of the stage (14r–14v). Tepalcingo's variant text here has Judas rush over to the council as soon as he hears of the proclamation. No price is discussed yet, but Judas demands a kind of promissory note. Caiaphas orders Notary to write it, and then they give this document to Judas (44–45).

Notary's next possible role is as courtroom recorder during Caiaphas's evidence-gathering session, or *información*, a concept Tlatlauhquitepec's Caiaphas renders into Nahuatl: *inechicoloca in itlahtlacol* 'the gathering together of his sins (or crimes)' (8r). Caiaphas has a notary only in the Penn, Amacuitlapilco, and Axochiapan plays. Their interactions are formulaic: as witnesses offer testimony, Caiaphas orders Notary to write down what they are saying, and he replies that he is doing just that (see III.iv.11–17). This formula recurs when it is Pilate's turn to hear the witnesses (IV.i.14–20). No play indicates that the Jewish high priest and the Roman prefect have different notaries, but a director could choose to cast two men or have the actor switch some costume elements.

Tlatlauhquitepec's Pilate, however, needs no notary, as the writer streamlined this scene. Even with no notary scripted into his own interrogation, Caiaphas did record the procedure somehow. Pilate asks if *probanzas sumarias* 'summary (of) proofs' have been properly prepared. Caiaphas replies, "O my noble, it's all been completed. All his bad deeds are in this piece of writing. These proofs (*probanzas*) were carried out with many witnesses" (11r).[6] Evidently, the actor is to hand Pilate a document purporting to summarize the evidence from Caiaphas's *información*.[7] Pilate then proceeds directly to his own questioning of Jesus (as in IV.i.22).

Having edited Pilate's notary out of the interrogation scene, the Tlatlauhquitepec scriptwriter then edited him into the later scene where Pilate orders that Christ be whipped. Pilate hands Notary a "Sentence of Lashes" (*sentenciah de azotes*), which Notary then reads aloud; we do not see him writing it (12v). No other notaries reappear on stage until Pilate issues his death warrant against Jesus. It is always Notary, rather than Town Crier, who is called upon to read that document aloud (IV.iv.25–28). As the death sentence is the lengthiest and most consequential reading performance in the four plays that include it, it merits a closer look.

The notion that Pilate made some sort of proclamation, rather than just hand Jesus over to his enemies as he does in each Gospel, extends back at least to the fourth-century Gospel of Nicodemus (James 1924, 103). Here Pilate says to Jesus: "Thy nation hath convicted thee (accused thee) as being a king: therefore have I decreed that thou shouldest first be scourged according to the law of the pious emperors, and thereafter hanged upon the cross in the garden wherein thou wast taken: and let Dysmas and Gestas the two malefactors be crucified with thee." In the Cervera Passion play, as in French Passion plays, Pilate delivers an oral death warrant, similarly limited in scope to the flagellation and crucifixion, containing 134 words in the Cervera case (Duran i Sanpere and Duran 1984, 111–112; Blecua 1988, 105). One of the early, fragmentary Passion plays in Catalan, from Majorca, has a notary (*escribano*) deliver its brief death sentence (Blecua 1988, 105n33). Hence, use of a notary character in this context had at least one precedent in Iberian circles, but *altepetl* notarial practices would have fostered the use of a written text and casting of an Escribanoh in these scenes, regardless of whether a Spanish source text featured this detail.

At 434 words, the Toledo Passion's *sentençia* (Torroja Menéndez and Rivas Palá 1977, 174–176) is much more developed than that of the Cervera Passion. No stage directions indicate whether it is to be spoken by Pilate or a town crier. Alberto Blecua (1988, 105–107) notes how it is patterned on juridical models that appeared in notarial guides in the thirteenth century—declaring Pilate's name and title, the proof of the crime, the type and method of punishment, a protestation (in which Pilate accepts responsibility), and a final pronouncement. We can see echoes of these formulas even in the simpler Nahuatl death sentences: the cognate versions in the Axochiapan (105 words; 34v–35r) and Tepalcingo plays (109 words; 107–108). Axochiapan's Notary reads:

> I, Pontius Pilate, president here in Jerusalem by order of my ruler, Caesar, always venerable. Before me have passed all the legal actions, the proof, the accusations, the demands of the Jews who have accused Jesus, who is called Christ. They have said how he goes around bewildering people here in Jerusalem. And I have seen all the actions, the evidence, the complaints made against him. By my order he was flogged, he was tormented. But they were not satisfied with that. Again they said that he is to die, so that many people will take an example from him. They strongly insist that they will make him stretch his arms. And I have accepted their demands. And I have left him in their hands. They will do to him as their hearts desire. This sentence was issued here in the *altepetl* of Jerusalem at the end of the month of March.[8]

A text that appeared in 1580 gave new vigor to the notion of a written death warrant, expanding on this basic formula with much new legalese and authoritative-sounding trimmings. This new death warrant found its way into Nahuatl Passion performances by 1750, if not 1732 or earlier, and into Spanish-language performances by 1766.[9]

This text was allegedly discovered, written in Hebrew on sheepskin, in the ruins of an ancient house in L'Aquila in the kingdom of Naples, near the ancient city of Amiternum, Pilate's supposed birthplace (Beskow 1983, 19). Although the Neapolitan jurist Camillo Borello soon deemed it inauthentic, his commentary and Italian translation were not published until 1588, while translations in French and German were circulating as early as 1581 and in Spanish by 1583 (Beskow 1983, 19–20; Berliner 2003, 50–52; Yepes 1583, 86r–88r). Continued or renewed interest in Spain accounts for a Spanish translation made by Domingo Valentín Guerra, Archbishop of Segovia from 1728 until his death in 1742 (Guerra n.d. 284v–288r; Santos Otero 1956, 566–569),[10] which resembles a copy in garbled Italian (as if transcribed by a Spaniard) housed in the Archivo General of Simancas, Spain (Sutcliffe 1949).

Two versions of the L'Aquila death warrant were swept up in the Inquisition investigation. Fray Francisco Larrea mentions them in his report for the case, opining that this warrant "is not recorded in sacred history"; nor is the earlier proc-lamation warning people not to let Jesus into their homes.[11] These documents came from Ozumba and Amecameca and apparently were intended to accompany the plays from those two towns. All four Spanish-language scripts have Pilate provide a written sentence. Stage directions in the Ozumba play suggest that the separate document is to be recited. The script from Tenango includes a version that, though brief, tracks closely with the content of the L'Aquila warrant; it is also to be read by a Notary character, the only one in the Inquisition corpus. In Cuaderno 1 and the Amecameca play, however, Pilate signs a document and Jesus kisses it—as occurs also in Tenango—but it may have been displayed without the action necessarily pausing for a reading.[12] The Amecameca death sentence is written on a large piece of paper and formatted to look like an official proclamation.

The Nahuatl script from Amacuitlapilco, like the Spanish one from Ozumba, calls for the reading of a death sentence that is not included in the text itself, although the "I, Pontius" added after the end of the play indicates that someone had a hast-ily abandoned intention to copy a version there. Even though the Amacuitlapilco play bears the date 1732, like the Axochiapan play, it is possible that a version of the L'Aquila warrant had come into the scriptwriter's possession and he meant for his Notary to read it rather than the shorter text used in nearby Axochiapan and Tepalcingo.

The Princeton and Penn plays, however, prove that the L'Aquila text was fully adapted into Nahuatl by at least 1750 and was circulating in different versions. The Penn death warrant resembles the Amecameca one in the Inquisition file, while the Princeton warrant is closer to the one from Ozumba, but in no case is one translated directly from another (the two Nahuatl versions are merged in IV.iv.28). Tlatlauhquitepec ends before this scene, but in the surviving part, Caiaphas has a war leader, Quinto Cornelio (6v), whose name comes straight from the L'Aquila forgery (see IV.iv.28), suggesting—as does the invention of a written "Sentence of Lashes"—that the complete play included a version of it.

This lengthy pronouncement (433 Nahuatl words in Princeton, 421 in Penn) gives Notary a turn at speech rivaling Judas's soliloquy (II.vi.2) or Christ's after-dinner address (II.5.12). It also gives him a name. The L'Aquila warrant teems with the names of Roman and Judean officials—like the Quinto Cornelio (or Quintus Cornelius) character mentioned above. The Mexican adaptations eliminated most of these names, but one that remains in the Nahuatl (but not the Spanish) ver-sions is that of Roman notary Lucius Sextilius, or Lucio Sextilio in Spanish and Italian translations. Penn's Notary renders this name as Lesio sestilio (32v) and lucio Sestilio (34r), while Princeton's Notary here calls himself losio textillo (41r), his surname reading as "milled" or "crumbled."[13]

Whether in longer or shorter form, Christ's death sentence makes a powerful finale for the performances of literacy. One more document reading is shared by the Amacuitlapilco (48v–49r) and Axochiapan (37v) plays (V.ii.14–16). Once Christ has raised the cross onto his shoulder, the leader of the Jewish soldiers orders Town Crier to read a brief document (46 words in Nahuatl) to the people of Jerusalem. In the case of Amacuitlapilco, where Pilate orders Notary to read the death sentence but the text is not provided at that point, Town Crier's proclamation would partially fulfill the same purpose if no separate document was available to the actors.

All of Notary's and Town Crier's writings and readings interrupt the action of the play to highlight the importance of reading and writing, with pieces of paper serving as important props. But everything that is written or read redounds to Christ's harm. Simply obeying orders and fulfilling their duty, these characters are complicit in the miscarriage of justice that ends in Christ's death. While alphabetic literacy was in many ways a boon for Indigenous Mesoamericans, the scriptwriters—whose training set them apart from most of their neighbors—chose to stage evidence of its darker side.

OF ANGELS, ORANGES, AND OTHER FLOURISHES

This section maps out a miscellany of additional stage effects that are neither called for by the Gospel story nor discussed elsewhere in this book but that rendered a particular production more engaging to the audience's sense of sight or sound. They provide hints of the kinds of things actors might do more commonly but that were not included in the written scripts. They also demonstrate, in small ways, the creative leeway individual scriptwriters enjoyed.

Christ always rides a donkey to Jerusalem, as specified in the Gospels,[14] but what of her gear? Tepalcingo's Jesus has the forethought to tell Peter (not James in this case) and John to use a halter or bridle (*tenilpihticah* 'she is lip-tied'), but there is no mention of a saddle (1). Elsewhere, the students follow Luke 19:36 by putting items of their clothing on the donkey. In the Penn play (4v), James proposes *Ma toconpepechtican in totilmah* 'Let us go saddle her with our cloaks.' Then they lift Jesus onto her back. Axochiapan (1v–2r) and Amacuitlapilco (8v–9r) draw out the saddling issue, having the apostle Andrew—who has no other line except in the Last Supper's "Is it I" sequence—milk his moment in the spotlight by speechifying upon Jesus's humbled condition and onlookers' supposed indifference to it, a contemplative aside more typical of sermons than of these plays (see I.ii.33). Then they saddle the donkey, with Amacuitlapilco dressing up the scene by using fancier cloths: John brings a white cloak and Andrew brings a piece of taffeta. Another random but revealing use of cloth occurs in the Penn play, when Gamaliel, the

Last Supper host, is to spread his turban on the ground (9r; II.iii.9). He is fidgety because he is fretting about Christ's welfare. This detail indicates that actors playing men of Jerusalem might be wearing turbans, consistent with the dress of Pontius Pilate and other men in colonial depictions of the Passion.[15]

The donkey is not the only equine in the corpus. Horses tread the space between the stage and Calvary in two plays. Princeton's Captain drags Christ from horseback (43v). Amacuitlapilco's scriptwriter sends Annas, Caiaphas, Joseph, Simeon, and Samuel to Calvary on horseback, where they are to react with distress to Pilate's signboard reading "Jesus of Nazareth, Ruler of the Jews" (53r–53v). Perhaps the scriptwriter knew five horses could be borrowed or else rented at low cost, as this could be a significant expense—at least according to Tlatelolco's fray Miguel Camacho Villavicencio, who thought his parishioners spent too much money to rent the horses that carried the Three Kings in Tlatelolco's Epiphany play.[16]

Obligatory in Peter's denial scene is the fowl that crows after his three repudiations. Nahuas heard nocturnal bird cries as harbingers of ill fortune. The verb all the plays use here, *tzahtzi* 'to cry out' or 'to shout,' was associated especially with ominous cries of the barn owl (*chicuahtli*) (García Garagarza 2020, 463, 465), but the plays follow the Gospels in designating a domestic fowl, not an owl, as the crying bird. The prescribed sound may be that of a rooster, named with the variant Nahuatl borrowings or neologisms *oquichcuanaca* 'male chicken' (*cuanaca* 'head flesh' refers to the chicken's comb and, by extension, to the whole bird), *caxtil* 'Castile' (shortened from the earlier usage *Caxtillan huexolotl* 'Castile male turkey'), and *oquichcaxtilih* 'male Castile'. Or it might be the clucking of a hen (*caxtillan totolin* 'Castile turkey hen'). Presumably, a stagehand imitated the sound or perhaps blew a whistle.[17]

Every play has an angel consult with Christ in the Garden of Gethsemane, taking two turns at speech. The Gospel of Luke (22:43) places an angel in the garden, who "strengthens" Christ but is not quoted. The Penn Passion provides the angel not only with dialogue but also with a name—Saint Michael (San Miguel)—and he brings a number of props to the encounter (20v–21r; III.i.14–18). This digression from the general model deserves some consideration.

Saint Michael the archangel appears elsewhere in Nahuatl theater in his role as the angel who will call the dead from their graves at the time of the Final Judgment and who assists Christ when he passes judgment on the souls of the dead (Sell and Burkhart 2004, 90–91, 200–203, 180–189; Leeming 2022). Stepping outside his usual job description, Michael intervenes in the exuberant 1539 Tlaxcalan battle drama *The Conquest of Jerusalem*, which enacted an imagined Christian (and Tlaxcalan) conquest of Jerusalem. When the archangel appears, Moors and Christians alike cower and cease their combat. Michael then announces that God

will be merciful to the Moors if they accept Christianity, which, led by the ironi-
cally named Sultan Cortés, they proceed to do (Motolinia 1979, 72; on this event,
see Díaz Balsera 2008). In the Epiphany play *The Star Sign*, as redacted in Metepec
in 1724, Michael warns the Three Kings of Herod's ire and urges them to bypass
Jerusalem on their way home. Both the earlier version of that play and the similar play *The Three Kings* deploy an angel here—in contrast to the dream-conveyed
warning in Matthew (2:12)—but in those plays the heavenly envoy remains anonymous (Paso y Troncoso 1902, 102, 122; Sell and Burkhart 2009, 110–111; Burkhart,
de la Cruz, and Sullivan 2017, 87).

Michael's familiarity may have been enhanced by the fact that many Nahuatl
versions of the General Confession (or *confiteor*), part of the basic catechism,
include him among the several saints it invokes (to cite a Franciscan, Dominican,
Augustinian, and Jesuit example, respectively: Molina 1678, 14r; León 1611, 102r;
Anunciación 1575, 226; Paredes 1758, 52).[18] He is the only angel in the catechism
and also the only angel whose images appear among the bequests made by testators
in the corpus of eighteenth-century wills from the Toluca Valley (Pizzigoni 2012,
43). The story of Michael's defeat of Lucifer and the other rebel angels was told in
Nahuatl, for example, in the *Psalmodia christiana* and *Colloquios y doctrina christiana*, to explain the origin of the demons and, thus, the Indigenous gods (Sahagún
1583, 179r–181v; 1986, 196–201). Figure 2.5, from the *Psalmodia*, shows him standing victorious over Lucifer.

The archangel Gabriel was the more standard angel emissary, such that the
Psalmodia christiana, before recounting his Bible-based visits to Daniel, Zechariah,
and Mary, calls him *in huei teuctitlantli* 'the great lordly messenger' (Sahagún 1583,
47r). Gabriel appears in one extant Nahuatl play—an adaptation of Lope de Vega
Carpio's *The Mother of the Best* (in Sell, Burkhart, and Wright 2008)—and in
recorded descriptions of two others (Horcasitas 1974, 237–241). He would be seen
in any depiction of the Annunciation. But he was not as well-known as his fellow
archangel. If someone wanted to give an angel a name, Michael was the more obvious choice. Hence, he usurps Gabriel's intermediary role in *The Star Sign* and here
in the Penn Passion.

Michael comes to Penn's Gethsemane bearing baggage. The first item is a chalice (*cáliz*), and Michael says, "Here is the chalice from which you will drink bitter
water."[19] This is the cup (*calix*) that, in Matthew (26:39) and Luke (22:42), Jesus
prays might pass from him (see figure 2.1)—a metaphor for Christ's painful destiny[20] manifested in a stage prop. Similarly, the Toledo Passion play's unnamed angel
brings *queste cáliz d'amargura* 'this chalice of bitterness' (Torroja Menéndez and
Rivas Palá 1977, 163). The second item is the cross, as *cuauhnepanolli* 'crossed-wood
device.' The Passion play from Villasinta, León, has the angel bring the chalice and

Figure 2.5. Saint Michael with the defeated Lucifer. In his left hand he holds the scales with which he weighs human souls. Woodcut in Bernardino de Sahagún, *Psalmodia christiana*, 1583, 179r. Courtesy of the John Carter Brown Library, Brown University, Providence, RI.

the cross (Lozano Prieto 1985, 84). Penn's Michael also presents the nails, the rope with which Christ will be whipped, the crown of thorns, and the lance—which Michael equates with a key for opening heaven.

If the stone column, in place of the (more portable) rope, were to serve as the metonym for the flagellation, these would be the same five Passion implements the Holy Fathers in limbo send, through angel messengers, to Mary in the play *Holy Wednesday* (Burkhart 1996). On a smaller scale, angels carrying a cross and a lance attend Christ when he appears on earth in the play *The Life of Don Sebastián* (Sell and Burkhart 2004, 278–283). Michael's cross might be a full-size one put in place by stagehands or a small one the actor could carry along with the other items, as is probably the case with the cross Magdalene brings Jesus in the Princeton and Amacuitlapilco plays (see chapter 3). The other props could well be the same ones used later in the play, with the lance handed off to one of the actors who are about to stage the arrest scene.

Generic angels carrying instruments of the Passion appear in Indigenous Christian art, but Michael's association with warfare may also have informed the scriptwriter's choice to burden him specifically with this array of items. The Passion implements were known collectively as the *arma Christi* 'weapons of Christ.' Michael, a mythic warrior, comes to "strengthen" Christ as armed soldiers, chosen for their own strength, approach the garden. He emphasizes this role just before he presents his grievous gifts, saying, "Be strong! Exert all your effort! You are great, you are valiant. The pain and torment that you are about to suffer are great."[21] He is, in effect, arming Jesus with weapons that will allow him to meet the challenge that has just left him so frightened that he sweated blood and asked to be excused.

While Michael's cameo is a particularly interesting angelic intervention, it is at least built upon a biblical precedent. Scriptwriters showed a fondness for these avian beings by adding them elsewhere in the script, giving Christ and, in one case, Mary stalwart and well-informed heavenly friends to complement their sometimes less reliable earthly companions. The same costumed actors might appear in multiple scenes. These cast members give a solid and, in their proliferation, everyday reality to ethereal, celestial beings. In Nahuatl theater, only Passion plays place so many angels onstage without also marching out demons to vie with them for human souls.[22]

While Jesus is in jail, he receives two angelic visitors in Amacuitlapilco (35r), Axochiapan (35v), and Penn (24v–25r). A curious fact about this scene is that while the two plays from Jonacatepec are, as in so much else, nearly identical in this instance, the Penn Passion's version is a separate composition—unlike some other content these three plays share in which Penn seems to preserve a template the others have somewhat minimized and altered. In this case, a possible scenario is that the jailhouse angel scene was at some point added to one performance tradition, and then someone took the idea—but not the scripted lines—and added it to their own practice. The speeches are quite different, and so are the turns at speech: in Penn, one angel speaks and Jesus responds; in the other plays, both angels speak and Jesus remains silent (the versions are merged in scene III.v). The author of Cuaderno 1 may have taken a cue from a performance similar to the Penn play. An archangel—Gabriel in this case—visits Christ in jail (212r). He offers Christ assistance, though in terms quite different from those in either Nahuatl version; Christ declines the proffered aid, departing from the Spanish plays' relative terseness by speaking at much greater length than his counterpart in the Penn play.

Penn's Jesus tells his jailhouse visitors, "And as for you, keep my beloved mother company, stay with her" (25r).[23] The scriptwriter fulfills Jesus's request by having two angels come to the crucifixion. Although they respond immediately to Mary's own appeal, they are also answering this earlier command. The angels offer Mary support and explain that one last ordeal—the lancing of Christ's side—remains before his body can be taken down for burial (41r–42v; V.iii.59). Depictions of angels in attendance at this scene, where they often hold chalices to collect the blood streaming from Christ's wounds, could have inspired the decision to add angels to this staging of the crucifixion (see figure 5.4). The Penn scriptwriter (or a predecessor) also ordered an angel to pop in at the Last Supper, where he is to snatch the blessed host from Judas's mouth with a napkin or handkerchief (ce panoh, 11v; II.iv.7) and show it to the audience. This angel has a Spanish-speaking analog in the play from Ozumba, where an angel takes the host from Judas and puts it back with the others (247v).

The Princeton Passion presents its own unparalleled angelic intervention: three angels visit Christ and the apostles shortly after he has driven the merchants from the temple. Each speaks in turn, the first two conveying messages from God the Father and the third just offering encouragement, and then Christ gives a brief response acceding to his father's will (8v–9r; scene I.v). The preceding stage direction says he will go back to a huerto ycales, possibly to be read huertoh icaliz 'orchard (and) his chalice' or huertoh in caliz 'orchard, chalice.' These terms suggest the Garden of Gethsemane and the chalice that Jesus there prays he might avoid. This is out of place, since Princeton's Gethsemane meeting with the angel does not occur until folios 25r–26r, where the dialogue is consistent with the garden scene in all the other plays: there is only one angel, and he recounts how he and all the other angels of heaven have already asked God to excuse Christ from further suffering (III.i.15). This earlier exchange, with the three angels, could be borrowed from another text's Gethsemane scene. Third Angel's speech (I.v.4) warns about the sinners coming now to dishonor Jesus, as if he is about to be arrested, which is not the case at this point in the play. Jesus's submissive speech (I.v.5) could substitute for its Gethsemane analog (III.i.16). The Princeton scriptwriter or a predecessor may have added this exchange out of a fondness for angelic visits, to foreshadow Christ's imminent tribulations, or for some other reason.

Angels traffic in weighty messages and uphold moral order, but other creative flourishes convey a sense of playfulness. In the Axochiapan script, when Judas comes to bargain with the Jerusalem council, he finds some of the Jews amusing themselves with oranges (19; II.vi.3)—perhaps tossing them back and forth, juggling, or just enjoying a snack. The Penn and Amacuitlapilco plays place oranges on the Last Supper table, and Axochiapan stagehands could have transferred oranges from their own supper spread to these actors. In the Princeton play (29v), the three men who provoke Peter into his denials of Christ are instructed to be smoking. The fire at which they are warming themselves would presumably have provided the light for their pipes or cigars. Later in the Princeton play (38r; IV.iii.11), after the "Jews" have dressed Christ in the red cloak and crown of thorns, they are to amuse themselves with his shirt, using a sword to, we might imagine, toss it around, tear it, or—perhaps, given the legendary powers associated with the seamless garment[24]—try but fail to divide it into pieces.

Oranges aside, Judas's errand to the council of priests can be drawn out in a way that parodies the bureaucratic rigmarole associated with *altepetl* proceedings and other interactions with dignitaries. In all plays except Tepalcingo's, a porter named Reuben[25] conveys Judas's messages to the chief priests, and their queries back to him, in direct quotation. This flunky-mediated back-and-forth was a dramatic formula: in both Epiphany plays, the Three Kings face a similar process when they arrive in Jerusalem and seek an audience with Herod (Sell and Burkhart 2004, 118–122; 2009, 84–86). The Reuben character evidently comes from a Spanish model text, as a porter called Rubén appears in the 1548 Passion play from the Catalonian town of Cervera.[26] This play has no scene of Judas with the council, but Rubén assists the priests as they deliberate over Jesus's fate and is obliged to publicize the resulting *citació* 'summons'—much to his distress, as he is a secret follower of Christ (Duran i Sanpere and Duran 1984, 35, 50–65). Three hundred years later, a porter named Roboán mediates Judas's visit to the council in the play from Villasinta (Lozano Prieto 1985, 81–82). The Tepalcingo play's divergent council scene omits Reuben; however, he turns up later, as one of the characters who harass Peter during the denial scene (86).

With or without Reuben, the priests question Judas's credentials. Their suspicion turns to fawning delight when they learn he is Christ's student and willing to betray his teacher for cash. Only in Tepalcingo does Judas simply demand thirty pieces of money (44). Tlatlauhquitepec's Annas suggests a payment of thirty pieces, and there is no further discussion (6r). The other four plays stretch out the negotiation: Judas is sent out of and called back into the room twice, with Reuben fetching him; Annas offers only twenty pieces of *teocuitlatl* 'gold or silver' at first; Judas rejects that offer but then accepts thirty (see II.vi.4–44).

In the Nahuas' vigesimal counting system, twenty was a nice round number: *cempohualli* 'one count.' This could seem like a reasonable amount of payment, as a *tlatemantli* 'piece' could be worth much more than the shekels paid to Judas in the Gospels.[27] In the first Tulane Passion text, Judas says to Caiaphas and the others, "O my noble, I am a rotten *macehualli*. O how wretched I am! I go about afflicted. By your leave, have compassion for me with something." The priests respond, "May it be so. Very well. Twenty pieces of silver is what we will we give you." And he replies,

"O my noble, you (all) have shown me favor. It will be done when you want" (*Pasión en lengua mexicana* n.d., 20v).[28] In contrast to the plays, the priests specify that the payment will be in *iztac* 'white' *teocuitlatl*, meaning silver, rather than simply *teocuitlatl*, which includes both silver and gold.

Once all are agreed on the payment, it must be issued. *Altepetl* officials encompassed a majordomo (*mayordomoh*) and also a porter (*porteroh*), so these roles were not alien despite their Spanish titles (Lockhart 1992, 42).[29] Majordomos collected tribute and kept one of the keys to the community coffer, to ensure that any cash withdrawals were authorized by the proper officials (Haskett 1991, 108–109). Confraternities also put majordomos in charge of communal funds; some acted as itinerant alms collectors (Truitt 2018, 153; Osowski 2010, 100). Robert Haskett (1991, 122) cites the case of a confraternity majordomo in Jonacatepec who also worked as a traditional healer, for which he was convicted of witchcraft in 1746, eleven years before Jonacatepec's priest confiscated local Passion scripts. The plays' Majordomo plays the role of money dispenser (II.vi.45–51) and also takes charge of the money when Judas returns it (III.viii.14–15). In both cases he responds to orders from the Jewish council, with Reuben going to fetch him in Tlatlauhquitepec (6r–6v).

Every play has stage directions calling for the money to be counted, not just handed over, so we can imagine that Majordomo counts out each (imitation) silver coin from one to thirty in the rather wordy Nahuatl numeration system—except perhaps in the Princeton play, where the counting is to be done *ihciuhca* 'quickly' (23r). In Axochiapan, Majordomo tells Judas to wrap the money in his cloak (*ximocuixantih*)—the same way he carries off the Last Supper leftovers in the Penn play (12r) or Juan Diego carries the roses to Bishop Zumárraga before Our Lady of Guadalupe's image is revealed on his cloak (Sousa, Poole, and Lockhart 1998, 78–79; Sell, Burkhart, and Poole 2006, 94). In Amacuitlapilco, Judas lifts up a sack (*coxtal*, from Spanish *costal*), befitting his Gospel role as the carrier of the disciples' common purse (28r; see figure 4.1).

In every play except Tepalcingo, with its variant source for this part of the story, Judas's villainous purpose does not override his manners: he makes a polite speech thanking the rulers for their largesse (II.vi.53). All six plays have Judas delight in his new wealth during an aside (II.vi.57). In the four Spanish-language plays, Judas enlists an anonymous soldier or centurion to gain him entry to the council, requests or accepts an offer of thirty *reales*,[30] gets paid—by a *mayordomo* in the Amecameca and Tenango plays—and moves right on to organizing the arrest, neither expressing gratitude nor exulting in his good fortune.[31]

All the plays have Peter's three denials of Jesus and at least one witness who presents as testimony against him Jesus's claim that he could tear down the temple and raise it again in three days, from John 2:19 (see scene III.vi, III.iv.14, IV.i.18).

Jesus also predicts his resurrection after three days (I.i.13, I.vii.11), and Mary may recall the time she lost him in the temple for three days (I.viii.7). According to Matthew 26:39–45 and Mark 14:35–41, Jesus prays to his father three times in Gethsemane, checking on the sleeping apostles before the second and third appeals (see scene III.i). The scriptwriters saw some leeway in the pacing here, as Jesus may check back on the apostles only once (Amacuitlapilco, 29r–29v; Axochiapan, 22r; Penn, 20r–20v; Princeton, 24r–25r), twice (Tlatlauhquitepec, 7r), or three times (Tepalcingo, 65–66). Conversely, while John 18:6 says the soldiers coming to arrest Jesus fall down when he says he is Jesus of Nazareth, some scriptwriters liked this effect so much that they have the soldiers plop down on the stage two or three times before they proceed to take Jesus into custody.[32] The second Passion text in the Tulane manuscript also has Jesus return to the sleeping apostles three times and makes his pursuers fall down and get up three times (*Pasión en lengua mexicana* n.d., second pagination, 23v, 27r–v).[33]

Only Amacuitlapilco's scriptwriter makes sure to have his Christ fall three times while carrying the cross, in accordance with the Stations of the Cross—although he cites "the sacred words" as his source (*iuh cah teotlahtolpan*, 51v; V.ii.46). He adds other triple flourishes: Magdalene kneels three times as she approaches Christ (15v), Christ (or possibly the Last Supper host) kisses each apostle's feet three times (20v), and Judas looks three times to make sure everyone else has exited the stage before his soliloquy (23r; II.v.21)—while in the Penn Passion it is Jesus who looks back at Judas three times, as if giving him a chance to change his mind (14v). Amacuitlapilco's rooster (36v; III.vi.9) and Axochiapan's angel (26v) cry out three times, as if once for each of Peter's denials.

While the repeat-three-times flourishes are fairly simple and use a Christian/European formulaic number that recurs in many devotional contexts (Larkin 2004, 503–505), some scripts play with much larger Nahuatl numbers. The Nahuatl version of the *Via Crucis* likewise manifests an interest in fancifully large numbers that deviate from standard Nahuatl numeration. Either Vetancurt or the Nahua redactor of the extant manuscript added numbers to a litany of Christ's torments, which go unnumbered in Spanish versions of the text. The two largest are the 362,460 drops of shed blood and the 130,000 times he paid for people's sins with his blood (Schwaller 2017, 136). Four of the Passion scriptwriters include their take on the twelve legions of angels that Jesus, in Matthew 26:53, tells Peter he could summon from heaven if he wished to avoid arrest. One Roman legion numbered 6,000 soldiers (Gundry 2010, 121), so twelve legions amounted to 72,000. In the Nahuatl, the counting system's largest numerical category, *xiquipilli* '8,000,' is multiplied by ten or twelve, as per standard Nahuatl counting, as if a legion corresponded to one *xiquipilli*—but then this sum is further multiplied through the use of *tecpantli*, referring to a file of twenty, or simply *cempohualli* 'twenty,' yielding numbers approaching 2 million: 10 × 8,000 × 20 (Amacuitlapilco, 31v) or 12 × 8,000 × 20 (Penn, 22r; Princeton, 27v; Tepalcingo, 73; III.ii.29). As John Frederick Schwaller (2017, 136–137) notes, contemporary Nahuatl speakers consider the ability to render large numbers in their system to be a sign of linguistic mastery, but the writer(s) of the *Via Crucis* text "got carried away in expressing large numbers and began to simply make them up." The scriptwriters indulge in similar excess.

Pilate's death sentences in the Penn and Princeton scripts also present fanciful numbers, but here the European versions of this text traffic in even more strange numerology, tracing the time elapsed between the creation of the world and Christ's death in different calendars. The Nahua writers simplify matters by throwing in just one big, arbitrary number. The Princeton script (41r; IV.iv.28) gives the year of Christ's death as 2187—a number that might have seemed oddly futuristic in the mid-1700s—while the Penn death sentence (34r) asserts that 40,405 days have passed since the world began, placing Jesus's life at a very ancient moment in the history of the world.[34]

MUSIC: DRUMS, TRUMPETS, AND SINGING IN *LATINTLAHTOLLI*

From the very beginning, when Franciscans offered them melodies for chanting the Catholic catechism (Motolinia 1979, 25), Indigenous Mexicans transferred into their Christian practice the use of instruments and song to delineate sacred space and time. Chimalpahin noted that in 1609, when just two Franciscan friars left Mexico City to start a mission in New Mexico, they brought along not only printed catechisms but also cornets, *chirimías* (shawms), trombones, bells, and an organ (Lockhart, Schroeder, and Namala 2006, 157): they assumed there could be no mission without a mission band.[35] Instrumental music sounded in many Nahuatl plays, often at scene changes. Typically, the scripts say simply *tlapitzaloz* 'things will be blown' and/or *tlatzotzonaloz* 'things will be beaten.' The morality play *Don Rafael* sets the record for blowing things, with thirty-four instances, and *The Star Sign* for beating on things, with twenty occurrences (both in Sell and Burkhart 2009). The "blown" things can be any wind instrument. Where scriptwriters call for specific instruments, they are typically some type of trumpet: *clarín* 'clarion' often accompanies the beaten things in *The Star Sign*, *trompetas* sound in *Souls and Testamentary Executors* and *Don Rafael*, and *vacas*—identified as *cornetas*—ring out in *Dialogue on the Apparition of the Virgin Saint Mary of Guadalupe* (86–103, 377; Sell and Burkhart 2004, 188; Sell, Burkhart, and Poole 2006, 58, 72, 92).[36] But woodwinds also appear: the *tlapitzalli* 'blown things' that toot at the Jerusalem arrival of the title characters in *The Three Kings* could be flutes (of Indigenous or

European origin), *chirimías*, or oboes, according to Molina's definition of the term (Sell and Burkhart 2004, 122; Molina 1992, pt. 2, 132r); the Guadalupe play calls for *chirimías* as well as the cornets (Sell, Burkhart, and Poole 2006, 58, 90, 98). "Beaten" instruments would generally be drums of one kind or another but can be any instrument that is struck, including harps in the morality play about a grandfather and grandson (Silva Cruz 2001, 37) and the play about Emperor Constantine and Saint Helen (Sell and Burkhart 2009, 288) and the organ that *castizo*[37] priest and playwright Bartolomé de Alva includes in his adaptation of Pedro Calderón's *The Great Theater of the World* (Sell, Burkhart, and Wright 2008, 91).[38]

Compared to some Nahuatl plays, the Passions give rather sparse notations for these intermittent fanfares, though once musicians were on the scene, they might play more often than the script denotes. The Penn play calls for them only four times but helpfully specifies some instruments: *clarín* (8v, 22r), *cajah* 'drum'—the loanword suggesting a European type rather than the Indigenous *huehuetl* or *teponaztli* (16v, 22r)—and *roncah* (37r). Since it is to be blown, I surmise that this is a *trompeta ronca*, a variety of horn that Miguel de Cervantes mentions frequently (Salazar 1951, 73); the name suggests a snoring or snorting sound.[39] It is played when Town Crier briefly reiterates the death sentence against Jesus, just as he takes up his cross and begins the walk to Calvary. An obnoxious noise is appropriate. Amacuitlapilco specifies the playing of the *clarín* (15v) and calls for a *trompiteroh* 'trumpeter' to punctuate Town Crier's reading of the council decree against housing or befriending Jesus (14v–15r). The Tepalcingo play calls for the highest number of wind instrument flourishes, with a mere five, though all six plays have at least one.

The Princeton and Amacuitlapilco scripts provide an unusual touch when they have the "Jews" or the chief priests themselves, rather than attendant musicians, play instruments: winds when they exit their Amacuitlapilco council meetings (15v, 28v; II.vi.56); beaten and blown things when they arrest Jesus in Princeton's Gethsemane (27v; III.ii.25). This is the only drumming in the Princeton play and in the Passion corpus apart from Penn's *cajah* player(s), but it might account for the *Cajeroh* who tops the list of dramatis personae written on the play's inside covers. The loanword could refer either to a drummer or to a cashier, or keeper of the *altepetl* cashbox who might assist Majordomo with Judas's money. This character has one turn at speech, later in the play, when he joins First, Second, and Third Jew as they mock Christ after decking him out with the crown of thorns and reed scepter (38r). Oddly, if he is indeed a drummer, his misbehavior here consists of blowing some kind of wind instrument into Christ's ear (see IV.iii.11, IV.iii.16). Jews blowing on trumpets—whether in the crowd, at Jesus, and in his ear during this mocking—are a recurring motif in European Passion imagery (Marrow 1979,

153–161), so these Jewish characters raising a musical ruckus themselves may derive from some model text or image.

Only once are musicians instructed to play a particular instrumental piece. In the Penn Passion (8v), the *Misericordia* is to be "blown" (*mopitzaz*), after Town Crier has proclaimed the edict seeking Jesus's arrest and just before he speaks to his students of his impending doom. This would be a musical setting for Psalm 51 (50), which appeals to God for forgiveness of sins. The play *The Sacrifice of Isaac* also calls for the *Misericordia* to be blown, at the pivotal moment when Abraham is on the verge of killing his son (Sell and Burkhart 2004, 158). Requests for specific music without singing appear nowhere else in the known Nahuatl corpus.

The Passion scriptwriters include instrumental interludes in conformity with established Nahua theatrical practice, but none seems to have considered them so essential to his aesthetic vision that he called for them at regular intervals. This may be because, more than in any other Nahuatl theater genre, Latin choral music stole the thunder from these other sound effects. I turn next to these solemn incantations, which cast a sanctifying cloud of sound over at least some scenes in each play.

Latin liturgical music became part of Nahua religious practice because of its use in the Catholic Mass, church services, and canonical hours. Priests, spread thin across the colony, relied on Indigenous singers to fill their churches with appropriate sacred music. As James Lockhart (1992, 215–217) determined from his study of *altepetl* records, this role was institutionalized as a major function of Indigenous church staff, the *teopantlacah* 'church people,' with the singers denoted more directly as *cuicanimeh* or *cantores* (cf. Truitt 2018, 61–62). Singers earned some income and paid reduced tribute, and their special training allowed them to stay in office longer than other rotating officials. People dictating their wills typically left a little money to the church staff who would assist in their funerary rites, singing responsories for them as they conveyed their bodies to their resting places. The head singer, often called the *maestro de capilla* 'chapel master' or 'choirmaster' (like the Gregorio Eusebio named in the Princeton play), took charge of training other singers and preparing a choir of boys and men for service on Sundays and feast days.

Records kept by an Indigenous noble family of Tepemaxalco, in the Toluca Valley, reveal that an *altepetl*'s cohort of *cantores* could be major players in local affairs, for example by raising money from agricultural sales to purchase an organ and other musical instruments or to adorn the church and by using this respected position as a stepping stone to higher office (Lockhart 1992, 230, 233–234; Pizzigoni and Townsend 2021, 78, 85–89, 92). William B. Taylor (1996, 333–334) found the office of *cantor* to be a prestigious and profitable one for eighteenth-century Nahuas in the dioceses of Mexico and Guadalajara. The men earned money for each sung Mass and could attain political influence in their communities, especially if their skill and experience allowed them to remain in office even as new priests cycled into the parish.

Maestros de capilla or *cantores* may have had much to do with Passion play scripting and performance, but the preparation of the Latin choral music would always fall in their bailiwick. While these specialists were trained well enough in Latin to manage the church chants, scriptwriters did not necessarily share their facility in Latin, and their musical cues are sometimes so garbled or truncated as to be difficult to identify. But since in almost every case I have been able to match the suggested chant to a specific musical piece appropriate to the context, colonial Nahua music experts familiar with the performance genre and the music used in their churches would have had no trouble using any of these scripts as a guide for the choir.

While some selections appear in more than one play, the variety of choices is striking. It seems scriptwriters, perhaps guided by choirmasters (if they were not actually the same men), selected from a broad catalog of possible songs, based on local preferences and the availability of choir books. Writers felt obliged to include at least a few bits of Latin singing and could have as many as twenty. Manuscripts with less music might mark a loss of interest or of access to the required choral sources along some lines of transmission. The composite play includes most of the song cues in the corpus, so it displays more of them than does any single script.

The Latin singing in the Passion corpus can be divided into three somewhat overlapping categories. The first is the music from fray Juan Navarro's Passion chant book of 1604, with its plainsong extracts from the Passion accounts of each of the four evangelists. As I noted in the introduction to this volume, the Penn Passion so closely reproduces the opening of Navarro's *Passion of Our Lord Jesus Christ According to Matthew* as to leave no doubt as to its model (1v; see figures 0.1 and 0.2). Axochiapan titles itself with the opening words of the same text and calls two other times for what is likely the same Passion to be sung (1r, 2v, 5v), while Tepalcingo at one point calls for the chanting of the *Passion of Our Lord according to Matthew* (16–17). These later references leave vague which particular part of that Passion was planned. Furthermore, the reference in Tepalcingo and the first instance in Axochiapan occur at early points in the action that have no correspondence to the Gospel texts set by Navarro. It seems unlikely that the play would stop mid-action while the choir intoned an entire choral Passion, but what the scriptwriters had in mind is not clear.

In most instances, the scriptwriter wrote the first word or words of a particular passage, often noting that it was to be "raised" (*mehuaz*) or "sung" (*cuicoz*). I cannot be certain that Navarro was its immediate source, since the passages come from the Bible and some are also in the liturgy. However, given the evident connection between the theatrical corpus and Navarro's book, any chants that do appear in that songbook could be derived from it. This is the case in six later instances in Penn, one later instance in Tepalcingo, two chants in Tlatlauhquitepec, possibly two in Amacuitlapilco, and seven to fourteen in Princeton.[40] The last seven in Princeton (45v–46r; V.iii.15, 17, 22, 27, 43, 52, 54) correspond to the "seven sayings" or "seven last words" (*ultima septem verba*) of Jesus on the cross, which draw on different Gospels—and hence Navarro's different sung Passions. The source here may have instead been one of the choral settings of these seven Gospel verses, which happened to be available to the Princeton scriptwriter or his choirmaster colleague. In any case, the close alternation between Nahuatl dialogue and Latin chant staged here in Princeton, within barely more than one page's worth of the manuscript, is unique in Nahuatl theater. It would have given Christ's final moments the sacred aura of a church rite.[41]

The second category includes antiphons, hymn verses, and other chants from the liturgy or Mass that do not appear in Navarro. Liturgical books were imported from Europe, and smaller-scale imprints were also marketed, like the Mass score and song in honor of Saint Peter that don Pedro de la Cruz, Nahua governor of Tepemaxalco, commissioned his *altepetl's cantores* to purchase for two pesos (Pizzigoni and Townsend 2021, 87). For the full Latin and English text of the chants whose Latin titles I give in this section, see notes on the cited lines of the composite play.[42] These notes also indicate when chants found in Navarro share their words with antiphons in the liturgy.

Among Mexican music books, Navarro's work was preceded by the 1584 *Psalterium Ant[i]phonarium Sanctorale, cum Psalmis et Hymnis.* It holds only two of the antiphons in the Passion corpus: the "Miserere mei Deus" sung during Jesus's flagellation in the Princeton play (37v; IV.iii.11; *Psalterium* 1584, 44r) and the "Adoramus te Christe" sung at the end of the Penn play (45r; V.iv.37; *Psalterium* 1584, 201r, 224r–224v, 262r–262v). "Adoramus te Christe" is an antiphon in the liturgy for the feast of the Holy Cross, but some versions of the Stations of the Cross call for it to be sung at each station. These include one of the two versions known to have been circulating in New Spain in the seventeenth and eighteenth centuries, which includes this chant in Spanish.[43]

Choral directors of the Passion plays likely had recourse to handwritten collections of Latin sheet music that circulated among performing communities. Robert Stevenson (1964) describes nine such manuscripts collected from Indigenous communities in Guatemala; similar works probably circulated among Central Mexican *altepetl* as well. One of the Guatemalan texts shares a redactor with the seventeenth-century "choral music miscellany" held by Princeton University, a choirmaster named Tomás Pascual from the community of San Juan Ixcoy. He added notes in Nahuatl—the colony's lingua franca—to both manuscripts.[44]

The Princeton miscellany includes five pieces used in the Passion plays. One is the Palm Sunday antiphon that intones "Hosanna to the Son of David! Blessed is he that comes in the name of the Lord! Hosanna in the highest."[45] The text is from Matthew 21:9, where it is shouted by the crowd as Jesus rides his donkey into Jerusalem. Princeton places this in a stage direction, indicating a choral accompaniment (1v). Tepalcingo does the same but specifies that *Judiosmeh inpilhuan* 'the children of the Jews' will sing it (2). The Penn play takes the unusual step of placing Latin into the dialogue, having the Israelite children sing the text in Latin and follow it with a Nahuatl translation (5r; I.iii.2). Choirboys may have played these singing children.

Play characters sing in Latin on one other occasion, also a piece scored in Tomás Pascual's manuscript at Princeton (35r–35v). These are the three angels who pay that oddly early visit to Jesus in the Princeton play. As they leave, they sing the *Sanctus* from the Mass, the script reproducing the full Latin text (9r; I.v.6): *Sanctus sanctus sanctus. Dominus Deus Sabaoth. Pleni sunt caeli et terra gloria tua. Hosana in excelsis* 'Holy Holy Holy. Lord God of hosts. Heaven and earth are full of your glory. Hosanna in the highest.'[46]

Other Passion play chants include antiphons connected with Holy Thursday's foot-washing ceremony, the Mandatum. The Tlatlauhquitepec choir sings the antiphon "Domini tu mihi lavas pedes" (3r), while the Penn script (12r–v) instead requests "Mandatum novum do vobis" and "Dominus Jesus postquam cenabit" (see note at II.v.2). The Tepalcingo play calls for "Pascua surrexit," which does not seem to name a chant but may telescope into two words another Mandatum antiphon, a reworded excerpt from John 13:1–9 that contains the words *paschae* and *surrexit*.[47] Another cryptic cue placed at the foot washing is the Princeton play's *que confundatur*, which might be read *qui* or *quem* plus *confunditur* or *confundetur* (16v). This exact phrase does not occur in the Vulgate Bible or the Latin liturgy. A possible source is the phrase *omnes qui credit in eum non confundetur* 'all who believe in him will not be put to shame,' which appears, with slight variations, in Romans 9:33, Romans 10:11, and 1 Peter 2:6. As Jesus is about to speak of how his students will fare after his death, such words are not entirely out of context, but I have not traced them to a musical source.

Scriptwriters also called for hymns. Instead of singing the Hosanna text, Princeton's choir is to sing part or all of the hymn "Gloria, laus, et honor," from the Palm Sunday liturgy, as the actors carry out the triumphal entry celebrated in the hymn (5r). The Penn play calls for "Pange lingua" and "Tantum ergo" to be sung as Christ blesses and distributes the tortillas and wine (11v; II.iv.7, II.iv.9). The latter text is actually the last two stanzas of the six-stanza "Pange lingua gloriosi," a Eucharistic hymn attributed to Thomas Aquinas and included in the liturgy for Corpus Christi. Tomás Pascual's choir book contains this hymn (see figure 2.6).[48]

In the third category of Latin songs are the several motets found in the Passion corpus. Sacred music composers of the Renaissance and Baroque eras, including the

Figure 2.6. Scoring for the first stanza of "Pange lingua gloriosi," in seventeenth-century choral book annotated in Nahuatl by choirmaster Tomás Pascual of San Juan Ixcoy, Guatemala. Choral Music Miscellany, Garrett-Gates Mesoamerican Manuscripts, no. 258, Special Collections, Princeton University Library. Courtesy of Princeton University Library, Princeton, NJ.

renowned Spaniards Francisco Guerrero (1528–1599) and Tomás Luis de Victoria (ca. 1548–1611), used these short, polyphonic songs to showcase their talent and devotion. The pieces appealed as well to Nahua *maestros de capilla*. The Tepalcingo script calls for two, the first shared with the Princeton choral manuscript. This motet, "O Bone Jesu," is to be sung as Jesus and his three companions enter the Garden of Gethsemane (64), although it has no particular narrative connection to that moment.[49] The second is "O Domine Jesu Christe," a motet associated with both of the Spanish composers just mentioned. The scriptwriter, designating it a motet (as *motentes*), inserted it just after Longinus is to lance Jesus's side (115; V.iii.66). As the motet sings of Jesus wounded on the cross, it is aptly placed.

Axochiapan (13r) calls for a musical piece labeled "O Domine" but places it just before Jesus dispatches John and James to find and prepare the Last Supper site. I have not found a liturgical chant with this phrase that is appropriate to that context. It may be that, as with his vague earlier references to Navarro's Saint Matthew Passion, he is not paying much attention to the precise contextualization of his choral cues and is simply tossing the "O Domine Jesu Christe" motet in here. The same could be said of "O vos omnes," another motet associated with Victoria, which

Axochiapan's singers are asked to perform as Jesus enters the Garden of Gethsemane (21v). The text, Lamentations 1:12, beseeches people passing on the road to contemplate the singer's sorrow. It is better placed where it appears in the Penn Passion: as Jesus is embarking on the road to Calvary and falling for the first time (37v; V.ii.17). As this lament featured prominently in the liturgy for Holy Week,[50] the source could be a liturgical work rather than the motet.

The writer of the Amacuitlapilco script calls for choral music only twice. He cues motets, using *motete*, but seems to be applying the term to any choral interlude. Perhaps his limited musical knowledge is related to the sparsity of singing in his text. His first "motet" is labeled *recordatus*, referring to Peter recalling Christ's prediction of his denial, which the Peter actor is about to enact in the script (36v). The most likely source is not a motet but Navarro's Saint Matthew Passion (1604, 15v), which scores this passage from Matthew (26:75); the Penn play also uses it (25v; III.vi.9).

Amacuitlapilco's second alleged motet is cued with what seems to say *tuan Crusen*, placed when Christ is about to speak to the cross (38v; V.ii.13). I have two possible interpretations. One is to reverse the order of the words and read this as *[per] crucem tuam* '[by means of] your cross,' a phrase in the "Adoramus te Christe" antiphon that closes the Penn play. The second, more of a stretch from *tuan crucen* but precisely appropriate to the context, is to link it to John 19:17, scored by Navarro (1604, 74v), which reads *et baiulans sibi crucem exivit in eum* 'and he went out, bearing his own cross'; the *tuan*, then, is a Nahuatlized (/b/ changed to /t/) remnant of *baiulans*. I lean toward this reading, as it maintains the order of the two words and also reduces Amacuitlapilco's music to one source—Navarro—which we know the Passion performances drew upon extensively.

Perhaps the exception will prove the point that Latin was favored as the language of song. Penn (5v) calls for the singing of a song called "Ma cenquizcayectenehualo" 'Let [someone] be utterly praised.' This may be a Nahuatl translation of the popular hymn "Te deum laudamus," sung in Latin elsewhere in Nahuatl theater: the souls of the righteous sing it with the saints in heaven at the end of Fabián de Aquino's *Antichrist and the Hermit* (Leeming 2022), and the choir sings it when Christ calls upon Saint Michael to raise the dead in *Final Judgment* (Sell and Burkhart 2004, 202). We can also mention here the Hosanna singing in the Penn Passion, as it is possible the children were to sing the Nahuatl translation as well as the Latin text (5r; I.iii.2).

Nahuatl theater overall staged little Nahuatl-language singing. Demons sing in Nahuatl—we can hardly expect them to know Latin—in Aquino's other play, *Antichrist and the Final Judgment* (Leeming 2022). In his *Colloquy of How the Fortunate Saint Helen Found the Precious and Revered Wooden Cross*, the Nahua priest don Manuel de los Santos y Salazar[51] presents the portentous chants in Nahuatl, as he frames the Roman emperor Constantine as a figure comparable to the Tlaxcalan leaders who defeated their Mexica enemies in 1521 (Sell and Burkhart 2009, 280, 282, 288, 294; Burkhart 2016). Bartolomé de Alva adapts sung Spanish dialogue into Nahuatl in his plays and also offers a Nahuatl rendition of "Tantum ergo" (Sell, Burkhart, and Wright 2008, 91, 93, 149, 288–297, 313, 377). His only Latin song is the silly doggerel in his comic intermezzo (158).

The theater corpus as a whole has more singing in Latin than in Nahuatl, but nowhere with such frequency and variety as in the Passion plays. Morality plays, in addition to the "Te Deum" mentioned above, can solemnize their proceedings with responsories for the dead and, in one case, a verse from Psalm 24 (25), used in the Office for the Dead (Sell and Burkhart 2004, 168, 172, 238, 264; 2009, 328). Otherwise, all the Latin singing is in praise of the Virgin Mary. The Marian song "Ave Maris stella" ("Hail, Star of the Sea") is intoned as Mary comes onstage in *How to Live on Earth* (Sell and Burkhart 2004, 227). Joseph Pérez de la Fuente, the *criollo*[52] priest who wrote the Guadalupan verse play *The Wonder of Mexico*, requested the singing of a Marian song during each of Mary's apparitions: a setting of the catechistic prayer "Salve regina," the hymns "O gloriosa domina" and (again) "Ave Maris stella," and the Litany of the Blessed Virgin Mary (Sell, Burkhart, and Poole 2006, 116, 134, 144, 168). In addition to their relative scarcity, none of these other Latin lyrics plays a storytelling role the way most of the songs do in the Passions, with the singers intoning bits of the story in Latin just before or at the same time as the actors speak corresponding lines in Nahuatl or perform appropriate movements.

For a final point of comparison, we can ascertain how much of this musical practice overlaps with the Spanish-language Passions from the Inquisition files. The answer is: very little. All four Spanish plays accompany Jesus's donkey-mounted approach to Jerusalem with the singing of a "Hosanna" song, but in all except the play from Ozumba (245v) this is a Spanish adaptation of Matthew 21:9 rather than the Latin text. Another Spanish song, "Nuestro amado Jesús" ("Our Beloved Jesus"), accompanies the foot-washing scene in Cuaderno 1 (207r) and the play from Amecameca (282v). The Tenango play instead has the disciples themselves sing Psalm 113 (114), "In exitu Israel," apparently in Latin, before departing for Gethsemane (263r). Cuaderno 1 has additional musical interludes: "sad music," perhaps instrumental, is to sound when Jesus prays in the garden (209v); and the singers are asked, like those of the Princeton Passion (37v; IV.iii.11), to sing the "Miserere" at the time of Christ's flagellation (216v). Music there is, but with only one to three songs per play and Spanish songs outnumbering Latin ones by five to three, the Spanish playwrights presented an impoverished soundscape of sacred music compared to their Nahua counterparts. The contrast points to the more ritualized character of the Nahuatl productions: the Latin liturgical music carried the church's sacrality out into the cemetery or another outdoor venue.

PRODUCTION VALUES

Nahuatl Passion plays kept choristers, trumpeters, donkey wranglers and other stagehands, costumers, set designers, and property masters busy preparing for and participating in these productions. This chapter has reviewed some of the staging strategies and effects that helped keep these productions visually and aurally interesting and appropriate to their *altepetl* settings. Scriptwriters vary the pacing by interposing quieter moments like the filling of a water jug or the counting of coins; calling for the reading, sometimes repeated, of documents; and deciding how many times Jesus will go into and out of the Garden of Gethsemane or the arresting soldiers will fall down in front of him. They split the stage among multiple sets, juxtaposing scenes of godliness and of villainy. And they cast a *teoyotica* aura—a sense of sacred, church-related things—through the Latin music and the winged emissaries from the sky realm who drop in for occasional visits. Actors pose in iconic tableaux, such as Christ on the cross flanked by Mary and John or seated among his students at the Last Supper or praying in the garden near his dozing disciples, as live theater imitates familiar sculpted or painted scenes.

All these variations prove that the Passions represent a *tradition*: there is a core story and a core cast of characters that no scriptwriter essentially alters, while each version adds or subtracts or changes enough things to show that this was a living, developing performance practice moving through time and space. Participants felt no obligation to reproduce a single, authoritative dialogue or mise-en-scène. Scriptwriters thought about how their play would be staged and how to improve upon versions from the past, even if that meant eliminating or simplifying certain things.

The production values reflect the value *altepetl* leaders and play participants placed on this tradition, whatever combination of camaraderie, piety, prestige seeking, or desire to wreak norm-breaking havoc might motivate a particular man, woman, or child to take part. As each of the five complete Passion plays is longer than any extant Nahuatl play from another genre, the sheer amount of material to be memorized and staged also speaks to the value placed on these plays. So does the size of the cast—or at least the number of roles, if we allow that some actors might play more than one part. Passion plays have double the number of roles found in nearly any other colonial Nahuatl play. Each of the five complete plays calls for between fifty and fifty-five characters, not counting any unscripted extras such as additional soldiers or generalized Jerusalemites. This is a remarkably consistent number, considering the many variations among the scripts. What survives of the Passion from Tlatlauhquitepec suggests that it had pretty much the same cast range as the complete plays. The Spanish-language plays also have rather large casts, numbering, roughly, in the forties; various plural references to centurions or pontiffs and the like preclude an exact count.

The only Nahuatl plays that compete with the Passions in cast size are Fabián de Aquino's two idiosyncratic plays, *Antichrist and the Final Judgment* and *Antichrist and the Hermit*—so titled by Ben Leeming (2022) in his comprehensive study and translation. Leeming dates the plays to the mid- to late sixteenth century, making them the earliest extant Nahuatl scripts. For the first play, Aquino writes that fifty-one people are required. Leeming estimates that it could be staged with as few as forty people, as only seven characters speak as individuals while the others break into clusters of Converts, Demons, Damned, Blessed, and Apostles, supplemented by a pair of angels and possibly Saint Mary. Thirty-one individual characters have lines in *Antichrist and the Hermit*, and there are also several groups who speak in chorus: six Fire Priests, six Martyrs, and an unspecified number of converts and additional martyrs—if six each, the parts would total fifty-five (Ben Leeming, personal communication, June 17, 2020). Large casts indeed, but we may note that even in *Antichrist and the Hermit*, individually named characters who speak solo lines are substantially fewer than in the Passions.

Among the seventeenth- and eighteenth-century scripts more typical of the extant Nahuatl corpus, the most highly populated productions are *Colloquy of How the Fortunate Saint Helen Found the Precious and Revered Wooden Cross*, with twenty-eight speaking parts and some silent soldiers; the Epiphany play *The Star Sign*, with twenty-four; the morality plays *The Merchant* and *How to Live on Earth*, with twenty-four (if the seen-and-not-heard children number only two) and twenty-three, respectively; and Alva's Golden Age adaptation *The Animal Prophet and the Fortunate Patricide*, with twenty-three—if we count two disembodied voices and the talking deer. Morality plays could have as few as twelve roles, in the case of *The Life of Don Sebastián*, while *The Three Kings*, with only ten roles, looks understaffed compared to *The Star Sign*. The two Guadalupan plays have only thirteen and sixteen parts, and *The Destruction of Jerusalem* manages to stage the siege and fall of the holy *altepetl* and the trial of Pilate with only fifteen speaking roles.[53]

These numbers capture the scale of the Passion dramas as spectacle and as community theater. As spectacle, their length and their assemblage of scenes and dialogue outdo anything else in the surviving records. The remaining chapters in this book explore many more of the sensational moments that hit notes of pathos, compassion, violence, ritual, and legal drama. As community theater, the Passions gave as many as fifty-plus players a chance to strut and fret their hour—or at least their scene or two—on the stage, their work facilitated and enhanced by the various support personnel and special effects. Fray Miguel of Tlatelolco did not like to see Indigenous people, with their very modest means, spend money to put on shows.[54] We can read his criticism instead as evidence of the intangible value these productions had for the sponsoring *altepetl* and for each of its resident *macehualtin* who chose to join the cast or crew.

3

Sadness and Solidarity

The Women of the Passion

THE LEAVE-TAKING

Every play follows the Gospels in placing the Virgin Mary and Mary Magdalene at the crucifixion, but otherwise women characters' presence in the play varies quite a bit. One major decision in this regard was whether and how extensively to stage Christ's farewell to his mother (scene I.viii). I begin by considering how this scene entered medieval tradition, and how its origin illuminates the role of gender in Passion devotions.

In European Passion literature, this leave-taking occurs at the Bethany home of Mary—identified with Mary Magdalene in Christian tradition—and her sister, Martha, before Jesus returns to Jerusalem prior to Passover. Jesus's association with the sisters and their brother, Lazarus, derives from Luke 10:38–41 and John 11:17–27. The leave-taking, however, stems not from the Gospels but from the fourteenth-century *Meditations on the Life of Christ* (McNamer 2018), a key text in the development of contemplative Passion devotions. Although the work was traditionally ascribed to the Franciscan Saint Bonaventure, modern scholars have usually attributed it to Giovanni da Cauli (or Johannes de Caulibus), a Franciscan friar from San Gimignano, Italy (e.g., Peck 1980, 140–142). In contrast, Sarah McNamer's (2010, 111–113; 2018) meticulous analysis of early manuscript versions leads her to conclude that the original text was written in Italian by an anonymous nun—possibly but not necessarily a Franciscan Poor Clare—and directed to a fellow nun: the author refers to herself and her addressee as "brides of Christ." This text was then enlarged

https://doi.org/10.5876/9781646424511.c003

and Latinized, possibly by da Cauli, who aimed his accretions at toning down the text's affective dimensions, "colonizing and containing" (McNamer 2010, 115) its feminine sensibility. The expanded text, which nevertheless retained the dialogical character and emotional pull of the original, came to be considered a quintessential Franciscan work (chapter 3; cf. McNamer 2009, 2018).

The unrecognized female authorship of the *Meditations* is but one example of how the role of women in the later medieval development of European Passion devotions had been overlooked. McNamer (2010, 1) sees the practices of nuns and anchoresses as a driving force behind the rise of affective meditations on the Passion, which "ask readers to imagine themselves present at scenes of Christ's suffering and to perform compassion for that suffering victim as a private drama of the heart." Many of the early texts in this mode were written by men, but they were explicitly directed to women religious; as McNamer (80) puts it, "male authors were less inventors of the genre than go-betweens in the marriages of aspiring *sponsae Christi*." As "brides of Christ" hoping to be united with him in heaven, these women sought to prove themselves worthy of their husband's love by cultivating intense emotions on his behalf. Since women, as a gender, were defined as more carnal and emotional than men, they could claim a particular predisposition to affective devotions that focused on Christ's bodily experiences (15; McNamer draws on Bynum 1988).

The new devotional mode spread to male monastics and then to the Franciscans and to laymen and laywomen. However, compassion, as an emotion, remained so female-gendered that male participants had, in effect, to "feel like a woman"—to experience female-gendered feelings—to participate in this cathartic experience. Often, the identification was mediated through the figure of Mary: a woman could imagine her tender maternal love, and a man could sympathize with her suffering secondhand without feeling that he was wallowing in feminized emotion (McNamer 2010).

Passion literature augmented Mary's suffering along with that of her son, rendering both experiences extreme and hers so intense that it rivaled his, such that she underwent a kind of co-Passion and became a "co-redemtrix of the human race" (Bestul 1996, 113; cf. Warner 1976) while also, in Miri Rubin's (2009, 246) words, "encompass[ing] all the pain associated with the Crucifixion as a drama of loss and bereavement." Trends outside Passion literature contributed to her exaltation: Thomas Bestul (1996, 113–114) links it to the simultaneous development in secular, courtly literature of a fixation with aristocratic ladies—"idealized paragons of virtue, yet largely governed and defined by their appearance, emotions, desires, and physicality"—that went along with the seigneurial class's increasing wealth and power. Rubin (2008, 53, 59) connects the growing emphasis on Mary's purity and her maternal suffering to hatred of the Jews held responsible for causing it. The purer Mary became, the more perverse were her detractors; the more she suffered, the more responsibility they bore.

Positing a sad farewell between Jesus and Mary provided "brides of Christ" and other devotees with another occasion for identifying with Mary and feeling the painful emotions wrought by her son's death. The popularity of the *Meditations* ensured that this poignant scene would find a place in various other Passion narratives and devotional miscellany[1] and become a subject for Passion-related art (for example, figure 3.1). Imported to New Spain, the farewell appears in early narrative sources (such as the Tulane Passion manuscript and the "Historia de la Pasión de Nuestro Señor Jesu Christo en lengua mexicana") and in one of the oldest surviving Nahuatl dramas. Around 1582, the Valencian poet Ausías Izquierdo Zebrero recast the farewell scene as a one-act religious play called *Beacon of Our Salvation*,[2] and this piece was adapted into Nahuatl, probably at Tlatelolco. In the 1590s an Indigenous copyist inscribed this drama into a Franciscan manuscript under the simple Spanish title *Miércoles santo 'Holy Wednesday'* (Burkhart 1996).

The Spanish play revolves around Christ's request that Mary grant him permission to proceed with his predestined death. She protests and petitions him to somehow avoid dying. After some disputation, an angel interrupts their conversation to read to Mary five letters sent from Adam and other ancient figures who are waiting in the Limbo of the Holy Fathers for Jesus to come and take them to heaven. Each presents Mary with one of the implements of the Passion (cross, crown of thorns, nails, stone column, lance) and implores her to let her son fulfill his destiny. She ultimately accedes, resolving the conflict. In the Nahuatl adaptation, Jesus expresses greater filial obedience and deference. He never requests permission, and she does not grant it. Mary is more authoritative and knowledgeable than her Spanish counterpart. The tenor of the interaction between mother and son emphasizes love and solidarity over disagreement and conflict. The Nahuatl Christ also places more emphasis on the prophecies that predetermine his fate, a strategy that makes him seem more submissive and less willful than his Spanish model (Burkhart 1996, 89–91; 2000, 80–85).

While Christ in the Passion plays follows this model of deference to his mother and to the force of prophecy, of necessity his farewell scene is much briefer. The leave-taking scene appears in four of the complete plays. In addition, the one-leaf play fragment from Atlihuetzia (Macuil Martínez 2016, 233 fig. 2, 241–244) happens to preserve the latter part of this scene. However, since the redactor of the Axochiapan play saw fit to leave it out, we can surmise that the exchange was not considered absolutely essential to the staging of a Nahuatl Passion.

The Tepalcingo play locates the scene after Christ's Palm Sunday entry into Jerusalem. The Atlihuetzia fragment, which is slightly more elaborate than its close

Figure 3.1. *Christ Taking Leave of His Mother.* John, Magdalene, and Martha hold on to the swooning Mary, while Peter and James attend Jesus and the donor, Elisabetta Rota, kneels in the foreground. Painting by Lorenzo Lotto, 1521. Gemäldegalerie, Berlin. Courtesy of Wikimedia Commons.

cognate in the Tepalcingo text, suggests the same, as it likewise ends with plans to walk to Jerusalem, not to fetch the donkey. This placement is consistent with the European tradition that placed this visit after Palm Sunday and before Thursday's Last Supper. I follow this sequence in the composite play for two reasons. First, if the scene existed in the model Passion—and it may not have—it was probably located here for consistency with Old World models. Second, as discussed in the next section, Tepalcingo and Axochiapan show Mary Magdalene repenting her immoral ways (I.v.22), and this event logically precedes the devotion to Christ and Mary that she expresses in the farewell scene. In contrast, Penn and Princeton begin with the leave-taking, and Amacuitlapilco places it right after a brief opening exchange among Christ and his students, unique to that play (scene I.i). One or more redactors may have decided the original placement was illogical because the characters discuss Jesus going to Jerusalem when that has already been staged, with much fanfare, and therefore showed Jesus taking leave of his mother prior to his Jerusalem-bound donkey ride.

Placed at different points in the story, the versions also vary in length, in precisely which counterarguments Mary makes to Christ's announcement of his impending death, the degree to which Magdalene and Martha participate in the scene, and whether the students come in toward the end and add their own pleas. The high degree of variation supports the idea that the scene was not part of the original play. Even in Tepalcingo, where its placement fits the European tradition, annotations suggest the scriptwriter may have copied it from a source separate from the main text he was recopying or editing. He instructs "Caiaphas and all the Jews" to enter for the scene in which they plot Jesus's arrest (scene II.i) but then decides, or remembers, to insert the leave-taking before proceeding with the priestly council's meeting (16). Moreover, the Amacuitlapilco play, which is almost entirely cognate with Axochiapan except in some scenes in which it mirrors Tepalcingo, has a distinct version of this scene linked more closely to the Penn play (4v–7r).

Tepalcingo and the Atlihuetzia fragment present the most elaborate staging of the scene. It tracks so closely with the leave-taking narrative in the sixteenth-century Nahuatl Christian copybook at Tulane, most of which consists of dialogue, that we can trace it to either that source or another copy of the same narrative (see my translation in Burkhart 1996, 255–259). This connection to a separate textual tradition suggests that the scene is an independent piece with its own history. The original playwright(s) may have included it, augmenting their other source or sources, but it is at least as likely that some later scriptwriter wanted to expand Mary's role and had access to some version of the text preserved in the Tulane manuscript.

The Penn and Amacuitlapilco leave-takings, though not identical to each other, are similar enough that they must derive from the same variant. This in turn may have originated from an earlier inscription of the Tepalcingo-Atlihuetzia text, but, if so, the scene has been extensively reduced and rewritten. Martha and the students are absent, while some new material is added. For example, Mary reminds Christ of the difficulty she endured when she had to flee with him to Egypt to save him from Herod (Amacuitlapilco, 5v; Penn, 2v; I.viii.7), a point she makes in the *Holy Wednesday* play (Burkhart 1996, 123) but not in the Tulane text. In Princeton (1r–1v) the scene is so truncated that Christ and Mary take only two turns each at speech, including the brief blessings they make to each other. No one else is present, and Mary offers only one feeble protest, regarding how the people of Jerusalem hate her son—a misgiving voiced by John in the Tepalcingo-Atlihuetzia variant (I.viii.28) and by Jesus's students collectively in the Tulane source (Burkhart 1996, 259).

Variations aside, the inclusion of especially the more elaborate forms of this scene, in which Mary speaks more than she does in the rest of the play, highlighted Mary's importance in her son's life and in the Passion story. She can protest his plans, claim authority by enumerating previous actions she has taken for his benefit, and offer alternative scenarios. These are rejected, but in refusing them Jesus does not simply override maternal authority with his own or his father's. To his father's demands he adds the force of both prophecy and the sacred written word. These three paramount authorities and not his own willfulness explain his actions. The blessings and embraces he exchanges with his mother enact mutuality rather than the submission of one to the other.

The presence of other women in the scene creates a feminized space onstage, into which Jesus enters, sometimes later joined by his students (en masse, in Atlihuetzia, or, in Tepalcingo, only Peter and John). When Magdalene adds her voice to Mary's, she echoes the older woman's tones of both lamentation and resistance—a joint effort that recalls the earliest inscription of the story by the anonymous Italian nun, before male writers made Mary's protests more soft-spoken than Magdalene's (McNamer 2010, 109). It is the province of the women to be steadfast in their love for Jesus, to express dependence on him for their own contentment or even existence, and to display their concern through bodily actions: weeping, fainting, kneeling in entreaty. They also support one another, with Magdalene and Martha attending to Mary's distress and Mary addressing the two sisters as her daughters. In formal Nahuatl speech, addressing non-kin with kinship terms displayed affection and respect (Karttunen and Lockhart 1987, 43–45), a pattern Lisa Sousa (2017, 232) found in the more mundane context of criminal cases as well. Similarly, Jesus often calls his students "my children," which he never does in the Gospels.

We should not assume that in an Indigenous milieu, the women's words and gestures display feminized weakness or gendered emotionality. There is no reason to believe that compassion was particularly female-gendered in Indigenous categories of emotion. Women were more closely identified with the earth and its deified manifestations than men were, but this was not the material-versus-spiritual or terrestrial-versus-celestial opposition that fostered the body-based penances of medieval nuns. Gender itself was less body-based and more of a performance, grounded in self-presentation through dress, labor, and ritual roles (Sousa 2017, 30, 49). Gender complementarity extended to parenting: while mothers had primary responsibility for babies, Nahuatl orations composed in the voices of both mothers and fathers express tender feelings for children, and parents were responsible for educating and disciplining children of their own gender (239–242; Marín-Guadarrama 2012).[3] Nahua compassion is also distinct linguistically: the Nahuatl term used is *tetlaocoyaliztli* 'feeling sad on behalf of someone,' while compassion (Spanish *compasión*, from Latin *compassio*) adds *com* 'with' to the same Latin root as the word "passion" itself (*patior* 'suffer'). Even if this nominalized form of *tlaocoya* 'to be sad' was used principally in Christian contexts, sympathetic sadness is not the same thing as the co-suffering that sent European devotees into ecstasies of agony.

Thus, while the European tradition of affective Passion devotion passed into the Nahuatl plays, accounting for the farewell scene and other plaintive episodes, these scenes may have played differently in Nahuatl. Mary and the other women cannot stop Jesus from fulfilling his preordained responsibility. But passivity was not female-gendered: colonial Indigenous women engaged in and even led violent uprisings when faced with injustice or threats to their livelihood or lifeways (Sousa 2017, 205; Taylor 1979, 116). The women in the farewell scene, neither weak nor over-emotional, model a mode of behavior that is much more attuned to the events at hand than that of the apostles—who despite their protestations will soon abandon Jesus—or of the enemies who are plotting to kill him. The tears of the women are prescient, foreseeing the upcoming events as well as setting the lamenting tone with which Christians in the future, Indigenous as well as European, will recall Christ's torment and death. The women, in effect, pose a counter-narrative of love, devotion, and solidarity to the narrative of hatred, torture, and abandonment to be carried out by men—violence that is illegitimate, not directed to a righteous cause. And they keep this alternative alive across the rupture rent by Christ's death. As embodiments of benevolent saints, they may help to preserve some degree of cosmic and social order that protects the *altepetl* from dangerous effects the violent enactment of the deity's death could otherwise precipitate.

Spanish-speaking performers granted enough importance to the leave-taking to stage it in each of the four plays from the Inquisition file. Hewing to the European model, the scripts place the conversation just before the Last Supper. The play from Amecameca (281r) and Cuaderno 1 (206r) share a brief exchange in which Jesus requests and Mary grants a blessing, with the two speaking a total of 154 and 152 words, respectively. The plays from Ozumba and Tenango stage a longer conversation, with Mary speaking twice and Jesus once in Ozumba (839 words of dialogue; 246v), and each taking a single turn at speech in Tenango (592 words; 258r–258v). In Ozumba they speak in terms of a mystical union of body and soul quite alien to the Nahuatl dialogue. In Tenango they exchange words of encouragement and sympathy. Strikingly, no Spanish-speaking Mary dares suggest that Jesus should find a way to avoid his fate. In the Spanish plays, mother and son may kneel and Jesus may take Mary's hand, but they never embrace. Magdalene's presence is always noted but she never speaks or is spoken to, while the Spanish-speaking playwrights omitted Martha entirely. Collectively, the Nahuatl plays stage considerably more female agency in this scene.

MAGDALENE AND THE PRECIOUS *PAHATL*

Mary Magdalene—nearly always called simply Magdalene (Magdalena) in the plays—is named in each of the Gospels. A follower of Jesus from whom he had cast out seven demons (Luke 8:2), she was present at the crucifixion and was one of the women to discover the empty tomb on Sunday morning. She also had the particular distinction of being the first person to whom the resurrected Christ appeared (John 20:17–18). Christian tradition combined her with two other female friends of Jesus: Mary of Bethany, sister of Martha and Lazarus, and the unnamed woman who anoints Christ with a pricey and fragrant ointment (Farmer 1992, 329–330; figure 3.2). This scene occurs in each of the four Gospels (Matthew 26:6–13; Mark 14:3–9; Luke 7:36–50; John 12:1–8). In Matthew and Mark, the woman pours the ointment on Christ's head, while in Luke she is a sinner who washes Jesus's feet with her tears, dries them with her hair, and then anoints them with the ointment, after which he pardons her sins. In John she anoints his feet and wipes them with her hair. John differs from the other Gospels in placing this event at the home of the Bethany siblings rather than that of Simon the leper (or, in Luke, an unspecified Pharisee, presumably Simon). This change lends some justification to the later identification of this anonymous woman as Mary Magdalene, although nowhere in the Gospels does Magdalene bear the sinful attributes she would acquire in medieval Christianity.

In the Gospel accounts, Simon the Pharisee (in Luke), the disciples in general (in Matthew), "some" (in Mark), or Judas (in John) consider the woman's behavior wasteful, as the price of the unguent could have been used to help the poor. Jesus defends his devotee's act. In Matthew and Mark, Jesus remarks that they will always have the poor with them, but he will not be around much longer. He notes that she has anointed his body for burial, adding, "Truly, I say to you, wherever the gospel is preached in the whole world, what she has done will be told in memory of her."[4]

Figure 3.2. *The Meal in the House of Simon the Pharisee.* Mary Magdalene, shown with her jar of ointment, dries Jesus's feet with her hair. Painting by Frans Francken the Younger, 1637 (cropped). Museum of Fine Arts, Rennes, France. Courtesy of Wikimedia Commons (license: Creative Commons—Attribution-ShareAlike 4.0 International—CC BY-SA 4.0).

In Christian iconography, the jar of ointment became an emblem of Magdalene, who was often depicted as a luxuriously adorned woman. Her presumed sinful past justified the legend that she spent the rest of her life in penitential retirement, alone in the woods but visited and fed by angels—a story included in the 1583 Nahuatl *Psalmodia christiana* (Sahagún 1583, 119v; figure 3.3). For European Christianity, Magdalene was the "prototype of the penitent sinner" and "patron of all sinners" (Sticca 1970, 137). While Nahuas might gather that her sexual excess put her into a dangerous state, which she corrected by turning to Jesus and his teachings, she may have served less as a model of penitence than as a prestigious female presence within the Christian divine.

Four of the five complete plays include the scene of Magdalene and the ointment. Hence, like the leave-taking, it was not considered essential for every Passion enactment but did enjoy widespread performance. In contrast, none of the Spanish plays from the Inquisition file presents the scene. The Gospels place this event at different times, with only Matthew and Mark scheduling it after Palm Sunday; it was by no means essential to a recounting of Holy Week. The scene's scripters and probably the original playwright(s) found something interesting in this interchange that justified staging it.

Including the Magdalene encounter could serve two purposes in Passion accounts. First, the motif, from John, that Judas is the one to get angry and raise

Figure 3.3. Mary Magdalene at prayer in front of a crucifix, her ointment jar near her knees. In the upper left, angels carry her. Woodcut in Bernardino de Sahagún, *Psalmodia christiana*, 1583, 117v. Courtesy of the John Carter Brown Library, Brown University, Providence, RI.

objections serves as a motivation for his betrayal of Jesus. John here (12:6) accuses Judas of stealing from the disciples' money box, and later tradition affirmed his identity as a habitual embezzler of the group's funds, this thievery helping to establish his evil character: he wants to appropriate some of the money he claims would go to the poor.[5] In Matthew and Mark, Judas marches off to make his arrangement with the chief priests immediately after this meal. Second, the account foreshadows the moment, in narratives or plays that extend to Easter, when the women coming to anoint Christ's body find the sepulcher unoccupied.

The second of the two Tulane Passion texts, less a narrative than a collection of Passion-related moral lessons, recalls this dinner for the sole purpose of vilifying

Judas (*Pasión en lengua mexicana* n.d., second pagination, 25v–26r). Magdalene is not even named; she is just a *cihuatzintli* 'dear (or respected) woman.' She spreads her *pahatl cencah ahhuiac cencah tlazohtli* 'very fragrant, very precious unguent' on an unspecified part of Jesus. As for Judas:

> And when Judas saw it, then he became very angry. He said, "Why is she doing this? She just wasted it. If we had sold it, would we not have gotten a great deal of gold [or silver] with which we could have had compassion for the poor?"[6] This is how Judas spoke, the wretched thief. It is not true, what he said. If they had sold it, they would not have had compassion for the poor with all of it. He just . . . would have stolen some of it.[7]

Jesus defends the *cihuatzintli*'s actions, and then, "Judas was very jealous. And that is how it is clear that Judas is a very covetous one, and a very jealous one, and a very thieving one. And that is why he sold our lord, as he loves gold [or silver] very much."[8] One of the Passion narrative fragments inside the Christ statue from Mexicaltzingo also speaks of Judas's greed and thievery (Carrillo y Gariel 1949, vol. 2, 71).

It may be that the scene was included in the model Passion play to provide this bit of backstory regarding Judas's motivation. But if the dialogue or stage directions made any reference to Judas helping himself to communal funds, this was dropped as the play was revised over time. And Magdalene claimed more of the limelight.

The Axochiapan play's writer skipped the leave-taking but, like the cognate section of Tepalcingo, included an extended treatment of Magdalene that begins with her attendance at Jesus's Jerusalem preaching (3r–5r; I.iv.20–23). When she hears him say, "Your beauty, your good looks, that you fit on yourself will all turn into red-hot coals in the place of the dead" (I.iv.21), she regrets her sins and casts off her adornments—suggestive of both wealth and feminine attraction—because they are now burning her. This transformation comes not from the Gospels but from a convention of Nahuatl theater. Some Nahuatl morality plays showed women guilty of sexual misdeeds condemned to the place of the dead and tormented by underworldly replacements of their former feminine gear. A childless noblewoman—it is hinted that she had abortions—is beset by "fire lizards" that replace her earrings, a "fire blouse," and "fire butterflies" that suck at her breasts in place of the children she did not bear, while snakes replace her hair ornaments and necklaces (Sell and Burkhart 2009, 329). Lucía, the woman in the play *Final Judgment* who neglected to get married (while, apparently, not practicing abstinence), wears fire-butterfly earrings, a fire-serpent necklace, and another fire serpent around her waist that signifies her former pleasures (Sell and Burkhart 2004, 207). The actor playing Magdalene could have displayed similar items and thrown them away from her body, although no stage directions so specify.

Magdalene then follows Jesus and his students to the home where they have been invited to dine. Tepalcingo's host is Simon (7–8), but in Axochiapan, though the name Simon is retained in a stage direction (he sets out the table), someone decided that the same man could and should host both this meal and the Last Supper, and the host's role goes to Gamaliel (4r–v; see chapter 4). Magdalene gains admittance to Jesus's presence, then proceeds to wash his feet with her tears and dry them with her hair (I.vi.4–12). Next, however, occurs a striking inversion of the canonical story. Jesus, not Magdalene, provides the costly unguent—not merely costly but in these two plays of otherworldly, presumably celestial, origin—and he spreads it on her head, not she on his feet or head (I.vi.13–16). Given the overall consistency of the plays with Gospel models, I suspect this change occurred at some point in the process of recopying and revision. Since Nahuatl does not have grammatical gender, "he will spread it on her head" and "she will spread it on his head" are the same words (*icpac quimotequiliz*), so there could have been some ambiguity in a third-person stage direction or in an earlier narrative source adapted to the stage. But there is no ambiguity when Christ says, "Bend down. Let me spread the precious unguent on your head" (Axochiapan, 5r),[9] especially when he has just obtained it from John's hands. When Judas complains about the wastefulness, Christ responds somewhat as he does in Matthew and Mark, referring to Magdalene's future renown (I.vi. 17–18). But he does not mention his burial, here or in any of the other plays. This motif, if it was in the original play, had to be dropped once Magdalene became the anointed one.

The Princeton and Amacuitlapilco plays present a briefer encounter. Magdalene approaches when Christ is with his students, and they each make just one speech. A stage direction in Amacuitlapilco instructs her to bring an unguent, but what she presents to Jesus is instead a cross, as she does also in Princeton. That stage direction may be a vestige from before the ointment switch was established in the performance tradition. Magdalene's proffered cross probably derives from the cross in front of which she is typically depicted in penitential poses (as in figure 3.3) and simply replaced the unguent she brought in earlier versions of the play. It is in line with other scenes in which implements of the Passion are presented to Christ or Mary (for example, Michael's display in III.i.17, from the Penn play, or the implements sent from the Limbo of the Holy Fathers in *Holy Wednesday*). Amacuitlapilco's Christ presents the unguent to her: "Here is a precious unguent, which I will spread on your head" (16r).[10] Princeton's Jesus tells Magdalene that "you" will put the unguent on "your" head, but here the stage directions indicate that he is to put it on her; either way, it is she who receives the gift (10r). Amacuitlapilco includes Judas's objection but not until a little later on, when he is alone onstage: "Why did the teacher want the very good, precious unguent to be wasted? I think you just want to give me problems thereby. But nevertheless, you will pay the price of it. If not, let my name not be Judas Iscariot" (17r; I.vi.20).[11]

The ointment inversion has two principal effects. One is to elevate Mary Magdalene in Christ's esteem and in front of the audience. His pardon of her sins is materialized by his application of a *tlazohpahatl* 'precious medicinal liquid' that could be seen to purify and heal her and perhaps even extend its pleasing fragrance to people standing near the stage. There is a reciprocity in their actions that lessens the distance between his masculine and divine status and her female and human one: she performs a service to him, and he performs one on her. Her tears on his feet, an act of bodily purification, are exchanged for a precious liquid on her head. We can also see this soothing unguent as a heavenly balm for the pain caused by the burning adornments she cast away, especially if one of those bits of finery was a head or hair ornament.

The other effect is to rationalize Judas's anger. If it was Magdalene's own ointment, why should she not do as she pleased with it? But if it belonged to Jesus and his students, Judas has some claim to its value; he just cannot see that this dear woman is indeed worthy of the gift. He is angry not because he is inordinately evil or, as far as the plays tell us, because he wanted some of the money for himself. But as in the larger tradition, this anger feeds his decision to betray Christ. All six plays present a very similar, lengthy soliloquy in which Judas struggles to make up his mind whether to inform on his teacher (II.vi.2; see fuller discussion in chapter 4). Near the end, he voices his displeasure over the wasted ointment and laments the 300 pesos it could have been sold for.[12] This issue seems to clinch his argument with himself, and he resolves to proceed with his betrayal. Here, the third-person reference carries the ambiguity noted above: Judas could be saying "she spread it on his head" or "he spread it on her head." Thus, in performances where the scene was not actually staged, auditors could interpret his words either way. The latter reading, though, better validates the anger at Jesus that drives him on to seek an audience with the chief priests and is also more in keeping with the derogatory word he applies to Magdalene in five of the six cases: *cihuatontli* 'wretched little woman.' In Tlatlauhquitepec he calls her a *cihuatl* 'woman,' but even that is at odds with the polite *cihuatzintli* Jesus and his good followers use for the women in the story. Judas, then, betrays Christ mainly because he is angry about a woman. His resentment of Magdalene adds a tone of misogyny that definitely does not model proper behavior and also alienates him from the order, stability, and loving kindness the Passion women, collectively, represent. The fact that he goes on not only to betray Jesus but to die by his own hand argues powerfully for the importance of gender harmony in the Nahua worldview.

THE WOMAN CAUGHT IN ADULTERY

After the scene with Magdalene, Tepalcingo and Axochiapan continue with shared text as Jesus goes out to preach to the people of Jerusalem (I.vii). The high priest Caiaphas and the "Jews" challenge him by bringing a woman imprisoned for adultery and demanding that he pass judgment on her. Citing ancestral authority, they recommend stoning her. This scene comes from John 8:1–11, where the antagonists are anonymous "scribes and Pharisees" and the encounter occurs in Jerusalem but—like Luke's and John's versions of the ointment exchange—prior to Christ's Palm Sunday re-entry to that city.[13] Here, there is a more deliberate departure from Gospel chronology to include a scene with a woman, and in this case there is no obvious connection to the Passion story. Although more associated with Jesus's admonition "he that is without sin among you, let him first cast a stone at her," absent from the Nahuatl texts, the account in John also includes the mysterious writing on the ground that the Nahuatl versions highlight (I.vii.6–8). In John 8:9, the woman's persecutors slip away one by one after seeing the written message. In the plays they run off quickly, heightening the drama while also reinforcing impressions of these characters as disorderly and immoderate.

The Jews and Caiaphas insult the woman as a *cihuatontli* 'wretched little woman' and a *cihuatlahueliloc* 'despicable woman' or 'female scoundrel.' But Jesus addresses her, as he does Magdalene, with the polite *cihuatzintli*: she is a person worthy of respect even though we do not see her expressing regret for her deeds, as Magdalene does. The different terms add shades of honor and opprobrium to what in the Bible source is simply "woman" (*mulier* in the Vulgate). As well as admonishing her to reform her behavior (from John's "go, and sin no more"), Jesus comforts her and promises her membership in his elect, saying "you will be one of my beloved ones" (I.vii.9).[14] Though not as strikingly as in the unguent scene, Jesus again raises the status of a female character well above the way she is represented in the Bible.

The laws of Moses are mentioned multiple times in the Nahuatl plays, so it is worth noting that here, whereas John 8:5 refers to what "Moses in the law commanded us," Caiaphas in the plays instead invokes *in tocolhuan in tocihhuan* 'our grandfathers, our grandmothers.' Although this is a formulaic phrase for ancestors, it occurs nowhere else in the corpus of Passion plays. Why here? As it happens, various sixteenth-century reports, including pictorial manuscripts and the *Relaciones geográficas* commissioned by Philip II, indicate that adultery was punished with death—by stoning, according to some sources—in Post-Classic Mesoamerica, a chance correspondence to the stoning prescribed in Leviticus 20:10 (Sousa 2017, 158–162; López Hernández 2017; one well-known image of stoning is in Codex Mendoza [Berdan and Anawalt 1992, vol. 3, 71r]). The usage fosters a conflation of Jewish with pre-Columbian law—at least as it was represented and perhaps reinvented in these sources. While I do not think the Passion plays—even though Christ and his followers may be seen as Indigenous people—develop a Jerusalem-as-Tenochtitlan analogy as pervasively as do the Epiphany plays or the play *The Destruction of Jerusalem* (see Burkhart 2008, 2010; Brown and Terukina Yamauchi 2017), this is one hint that such an identification could be operating. Eighteenth-century Nahuas staging these plays may have had no inkling that pre-Columbian Nahuas reportedly stoned adulterers, but the authors of the original play may have known that this practice was attributed to their forebears and was a point of similarity with ancient Judeans.

Sousa's investigation of criminal cases demonstrates that extramarital relations were still considered a crime in the colonial *altepetl* but not a capital one—although a husband who killed a wife he caught in the act could be excused for her murder, as in Spain. A wife's philandering was subject to more opprobrium than a husband's, and she could be beaten and punished for adultery even if she was raped. Interestingly, Indigenous men and women did not attempt to bring rape charges against non-Indigenous men, unless the violator was a Catholic priest (Sousa 2017, chapter 6). This last point is relevant here as it suggests that Indigenous people were not passive in the face of ecclesiastical hypocrisy and abuse.[15] In the play it is, after all, the chief priests who are planning to kill the imprisoned woman.

In leveling his accusation, Caiaphas recounts a couplet of sexual sins: *otetlaxin omomecatih* 'she committed adultery, she took a lover' (I.vii.5). The verb *(te)tlaxima* was established early on as an equivalent for *adulterar* and the noun *tetlaximaliztli* as *adulterio* (as in Molina's dictionary, 1992, pt. 1, 5r; pt. 2, 146r). The root is *xima* 'shear' or 'shave,' applied, for instance, to cutting hair or planing wood. Miriam López Hernández (2017, 197) interprets the usage as suggesting that the unfaithful spouse cuts or divides the marriage. Julia Madajczak (2017, 71) reads *tetlaximaliztli* as *tetlaxximaliztli*, from *tlantli* 'tooth' and *xima*, referring to the planing of teeth; it would be by some metaphorical or metonymical extension that this acquired a sexual meaning. What we can say for sure is that in Nahuatl doctrinal texts, this activity receives frequent and vehement sanction.

So does the second concept Caiaphas invokes, with his *momecatih* 'she tied herself': that is, she took a lover. The "Jews" on the scene taunt the woman, in unison, that Jesus is the man with whom she shares this relationship—a detail certainly not present in the Bible (I.vii.4). *Nemecatiliztli* 'tying oneself' referred to an unmarried person taking a lover in a free union that did not carry a heavy burden of social disapproval and would often lead to marriage; loss of virginity was not an impediment to a legitimate union (Burkhart 1989, 150–151; Sousa 2017, 149). Excessive or illicit sexual activity was seen as dangerous and polluting for the individual and people close to them, but for the *altepetl* adultery was a problem not so much because of its sexual nature per se but because it threatened the cooperative relations between married partners that were fundamental to social stability (Sousa 2017, chapter 5). "Tying oneself" was a less problematic and completely different matter, even though Christian preachers appropriated the term to convey the sinful act of concubinage, or a*mancebamiento*.

The only way the woman in the play can be guilty of both sins is if she is single and her lover is married, since Indigenous people considered both parties in an extramarital affair to be guilty of adultery (Sousa 2017, chapter 5). However, I find it unlikely that this specific situation was intended, especially if the bachelor Jesus could be accused of being the lover. More likely, the author(s) intended simply to cast her as a sexual sinner, with the paired terms serving as a synecdochic shorthand for the general category of sexual acts whose practice the Catholic Church sought to discourage. Thus, Caiaphas's phrase is less a specific accusation than a recognizable Christian preaching formula imputing imprecisely defined sexual misdeeds—all of which were condemned by the Church—to the jailed woman.

This "dear woman" whom Jesus saves from so dreadful a death makes a brief cameo earlier, with no Gospel model. After Magdalene flings away her finery, she falls facedown on the ground. The unnamed woman, alone in Axochiapan and in concert with Martha in Tepalcingo, comes to assist her, addressing her as a friend in Axochiapan (I.iv.23–25). Martha, Magdalene's sister, could appropriately proffer this aid on her own. Placing the unnamed woman in this scene does two things. Having women witness Christ's onstage preaching and take part in the dialogue highlights the gender inclusiveness of his followers. Second, to the extent that the audience understood Magdalene's sinfulness as sexual in nature, she has a colleague in this second woman to whom sexual misdeeds are imputed. That means Jesus takes into his circle of particularly beloved followers not just one but two women who are sexually active outside of marriage. While we can see this as an effort to encode Christian moral teachings into the play and thus urge other women to "sin no more," Indigenous viewers could see in Christ's tender and respectful treatment of these women a counter-narrative to the Church's derogation of female sexuality.

Not all scriptwriters viewed this woman so fondly, as her scene was omitted from the other plays (or their intervening sources). The scene is a bit anomalous, as it does not properly pertain to Holy Week, but it may have been dropped for other reasons. Someone seeking to shorten the performance might deem this interaction nonessential. Someone less invested in gender inclusivity might seek to reduce the presence of women onstage—especially as that in itself was a locus of controversy with Church officials. Neither the leave-taking scene nor the ointment scene was retained (or added) in every play. Choices were made in each script about which of the woman-centered scenes to stage and which to omit.

JOHN AND THE WOMEN

Each of the six plays uses the same mechanism to bring Mary and two (or more) other women to Jerusalem to witness Christ's death. John, on his own initiative, goes to fetch them from a location we can understand as Magdalene and Martha's house in Bethany, where Jesus had previously bid his mother farewell, though the Bethany location is specified only in Penn (34r; scene V.i). John's presence at the crucifixion in the company of women (discussed later in this chapter) made it logical for him to play this messenger role and escort them there, as he does in the *Meditations on the Life of Christ* (McNamer 2018, 121) and many other sources. In the Spanish model for the Holy Wednesday play (though not in its Nahuatl adaptation), Christ promises Mary that John "will take you to where you can find me" in Jerusalem (Burkhart 1996, 154).

At this point in the play, John is the only one of Jesus's students who continues to appear onstage. Separated from the other disciples, he joins the women and remains with them to the end, as he too enacts steadfast devotion to Jesus. In the Princeton play, he even swoons in tears when he reaches the women (41v; V.i.7), an emotive act otherwise restricted to Mary. Weeping (without swooning) is not a strongly gendered act in the plays. Penn's Jesus weeps as he addresses the Jerusalemites after he arrives on the donkey (5r; I.iv.1) and again in the Garden of Gethsemane (20r; III.i.12). In the Tepalcingo play, the apostles exit the stage weeping when Christ has been arrested (74), an instance that may accord with the women's sadness on Christ's behalf, their *tetlaocoyaliztli*. Since the apostles voice no articulate lament, their weeping could also be seen as a solicitation of divine help for themselves or Christ or as stemming from remorse for their failure to protect him. In Princeton, Judas weeps, in remorse and desperation, as he heads toward his suicide (32r; III. viii.16), and Peter weeps, as he does in Matthew 26:75, when he repents his denial of Christ (30r; III.vi.9)—a show of tears also staged in Cuaderno 1 (213r). Unlike these weeping disciples, John is blameless and his tears, like those of the women, come from sadness over Christ's suffering—as Christ's own come from sadness for the fate of Jerusalem. The same can be said of Joseph's and Arimathea's tears, in Amacuitlapilco, when they come to take Christ down from the cross (43v; V.iv.23). As noted in chapter 1, for Nahuas, weeping had positive effects in restoring equilibrium and obtaining divine assistance. It was part of the armature of stability and positivity the women, joined now by John, deploy to counteract the destructive violence other men enact.

The feminization of John is not a Nahua innovation. In Western European art, he was often depicted as youthful, beardless, and androgynous; Indigenous artists followed these conventions. To Indigenous viewers, his long hair, in the absence of a clearly masculine (and European) beard, gave him the look of an unmarried girl—even though he was San Juan, never Santa. McNamer sees the portrayal of John in Passion literature as an important avenue by which male devotees could participate in the female-gendered compassionate feelings needed to enter emotionally into Jesus's experience. A man could "feel like a woman" by sympathizing with Mary. But he could also do so by identifying with the feminized—but still male—John, whose youthfulness granted him the freedom to perform in both feminine and masculine modes, weeping with the women but also issuing challenges to men who afflicted Jesus or Mary (McNamer 2010, 142–146). His liminal condition, she notes, is expressed quite literally, as he is often pictured at the doorway of Magdalene's house—the *limen* 'threshold' itself (144).

Although McNamer is here discussing Middle English Passion literature specifically, this gender ambiguity comes through in the Nahuatl context also—including, in some plays, his placement at a doorway (V.i.3).[16] But since Nahua men did not require a license to "feel sad on behalf of someone," John's liminal position would read differently. By passing between the male and female realms and embodying gender fluidity, John prevents these interdependent spheres from becoming sundered one from the other, all complementarity lost, as the violence and mayhem accelerate toward the end of the play. By decamping into the women's space and then bringing them back to the epicenter of the action, he ensures that female power will counterbalance male power at the time of Christ's death, maintaining some continuity and complementarity and, once the crisis passes, permitting recovery and renewal. Although he does not perform gender ambiguity as overtly (or even obscenely) as do the cross-dressing dancers and other ambiguously gendered participants who mark period-ending rituals in many Mesoamerican contexts, past and present, as analyzed by Cecilia Klein (2001, 185), his own gender crossover may serve a similar purpose: facilitating the passage from one "temporal phase into another" and the restoration of "social and cosmic order." Easter morning is not staged in the Passion plays, but the role of the women who find the empty tomb and of Magdalene, to whom the risen Christ first shows himself, would also confirm the necessity of female presence and power to cosmic continuity.[17]

We would expect the women in Bethany to include Mary, Magdalene, and Martha—like in the fuller versions of the leave-taking scene—since Magdalene and Martha live in this house.[18] This is the case in Axochiapan, Penn, Tepalcingo, and Tlatlauhquitepec (in which the leave-taking, if it had one, was in the lost opening segment). The sixteenth-century Nahuatl "De la passion de noestro señor ie. xºꝰ" (n.d., 209v–210v) puts Martha in this scene, but only Mary and Magdalene then travel to Jerusalem with John—as is the case in the Axochiapan play. Since no Gospel places Martha at the crucifixion, she is not essential to these later scenes, and

Passion plays that did not already have an actor playing Martha in the Jesus-Mary farewell scene did not bother to cast a Martha if she would appear only in this second Bethany scene. The Princeton Passion, in which only mother and son participate in the farewell, replaces Martha with Veronica, moving her into the circle of Mary's intimates and accounting for her presence on the road to Calvary later in the play. Amacuitlapilco, in which Magdalene but not Martha participates in the leave-taking scene, substitutes Mary Salome. We may surmise, then, that Martha's presence here in the Tlatlauhquitepec play suggests that she had already been cast in a farewell scene in the script's lost opening section. Whoever they may be, though, there are always three named women in this scene, with Martha or her substitute having one or two turns at speech (V.i.14, V.i.23).

Mark 15:40 names Salome among the other women looking on at Jesus's death, while Matthew 27:56 instead mentions "the mother of the sons of Zebedee"— that is, John and James. These two were then assumed to be the same woman and to also be the sister of Mary mentioned without a name in John 19:25; this accorded with the tradition that these two apostles were Jesus's cousins (Driscoll 1912). John 19:25 places another Mary, the wife of Clopas,[19] also known as Mary Jacobe, at the scene. Clustered with the Virgin Mary, Mary Magdalene, and Mary of Clopas, Salome became a Mary too and is known in the Catholic Church as Saint Mary Salome. The medieval tradition of the "Three Marys" made the Virgin Mary, Mary Salome, and Mary of Clopas all into daughters of Saint Anne, with three different fathers (Roten n.d.).

Whether the model play had no third female speaker here, cast Mary Salome or Mary of Clopas, or did already have a farewell scene with Martha and thus gave her this later role is difficult to say. Whatever the case, multiple women appear here with Mary and accompany her to Jerusalem. In the performance tradition, Mary Salome and Mary of Clopas could have been represented by actors regardless of whether they had scripted lines. A stage direction in Tepalcingo directs the *Mariameh* 'Marys' to follow John offstage at the end of this scene (85). Similarly, the stage direction that closes the Penn play instructs the *Mariasmeh*[20] 'Marys' to accompany Jesus (now simulating a dead body) as he is carried away (45r; V.iv.37). Depictions of the crucifixion also showed two women clustered with the Virgin Mary, representing Mary Salome and Mary of Clopas, and play directors may have considered them necessary to the scene (see figures 3.5, 5.4).[21]

John may go up to a stage-set door and call out or simply call to Magdalene or to Mary. In every play he addresses Mary as his mother, and she addresses him as her nephew and in three plays as her child as well. This may reflect the actual kinship ties that Christian tradition assigned them or the Nahua custom of extending kinship terms to non-kin in affectionate discourse. As Mary calls her unrelated female companions her daughters, we cannot assume she means that John is her biological nephew. The loving and lamenting tones with which the women greet John's news of Jesus's condition echo the leave-taking scene, replaying (or, for Axochiapan, introducing) their gendered role of unwavering devotion to Jesus and identification with his suffering. And as at the leave-taking, the encouragement and support Mary receives from her fictive daughters also model female strength and solidarity.

There were two options for where to place this scene. Tepalcingo and Tlatlauhquitepec place it after Christ's arrest and interview with Caiaphas. This means we would insert it after scene III.iv in the composite play. The other four plays wait until Jesus has been sentenced to death and the crucifixion is imminent. At this point the women must indeed hurry to Jerusalem or they will be too late to bear witness. They arrive just as Christ's journey to Calvary is unfolding, allowing a smoother flow of action. The earlier placement shows them setting off and then remaining offstage, or at least silent, for quite some time, with the sense of urgency fading.

One constant in the scene is John's substantial speech (V.i.15) that recaps for the women what has happened since the leave-taking: the Last Supper, the visit to the garden, and the arrest—news to these characters, though not to the audience that has just seen these events staged. This speech is very similar across the corpus, and the recap never extends past Jesus's arrest—even when the scene comes after the entire round of interrogations, the flagellation, and the sentencing. This makes it likely that Tepalcingo and Tlatlauhquitepec retain the original placement, and the other plays reflect a decision to place the scene later for dramatic effect. John does not take on this mediating role in the Spanish-language plays.[22]

MARY ON THE ROAD TO CALVARY

The Stations of the Cross devotion codified Mary's meeting with her son as the Fourth Station. There is no such meeting in the Gospels, but every play stages this encounter. Amacuitlapilco, Axochiapan, and Penn show Mary actively seeking Jesus, stopping one or two passersby (Reuben, or Reuben and First Jew) to ask where she might find him (V.ii.1–5). They are polite, addressing her as *cihuatzintli* or *cihuapilli* 'noblewoman.' As an identifying clue, she tells them either that her son looks like her or that he is very good-looking, like a roseate spoonbill, a bird of beautiful pink and white plumage invoked—like flowers and other colorful birds—in Nahuatl song. Reuben tells her how altered her son's appearance is now, with messy hair and his face no longer visible—a tame description by the standards of European Passion literature, as it says nothing of blood, saliva, or other substances that obscure his visage.

Soon afterward, though delayed in Tepalcingo until after Veronica's interaction with Jesus, Mary meets her son and speaks to him. She asks why he must suffer this fate and wishes to die along with him (V.ii.18). He, in turn, makes one brief speech of encouragement (V.ii.22). In Princeton, First Jew yells at and even kicks Mary between her turn at speech and Jesus's reply (43r; V.ii.19–20). Elsewhere in the corpus, the worst disrespect shown to her occurs during the crucifixion, when Princeton's Centurion tells her to get out of the way and calls her a *cihuatontli* 'wretched little woman' (48r); Malchus mouths the same epithet in Amacuitlapilco (54v) and Axochiapan (42r).

In Tepalcingo we trace a scriptwriter's decision to streamline Christ's interactions with women, as if to make up time after transcribing the most developed Veronica scene in the corpus. Here, Mary meets her son and speaks to him, but he replies not to her alone but to the women collectively. This is the speech to the daughters of Jerusalem, from Luke 23:28–30, commemorated as the Eighth Station of the Cross. Only in this version of her speech does Mary refer to herself and her traveling companions as *timohuanyolqueh* 'we your relations'—either figuratively or suggesting the kin ties she has with John and with Mary Salome and Mary of Clopas, if they number among her companions. This collective self-reference invites and justifies Christ's collective reply.

VERONICA

The legend of Veronica reaches back to the woman who touches the hem of Jesus's garment and is thereby healed of "an issue of blood" (Luke 8:43–48). But it was a long time before she took on her role in the Passion, meeting him on the way to Calvary and wiping his bloody, sweaty face with a cloth on which his visage remains miraculously imprinted—the touch of his garment replaced by a garment he touched. In the fourth century, the apocryphal Gospel of Nicodemus gave the name Berenice to the hemorrhaging woman, and Eusebius of Caesarea shared a story that has her erect statues of herself and Jesus in gratitude for her cure (James 1924, 102; Kuryluk 1991, 5).

When her miraculous cloth enters the tradition in the Western Church, it has healing power but is not connected to the Passion. Stories from the eighth century and later have her and her cloth fetched to Rome to heal an emperor or a relation of his. As traced by Alvin E. Ford (1993, 6–7), versions vary as to whether the emperor is Tiberius, Vespasian, Titus, or two or three of them; whether the disease is leprosy, cancer, both, or an unspecified ailment; and who is dispatched to Jerusalem to track down Veronica. The miraculously cured emperor then, according to the legend, converts to Christianity—centuries before Emperor Constantine's actual deathbed baptism in 337.

This Veronica-heals-the-emperor story continued on its own trajectory, form-ing part of the "Vengeance of Our Lord" tradition, which retold the conquest of Jerusalem under Vespasian and Titus in AD 70 as a tale of revenge against the Jews for Christ's death, building on the Gospel texts in which Jesus warns of loom-ing destruction. This anti-Jewish story gained particular popularity in the four-teenth and fifteenth centuries and was well-known in Spain (Livingston 2004, 5). It found its way to Mexico and into the Nahuatl play *The Destruction of Jerusalem* (Sell and Burkhart 2009, 242–279; Burkhart 2009, 20–30; 2010). Originally writ-ten probably no later than the mid-sixteenth century (2010, 75–80), this play was adapted from a prose narrative called "La destruycion de Jerusalem," published repeatedly in Castilian in the 1520s and 1530s (Delbrugge 2020, 31–46; Ferrrer Gimeno 2011, 281; Hook 2000).[23] Although Veronica has no scripted lines in this Nahuatl drama, she and her miraculous *neixpohpohualoni* 'face cleaner,' with which she is said to have already cured many people, are fetched from Jerusalem to heal Emperor Vespasian.

As Neil MacGregor (2000, 90–92) explains, the cloth image held in Rome since at least the eleventh century started its career as a *sudarium*, or sweat cloth, with which Jesus was believed to have wiped his face in the Garden of Gethsemane. Around 1200 it was re-evaluated as a wondrous portrait of Jesus—a *vera icon*, or true icon. After Pope Innocent III, in 1216, offered indulgences to anyone who prayed in front of the cloth, throngs of pilgrims flocked to Rome for the occasions on which it was put on public display, and reproductions of the image proliferated across Europe. Although these reproductions of what was believed to be a direct likeness of Jesus's face varied considerably, they did contribute to a shared concep-tion of what he looked like—for example, that he had a beard. A thirteenth-century French text relocated Veronica's encounter with Jesus onto the road to Calvary, and thereafter the story of the pious woman who wipes Jesus's face became part of the expanding devotion to the Passion and to the *Via Crucis* (Kurylak 1991, 123).[24]

The later history of the Roman image is uncertain: it may or may not have been stolen by Lutheran soldiers in Charles V's army during the sack of Rome in 1527. It may or may not have been returned to Saint Peter's, only to, perhaps, disappear when it was removed from its shrine to be installed in the new basilica in the early 1600s. Or the icon may still reside in its official location: one of the piers supporting Michelangelo's dome. Whatever the case, the cloth held in much secrecy in Rome today bears little or no trace of the image attributed to it for the past millennium or so and reimagined in many Renaissance and Baroque works (figure 3.4).[25]

The many later medieval reproductions of Veronica's cloth include two that are still venerated in Spain: the Santa Faz, acquired by Pope Nicholas V in 1453 and given to a monastery in Alicante in 1489, and the cathedral of Jaén's Santo Rostro,

Figure 3.4. Saint Veronica with the Veil. Painting by Mattia Preti, made between 1655 and 1660. Los Angeles County Museum of Art. Courtesy of Wikimedia Commons.

placed there in the fourteenth century.[26] A Spanish variant of the legend claimed that both of these images were authentic, Veronica's veil having been folded with three layers, each of which captured the image of Jesus's face (Matthaeis 2018).

The story of Veronica and the miraculous image came to be enshrined as the Sixth Station of the Cross, a context from which the motif of healing is absent. The Spanish source that Vetancurt adapted into Nahuatl included the triple image. In the manuscript copy of Vetancurt's book, the Veronica encounter is recounted as follows: "6. The sixth place of kneeling [or] Station, 91 steps that our deity goes walking, here is where an honored person named Veronica went to meet our savior on the road. When she saw how very full of swellings, blackened in various places, and livid in various places his precious face was, his eyes (?), then she whipped out a fine white cloak for him, in order to clean his painful face. And by a very great marvel it happened that in three places the cloak was filled. The precious face of our savior was copied in three places."[27]

The motif of the triple image was, then, circulating in Nahuatl in the late seventeenth and early eighteenth centuries. Artists represented it as well, including the Indigenous painter Miguel Antonio Martínez de Pocasangre.[28] But many other images, mostly one-faced, could be seen in colonial Mexico, and cloth props were used in processions as well as plays: one of the figures in the confraternity procession mural at Huejotzingo holds a re-creation of Veronica's cloth, while figures on either side carry other Passion accouterments (Webster 1997a, 18, fig. 4). Agustín de Vetancurt (1971, pt. 4, 134) reports that an image of Veronica in San José de los Naturales exuded large drops of sweat for four months in 1635.

In European Passion plays, Veronica may seek a remembrance of Jesus or simply to clean his dirty face (Kurylak 1991, 123–124). Nahua Veronicas express similar motives. Although the Passion play from Toledo omits Veronica, she speaks twenty-six lines of verse in the Catalan Passion from Cervera (Duran i Sanpere and Duran 1984, 115–117). She approaches Christ, remarking on Mary's weeping presence. He asks her to clean his face (*cara*), then states that his face (*fas*) on the cloth will be a record or remembrance of his pain (*recort de ma dolor*). She remarks on his great mercy in leaving his face for the world and her own regret for her past behavior. Then she displays the cloth to the people while speaking of the cruelty shown to Christ and the pain felt by Mary. The 1856 play from Villasinta, León, features her even more prominently. In a gushy fifty-four-line, uninterrupted speech, she addresses, in turn, Jesus, the soldiers, mothers in the audience, and Jesus again. Then, after employing her headcloth, she exults in the prodigious appearance of the image before rushing off the stage (Lozano Prieto 1985, 101–102). Apart from calling herself *tu sierva indigna* 'your unworthy servant,' she expresses no repentance. Neither play mentions illness or cure.

Unlike most of the scenes already discussed in this chapter, Veronica's encounter with Jesus occurs in each of the complete plays (V.ii.31–40). All scripts agree that the image on the cloth is a *tlamahuizolli* 'marvel' or 'something to be marveled at,' the Nahuatl rendering of "miracle," or even a *huei* 'great' one. In all the plays, only one other staged event receives this designation and only in one play: Malchus in Tlatlauhquitepec calls the restoration of his ear a *tlamahuizolli* (7v; III.ii.31). The term does not appear when Jesus restores the vision of the blind supplicant (Penn play only, 4r; I.ii.1–9) or of the blind man who spears his side (V.iii.64–67). Herod's request that Jesus perform some *tlamahuizolli* just for him goes unheeded (IV.ii.11).

There were options for how Veronica's miracle was framed, in respect to who initiates the encounter, the motivation for it, and how much the image's wondrous origin or curing power is emphasized. The scenes fall into three types: (1) Tepalcingo; (2) Amacuitlapilco and Axochiapan, plus the similar but longer Penn version; and (3) Princeton.[29] Given how distinct these three variants are, Veronica may have been added to the cast after the original play was disseminated, due perhaps to influence from the Stations of the Cross. Some similar wording is used.

This terminology, however, links the scene also to the story and image of Our Lady of Guadalupe. Nahuas had gained increasing familiarity with this devotion after the narrative was published in Nahuatl in 1649 by Luis Laso de la Vega (1649; Sousa, Poole, and Lockhart 1998) and widely propagated beyond the Mexico City area by clergy in the later seventeenth century (Taylor 1987, 2016). At least two Nahuatl plays dramatized the apparition story in the early eighteenth century (Sell, Burkhart, and Poole 2006). The devotion grew even more prominent in the wake of a 1737 epidemic that Our Lady of Guadalupe was credited with abating, while Indigenous people were encouraged to identify with the Nahua protagonist of the story, pictures of whom begin to accompany the main image in the late seventeenth century and become more common in the eighteenth century (Taylor 2010, chapter 4; 2016, 173–182).

In the Guadalupe narrative, the Virgin Mary leaves her image imprinted on the *tilmahtli* 'cloak' of a Nahua commoner named Juan Diego, after appearing to him on multiple occasions and also healing his uncle of a severe illness. This transformation was touted as a *tlamahuizolli* right in the title of Laso de la Vega's book, which begins *Huey tlamahuizoltica* 'By means of a great marvel.' The Nahuatl *Via Crucis* text on Veronica echoes this language, as it is also *huei tlamahuizoltica* that Christ's face is copied on the *iztac canahuac tilmahtli* 'white, thin (or fine) cloak' with which Veronica wipes it. In both stories, a sacred being's image appears in a wondrous fashion on a garment that is a marker of Indigenous identity, and this image is associated with healing.

The Spanish source for the Nahuatl *Via Crucis* calls Veronica's cloth a *lienzo* (Schwaller 2021, 123n50). Three of the five Nahuatl plays employ instead the word *panoh*, from Spanish *paño*, a somewhat generic term for a kerchief- or dish-towel–size piece of cloth, typically applied to Veronica's veil in Spanish.[30] But in every play, Veronica's cloth is called a *tilmahtli* or a *tilmahtzintli* 'little (or honored) cloak' at least one time, even though a *tilmahtli* was a predominantly male-gendered garment as well as a sign of Indigenous ethnicity.[31] In Princeton, Jesus twice calls the cloth a *tilmahtzintli* while Veronica calls it a *panoh* and a *tzohtzomahtzintli* 'raggedy little cloth' (44r)—the latter term emphasized its humble nature and thereby the magnitude of the favor bestowed upon her. This designation accords with the Juan Diego story, as the rusticity of his palm- or maguey-fiber (not soft cotton) cloak helps establish his humble status. Penn, in contrast, echoes the "white, thin cloak" of the *Via Crucis* (39r), and a later editor of the Amacuitlapilco play modified *panoh* with "white, thin" (50v), as if in their view both Veronica and the visage of Christ merited a finely woven rather than a coarse cloth. All the plays also use the verb *copina* 'copy,' like the *Via Crucis* text, with Axochiapan suggesting a multiple image through the frequentative form of the verb (*cohcopina*). Another shared feature, though worded differently, is Veronica's confident proclamation of the miracle and display of the image to all onlookers (V.ii.39).

While agreeing about the miraculous copy on the *tilmahtli*, how do the dramatizations differ? Tepalcingo features the longest treatment, striking also in that Veronica takes all the initiative and does all the talking while Jesus remains silent. Approaching Christ, whom she refers to as her teacher, she remarks on how dirty his face and head are: *ca zan ixtlaltzin, ca zan cuatlaltzin* 'just face earth, just head earth' (108). It is the dirt that motivates her, so her act is primarily one of purification. She kneels before Jesus and cleans his face, exhorting him to bear up under his suffering. She then shows the imprinted image to Mary, John, Martha, and Magdalene and speaks to Mary (109–110; V.ii.37). Veronica then holds up the cloth and speaks with authority about Christ's actions, telling all the people of the world to look at "the precious visage of the ruler of the world" and be grateful to him for his compassion, for he there "shows he is human: his precious face and his precious body" (110).[32] The materiality of Christ's body as well as of the cloth itself is thus highlighted. There is no mention of sickness and healing.

Veronica takes the initiative in the Penn, Axochiapan, and Amacuitlapilco plays as well. She approaches Jesus, laments his suffering, and asks him to give her something with which to remember him: she is motivated by love and by regret at the impending loss of her benefactor.[33] It is Jesus who suggests she wipe his face. He also promises her that the resulting image will cure her illness, so this aspect is included (V.ii.32–33). The Princeton play differs in that Christ initiates the encounter, but, as in Tepalcingo, dirt is the motivating factor. He calls Veronica to him to clean his face, and we learn from her that the cloth actually belongs to Christ. Veronica did his laundry, apparently, but was not able to get the cloth washed in time to return it to him earlier—and now he is so dirty that he truly needs it. Here too, he promises that the cloth will heal her illness.

In both the Magdalene and the Veronica scenes, a woman who performs an act of bodily care and cleansing receives an outsized award, whether a heavenly unguent applied to her own body and a promise of enduring fame or a miraculous cloth image with, usually, healing power. Both of the cleansers are cleansed: Magdalene of sin, Veronica of sickness. Although Simon of Cyrene helps Christ carry the cross (V.ii.26–31; see figure 1.2) and Christ and his mother embrace (I.viii.31, 35), only these women directly touch Jesus's body with alleviating acts, countering—albeit only in a small way—the many acts of violence and pollution perpetrated upon him by men. The media are female-gendered: Magdalene's long hair; Veronica's cloth—an item spun and woven by women, worn or washed by Veronica, even if men more customarily wore *tilmahtli*.

Among the four Spanish-language plays, Cuaderno 1 (218v) and the Ozumba play (252r) give a part to Veronica, but her role is a reduced one in comparison to what Nahua scriptwriters provided to their own Veronicas. In both Spanish plays, Veronica approaches Jesus and makes one speech. While the versions differ, in both she expresses her desire to be so daring as to clean his face with her *tocas* 'headcloths.' She then does so, and that ends the encounter: he does not speak to her and she does not announce the miracle or, per the stage directions, lift up the cloth for general viewing. Neither a memento nor a cure is mentioned. These differences further highlight the greater visibility and empowerment Nahua dramatists granted to the women of the Passion.

THE DAUGHTERS OF JERUSALEM (*ICHPOCHHUAN JERUSALÉN*)

As noted above, Jesus's portentous address to the "daughters of Jerusalem" (Luke 23:28–30; V.ii.44) is enshrined as the Eighth Station of the Cross. Luke (23:27) describes the addressees as "women who bewailed and lamented him," among the "great multitude" who were following Jesus as he trudged toward Calvary. Every complete Nahuatl play, like all four Spanish plays, has a version of the speech, which tells the women to save their tears for a future calamity—interpreted as Rome's upcoming siege of Jerusalem. Mothers will wish themselves childless and desire the mountains to collapse on them. Only Penn and Tepalcingo attempt to render the subsequent statement about wood: "For if they do this when the wood is green what will happen when it is dry?"[34] Amacuitlapilco (50r–50v) and Axochiapan (38v) instead take the opportunity to add a little more moral preaching at women in terms familiar from doctrinal discourse: "Who are you who are standing here among the others, you sinner? Loosen the black rope from around your neck, with which you tied yourself."[35]

Christ's speech necessitates that there be a group of women to hear his words. Directors had the option to include only Mary, Magdalene, Martha or Mary

Salome, and Veronica, who are there anyway, or to include Mary of Clopas and unnamed extras to augment the lamenting chorus. Two plays innovate within Veronica's lines to provide more context for the women Christ is about to address collectively. When Veronica in the Penn play says to Jesus, "O my lord, O my ruler, my beloved savior, all this time you dearly loved me [and the other?] daughters of Jerusalem" (38v),[36] she enunciates Jesus's particular bond with his women followers. Similarly, in Tepalcingo (110–111; V.ii.39) she places herself among this group of women: "May you, my women friends, you daughters of Jerusalem, encourage him. Let all of us follow behind him, because of his precious suffering."[37]

Given the enigmatic nature of the passage and its only approximate renderings in Nahuatl, we may wonder how Indigenous auditors understood it and whether it could have been read as just another example of Jesus showing attention and favor to women, reflected in the polite way he addresses them, as *ancihuatzitzintin* 'you dear women,' in Princeton (44v), Amacuitlapilco (50r), and Axochiapan (38v). Earlier in the story, Princeton's Jesus voices a positive view of these women not as future siege victims but as enlightened critics of Jerusalem's male leaders. Berating the Pharisees after he drives the merchants from the temple, he says, "And as for you, you who pass sentence on people, for a great many things do the daughters of Jerusalem mock you" (7v; I.iv.16).[38]

WOMEN AT THE CROSS

John's Gospel is the only one that places Mary or any of Jesus's disciples at the crucifixion. The other Gospels place only women at the cross, without naming Mary. In John 19:26–27, Jesus speaks from the cross to Mary and "the disciple whom he loved," saying, "Woman, behold your son" and, to the disciple, "Behold, your mother." This disciple is assumed to be John, accounting for his presence at the cross in Passion iconography and literature—which, as seen above, expanded his role such that he summons the women to Jerusalem, himself becoming something of an honorary woman. When Mary acknowledges John's particularly cherished status in V.i.9, she echoes this "disciple whom he loved" appellation. Roman Catholic tradition had John reside with Mary in Ephesus and care for her until her death.

Tepalcingo, having attended so thoroughly to Veronica, now moves rapidly to the play's end after the "daughters of Jerusalem" speech, with no more references to women. The four other complete plays represent the exchange among Jesus, Mary, and John at least in part. In Princeton (46r; V.iii.22), the choir is instructed to chant *Ecce mater tuam. Ecce filius tui,* 'Behold your mother. Behold your child,' possibly extracted from Navarro's (1604, 86v–87r) Saint John Passion. However, Christ's words are only partially staged: Christ says "O noblewoman, here is your child."[39] Since John is neither named nor spoken to, Jesus seems to be referring to himself.

The Penn Passion (40v) follows the model in John but—in accordance with the dialogical bent of Nahuatl style—frames Jesus's words within a brief conversation, as seen at V.iii.19–24. Mary initiates the exchange with a brief lament, in response to which Jesus says, "Dear woman, here is your child. Look at him. And you, John, here is your mother."[40] Then John reassures him with a short statement of compliance. Like the Penn play, the nearly identical versions in Amacuitlapilco (52v–53r) and Axochiapan (39r–40v) have Mary speak first, then Jesus, then John; as in various other scenes, these plays here seem to share a common ancestor with Penn. However, the content departs substantially from the Gospel model, the import of which was either misunderstood or ignored. Mary's brief lament echoes Penn's: "Oh, you my beloved child, now you are leaving me, I your mother." Her son plays a proper filial part by reassuring her: "O my beloved mother, I am not leaving you. Be strong." Then John says, "O my beloved teacher, here is your beloved mother."[41] This bit of dialogue rationalizes John 19:27 into a simple statement of fact rather than the establishment of a fictive parent-child relationship.

The affinity among Penn, Amacuitlapilco, and Axochiapan continues as, just after this exchange, Magdalene steps forth to take her place at the foot of the cross, where Passion art often places her (see figures 5.3, 5.4). Penn's stage directions have her kneel. Amacuitlapilco sends her to the foot of the cross, which she is to embrace. Axochiapan specifies just that she embraces the cross. She then speaks, most elaborately in Penn (40v; V.iii.26); in the other plays she just expresses her desire to die along with her benefactor. Christ does not answer, addressing his father instead (V.iii.28). Magdalene remains a silent bystander in Tepalcingo and Princeton.

Mary does not speak again until Jesus has uttered his dying words (V.iii.52–55). It is the Penn play that gives her the largest role in what remains of the action (42r–45r). First, she reacts to the breaking of the two thieves' legs to hasten their deaths (V.iii.48–50; John 19:31–32) with the speech at V.iii.57. Wondering how she may bury her child, she calls on the angels, beings that elsewhere in the play appear unbidden and speak only to Christ. Two come at her call—presumably the same two whom Jesus earlier asked to attend to his mother, when they visited him in jail (25r). They encourage her and speak of the importance of the blood he is about to spill (V.iii.58–59). This leads to the lancing, staged in every play and source of the stage blood that, as we saw in chapter 1, fray Miguel Camacho Villavicencio said was sopped up and kept for use in curing. Quite a large bag of red liquid might have been punctured to produce this special effect, attached to the cross or the actor's body before the cross was raised up. In Penn, Mary then speaks to Jesus and comments on the spilling of "all" his blood (V.iv.2).

While Penn then interposes its brief signboard scene, attention quickly returns to Mary and Jesus's body. Seeing people approaching, she fears further harm to her dead son, but they turn out to be friends. Now we see the odd splitting of Joseph of (Latin *ab*) Arimathea—the Jewish council member who in each of the Gospels provides a tomb for Christ, having gained Pilate's permission to do this—into two people: Joseph *and* "Abarimathea" (Aberematias in Penn). The conjoining of *ab* with Arimathea has precedents in Iberian Passion literature, such as the *Gamaliel* (Delbrugge 2020; on this text, see chapter 4) and *El Libro de Josep Abarimatia* (Pietsch 1924; Bogdanow 2009), but I have not found this splitting into two people outside of the Nahuatl Passions. This Joseph is the man who in II.i.21 defends Jesus before the Jerusalem council, seconded by the Pharisee Nicodemus in Tepalcingo (35; II.i.23). A few references in this latter scene to Nicodemus, who assists Joseph with the burial in John 19:39–42, suggest that the original play assigned this role to him, with "Abarimathea" replacing Nicodemus at some point in transmission. We see this in John's speech at V.iv.5, from Penn, and a later stage direction in Penn sends Joseph and Nicodemus to Pilate's house, even though the associated dialogue replaces Nicodemus with Joseph's alter ego.[42]

The two men secure Pilate's permission to take Christ's body down from the cross and bury it.[43] Then Joseph fetches a sheet (*sabanah*) to serve as a shroud, and Arimathea obtains the myrrh that Nicodemus provides in John 19:39 (43v; V.iv.23). No other Passion play mentions either item, but they hark back to the gifts of the Magi. In the Nahuatl play *The Three Kings*, Balthasar offers the infant Jesus "a very precious bitter potion, called myrrh. And when your precious and wondrous body is buried in the sepulcher, they will anoint you with this" (Sell and Burkhart 2004, 142–143). In *The Star Sign*, Balthasar provides the shroud as well: "Here is a little bit of a precious potion that you will need when they lay you in the supreme sepulcher and a fine white cloak with which they will cover your supremely good body" (Sell and Burkhart 2009, 106–107; Burkhart, de la Cruz, and Sullivan 2017, 85). His words resonate not just with Arimathea's myrrh but with Magdalene's precious potion or unguent (*tlazohpahatl*) and Veronica's fine white cloak.

Next, the two men request Mary's approval for their plan, which she graciously grants (V.iv.24–26). This is the only play in which Mary exerts such authority over her son's body. Her claim is not a trivial matter, for this moment had a history in European literature, which Thomas Bestul (1996, 137) links to women's increasing involvement in litigious property disputes. In the very influential text *Quis dabit capiti meo aquam* by Ogier de Locedio (died 1214), Mary, in an "ecstasy of self-annihilation," desires to be buried with Christ and a dispute over his body ensues, ending in her submission to John and Joseph of Arimathea (131–133). Intimate, even eroticized, contact with the bloody corpse then became a motif in women's spiritual writing (134–136). In contrast, the English mystic Margery Kempe in the early fifteenth century restores Mary's decorum and rationality in this scene: Mary accedes to the men's request because they ask her so beautifully (139–140). The Penn play treats Mary with similar dignity.

The Penn play then proceeds with the poignant scene in which Joseph and his double climb a ladder (or two) and, following John's instructions, gently remove the signboard, the crown of thorns, and the nails. They hand each item in turn to John, who then speaks to Mary and, urging her to be strong, entreats her to look at and even kiss them (V.iv.27–32). Finally, they take down the body—that is, the stiff and weary actor who has been obliged to play dead through all of this—and lay him in her arms (V.iv.33–35). These actions may have been modeled on descent ceremonies, in some of which insignia removed from the cross were placed in the hands of a statue of Mary, after which the Christ statue was taken down—using long towels—and laid across the Mary image's lap (Webster 1997b, 72).

Penn is the only play that stages this familiar tableau of Mary lamenting over her son's body (figure 3.5).[44] She makes the loving speech seen in V.iv.35. Then some of the actors wrap the Jesus player in the sheet that Joseph has brought and carry him off, the "Marys" following.

Amacuitlapilco (55r) and Axochiapan (42v) retain Mary's initial speech (V.iii.57) in a reduced form—no angels—and have a version of V.iv.2, but then the remainder of the play consists of the interchanges among Joseph, "Abarimatia," and Pilate. A choice was made either to expand Mary's role in the Penn play or its model or to reduce it in the source for these two versions. The two plays end as Joseph and Arimathea are about to take down the body; there is no indication that they actually do so.

Princeton also assigns Mary two speeches toward the end of the play. One, like V.iii.57, expresses dismay at the approach of others, but she is reacting to the Jewish leaders and Pilate who come to examine the signboard—a scene placement unique to Princeton (47r–47v). The second speech, Mary's last, immediately precedes the lancing: Mary beseeches Centurion not to torment her child any further, but he tells her to get out of the way and calls for Longinus (47v–48r). Then Mary faints, weeping, and John closes the play with a long soliloquy (48r–50v), even longer than that of Judas.

The beginning of John's speech (see V.iv.3), addressed to Jesus's tormentors, is connected to the preceding action and has analogs in the other three plays. Penn's John continues right on with the speech as shown in V.iv.9. His *O, in amehhuantin in ampilhuahqueh* 'O, you who are parents' transitions from theatrical dialogue into a preaching voice. Meanwhile, the action freezes into a silent tableau like a painted or printed image for the devotee to contemplate: the Jesus actor motionless

Figure 3.5. Mary holds Jesus's body, accompanied by the other women and, to the right, John, with his hands in prayer. The cross and a ladder are depicted in the rear. Woodcut in Pedro de Feria's *Doctrina christiana en lengua castellana y çapoteca*, Mexico, 1567, f. 34v. Courtesy of the John Carter Brown Library, Brown University, Providence, RI.

on the cross and the Mary actor collapsed below. John then shifts into the genre of affective Passion meditation, encouraging the audience members, whether men or women, to identify with Mary's pain and imagine that a child of their own had undergone such suffering, which he recaps for them. He guides listeners toward the desired response, using such words as "And so, weep with anguish, let your tears flow. Let your sadness reach inside you" (49v).[45] He urges them to speak to Christ, begging for pity and compassion. He then addresses Mary and the audience together, merging contemplative and theatrical modes and inviting the audience to accompany Mary. The apostles are now to take Jesus down from the cross and "then the procession will begin."[46] It seems the audience, having been invited into the theatrical frame, may join in this procession—even though John's final words resonate in a preachier mode, as he doubts the listeners' devotion to Mary and casts aspersion on the "people of earth" who do not heed his admonition.

Having noted several instances in which women are more prominent and respected in the Nahuatl plays than in the Spanish-language ones, I want to acknowledge a departure from that pattern: the strong speech with which Mary closes Cuaderno 1 (219v), drawing on the *planctus Mariae* tradition and acting in her role as modeler of correct emotional responses to the Passion. In a 107-word speech that draws on Matthew 27:51–52, she calls on inanimate matter to show the appropriate response to her son's death that men, though capable of reason, have failed to display. She commands the heavenly orbs to stay their course, the rocks to split, the graves to open, and the temple veil to split in two.

THE WOMAN AT PETER'S DENIAL

One final woman merits a brief mention. When Peter denies his affiliation with Jesus, three of the Gospels make at least the first of his interlocutors a woman, a maid in Caiaphas's employ according to Mark 14:66 (see also Matthew 26:69, Luke 23:56). This servant woman turns up as the *ançilla* in Alonso del Campo's play from Toledo and the *moza* in the 1856 play from León (Torroja Menéndez and Rivas Palá 1977, 166–167; Lozano Prieto 1985, 91–92).

Tlatlauhquitepec (10r) is the only play that retains a female character in the scene with the three denials (III.vi.2). Princeton preserves a truncated version of the scene, in which a woman questions Peter when he trails the arrested Jesus to Annas's place. She asks, "Aren't you also a student of the one they brought in here?"[47] He denies it, and the action proceeds with the interrogation before Annas (28v). This woman, as *Judiocihuatl* 'Jewish woman,' is included in the list of dramatis personae on the manuscript's inside covers. But the full scene with three interlocutors—all male—and the crowing rooster, followed by Peter's lament, occurs later (29v–30r). The scriptwriter chose to retain this woman but to separate her from the scene that fulfills Jesus's prophecy and displays Peter's painful regret.

Across the corpus, Peter's male interlocutors vary among Reuben, Malchus, First Jew, and Centurion: there was no shortage of male characters available to harass Peter. If the original play, following the Gospels and consistent with Spanish practice, had a woman, why was she dropped—or at least separated from the full scene of Peter's despair—in the larger part of the tradition? A simple bias toward male roles and actors could account for this. The Spanish plays have all males in two cases, but a "maid (*criada*) of the pontiff" appears in Ozumba (250r) and a "female slave (*esclava*) of Pilate" in Amecameca (287v). We would not expect the Nahuatl plays to be more male-centered than the Spanish-language ones, given their fuller attention to women characters overall. Alternatively, we may note how this annoying woman violates the pattern set by all other women in the Nahuatl Passion corpus, who overwhelmingly express devotion to Jesus and all of whom he treats kindly and includes among his beloved ones. Harassment and injury to Christ or his students are the province of men. The near-elimination of this woman from the performance tradition could be a matter of consistency in how roles were gendered.

THE WOMEN'S CHORUS

Women have crucial moments onstage in every play, even while (presumably male) scriptwriters made many different choices about which such scenes to include and how to cast and script them. Female characters were greatly outnumbered by male ones, but they were essential to the production. They did not merely help to tell the story, filling the roles derived from scripture and legend. They serve as models of and for devotion to Christ, accompany him through the later parts of his ordeal, and—more than the apostles—both recognize his divinity and understand the magnitude of what is happening. Their laments and tears are not futile displays of feminized emotion. They are entirely called for, given the reality of the situation, and help to counteract the forces of destruction. As events hurtle toward their fatal conclusion, women keep love, devotion, and order alive.

European Passion literature and practice gave a privileged place to lamenting women, Mary in particular, as a vehicle by which the devout could enter empathetically into Christ's bodily torments and perhaps achieve a mystical union with God. Bestul notes that devotees could find in these representations varied messages about gender. For some, the texts confirmed expected gender differences, painting women as emotional, irrational, weak, grounded in their physicality. Yet the literature placed Mary and other women at the center of the redemption, which itself was now centered on bodily experience—whether Mary's or Christ's. Mary's laments could be experienced as empowering, a use of emotion to show strength and assert authority. Misogyny and resistance to it could coexist in the same text; and an audience differentiated by gender, class, and other criteria would interpret any given text in different ways. Individual readers might hold contradictory beliefs and values (Bestul 1996, 116–118, 132).

Indigenous people came to the Passion plays without all the cultural baggage of later medieval Western Europeans, so they had perhaps even more latitude to construct their own interpretations of their plays' gendered messages. In their own society, as Susan Kellogg (1995, 1997 cf. Sousa 2017) has established, gender complementarity had been partially undermined by the Catholic Church and colonial institutions, but the plays themselves document no simple acceptance of patriarchy. Individuals who had come to share, to any extent, the European devotional orientation toward identification with Christ and Mary found plenty of emotional sustenance in the performance of these plays. They might weep as they witnessed the Mary and Jesus actors enacting so much suffering, regardless of whether the experience resonated with their view of their own moral status. The preachy bits about female sexual morality also stem from European attitudes and may or may not have made the desired impression on female spectators.

The Indigenous authors who wrote and rewrote the plays innovated upon the received material by choosing to retain or add woman-centered scenes that either are not in the Bible or, if there, do not take place during Christ's final days. They made women more outspoken and assertive than their counterparts in the Spanish-language plays from the same general time and place and made Jesus treat them with more respect and affection. He has a special relationship to women, even beyond what the Gospels express, that contradicts the patriarchal structure of the Roman Catholic Church, while those women exhibit superiority to the male characters in knowledge as well as in feeling. Since the plays taught more of the Passion story than most Indigenous people experienced anywhere else, they were a vehicle not just for affective identification with the suffering characters or worry for a world turned so violently topsy-turvy but for an understanding of what sort of god Jesus Christ is and what he did. He is a god who is centered in a circle of female kin and friends as well as the circle of his male students, who talks with women, and who bestows helpful blessings upon them regardless of how sexually experienced they are. Christianity offered no female deities; nevertheless, it did offer not just Mary and the other stalwart women of the Passion but a male god who did not hold himself apart from or superior to women. As the writers, responding to their own or community preferences, altered the gendered balance of power and authority in their scripts, the Indigenous players—known and often prominent members of the community—also represented a more gender-balanced model for social relations in the *altepetl*.

4

Thursday at Gamaliel's

Staging the Last Supper

TO GAMALIEL'S HOUSE

The story of Jesus's Passover meal with his students the day before his death is not a story of suffering. Passion texts that omit it, whether beginning their action with the trip to the Garden of Gethsemane or starting with earlier events but skipping the supper, include the early plays from Cervera and Toledo and the long early Passion tract in Nahuatl (Duran i Sanpere and Duran 1984; Torroja Menéndez and Rivas Palá 1977; León-Portilla 1994). The Nahua scriptwriters too could have left it out, even if it was in the original play, but all six plays stage the scene, as do the four Spanish-language plays.

Ritual feasting formed an essential component of *altepetl* relationships. Lisa Sousa (2017, 190–192) observes that the exchange of food between humans and the divine was "essential to maintain life," while the sharing of food among people was "necessary to civilized existence." Food and drink were metaphorically identified with eloquent speech, while feasts provided showcases for oratorical skill (192). Christ's eloquence before, during, and after the meal supports his identity as a sage teacher. The host household feeds the embodied god and his retinue, and the god provides sacralized sustenance to his followers. This supper, the last time Jesus and the twelve original disciples will be together, is indeed an interlude of "civilized existence" staged before everything goes haywire. It is not disconnected from the larger story: Judas's betrayal is set in motion, while Jesus's prediction of Peter's denial will come true later that night. The scene where Jesus washes the feet of his students

https://doi.org/10.5876/9781646424511.c004

explains the origin of the Mandatum, or ritual foot washing, that will be enacted at churches later in the week, on Holy (or Maundy) Thursday.

But the most important event at the supper occurs when Jesus turns bread and wine into his body and blood and orders his friends to do the same in his memory. This action is the foundation for both the Roman Catholic Mass, in which the priest repeats the transubstantiation of bread and wine into body and blood, and the Church's most holy sacrament—communion—when the faithful ingest what the Roman Catholic Church, in the face of Protestant rebellion on this point, insisted only more strongly was the result of this miraculous metamorphosis. When Indigenous actors mimicked this most holy transformation, exclusively the province of ordained priests, they challenged Church authority perhaps even more than when they put an Indigenous Jesus up on a cross.

At this point in the action it is, according to the Gospels, the first day of the Feast of Unleavened Bread, and the disciples have asked Jesus, "Where will you have us go to prepare for you to eat the Passover" (Matthew 26:17; Mark 14:12). Hebrew *pesach* 'Passover' is *pascha* in Greek, and the latter form is retained in the Vulgate Bible's Latin text. The Spanish equivalent is *pascua*, and this word was adopted into Nahuatl. While I translate *pascuah* as "Passover" in the composite play, we must note that for Nahuas, it may have had more Christian than Jewish connections. Like the English word Pasch, *pascua* refers to Easter as well as Passover and to a lesser degree Christmas; Nahuas heard it applied to Christian holidays more often than they had any cause to think of Jewish holy days. A Last Supper sermon—if they heard one—might explain the origin of the festival, as does a sermon in the sixteenth-century *Sermones en mexicano* (n.d., 104r–104v). Here, the preacher recounts the Passover story and tells how Jesus has taken the place of the sacrificed lamb. He expresses continuity between the two festivals: "And the people of Jerusalem rejoiced greatly. They would celebrate the festival of *pascua* every year. And so today we celebrate *pascua*."[1] As in other Nahuatl texts where the Jewish people are presented in a positive light, the sermon avoids the word *judío* in favor of "children of Israel" and "people of Jerusalem." Likewise, the plays' usage of the word *pascuah* would not necessarily lead people to see Jesus as a Jewish man.

Like the quest for the donkey Jesus will ride to Jerusalem on Palm Sunday (I.ii.9–28), the supper story now proceeds with an errand for a pair of apostles. Only Luke (22:8) names the messengers; they are Peter and John, dispatched also in most of the Nahuatl plays. Amacuitlapilco and Axochiapan choose John and James, who do the donkey fetching there. Once again, Jesus knows exactly what will happen: as in Mark (14:13–14) and Luke (22:10–11), upon entering Jerusalem the messengers will see "a man carrying a jar of water" and follow him home to the house where the whole group will sup. As discussed in chapter 2, the scene with Water Carrier can be staged in a variety of ways, but always the two students follow him home, convey Jesus's message to the owner of the house, and are warmly welcomed (II.iii.11–24).

None of the Gospels names this friendly host. Nor do three of the four Passion plays in the Inquisition file name him; he is simply the *aposentador*, the provider of hospitality.[2] The exception is the play from Tenango (258r, 259v), where he is John Mark (Juan Marcos). Perhaps because the Nahuatl plays overall exhibit less of a hierarchy between major and minor characters, they all give this man a personal name. In the Tepalcingo play, he shares the name John Mark with that one Spanish counterpart.[3] In all the other Nahuatl plays, he is Gamaliel.

Rabban Gamaliel (or Gamliel) the Elder was a prominent first-century law expert, teacher of the law, high-ranking member of the Jerusalem Sanhedrin, and grandson of the famous sage Hillel.[4] But because he appears twice in the Acts of the Apostles (5:34–39 and 22:3), first encouraging leniency toward the apostles and then as teacher of Jewish law to Paul, he was guaranteed a long and fantastical afterlife in Christian legend, becoming baptized and even canonized. According to the apocryphal gospel "The Revelation of Stephen," he and Nicodemus were stoned to death along with Saint Stephen, and Gamaliel later revealed their burial place to the text's narrator in a vision (James 1924, 565–567). Gamaliel had his own apocryphal, Coptic "Gospel of Gamaliel" (151).

In Iberia, a popular devotional miscellany called the *Gamaliel* kept this first-century personage's name familiar to many (Delbrugge 2020; Ferrer Gimeno 2011, 277). It is so anti-Jewish that its recent editor, Laura Delbrugge (2020, 70), concludes that "it was clearly written to establish Jewish culpability for Christ's death." The *Gamaliel* was so named because it opens with a Passion narrative centered on this character, who either witnesses the events directly (changing his outfit or lurking in doorways to avoid suspicion) or hears about them from his nephew Nicodemus or from Joseph of Arimathea. Gamaliel supports Christ and blames the unbelieving Jewish leaders for his death. The content derives largely from the fourth-century Gospel of Nicodemus, but it is dressed up with vivid and sensational details that made it enjoyable to its readers and thus profitable to its printers (3, 49).

One of the texts associated with the *Devotio moderna*, the *Gamaliel* circulated in Catalan in the fourteenth to early sixteenth centuries in manuscript and then in print. Juan de Molina translated it into a Castilian version published at least a dozen times between 1517 and 1558 (Delbrugge 2020, 3, 31–46; Ferrer Gimeno 2011, 281; Molina 1536). For its apocryphal content (not its anti-Jewish bent), the *Gamaliel* became one of the first twenty-seven books burned by the Spanish Inquisition in 1558, and it appeared on every official list of banned books from 1559 to 1790, even though it continued to be reprinted and read for centuries (Delbrugge 2020, 3, 68; Ferrer Gimeno 2011, 274). Although this narrative was not a model for the

Nahuatl Passion plays, copies of the work were likely imported to New Spain. The second piece in the volume, the similarly anti-Jewish narrative "The Destruction of Jerusalem," was the source for the Nahuatl play of the same title, either directly or through a previous adaptation into dramatic form (Burkhart 2010, 75). Some of the Castilian editions were published by the Crombergers of Seville (Delbrugge 2020, 38–39, 46), who operated a press in Mexico and may well have exported the title to the colony.

The *Gamaliel*'s influence accounts for the rabbi's role in the Catalan Passion from Cervera. Here, he joins forces with Nicodemus and Joseph of Arimathea to defend Jesus in the council meeting and, later, to gain Pilate's permission to bury Jesus. The three then remove him from the cross, lay him in Mary's arms and then on a board, and carry him away (Duran i Sanpere and Duran 1984, 53, 135–137). More than 300 years later, Gamaliel shows up in the Villasinta play as a Jerusalem townsperson. He observes Peter's denial and later watches helplessly when Jesus is flogged, reminiscing to his companion, Joab, about miracles he witnessed firsthand—the water into wine and the raising of Lazarus—and commenting, "they say he is the Son of God"; Joab is convinced and they resolve to pray on Christ's behalf (Lozano Prieto 1985, 91, 97).

In the *Gamaliel* Passion narrative, Gamaliel does not host the Last Supper, but he observes the meal and subsequent foot washing. At the latter event Jesus, spotting him in the doorway, tells him he will receive the Holy Spirit along with the apostles (Delbrugge 2020, 108–110). If a writer wanted to provide a name for the host of the Last Supper, Gamaliel could seem like a good choice: an elite citizen of Jerusalem transformed in popular apocrypha into a supporter of Jesus and witness of many Passion episodes.

But John Mark is an alternative name, found in the Tepalcingo play and the Spanish play from Tenango. Tepalcingo also differs in that it lacks the speech shown at II.iii.10—shared by all other plays—in which Gamaliel, before the messengers arrive, worries about the well-being of the Messiah and wishes that he could offer him hospitality. Gamaliel's use of the Hebrew-derived word *mesías* marks him as a Jew who recognized Jesus, as does his statement, retained in the Penn play only, that the great teacher *ye huehcauh chiyalo* 'has been awaited for a long time' (10r).[5] John Mark is also the only host who does not call upon his servants to make preparations for the meal, with stage directions then indicating the preparation—simple or ornate—of a table (II.iii.24–25). The Tepalcingo scriptwriter may have been working from an alternative text that used recognizable Spanish saint names, making the host less of a Jewish other. The Tlatlauhquitepec scriptwriter seems to have had knowledge of this alternative version as well, for he waffles at first: a stage direction says *hualquizaz in Marcos itoca Gamaliel* 'Mark, whose name is Gamaliel, will come out' (1v), but then the actor gives the Messiah speech and thereafter his character is always called Gamaliel.

Although he lacks Gamaliel's twisted history, John Mark was another Jerusalemite who was mentioned in the Bible and could conceivably have bucked the authorities to wine and dine Jesus. This man is named several times in Acts, sometimes as "John whose other name was Mark" (Acts 12:12, 12:25). He traveled with Barnabas and Paul, and his mother hosted apostles in her home, making it a plausible Last Supper setting. In time, this man's identity merged with that of Mark the Evangelist (Farmer 1992, 322).

It seems that along at least one line of play transmission, John Mark was the host, but Gamaliel was preferred overall. Avoiding confusion with the unambiguously mean character Malchus, whose role is rooted in the Gospels, could have been one motivation. Malchus is Malco in Spanish. With no phoneme /r/ in Nahuatl, Nahuas were prone to substitute /l/ for /r/ and sometimes to hypercorrect Spanish /l/ to /r/. Hence Malco could turn into Marco—as he does a few times in Axochiapan and repeatedly in the Tepalcingo play, where the scriptwriter at one point mislabels him San Marco (102)—and Marcos could come out Malcos. Gamaliel could not be confused with anyone else, even though scriptwriters tended to hypercorrect his name to Gamalier.[6]

GRAVE ERRORS: PRELUDE TO THE BREAD AND WINE

Once preparations are made at the host's house, the two messengers fetch Christ and the other students. Amid greetings and blessings between honored host and honored guest, which may involve kneeling or hand holding, the party makes its way to the table, where Jesus invites his students to sit down and rest (II.iii.28–38). What is a little odd here in regard to Nahua social etiquette is the absence of Gamaliel's wife from the greeting and serving of the guests, though he could be imagined to be a widower. The fact that he seats his guests at a big table, as in the Gospels and Christian art, also suggests a high social rank, as most ordinary Nahuas at the time would have taken their meals while seated on the floor, near the cooking fire in their small homes.

Only the detail-oriented Amacuitlapilco scriptwriter shares the seating plan. All are to line up on one side of the table (so it had to be quite long, as in Leonardo da Vinci's famous fresco), with Jesus in the middle, Peter to his right, John to his left, and Judas at the end (19v; II.iv.3)—exactly as in the Villasinta Passion play (Lozano Prieto 1985, 79). The actors are now assembled into one of the iconic tableaux that occur at certain points in the script, imitating scenes from Christian art (figure 4.1, figure 4.2).

Figure 4.1. The Last Supper. Peter is seated at Jesus's right and John stands at his left. Judas is in the left foreground, identifiable by the bag in his hand, which can be seen as the disciples' common purse or as his payment for the betrayal—which, in Matthew 26:15, he has just received. The scene captures the moment when Jesus gives Judas the morsel he has dipped (John 13:26). Woodcut in fray Alonso de Molina's *Confessionario mayor*, 1565, 73r. Courtesy of the John Carter Brown Library, Brown University, Providence, RI.

The next thing that happens is that Jesus utters some version of Luke 22:15–16, about his desire to share this Passover meal before he suffers and that he will not do so again until he is in the kingdom of God. The Nahuatl embellishes "kingdom" with the old phrase for rulership *in petlatl in icpalli* 'the mat, the seat' (II.iv.4). Only the Penn scriptwriter (11r–11v) digresses as in II.iv.4, having Jesus give a longer preview of the sacrament's importance and call it *in yancuic chalchiuhteocalli* 'a new jade temple' where his body and blood will be kept. This expression of preciousness is both distinctly Indigenous and distinctly material: there is no qualifying *teoyotica* 'by means of divinity' or 'in a sacred way,' the neologism used in Nahuatl Christian preaching to try to impose a distinction between material and spiritual realms.

After this, things get complicated. But first, let us note something that never happens: Jesus and his students do not eat a Paschal lamb. While the Gospels place the Last Supper during Passover, none states that the group partook of sacrificed lamb. There have been various interpretations of how the chronology in the Gospel accounts coincides with the Jewish festival calendar at the time and whether the

Figure 4.2. *The Last Supper.* Painting by Agostino Carracci, made between 1593 and 1594. The group dines on lamb, while John leans dozing on Christ. Museo del Prado. Courtesy of Wikimedia Commons.

Paschal lambs could have been eaten on that Thursday or not until Friday evening, after the trial and crucifixion had been completed. For present purposes, we can note that many depictions in art and literature have included a lamb at the meal (see figure 4.2), and in 2007 Pope Benedict XV considered it worth his while to officially debunk this popular tradition.[7]

We might presume that the model play followed the Gospels and restricted the enacted meal to bread and wine, with later redactors embellishing the table with the fruits and vegetables laid there in some stage directions. But scriptwriters may have known that lamb was an option and chosen not to add it in. In the Tepalcingo play, with its variant version of Judas's meetings with the Jewish council, Judas informs the priests that Jesus will eat the lamb at John Mark's house (49), so this motif was present in the narrative or play variant the scriptwriter used in this scene. In each of the four Spanish-language plays, Jesus divides and shares a lamb onstage; three plays specify that this prop is to be made of bread or dough.[8] Another Last Supper sermon from the manuscript *Sermones en mexicano* (n.d., 106r) assumes that lamb was on the menu,[9] as does one of the fragments of Passion text stuffed into the *pasta de caña* Christ statue from Mexicaltzingo (Carrillo y Gariel 1949, vol. 2, 70). And in the second Tulane Passion text, "the homeowner then laid the roasted lamb in front of him. It was in a very precious emerald bowl. And our lord then grasped it. Then he divided it in pieces. And then he commanded all the apostles to eat it, according to the command" (*Pasión en lengua mexicana* n.d., second pagination, 31r–31v).[10] The "command" here would refer to Jewish law, just as the Spanish-language plays refer to *la sena del cordero, según la ley* 'the supper of the lamb, according to the law,'[11] as well as *el cordero legal* 'the legal lamb' and *la cena legal* 'the legal supper.'[12]

Colonial Nahuas kept sheep; there was nothing particularly exotic about eating lamb, especially in the home of a high-status man. Further, Gamaliel's characterization would not be harmed if a fine vessel like that emerald bowl were to grace his table. But the scriptwriters move on directly to the more important matter of the tortillas—a food that, unlike imported Old World livestock, was the essence of Nahua subsistence. How the Jesus actor handles the blessing of tortillas brings us to the most controversial part of the supper enactment. Before examining these scenes, let us consider the issues.

Fray Francisco Larrea's 1768 report to the Inquisition unpacks the problems from the viewpoint of this paternalistic but not entirely unsympathetic Dominican. After opining that laypeople should never be allowed to perform representations of the Passion in churches, he extends his opprobrium to performances of the origin of the most divine sacrament, describing what, he alleges, happens in such enactments: "Seated at the table, the actor representing Christ, with those who play the roles of the twelve apostles, takes the bread, blesses it, and consecrates it with vulgar words of Castilian or Mexican [Nahuatl] language, and distributes it among the twelve. Afterwards he takes the chalice of wine, blesses it, consecrates it in the same manner, and tells all to drink of it: which certainly is an action full of errors and, consequently, intolerable among Catholics."[13] Next, he complains about how this mock sacrament is rehearsed on various nights, as late as midnight, which surely results in many improprieties. Then he returns to performance practices:

> And it must also be warned that at the time of acting out the consecration of the bread and wine, they sing the hymn "Pange lingua [gloriosi corporis mysterium" 'Tell, tongue, of the mystery of the glorious body'] translated into vulgar language, and as in the last verse it invites the church to adore the most divine with these words, *Tantum ergo sacramentum veneremur cernui* [We venerate, reverent, such a high sacrament], they kneel and thus adore the bread and wine that the actor playing Christ consecrated or intended to consecrate, or whose consecration is entirely acted out. If this is not a most grave error, what error can there be in the world?[14]

As mentioned in chapter 2, the "Pange lingua" hymn celebrates the Eucharist, and the last two stanzas of the hymn are sometimes separated off as the "Tantum ergo" (see notes at II.iv.7 and II.iv.9; figure 2.6). While irreverent imitation of these sacred events is Larrea's main concern here, earlier in his report the friar worries also that the singing of such songs will lead the poorly educated to imagine that they were sung back in Jesus's day, during the original events.[15]

When Larrea discusses Nahuatl Passion performances he had actually seen, when posted at Tepoztlán and perhaps other Dominican churches, he is supportive of Indigenous practice and critical of Archbishop Rubio y Salinas's crackdown. In regard to the scene with the bread and wine, he recalls: "I heard no words of consecration, and even if I heard them, I could not understand them. I saw only that the actor playing Christ, who could serve as a living example of patience, humility, and meekness, blessed the bread and wine and distributed them among those at the table, but no one knelt, or adored, nor was any hymn sung."[16] Larrea here admits, in effect, what limited many observers' comprehension of the plays: actors speaking Nahuatl, especially in front of a multi-ethnic crowd, could say words not everyone would entirely grasp.

Even though he was pleased with the demeanor of the Nahua players he observed, Larrea would prefer that rather than personify Jesus while performing these weighty acts, the actor would distance himself through third-person narration, saying something like this: " 'I who unworthily represent the character of our Lord Jesus Christ make known to you that on the night of the Last Supper he took the bread into his holy hands, blessed it, and consecrated it in the same way that the priests practice it on the altar, and he divided it among his disciples, like I do now with you'; and for the wine he say and do the same, *mutatis mutandis*."[17] Furthermore, the actors should not sing or kneel or adore the consecrated host in any way, "for it would be a pity if, because of an error that they commit with innocence and without malice, the performance be forbidden to them, which can be very useful to them for doctrine, for faith, and for good customs."[18]

Raised hosts and kneeling people arise elsewhere in the Inquisition inquiry: they are one of the concerns that led the judges to seek Larrea's opinion. The file contains identical reports purporting to describe Spanish-language productions by "people of reason" in Ozumba, Nochiztlan,[19] Cuauhtla de Amilpas, and Huejotzingo. Among other scandalous acts, each document mentions "the most grave circumstance that when they make the supper, this one [the Jesus player] raises a host and all kneel to adore it."[20] There was a concern that this kneeling "all" (*todos*) could encompass the audience along with the actors. That is why don Antonio de Guevara, the former Jesus actor from Huejotzingo, was obliged to testify not only that his *altepetl*'s play had been an all-Indigenous and a dignified affair but that "nor is it true that the whole audience used to kneel to adore the host whose consecration was simulated, because only those who had roles in the play would do it."[21] His recollection does support Larrea's assertion that kneeling and adoration could be part of the Nahuatl performances.

Larrea does not speak directly of "Judaizing" practices—the alleged traces of Judaism the Spanish and Mexican Inquisitions persecuted—but desecration of the host was one such imagined crime and also a common element in the false stories of Jewish ritual murder (Enriquez 2018, 289). Hence, there does not seem to be a fear that Indigenous performers were swiping actual communion hosts from churches to abuse in the plays. Nevertheless, this fear might have aggravated the anxiety that surrounded scenes of Indigenous or other unauthorized people handling objects that at least closely resembled the actual wafers.

We might expect the four Spanish-language plays seized during the Inquisition investigation to violate Larrea's stipulations, but they do so only to some extent. Singing, of an unidentified song, is called for only in Cuaderno 1 (208v). The Ozumba play speaks of "the elevation of the hosts (*hostias*)," but the other three instruct Jesus to look up to heaven while he holds the bread, not to lift it up. Ozumba also calls the bread *formas*, another Spanish word for communion hosts, as does Cuaderno 1 (208r). All but Amecameca use the verb *comulgar* 'to give or take communion.'[22] So the Jesus actor was generally understood to be performing this rite at least in imitation, but none of the plays calls for kneeling or requests a Eucharistic hymn.

THIS TORTILLA IS MY BODY

Larrea's 1768 report, like Archbishop Rubio y Salinas's 1757 decree, came later than any of the dates inscribed on the Nahuatl scripts. Nevertheless, variations among the plays indicate different levels of confidence regarding what could be safely staged and, possibly, previous interference from local priests. The Tlatlauhquitepec scriptwriter was the most cautious (2v–3r). There is no description of a table setting at all, let alone one stocked with tortillas and wine. Jesus invites his students to start eating before he utters his version of the Luke 22:15–16 passage, which he combines with the passage in Matthew (26:31–32) about the sheep being scattered, referring to how the apostles will abandon Jesus when he is arrested. When Peter protests, Jesus predicts his denial. This exchange normally comes later (see II.v.16–18). The scene then jumps back to Jesus's prediction that one of those at the table will betray him (II.iv.10). It seems the cast members are meanwhile to eat some food that is on the table, but there are no scripted lines about the blessing of the tortilla(s) and wine. However, the choir is to sing about the bread in Latin, for the script retains a cue for the chant, quoting Matthew 26:26, *Cenantibus autem eis, accepit Jesus panem, benedixit ac fregit, dedit discipulis suis* 'Now as they were eating, Jesus took bread,

Figure 4.3. The *cenantibus autem eis* chant in Juan Navarro's *Liber in quo quatuor passiones Christi Domini continentur*, 1604, f. 5v. Courtesy of the John Carter Brown Library, Brown University, Providence, RI.

blessed and broke it, and gave it to his disciples' (see II.iv.3), possibly taken from Navarro's Saint Matthew Passion (figure 4.3). It is possible that the actors would pantomime these actions or even improvise unscripted lines as loudly or softly as they chose. But no priest, reviewing the script, could claim that an unworthy man was to act too much like Jesus or like a priest.

At the other extreme lies the Penn Passion, which offers a scenario that Larrea would find "intolerable" and beset by "most grave error" and which also accords with don Antonio's testimony. The well-laid table includes not just tortillas and a flask of wine but one special white (*iztac*) tortilla for Jesus to bless and twelve *formas*, or communion hosts, for him to distribute among his students (10r–10v; II.iii.25).[23] After his speech with the "jade temple" figure, Jesus proceeds to grasp the host—in this case the specified single white tortilla, presumably—with both hands, bless it (or, in Nahuatl, "make it sacred") and raise it up. These gestures mirror what a priest does at the altar during Mass, at the moment of consecration. He tells his students, "See this tortilla. It is my precious body. And now, take it, receive it" (11v).[24] Only in this play does he make a simple equation between maize product and flesh. The second verb in his command, *xicmocelilican*, is the same verb used for taking communion, or Spanish *comulgar*; the Nahuatl noun form is the nonspecific *tlaceliliztli* 'receiving something.'

There was nothing scandalous about using the word *tlaxcalli* 'tortilla' or 'something toasted' (on a griddle) for the communion host: Nahuatl explanations of the Mass and communion typically called the consecrated wafer a *tlaxcaltzintli* 'revered (or little) tortilla' rather than impose the Spanish word *pan*. Tortillas were, after all, the Indigenous form of bread; the Our Father prayer's "daily bread" becomes tortillas in Nahuatl versions. Consecrated communion wafers were made of wheat, not maize (Earle 2010, 699).[25] But being flat and round, they looked like maize tortillas, not loaves of *pan*; in an Indigenous performance items called *tlaxcalli* could certainly be viewed as maize tortillas and the table be furnished with such by local women.

Priests do not seem to have understood that in allowing the host to be associated with a toasted maize (not baked wheat) product, they were confirming Indigenous views of maize as a sacred, living entity that embodied the divine nurturing and strengthening force of the sun, now linked with Christ. The loanword *pan* could have been used in the scripts and the table been laden with suitable loaves, were this indeed seen as an issue.[26] Appropriate to a meal eaten at the time of Passover, tortillas are unleavened. What is striking here is the use of the Spanish word *forma*, indicating that real or imitation communion hosts—tiny tortillas being an easily procured substitute—were to be blessed and distributed. This makes for a different and much more provocative staging than if the Jesus actor was to tear up an ordinary tortilla, like one found at any Nahua meal, and distribute the pieces.

The Penn play's stage directions now instruct the Jesus actor to have each of the twelve apostles "receive something," presumably one of the twelve *formas*, while a quick-acting angel impersonator is to snatch Judas's mini-tortilla out of his mouth. Meanwhile, the choir is to chant the "Pange lingua gloriosi" hymn (11v; II.iv.7). Jesus then drinks some wine from the flask on the table and blesses it, saying, "O my beloved children, look at this wine that I drink. It is my precious blood that will be spilled. Receive it" (11v).[27] The choir then sings the "Tantum ergo sacramentum," while the apostles, spread out on the stage on their knees, take sips of wine (11v; II.iv.9). Even though the singing was in Latin rather than a vulgar tongue, Larrea would have objected to this staging. But the fact that the apostles are to kneel now, for the wine but not for the tortillas, may reflect an element of caution.

The remaining plays fall between these two extremes. They also bear traces of the editing and rearrangement of the scene. Princeton's Jesus says his Luke 22:15–16 speech and then everyone eats, while the choir chants about the blessing of the bread (15v–16r). The cue for the music is *Hoc est corpus meum quod pro vobis* 'this is my body which for your sake,' a sequence found in slightly different responsories from the Corpus Christi liturgy.[28] Regardless of what the choir is singing, however, the actors move right on to the "Is it I" exchange and do not enact the tortilla blessing until after their foot-washing scene and Jesus's subsequent monologue. Since John tells of the foot washing and the other evangelists of the bread and wine, these events could be placed in either order. The foot washing precedes the bread blessing in the *Meditations on the Life of Christ* (McNamer 2018, 97–99); we find this order in the second Tulane Passion text (*Pasión en lengua mexicana* n.d., second pagination, 31v–37r) and in each of the four Spanish plays from the Inquisition case. The only thing strange about the Princeton script's ordering is the separation between the chant and the staged action. In chapter 3, I mentioned the truncated bit of Peter's denial scene that precedes the full scene in the Princeton script and in chapter 2 the early angel intervention that sounds as though it might come from another text's Gethsemane scene. This separation between the chanted blessing and the enacted blessing may be another example of how the Princeton scriptwriter was working from multiple models.

Princeton's Jesus tags these lines onto his monologue (17v–18r): "And now I am going to establish for you a sign, a model, so that you will always do as you will now see. I am going to leave you the localized embodiment of my body, my blood. Now I will bless this tortilla and wine. I myself reach onto them. I will remain here with you. This will become my localized embodiment forever."[29] *Machiyotl, octacatl* is a traditional parallelism referring to a wise example that people should follow; it would have an archaic ring. Jesus proceeds to designate the tortilla and wine not directly as his body and blood, as in the Penn play, but as *ixiptlahtzin*, their localized embodiment, image, representative, or substitute. Read with the latter definitions, this could seem a rather Protestant take on the Eucharist, but if we read *ixiptlahtzin* here not as a stand-in but in terms of how, in Indigenous religious thought, divine identities could be embodied in a dispersed fashion among multiple objects—what Molly Bassett (2015, 135–136, drawing on Alfred Gell 1998) calls "distributed personhood"—this is actually a very effective Nahua way to express how the consecrated host and wine could contain the person of Christ without resembling his complete self. In chapter 5, I apply this concept to the instruments of the Passion. Here in the Princeton play, we see a very sophisticated Indigenous adaptation of the idea of transubstantiation. The "I reach onto them" or "I arrive on them" (*ipan nahci*) construction suggests the action by which Jesus extends himself into these objects to effect this process of embodiment.

Then comes the stage direction "He will bless the tortilla" (18r). I have translated this and similar passages with a single tortilla, but since colonial Nahuatl did not pluralize inanimate objects, unless the scripts specify how many tortillas are involved—as Penn does here—it could be any number. The actor could take a stack of tortillas and distribute them, as diners at a Nahua meal would do. The resulting freedom of interpretation could give rise to unorthodox treatments like this one in the second Tulane Passion text (*Pasión en lengua mexicana* n.d., second pagination, 36r–36v): "When they had, thus, eaten the lamb, then there were only five tortillas. Then he said sacred words over them. He said, 'This is my body. Eat it, all of you.' When our lord said this, the tortillas, which were only five, then became his body. And all the apostles ate them."[30] The author could have been thinking of the story about Jesus feeding a multitude with five loaves and two fishes. He may have considered five, a number Mesoamericans associated with completion, to be the perfect number—or, given his repetition of *zan* 'only,' the minimum number to serve as a complete complement in so serious an undertaking. But no priest would have countenanced such an apportionment of bread, and we are left to wonder how the five transformed tortillas were to be divided among twelve disciples.

Princeton's Christ then tells his "beloved children" to receive (again, as if taking communion) and eat the tortilla(s), which now is (or are) considered, or counted as (*ipan pohui*), his body (18r). This is another way to express the connection between him and his new embodiments without making a simple identification. He moves right on to the wine, called *vinoh* in the stage directions but *xocomecatzintli* 'wild-grape water' in the Nahuatl (18r).[31] This is the only place in the corpus where the dialogue avoids this Spanish loanword, one that showed up in Nahuatl civil documents by 1553 (Karttunen and Lockhart 1976, 59). The substitution is a deliberate archaism meant to make the text sound more authentically and ancestrally Nahua; the general lamb avoidance may have served the same purpose. As to how Jesus's blood gets into this fruit beverage, Jesus now uses the *ipan ahci* 'it reaches onto' or 'it arrives upon' construction we just saw in the Penn play. Thus, the scriptwriter provides listeners with three Nahuatl linguistic formulas through which they may understand the transubstantiation: localized embodiment, being counted or considered as, and reaching or arriving on. *Ipan ahci* might also have been interpreted as a simple relationship of resemblance between the tortilla or wine and Jesus himself, that they are like to one another, with no magical sharing of substance.[32] If one does not make sense to an audience member, another might.

This scriptwriter goes on to provide some further explanation in regard to the blood-beverage, using words derived from Matthew 26:28: "for this is my blood of the covenant, which is poured out for many for the forgiveness of sins." The Nahuatl says, "With this your belief will be strengthened. It will be spilled on many people.

Thus their sins will be destroyed" (18r).[33] He definitely wrote "on them" (*inpan*; standard *impan*), not "on account of" or "for the sake of them" (*impampa*).

The Princeton play's scriptwriter has avoided the elements in the Penn play that would have seemed intolerable to Larrea. His Jesus does not raise up the tortilla(s); his apostles do not kneel down. His choir intones a liturgical chant but does not sing the "Pange lingua" or "Tantum ergo," and this chant is removed in time from the tortilla and wine blessings. Larrea's bugbears are all trappings that came from the Catholic Church; he just did not want Indigenous people exerting ownership of them. Even priests like Larrea, with experience in Nahua communities, might not have recognized the subtle processes of appropriation and interpretation of the Eucharist that are going on here in the Princeton play—and we should also recall that "jade temple" slipped into the Penn script. Christ may act less like a priest while at the same time becoming more of a Nahua god. He is a god of sustenance, blessing and providing the maize that is his own flesh, along with his life-giving blood, spilled directly on his followers. Or he is the sun god, which he remains for many people in Mesoamerica, whose heat (*tonalli*) flows into the maize and other foods, collectively called *tonacayotl*—'solar heat-ness,' basically—that in turn give strength and health to human beings.[34]

The three plays from Jonacatepec present two distinct models and, in the third case, a deliberate choice of one of those models over the other. Only the Tepalcingo play, however, calls for music: the same *Cenantibus autem eis* chant that was Tlatlauhquitepec's sole sign that something involving bread was happening. Tepalcingo's Jesus makes a simple one-to-one identification between his body and the tortilla, paired with another way of coming to terms with the body-tortilla connection. The actor says, "O my children, this tortilla is (alternatively, these tortillas are) my body; the tortilla is just filled up with it, which for your sakes will be made to stretch its arms upon the cross. Eat it, O my children" (53).[35] The reference to the imminent crucifixion intensifies the identification between the tortilla(s) about to be eaten and the body about to be tormented. As for the tortilla being "filled up" with Christ's body, another possible reading is "it (the tortilla) is just covered with it (the body)," as if Christ's flesh were a garment or a blanket.[36] "Filled up" makes the merger more complete and easier to grasp—one can imagine his substance infusing the foodstuff. This reading also seems more apt than the "cover" one when it is applied to the wine. When he speaks of the wine, Jesus again looks ahead to the cross: "O my beloved children, this wine is my blood. The wine is filled up (or covered) with it, which for your sakes will be spilled on the cross, so that the new way of living will become strong with it. Drink it, consume it all, O my children" (53).[37]

The Amacuitlapilco play, like Princeton, delays the tortilla and wine exchange until after Christ has completed his post-foot-washing remarks. He is to bless *ce chipahuac tlaxcalli* 'one pure tortilla.' Then "he will break it inside a gold (or silver) plate, so that he will cause everyone to receive something, each of the apostles" (22r).[38] This is the only case in which not only is there one special tortilla, as in Penn, but the actor is to break it, as Jesus broke (Latin *fregit*, from *frangere*) the bread in the Gospel accounts. This Jesus then offers yet another verbal construction by which his audience may perceive his action, using the verb *ehua* 'to rise, get up, get up to leave.' He says, "Obtain, eat, this tortilla that I have blessed. My body arises on it" (22r).[39] The wording might suggest a sudden surging of his substance onto or into the tortilla, not wholly unlike the filling or covering suggested by *tlapachihui*. Then, for his blood, he uses the *ipan pohui* construction, meaning to be considered or counted as, that the Princeton scriptwriter employed for his tortilla line: "Drink this wine that I have blessed. It will be considered my precious blood." Then, as in the corresponding speech in Princeton, he tells his students that this blood will strengthen their faith. But rather than being "spilled on many people," this Jesus gives the more conventional prediction that "the life forces, the souls, of all the people of the world will be purified with it" (22r).[40]

When the Axochiapan scriptwriter came to this scene, he first proceeded as in the Amacuitlapilco play, waiting until after the foot washing to set a cognate but somewhat stripped-down dialogue. A stage direction says Christ will bless the tortilla(s) and cause the apostles to receive something—nothing about a pure tortilla or a pricey plate. His Christ then instructs his students to eat the tortilla he has blessed but neglects to identify it as his body. This does not seem to be an attempt to water down the scene, as his subsequent line, concerning the wine that will be considered his blood, is the same as Amacuitlapilco's (17v). But then at some point the writer changed his mind, crossed these lines out, and inserted a partial sheet of paper earlier in his text (15r) on which he wrote the same dialogue found in the Tepalcingo play (though without cueing any music). He also excised some other lines from the earlier scene to help integrate the added half-page. As the two options are roughly equivalent enactments, staging the blessing and sharing of food and drink without any raising of the tortilla or kneeling of the apostles, there is no obvious reason for his choice other than a preference to set the scene earlier, when the group is seated at the table anyway. The result is that the scene occurs at this point in the action in four of the six scripts, in contrast to its later placement in all four Spanish-language plays.

Of the five plays that inscribe the body and blood transformations into the script, only the Penn play is content with the simple equation of food with body and drink with blood, as given in the Gospels. The lines lack any copula (the Vulgate's *est* 'is'), as none is needed here in Nahuatl. All the other scripts introduce one or another verbal construct to help listeners imagine how Jesus's substance gets into or becomes equated with the items on the table. Scriptwriters had options for how they would express this essential Christian notion. Other options for raising, kneeling, and singing were also available but were apparently subject to some degree of self- or local censorship.

JUDAS REVEALED

The blessing of tortillas and wine, though a prerequisite for Christ's death, does not advance the saga of his torment. But another part of the scene dispatches Judas to his act of betrayal. In each of the Gospels, Jesus reveals that one of his companions at the table will betray him, and they wonder who it could be (Matthew 26:21–25; Mark 14:18–21; Luke 22:21–23; John 13:21–22). In Matthew and Mark, each asks, "Is it I, Lord," and Jesus says it is the man who has dipped his hand or his bread in the dish with him. In the first three Gospels, Jesus says "woe to that man by whom he is betrayed," adding in Matthew and Mark, "it would have been better for that man if he had not been born." Except for the Tepalcingo play, where Judas meets with the chief priests earlier in the action, Judas has previously drawn attention to himself only for his reaction to Jesus's treatment of Mary Magdalene—a scene omitted in Penn. Audience members not very familiar with the Passion story may only now be learning or remembering that one man in Jesus's retinue bears so dangerous a grudge.

Tlatlauhquitepec's Jesus gives the mildest version of this speech, noting that one of those dining with him will sell him and adding that it would have been good if this man had never been born (3r). This seems to have been reduced from the original speech, more of which the other plays retain. If we combine the traces in the different plays, we can see how the model speech Nahuatlized the Gospel passage by adding semantic parallelism. The verbs *namaca* 'sell' and *immac tlaza* 'cast into their hands' or 'betray' can be paired, and Jesus's enemies are both scoundrels and Jews, though only Tepalcingo retains both nouns. By chance, Matthew's and Mark's pairing of *vae homini* 'woe to that man' with the statement that the world would have been better off without this person corresponds neatly to the Nahuatl Jesus's formulaic *omotlahueliltic* 'O how wretched he is' and *cualli yezquia in macamo tlacatini* 'it would have been good if he had not been born.' In I.iv.21, Jesus predicts that Jerusalemites who reject his teachings will say the same things about themselves when they are sent to the place of the dead. These phrases echo the remorseful speeches condemned sinners deliver in Nahuatl morality plays (Sell and Burkhart 2004, 183, 189, 207; 2009, 379). Jesus then asserts once again that he is bound to fulfill prophecy, ending with a semantic pairing—retained only in Axochiapan—of 'the sacred words, the books of the prophets' (see II.iv.10).

No scriptwriter wrote out each individual student asking Jesus if he is the guilty party. This is why the names of many of the twelve never appear in the scripts, though we can assume that the number twelve was well enough established that actors represented them onstage. Five scriptwriters instruct "each" apostle to speak; Penn gives a line apiece to Peter, John, James, and Bartholomew (12r; see II.iv.13–23). Christ's response to each, "It isn't you" or "No, sit down" or "No, be at rest," is scripted once or, in two plays, omitted entirely. In Matthew, Judas asks the question last and separately from the others, after Jesus speaks so disparagingly of his betrayer. He addresses Jesus not as *Domine* 'O Lord' but with the less reverent *Rabbi* 'Teacher' (the Vulgate retains the Hebrew word). In the plays, all the students call Jesus their teacher. Although Judas speaks immediately after the others, four of the plays follow Matthew in rendering his question less respectful, using Nahuatl grammatical options rather than different words. The other students address Jesus as *notemachticatzine* 'O my (dear or esteemed) teacher,' expressing a personal relationship and using the honorific suffix *-tzin*, while Judas says *temachtianie* 'O teacher,' neither honorific nor possessed. It is likely that the original play made this distinction, but the Princeton and Amacuitlapilco scriptwriters placed the same honorific epithet in Judas's mouth as in those of his fellow students, whether for consistency or because of the general practice of applying honorifics to Jesus. Later, though, in front of the priests, having resolved to sell Jesus, Princeton's Judas abandons honorifics and speaks of *in temachtiani* 'the teacher' who *notemachticauh ocatca* 'used to be my teacher' (21v).[41]

In Matthew (26:25), Jesus responds to Judas's question with "You have said so"; John (13:27) gives "What you are going to do, do quickly." All the Nahuatl plays retain the first response, and five of them add the second, phrased as a command to bring it to an end or do quickly what he is to do (II.iv.23). Only two plays retain a trace of the exchange in which Jesus reveals the identity of the betrayer, based not on Matthew's and Mark's remark about Judas dipping bread in the dish but on John's version (13:23–26). Here, Peter asks John,[42] who "was lying close to the breast of Jesus" as they reclined at table, to inquire; Jesus reveals to John, out of the others' hearing, that the betrayer "is he to whom I shall give this morsel when I have dipped it." He then dips said morsel and hands it to Judas (see figure 4.1). The *Gamaliel's* Passion account adds the detail that Jesus dips the bite of bread in the juice of a lamb that Judas purchased for the meal (Delbrugge 2020, 108). In the Tepalcingo play, prior to the "Is it I" recitation, John asks his teacher who has done this thing, and Jesus tells him it is the one to whom he will give the *paltic tlaxcalli* 'wet tortilla' (54; II.iv.12). The actors may then mime this, but the script does not so indicate; nor does it treat the exchange as confidential.

The other trace appears in the Princeton play (16r). After Jesus has dispatched Judas, a stage direction says *mocochitiz San Juan ipantzinco Cristo* 'Saint John will go to sleep on Christ.' Many paintings of the Last Supper, including figure 4.2, interpret "lying close to the breast of Jesus" as napping while leaning against Jesus or with his head on the table. John could not be dozing while also having a secret conversation. I suspect that Princeton's John is aping an image known to this or a previous scriptwriter, and this motif does not come directly from the original play or the Bible.

The second Passion text in the Tulane manuscript explains things in this scene about which the scriptwriters show no concern. Judas had to ask the "Is it I" question or he would have drawn suspicion to himself. Jesus, too, had to keep his betrayer's identity secret from the larger group of apostles, or they would have stopped Judas from carrying out his plans and the entire scheme of salvation would have been derailed. The text has the wet tortilla story, imagining a sauce bowl—such as may also have lain on the Tepalcingo play's table—but making the conversation secret, as in John's Gospel (*Pasión en lengua mexicana* n.d., second pagination, 35v): "And Saint John then secretly asked in our lord's ear, he said to him, 'O our lord, by your authority, tell me, who is it that will betray you?' And our lord then said to him, 'O my beloved child, how you will recognize him is that I will give him food that I will wet with sauce.' And then he took a tortilla. He wetted it with sauce. Then he gave it to Judas."[43] John continues (13:27), "Then, after the morsel, Satan entered into him." The Tulane text has "And when he gave him the tortilla, that was when the human horned owl entered inside him" (35v–36r).[44] The author then takes additional pains to explain how the other apostles remained unaware of Judas's intentions. When Jesus tells Judas to proceed with his errand, he does so without the others hearing, such that "they thought maybe he was going to do something with the tortilla, or maybe have compassion for the poor" (36r).[45] Even this text, which fits Mark Z. Christensen's definition of Category Three (or least orthodox) materials, hews closer to the Bible than do the plays in this moment, referring to the secrecy of the morsel-passing exchange and to Judas's demon possession while also intruding exegesis and rationalization into what in the plays is a smooth flow of action.

OF PETER AND CLEAN FEET

Every play retains the foot-washing scene from chapter 13 of John, whether placed before or after the tortilla and wine event. Figure 4.4 provides one example of how the event was depicted. In John, Jesus prepares by putting aside his clothes (*vestimenta*), wrapping a towel (*linteus*) around himself, and pouring water into a basin (*pelvis*). Some scripts say none of this. Penn (12r) gives Jesus a large towel (*tobajah*, from Spanish) and also a change of cloak (*tilmahtli*), plus a large earthenware tub (*apaztli*) and a washbasin (*palanganah*, from Spanish). Gamaliel goes to fetch the vessel of water in the Princeton (16r), Amacuitlapilco (20r), and Axochiapan (16r) plays.

Figure 4.4. *Christ Washing the Disciples' Feet.* Anonymous Italian painting, early eighteenth century. Courtesy of Wikimedia Commons, posted by Nagel Auction.

Amacuilapilco's Jesus has towels to lay over his shoulder (20r). Penn calls for the table and Amacuitlapilco for the benches to be moved aside to make room (II.v.2–3).

In John 13:6, Jesus then approaches Peter first and Peter objects: "Lord, do you wash my feet?" Most of the scripts have Jesus speak first, telling Peter either to bare his feet or to sit down so he can wash them (II.v.4). Peter then resists, the Penn scriptwriter instructing the actor to react with consternation (*huel momauhtiz*) (12r). Most Peters supplement the biblical model by saying that since Jesus is their deity and ruler, they cannot possibly permit this and even repeating the reason after Jesus explains that Peter will, at a later time, come to understand what he is doing (II.v.5–7). The extra dialogue helps frame Christ's behavior as an act of humility for people unaware of first-century Jewish etiquette. Jesus then recites his adaptation of John 13:10–11, assuring Peter—who now wants more of his body parts washed—that people who are otherwise clean need only their feet washed. He adds that "not all of you" are clean, based on the Gospel text's "he knew who was to betray him." Three of the plays omit this explanation of the "not all of you," while Amacuitlapilco (20v) and Axochiapan (16v) have Jesus say, "I know who my chosen ones are," words from John 13:18 that Jesus will repeat in his upcoming speech. Only Penn (12v–13r) has Jesus address Judas directly here, demanding to wash his feet and giving him a last chance to air his grievances directly (II.v.10). Peter is always first. Stage directions in Penn specify that Judas is to be last, also implied in Amacuitlapilco; this may have been the general practice. Penn also instructs the Jesus actor to closely embrace each apostle's feet and the Gamaliel actor to kiss them (13r). Amacuitlapilco's stage direction has someone kiss each foot three times, but it is unclear whether this is Jesus or Gamaliel. Judas apparently avoids this by moving out of the way (20v).[46]

Mendieta, in his account of Indigenous Passion observations in Mexico City in 1595, describes a Mandatum ceremony. Twelve impoverished and disabled Indigenous men took the parts of the disciples. After two Franciscans friars washed their feet, Nahua nobles dressed them in new clothes and fed them a meal, also feeding 100 or 200 other needy people (Mendieta 1980, 435–436). While such records are lacking for the eighteenth-century *altepetl* that staged the known plays, the occasion likely still provided an opportunity for local leaders to spread charity in their communities, even if on a smaller scale.

JESUS AND JUDAS: SANCTIFIED AND DISORDERED ORATIONS

Next, Jesus gives the speech shown at II.v.12, his longest in the play and a remarkably stable text across the corpus, probably remaining close to what the original playwright(s) composed. Jesus has some substantial speeches at the Last Supper in the Spanish-language plays, but they are not cognate with this one. This speech as a whole illustrates very effectively how the original playwright(s) wove different Bible passages together to compose fitting speeches for the play, how Jesus's words were reworked to make him speak like a skilled Nahua orator, and how different scriptwriters—over time and through space—recognized the artistic and authoritative character of such compositions and preserved them with few omissions or alterations. Although Tlatlauhquitepec's Jesus speeds things up by reciting this while he is washing everyone's feet (3r), which could also happen in Axochiapan, the other plays have him sit down again while he delivers this formal oration. The Penn play has Gamaliel kneel and also has Peter lay his head on the table (13r). Peter is an old man, perhaps in need of a nap, but the motif could come from the reclining John we saw dozing in the Princeton play. Penn characterizes the speech as *Evangelioh*, or Gospel reading. Nowhere else in the corpus does a speech receive this designation, however closely to the Bible it may hew.

The speech adapts several passages from the extended declamation Jesus delivers over four chapters of John, specifically John 13:12–19, 13:33–35, 15:18–20, and 16:20. The playwright(s) then selected the passage from Luke's Last Supper narrative where Jesus, addressing Peter, says that Satan demanded to have you (plural) in order to "sift you like wheat," as if to loosen their faith from them (Gundry 2010, 332), but Jesus has prayed for their faith to remain strong (Luke 22:31). The playwright(s) peppered this composite oration with parallelisms as they adapted it into Nahuatl, as the many verb and noun pairs in II.v.12 demonstrate. John 13:15's "example" becomes the traditional doublet *in machiyotl, in octacatl* 'sign, model,' which, we saw above, Princeton's Jesus uses for the transformed tortilla and wine. The Vulgate's *cribrare* 'sift' becomes *cehcemmana* 'scatter,' paired resonantly in three cases with *chahchayahua* 'strew' or 'sow.' Separating grain from chaff becomes the more familiar action of strewing seed, and three plays pair maize kernels (*tlaolli*) with the wheat (*trigoh*) to make the vocabulary even more accessible. Addressing Peter, Jesus adjusts to his Nahua context by replacing Satan with the familiar *tlacatecolotl* 'human horned owl,' and Peter's "brethren" become "your younger brothers," as Nahua siblings must be designated either older or younger.

Jesus in the plays often cites his obligation to fulfill prophecy, so it is no surprise that his speech here retains this passage from John 13:18: "I am not speaking of you all; I know whom I have chosen; it is that the scripture may be fulfilled, 'He who ate my bread has lifted his heel against me.'" That is, he excludes Judas from the counsel he is offering. The "scripture" allusion is to Psalm 40:10 (41:9): "Even my bosom friend in whom I trusted, who ate of my bread, has lifted his heel against me." The original playwright(s) knew to attribute this line to David, purported author of the Psalms. Four of the plays retain a parallelism that pairs, in some way, "sacred words" with the "sacred book of the prophet David." Tepalcingo (56) merely mentions "the sacred words of the prophets that lie written in their books," while Tlatlauhquitepec has "everything that lies written in the sacred books" (3v): both statements affirm the authority of scripture. The passage from Psalms was reorganized into two verb pairs: "one who eats with me, one who drinks with me" and "will kick me, will offend me." The first pair appropriately revisits the sharing of both tortillas and wine. The Nahuatl expression for "offend" itself incorporates a pair of locatives: *nixco nocpac nemiz* 'they will live on my face, on top of my head.' The verb *telicza* 'to kick' obviously equates to "lifted his heel"; the Tlatlauhquitepec scriptwriter considered the "offend" idiom sufficient in this context (3v).

The Amacuitlapilco scriptwriter inserted his compact tortilla and wine exchange immediately after this oration, delaying by a few turns at speech the response Peter makes at II.v.13, which clearly was originally written as an immediate reply to Jesus's long address. Except for the question at the end, the model for Peter's speech is traditional Nahuatl oratory, in which the recipient of an admonition politely thanks the speaker for their words of wisdom. For Peter to reply as abruptly as he does in John 13:36 ("Lord, where are you going?") would have been rude. While their ensuing exchange tracks with John 13:36–38, the playwright(s) also switched Gospels and inserted the speech at II.v.16, from Matthew 26:31–32 or Mark 14:27–28. This gave Jesus another opportunity to cite prophecy, in this case Zechariah 13:7: "says the Lord of hosts, 'Strike the shepherd, that the sheep may be scattered.'" This is read as predicting the disciples' abandonment of Jesus after his arrest. But the Nahua Jesus couches this prediction among words of support and encouragement; his tone is not one of anger or chastisement.

Jesus in all four Gospels then predicts Peter's denial, while Peter declares his steadfastness (Matthew 26:34–35; Mark 14:30–31; Luke 22:33–34; John 13:37–38). The Tlatlauhquitepec scriptwriter omitted this, perhaps accidentally, but all the other plays have an exchange something like II.v.17–19. Jesus will, of course, be proven correct; all plays stage the denial scene.

The supper party now breaks up. In most plays, Jesus invites his students to accompany him to his grandfather David's garden—that is, the Garden of Gethsemane, where he will be arrested (II.v.20). His statement has no biblical model, but Passion narratives could supply one, like the simple "Let us rise and go from here" in the *Meditations on the Life of Christ* (McNamer 2018, 105). In all the plays, this is when Judas parts company with the others. They exit the stage, while he remains in or in front of the set representing Gamaliel's or John Mark's house and launches into his soliloquy (II.vi.2).

In chapter 3, I discuss this speech in regard to Judas's animosity toward Mary Magdalene and his resulting isolation from the women's social network. But in the immediate context, the audience sees him separate himself from his former comrades, both in movement and in words. The supper, where food—some made sacred—was shared and the leader declaimed formal words of counsel, fails to integrate this personage into his social circle.

Coming so soon on the heels of Jesus's supper oration, the soliloquy naturally reads as some kind of counterpart or counterpoint to that. Whatever the original playwright(s) may have used as a source, it was not the Bible or any scene common in Passion narratives and plays, either in Europe or in the colony. Including this oration was a deliberate choice of the playwright(s) and retaining it a deliberate choice of each scriptwriter. The authors of the four Spanish plays opted not to include anything similar.

The first thing to observe about Judas's soliloquy is that it is, notably, more than twice as long as Jesus's preceding oration. It is also about 20 percent longer than the long versions of Pilate's death warrant.[47] Such a long discourse, delivered only to himself, in plays that are so interactive and dialogical bespeaks an untoward egotism and a severe social isolation, confirmed when he later commits suicide. The second thing is that, as in the case of Jesus's speech, its author(s) made sure to include many parallel constructions and traditional idioms, devices of formal Nahuatl oratory. Is Judas, then, an orator of Jesus's caliber? Definitely not, for the third thing to note is that the speech's content is entirely divorced from the purposes of good Nahuatl oratory. It does not offer counsel or consolation, appeal to divine or human authorities for assistance, or bestow praise on the addressee—who is merely Judas himself. While some of his concern is on behalf of his wife, children, or household, his speech is mainly about himself and his needs.

Fourth, the speech lays no claim to the self-confidence and authority normally projected by formal oratory. The uncertainty and constant self-questioning are not the self-deprecation a petitioner may express to elicit favor from a deity or social superior. Good orators may take time to assemble their array of choice images and metaphors, but they do not dither. Judas will remain uncertain about his own feelings even after he goes to the priests: he says it is "like" or "as if" he is happy and tranquil now rather than simply asserting satisfaction with his decision (II.vi.30). He does not know his own mind.

Fifth, while Judas is no giver of sage advice, neither is he a calculating villain launching a carefully planned plot. He is a bad guy: John denounces Judas as a *tlahueliloc* 'scoundrel' or 'despicable person' (V.i.11), and Jesus tells Pilate that he is blameless in comparison to Judas (IV.iv.13). But Judas is not a caricature of evil. He is acting on impulse and could have acted differently. Nor is he presented as demon-possessed. The only place he expresses hatred of Christ and his teachings is in the section of Tepalcingo based on an alternative council scene (43; see the lines in II.vi. 25 where he says he despises Christ and will never return to him). He never doubts Christ's divinity or resents his popularity. In contrast, the Judas in the Spanish play from Ozumba is possessed by a demon (245r)—as in John 13:27—and also speaks with a demon in human guise after Christ's arrest, acknowledging Christ's innocence and his own guilt (249r). In Cuaderno 1, he sees danger in Jesus's doctrine and sorcery in his actions (205r–205v). The Nahua Judas is a tormented soul, disordered by need and greed. Rambling and ranting to an audience of one, he provides an object lesson in what happens when someone puts their own welfare above that of their social unit and loses their identity as part of a collective. In a Nahua corporate community, this is a lesson worth the staging.

While periodically resorting to expressions of anxiety and self-doubt, Judas nevertheless constructs an argument to support his actions. He first notes, accurately, that Jesus has told him to carry through with his plan. Then he considers counterarguments: he observes that his planned betrayal is an immoral act that may condemn him, and he acknowledges that Jesus has been kind to him. This leads to an attempt to minimize what he is doing. He imagines that the damage he will cause may not be that great, for Jesus has been a benefactor of the Jews. Surely both the priests and the *macehualtin* will protect him, and the rulers will not keep him imprisoned for long. Here, he underestimates the priests' animus, but then he quite rightly observes that God could, if he chose, save Jesus and stop the entire process.

His next move is to contradict his previous statement about Jesus's kindness by complaining that his service to Jesus has not sustained him and his household materially. He is not content with the shared poverty of Jesus and his fellow disciples.

The audience sees him acting on his poorly controlled appetites elsewhere in the play. When he receives his thirty pieces of silver, he thinks immediately of the goods, property—even horses, in Princeton—and food and drink he can now lavish upon himself (II.vi.57). In the Penn (11v) and Amacuitlapilco (19v) plays, he is the first to begin eating at the Last Supper (II.iv.9), and in Penn he also walks off with everything that is left on the table wrapped in his cloak (12r; II.iv.24). If he took Gamaliel's tableware along with scraps of food, this would be one enactment of the thievery some Nahuatl texts attribute to him. These instances when Judas desires to increase his wealth or impolitely seizes more than his share suggest that such traits were, like social isolation, more of a threat to *altepetl* harmony than supposed possession by demons. Shared poverty was the lot of most eighteenth-century Nahuas, as it was of Jesus and his students.

Contemplating his poverty leads Judas to imagine the monetary reward he might receive from the priests. But, still torn between his devotion to Jesus and his self-concern, he backtracks and expresses confidence that Jesus will yet show him favor. Then he squashes that thought: "he favors me with nothing." Finally, he returns to his grievance about how the precious unguent was wasted on that *cihuatontli* 'wretched little woman' Magdalene. Back when the meeting with Magdalene occurred, Judas, sincerely or not, expressed concern for people beset by poverty or danger who could have been helped if the unguent had been sold (see I.vi.17). Here, he narrows his concern to himself and his fellow students, declaring that Jesus should have said "My children are poor. I will buy them something with it. Let it be sold." Elsewhere in the plays, when Jesus says "my children," this means the twelve disciples. Judas's stated desire here may not amount to the embezzlement that legend accused him of (Olko 2017), but he does want a share of what that imagined 300 pesos might have bought. With that thought, he finally throws all caution to the wind and heads off to find the priests.

The unusual length of this speech gives the audience ample time to ponder Judas's uncertainty, desperation, and isolation. In no other Nahuatl play is a character alone onstage for such a prolonged time. His speech is a kind of character study unique in Nahuatl theater. There must have been an interest in how someone could come to betray their peers and their divine leader, and the simplistic reasoning that he was bad or the devil made him do it did not suffice. Indeed, these writers reject the association preachers so often drew between the alleged sins of Indigenous people and their purported susceptibility to the devils' blandishments, for Judas could have easily been used to teach a lesson along those lines. Nor is he ever explicitly linked to Judaism, to align him with Judas's role in anti-Jewish hatred. Going to the chief priests, the *altepetl* authorities who are seeking Jesus, does not make him more overtly Jewish than other characters not labeled *Judiosmeh*. Further, he is not caricatured as a non-Indigenous outsider, like the contemporary Maya representations of Judas as both an anti-Christ and a Ladino—that is, a member of the Spanish-speaking political and economic elite (Nash 1968, 320–321; Bricker 1981, 161). If Jesus and his students are *macehualtin*, then Judas is too. The lesson is that anyone might carry such darkness in their heart.

Recall don Bernabel Bustamante, the Judas player whose untimely, drunken demise precipitated the abandonment of Passion performances in Huejotzingo—at least according to his erstwhile co-stars. He very likely delivered a version of this same soliloquy each year he performed. We may wonder if the thought of being all alone onstage, speaking these self-centered though uncertain words that culminate, finally, in the denunciation of Magdalene and the decision to betray Jesus, was part of what deterred any potential replacements for this actor.

FROM SOLIDARITY TO RUPTURE

A lot has happened at Gamaliel's (or John Mark's) house this Thursday evening: the daring host's life-risking invitation, the infusion of Jesus's body and blood into tortillas and wine, the establishing of the foot-washing ritual, Jesus's admonishments and advice to his students, Judas's deliberations and their fatal conclusion. The performers in some way—from just a Latin chant to a full enactment with raised tortilla and kneeling apostles—have relived the origin of the Eucharist with an Indigenous company. The use of tortillas brings maize, the sacred staff of Indigenous life, into the Jesus story.

Feasting and oratory should have brought this group together, strengthening their bonds and reinforcing their roles as consummate teacher, treasured students, and generous friend. But the Gospels told a different story, one with a traitor at the table, so the meal instead portends betrayal and abandonment. The contrast between Jesus's oration at II.v.12 and Judas's at II.vi.2 displays this rupture in the normal social order: Jesus speaks properly (and biblically) to an appreciative audience, but Judas misapplies the tools of Nahuatl oratory to his self-absorbed and self-addressed histrionics. Peter opens the way to this bigger rupture when Jesus, predicting his denial, exposes how empty are this apostle's attestations of fealty. In chapter 5, we will see how Peter's rash swordplay further breaches the students' solidarity with Jesus. The action of the play will now continue with, on one hand, Judas's deal making with the chief priests and, on the other, Jesus's angel-interrupted visit to the Garden of Gethsemane, which culminates in his arrest. The interlude at Gamaliel's was the calm before the coming storm of violence.

5

Violence and Anger

VIOLENCE AMONG JESUS AND HIS CIRCLE

The massive amount of anger, violence, and threatened violence displayed in the Passion plays paints Jesus's enemies as disequilibrating and dangerous personages. These words and deeds blatantly violate the ideals of respectful and moderate behavior encoded in early colonial *huehuehtlahtolli*, or models of proper speech and sociality (Sahagún 1950–1982, bk. 6; Bautista Viseo 1600; Karttunen and Lockhart 1987). From a later vantage point, the views of contemporary Nahuas also help elucidate how such behavior threatened not just Jesus himself but *altepetl* and cosmic stability. According to James M. Taggart and Alan R. Sandstrom (2011, 23), ethnographers who have conducted long-term fieldwork in, respectively, the Sierra Norte de Puebla and the Huasteca, Nahuas see social and cosmic order as fragile and easily undermined by disrespectful or aggressive behavior. For Huastecan Nahuas, a key ethical concept is *tlatlepanittaliztli* 'that which looks upon, sees, or regards things respectfully,' while "to be disrespectful or cause problems through disrespect is *axtlatlepanitta*" (Alan R. Sandstrom, personal communication, February 5, 2021). Colonial texts, including the Passion plays, express a similar sense with the idiom *ahtle ipan quitta* 'to see nothing in,' meaning 'to disrespect.' For the Sierra Nahuat, an analogous concept is *ilihuiz*, which "refers to behavior that is impulsive, excessive, and disorderly" (Taggart and Sandstrom 2011, 23). This concept is centuries old: Molina's 1571 (1992, pt. 2, 37v) dictionary defined *ilihuiz* as *sin consideracion y desuariadamente* 'without consideration and deliriously.'

https://doi.org/10.5876/9781646424511.c005

Nahua oral narratives "describe scenarios of disaster brought about by impulsive behavior, particularly of men" (Taggart and Sandstrom 2011, 23). In his analysis of the folktales told by Nacho Hernández, a storyteller from the town of Huitzilan, Taggart (1997, 196) was struck by how this master narrator consistently distanced himself from characters who embodied *ilihuiz*, in keeping with "his view of a precariously ordered cosmic and human structure that came unraveled in the past and may well do so again in the future." This interdependence between human behavior and cosmic order (or disorder) characterized Indigenous worldviews at the time of Spanish colonization and survived Christian evangelization to at least some degree. The Passion plays present a world rife with male anger, corruption, injustice, and violence—culminating in the killing of Christ: a gross inversion of the proper relationship of respect between people and divinities, even though his death is only temporary.

We saw in chapter 3 how the women characters act as a counterforce to the disorder, or *ilihuiz*, associated with male villains. Yet in three plays, Princeton and one of the cognate sections of Axochiapan and Tepalcingo, the first violent act is committed by Jesus himself. Matthew (21:12–13), Mark (11:15–17), and John (2:13–16) tell of Jesus cleansing the temple by driving out moneylenders and the merchants who sell sacrificial animals, overturning tables and, according to John, even brandishing a whip. Matthew and Mark place this event just after the triumphal entry into Jerusalem, as do the plays (I.iv.7–9), but in John it occurs early in Jesus's preaching career, just after the wedding at Cana where Jesus changes water into wine. In the plays, Jesus speaks of vendors selling unspecified wares and of cheating and mockery but makes no mention of moneylending or animals. All three scripts direct Jesus to "beat" (*huitequi*) the vendors (or "the Jews," in Axochiapan, 3r). Shortly thereafter, in Tepalcingo (5) and Axochiapan (3v), occurs the only instance when he directly attributes anger to himself, here directed toward the Jerusalem nobility (I.iv.21). In Princeton, Jesus's violence instigates the first violent actions against him: first a Pharisee, then "they," then Samuel slap him in the face (6v–7r; I.iv.9, 12, 18).[1] Given its Gospel basis, it is likely that the original model for the plays contained this scene. The scriptwriter(s) who chose to remove the scene, such that it is missing from Penn and Amacuitlapilco,[2] may have wished to avoid depicting Jesus as an angry man and a perpetrator of violent acts—however righteously motivated those might be.

The disciple Peter also commits one violent act. All four Gospels recount a moment during Jesus's arrest when one of his followers, tagged as Simon Peter in John (18:10), draws his sword and cuts off the ear of Caiaphas's servant Malchus. In Luke (22:49) this happens just after Jesus's companions have asked "Lord, shall we strike with the sword?" Then, according to Luke (22:51), Jesus "touched his ear and healed him," while in Matthew he says, "Put your sword back into its place, for all who take the sword will perish by the sword" (26:52). Jesus may then make some reference to the fulfillment of his destiny (Mark 14:50; John 18:11), noting in Matthew (26:53) that he could call on his father to send more than twelve legions of angels if he so chose.

All six plays stage this exchange, drawing on these elements from the different Gospels (and inflating the number of angels, as noted in chapter 2) and requiring a false ear that Peter appears to cut from Malchus's head and Jesus appears to stick back on, after calling on Peter to pick it up and give it to him (III.ii.26–30). Only Tlatlauhquitepec adapts Matthew's "perish by the sword" lesson (7v; III.ii.29). The swordplay and the special effect with Malchus's ear made for an attention-grabbing moment of stagecraft, which may be why all the plays retain this scene. Recall how Juan Luis Vives complained of European audiences applauding Peter's act (see chapter 1). The Nahuatl plays heighten the drama by having Malchus, a particularly obnoxious personage across the corpus, step out of his passive Gospel role. First, he orders his companions to determine who severed his ear, and then—after Jesus bestows a miraculous favor on him—he not only fails to express any gratitude but berates him and, in five of the six plays, slaps him in the face (III.ii.28–31). The Penn scriptwriter was so appalled by Malchus's behavior that his stage direction does not say simply "he will slap Christ in the face" but "And this Malchus will get right up and go slap Christ in the face just like that" (22v; III.ii.30).[3] We can note the parallel with the temple-purging scene, where Christ's one act of righteous anger instigates an immediate face-slapping response from one of the villains. While no scriptwriter prevented Peter from engaging in violence, his sword waving could be tied to his denial scene (III.vi): in drawing his sword, he has already begun to dissociate himself from Jesus and enter into a disorderly state.

As I discuss in chapter 4, Judas thoroughly dissociates himself from the circle of Jesus and his students when he separates himself from them after the Last Supper and delivers his self-addressed soliloquy (II.vi.2). Like his long and lonely speech, Judas's act of violence is self-addressed. In every play he decides, after seeing the desperate straits into which he has driven his erstwhile benefactor, that he must kill himself. He proposes two methods, making a parallel construction out of the two alternatives offered by the Bible: in Matthew (27:5), Judas "went and hanged himself," while in Acts (1:18), "falling headlong he burst open in the middle and all his bowels gushed out." Tlatlauhquitepec's Judas contemplates only hanging (10v), but the other five plays pair the verb *(mo)tepexihui* 'to hurl oneself off a precipice' with *(mo)piloa* 'to hang oneself.' The former term is half of a Nahuatl metaphor for a dangerously peripheral or liminal—though not necessarily evil or immoral—condition. Sixteenth-century Christian preachers adopted this figure of speech as a metaphor for sin, based on an analogy with "falling" into sin or into hell (Brylak 2019; Burkhart 1989, 62). Normally, *(mo)tepexihui* would be paired with *(mo)atoyahuia* 'to throw oneself into a torrent.' Even without its partner, however, *(mo)tepexihui* gives Nahua listeners insight into Judas's chaotic state of mind.

An intention to hang oneself certainly might also suggest a disordered mind. For the Roman Catholic Church, suicide was a mortal sin like the taking of any human life; as the suicide surrendered any opportunity to do penance for this sin and secure God's forgiveness, the act signaled a lack of faith and also sent the person's soul to hell. How one viewed violent acts of self-harm would affect how one evaluated Judas's desperate act.

There is no evidence that suicide bore any stigma in Indigenous morality apart from Christian influence. Indigenous histories told a few stories of warriors and rulers or larger groups who killed themselves rather than submit to defeat or humiliation, typically by jumping from a height (Johansson 2014, 85–92). For example, the Tlaxcalteca warrior Tlahuicole reportedly either leaped off the Tlatelolco pyramid (Durán 1994, 448; Alvarado Tezozomoc 1975, 645) or chose death on the gladiatorial stone in Tenochtitlan (Muñoz Camargo 1966, 125–128) rather than return ashamed to Tlaxcala.[4] Moquihuix, the last ruler of independent Tlatelolco, leaped to his death from his *altepetl*'s main temple pyramid when Tenochtitlan's army defeated his own—according to the Codex Mendoza (Berdan and Anawalt 1992, vol. 1, 33; vol. 3, 9v–10r) and one of Chimalpahin's chronicles (Chimalpahin Quauhtlehuanitzin 1997, vol. 2, 51), though other accounts say he was killed by the Tenochca (e.g., Durán 1994, 260). Another famous man said to have jumped to his death is Tlacahuepan, brother of Moteuczoma Ilhuicamina, after his capture by the Chalca (Codex Ramírez, in Alvarado Tezozomoc 1975, 64–65; Tovar n.d., 107r).

A similar—though apparently non-fatal—plunge occurred in May 1565. Don Luis Santa María Cipac, the last governor of Tenochtitlan from the Mexica ethnic group, faced a revolt against his rule when he failed to get Spanish tribute demands decreased. The uprising culminated in an attack on his palace, which he had to escape with the help of Spanish guards. Several months later, apparently still in a state of despair, don Luis went to the roof of his palace and spent the night brandishing his sword and making battle cries. According to the *Anales de Juan Bautista*, he fell from his roof (Reyes García 2001, 318–319; Sousa 2017, 285).[5]

Suicide by hanging had precedents in Nahua chronicles—though they were written after the Passion story had been introduced. The Toltec ruler Huemac, fleeing Tula after the fall of that great *altepetl*, reportedly hanged himself in a cave at Chapultepec in the year 1070 (Bierhorst 1998, 42). Some sources said the Mexica ruler Chimalpopoca hanged himself after his Tepanec overlord, Maxtla, captured him and confined him in a cage; however, accounts of Chimalpopoca's death vary and other scenarios—especially a coup engineered by his uncle and successor, Itzcoatl—seem more likely (Conrad and Demarest 1984, 31–32).

The only other suicide in Nahuatl theater is that of King Archelaus in *The Destruction of Jerusalem* (Sell and Burkhart 2009, 256–267; Burkhart 2010). This fictional monarch[6] kills himself by falling on his sword—stage directions detail the process—after Emperor Vespasian refuses to make peace and end the ruinous siege of Jerusalem. The men who report his death to Pilate say he killed himself out of sadness (*omotlaocolmictih*). Although the play is adapted from a Spanish source, this defeated ruler's choice is consistent with the stories of Indigenous heroes who would rather die than live with dishonor. A sin-and-forgiveness view, in contrast, occurs in *The Animal Prophet and the Fortunate Patricide*, a play about Saint Julian the Hospitaler that Bartolomé de Alva adapted from a Spanish play in 1640. Julian momentarily despairs that God will not forgive his inadvertent murder of his parents and aims his dripping dagger at his own body, but his wife stops him and he regains his faith in God's mercy (Sell, Burkhart, and Wright 2008, 260–263).

While Judas is treated as a betrayer and scoundrel, his choice to destroy himself could read as a reaction not to an internal sense of sin but to his loser status, shame over his error, and his humiliation by the priests from whom he sought favor. Nahuas might not see his act as inherently ignoble. As with his soliloquy, at his death he is not characterized as inordinately evil or demonic.

Every play's Judas announces his self-destructive intention, but only Amacuitlapilco's is told how to act it out. The scriptwriter directed: "Then Judas will go beside a tree. He will go to hang himself with a rope" (38r; III.viii.16).[7] Since this writer consistently provides the most extensive and detailed stage directions in the corpus, the lack of such instructions in other plays need not indicate that their Judases would not act out a death scene for audience members to contemplate. And the actor could evoke different emotional reactions by the way he played the scene. In contrast to the morally neutral or morally ambiguous Nahua staging, the Villasinta Passion brings Lucifer onstage to claim Judas's soul and then, after the suicide, shows both of them arriving in hell (Lozano Prieto 1985, 93–94).

FEAR AND LOATHING IN JERUSALEM

Villainy against Jesus follows divisions of rank, which in part mirror those of the Gospels. However, the Jewish leaders' plot to kill Jesus, staged in scenes II.i and II.ii, receives only passing treatment in the Gospel accounts of Holy Week. Luke (22:2) gives "for they feared the people" as a motivation. In John (12:19), the Pharisees, upon seeing the throngs who attend Jesus's triumphal entry to their city, remark, "You see that you can do nothing; look, the world has gone after him," attributing his popularity to the resurrection of Lazarus.

In the plays, elite characters justify their worry and anger in terms of the threat they think Jesus poses to their rule and their honor. They fear that the *macehualtin* who follow this son of a mere carpenter (II.i.4) will cease to obey them, which is both an immediate and—should Rome decide to impose a more direct form of colonial rule—a long-term threat. Herod (IV.ii.13) and Pilate (V.iv.14, 21) complain of the headaches Jesus causes them. But with only two exceptions, high-status characters do not themselves physically hurt Christ. Samuel's Princeton face slap was noted above. Samuel, a member of the Jerusalem council, is a non-biblical character who is frequently on the scene making observations and suggestions, but he is not of high enough rank to issue decrees. He has another disorderly moment when Judas rejects Annas's initial offer to Judas of twenty pieces of silver—an amount Samuel speculates may or may not be enough. Amacuitlapilco (27v), Axochiapan (20v), and Penn (19v) agree that Samuel is to jump up and strike the table; Amacuitlapilco adds that the actor is to look angry (II.vi.40).

That table received a previous smack from Caiaphas when he angrily threw Joseph and Nicodemus out of the council meeting (II.i.26). But Caiaphas's angriest moment comes later and traces to Matthew 26:65 (or Mark 14:63–64). After Jesus tells him "hereafter you will see the Son of man seated at the right hand of Power and coming on the clouds of heaven," Caiaphas tears his robes (Latin *vestimenta*) and declares this utterance to be blasphemy. Every scriptwriter puts some version of this cryptic speech into Christ's mouth—with "Son of man" becoming "maiden's[8] child" or, in Penn (24r), "God's child"[9]—and does his best to convey the cloud comment or else leaves it out (III.iv.19). Every Caiaphas then tears his clothing, but only Tlatlauhquitepec (8v) lets the moment pass without further elaboration. Penn (24r) and Princeton (31r) direct the choir to chant the "*Blasphemavit*" verse from (presumably) Navarro's Saint Matthew Passion. In the biblical context, Caiaphas's rending of his garment signaled grief over what he considered a grave offense to God (Brown 1994, vol. 1, 517–518), but scriptwriters emphasize disordered anger. In Tepalcingo (78), after Caiaphas tears his cloak (an Indigenous *tilmahtli*), an unspecified "they" slap Christ in the face. Princeton has Caiaphas leap up, be visibly angry, and tear his clothing suddenly (31r). Penn's Caiaphas is also supposed to be visibly angry and is to "rip up his *tilmahtli* and jump up and down on it" (24r). Amacuitlapilco's scriptwriter has Caiaphas leap up and tear his clothing in rage, and he wants to be sure the audience can see this: "it will be obvious in front of people" (34v). Axochiapan does the others one better by staging the second instance where an elite character physically attacks Christ: Caiaphas hits him in the face with his torn *tilmahtli* (25r; these reactions are partially pooled in III.iv.20).

Caiaphas's over-the-top anger echoes that of another Jewish ruler familiar in Nahuatl theater: the King Herod of the Epiphany plays, which staged the Three

Kings' visit to Jerusalem and Bethlehem. As a historical figure, this Herod represents Herod Archelaus; it is his brother Herod Antipas who ruled at the time of Jesus's death. Both were sons of Herod the Great. Herod in the Passion plays is historically confused when he recalls how his father, rather than his brother, once sought in vain to kill the infant Jesus (IV.ii.4). In the Epiphany plays, Herod insults and rages at the Jewish priests who tell him of Jesus's prophesied birth and birthplace. In one play he orders the massacre of all the children in the *altepetl* of Judea, and this is enacted onstage, with Herod's henchmen reporting back that they have destroyed all the babies. Early colonial Nahua histories ascribed inordinate anger to Moteuczoma as well, transforming the Mexica emperor into a scapegoat for the loss of empire and autonomy. The theatrical Herod's behavior resonated with that tradition.[10] Good rulers, then, do not make angry displays like Caiaphas's poor treatment of his clothing.

Pontius Pilate, the Roman governor of Judea, does not fear or loathe Jesus; rather, he fears his rowdy subjects who demand that he sentence Jesus to death and also the threat that Emperor Tiberius might get mad at him. He is reluctant to harm Jesus and repeatedly offers his opinion that Jesus is without *tlahtlacolli* 'something damaged,' the Nahuatl word used for sin or misdeed. While in all plays he orders the flagellation, sometimes calling for considerable brutality, his hope is nevertheless that this punishment will satisfy Christ's accusers and thus save his life. This soft portrayal of Pilate is consistent with the Gospels, especially those of Matthew and John, but at odds with his actual career: Pilate oversaw the crucifixion of hundreds of Jewish people without proper trial, resulting in his recall to Rome in the year 36 (Bishops' Committee 1988, 36). The soft portrayal is also at odds with the Roman use of flagellation as a customary prelude to crucifixion, not an alternative punishment available to clement judges (Hourihane 2009, 272–274).

The shorter versions of the death sentence, in the Axochiapan and Tepalcingo plays, are consistent with this softer view of Pilate, with Pilate's own aggression limited to the flagellation. But the scriptwriters who opted to use a version of the sixteenth-century death warrant from L'Aquila (see chapter 2) present a Pilate who is much more belligerent—and more historically accurate, even though the death warrant was fake. In these longer death sentences (IV.iv.28), Pilate does not merely grant his subjects permission to crucify Jesus. He lays out the whole scenario, from what the condemned man will wear to how he is to be marched through the streets while carrying the cross to how and where the crucifixion will be carried out. He asserts his total authority over the matter. While the full-scale death warrant distributes blame more evenly between the Judeans and their Roman colonial overlords, its preview of Christ's upcoming torments acts, like the recap John offers to the women in Bethany (V.i.15), to increase the total amount of violence either staged or spoken of. Scriptwriters who chose this extended warrant also make the Roman colonial government—easily compared to Spain's rule of their own lands—fully culpable in Christ's death.

In the Nahuatl plays, the Jewish leaders and their henchmen frequently characterize Christ's effect on their subjects as *tetlapololtia*. This verb derives from *poloa* 'to perish' or 'to be destroyed'; with the indefinite object prefix *tla-*, it has the sense of "to lose one's senses or to make errors" (Karttunen 1983, 202). The causative form *tlapololtia*, with the indefinite personal prefix *te-*, then, means to cause other people to lose their judgment or become confused.[11] Jesus does this so much that his enemies call him the *tetlapololtiani*, or one who habitually has this effect on people. I use the verb "bewilder" and the noun "bewilderer" to translate these terms, intending to capture not just the sense of confusion but also that of leading astray or luring off into the wilds, from the archaic English verb "wilder." Alternative English verbs include "derange," "confuse," "perturb," "disconcert," or "disquiet." The leaders of Jerusalem, fearing that the law of Moses and their own hegemony are being undermined, seek to crush dissent by making this perturbation a capital crime. Christ turns the term back at the priests on one occasion (I.iv.14) and also tells his students that they will enter this altered state when they abandon him after his arrest, scattering like sheep (II.v.16–17). But "bewilder" and "bewilderer" are overwhelmingly applied to Christ, thirty times in the composite play.

Nahuatl doctrinal texts often apply this verb to the devils' machinations aimed at leading Christians astray. For some examples we can draw on another theatrical genre, the Nahuatl morality plays. In the play about the childless noblewoman who is condemned to the place of the dead, demons report to their master, Lucifer, about how well they are corrupting the people of earth. One says "the things we do to bewilder people are not few in number," while another reports, "I go in and immerse myself among the people everywhere, so that I bewilder them about any sensible speech that I hear from them" (Sell and Burkhart 2009, 318–319). In the play *Souls and Testamentary Executors*, another subsidiary devil assures Lucifer that he and his colleague will make certain that a dead man's relatives squander his estate: "Do not worry, for we are going right now in order to bewilder them" (Sell and Burkhart 2004, 167). Guardian Angel in *The Merchant*, urging the title character toward a proper deathbed confession, says: "do not believe your enemy the human horned owl, for he just wants to mock you, wants to bewilder you, so that you will just die in your sins, so that he will take you to the place of the dead. Don't you see that he is a bewilderer, a deceiver, one who ambushes people? He has bewildered innumerable people" (Sell and Burkhart 2009, 262–263). Another angel, in the play *Don Rafael*, reassures people that the angels "are here to help you, so they [the demons] won't bewilder you," but in the next scene a demon laughs at the expense of the countless people who are so bewildered (the verb is reflexive here) that they will flub their Lenten confession and thus become his vassals (348–349).

Guardian Angel pairs "bewilderer" with "deceiver" in reference to the devil, as do, for example, the confraternity ordinances published by Molina in 1552 (Sell 2002, 84). "Deceiver" is, thus, another devil-linked word with which the Passion plays disproportionately malign Christ. On one occasion he calls the Jews "deceivers," and a Pharisee subsequently comments on this slur (I.iv.8, II.i.6). But his enemies refer to him as deceiving or a deceiver twenty-two times in the composite play. The verb here is *ixcuepa*, from *ixtli* 'face' and *cuepa* 'turn.' As a reflexive verb it means to lose one's way, as if turning one's face to the wrong path. One who does this to others makes them lose their way. Molina (1992, pt. 2, 45r) defines *ixcuepa* as *embaucar o engañar a otro* 'delude or deceive another.' In the plays, the verb nearly always appears as *teixcuepani*, Jesus being someone who habitually deceives others. And both "bewilder" and "deceive" carry a sense of disorientation, of deflecting people onto paths of delusion, the danger being not so much moral evil as chaos or disorder.

Another devil-associated word is distributed a bit more broadly in the Passions. Princeton's Jesus uses it for Lucifer himself (7v, 24v; I.iv.16), but the majority of its occurrences denigrate Jesus instead: twenty-nine of forty-six cases in the composite play. This is *tlahueliloc*, which I render, inadequately but succinctly, as "scoundrel." It denotes a thoroughly despicable and odious person who arouses fury in others, as well as possibly implying a tinge of madness. Agnieszka Brylak (2021) has contributed a thorough analysis of this term. It most likely derives from the verb *tlahuelia*, which Molina's dictionary glosses as "to have anger and hatred for another" and which in turn derives from the noun *tlahuelli* 'indignation, anger, or fury of one who is furious and full of blind rage'[12] (Molina 1992, pt. 2, 144r, 144v). This is anger to the point of derangement, suggesting a conceptual affinity with "bewilder" and "deceive." Brylak suggests that the preterit patientive form *tlahueliloc*—referring to someone who is the recipient of such distaste—could be a colonial coinage. Brylak's (2021, 355) examples display a broad range of usages that "oscillated between sinfulness and foolishness," with "negative connotations involving wrath, evil, hatred, wickedness, sinfulness, and folly." She notes the close association between the latter two concepts in Early Modern Europe, which may account for the element of foolishness or insanity associated with the Nahuatl term—for example, in Molina's (1992, pt. 1, 78v) Spanish-to-Nahuatl glosses for *locura* 'madness' as *tlauelilocayotl* and of *loco de atar* 'raving mad' as *tlaueliloc*. *Tlahueliloc* provided colonial moralists with a stronger word for the wickedness vital to Christian moral dualism than Nahuatl's bland *ahcualli* 'not good.' While sinners or anyone depicted as a villain could receive this epithet, it could also refer to the devil—whether used by itself, as Judas does in II.vi.2, or paired with another demonic epithet, as where Jesus threatens to cast the leaders of Jerusalem "into the hands of the scoundrel Lucifer" (I.iv.16).[13] *Tlahueliloc* retains this association with the devil for contemporary Nahuas (Abelardo de la Cruz de la Cruz, annotation on the Amacuitlapilco play).[14]

The chief priests and other tormentors of Jesus never associate him directly with the devil (*diablo* or *demonio*), or human horned owl (*tlacatecolotl*), as such beings were called in Nahuatl (see Burkhart 1989, 40–42). This is not the case in the Spanish plays, where, for example, a guard in Cuaderno 1 (215v) says that Jesus "is a very great sorcerer who has a pact with the demons."[15] But the words with which the Nahuatl-speaking leaders vent their fear and hatred suggest that as a scoundrel who bewilders and deceives, he is doing a devil's work. And since they often refer to his followers as *macehualtin*, connoting Indigenous people, their words also echo with the doctrinal discourses that accused New Spain's *macehualtin* of being especially susceptible to demonic "bewilderment." Since the priests are wrong and the *macehualtin*—who include Jesus—are right, these accusations ring hollow and may play as a critique of colonial discourse, inverting the categories of who is bewildered and who the scoundrels are.

VIOLENT HENCHMEN

While angry Caiaphas, peevish Herod, and ultimately, despite his misgivings, weak-willed Pontius Pilate order acts of mockery and violence to be carried out against Jesus, a bevy of lower-status characters does almost all of the actual dirty work. However much the actors may have striven to feign their aggression and minimize the Jesus actor's discomfort, these men had to speak in hateful tones and at least appear to slap, shove, knock down, tie up, spit on, drag, hair-pull, beard-tear, whip, beat with a stick, crown with thorns, crucify, and stab a man from their *altepetl*—all while he was embodying Jesus Christ. Nahua performers, thus, had to act out many of the graphic abuses with which the authors of European Passion literature slaked devotees' thirst for imagined agony.

However much later literature played them up, some of these torments are drawn from the Gospels and necessary to the story. Even some of the minor acts of violence occur in the Bible. For example, the exchange at III.iii.7–10 comes from John 18:22–23, with Malchus taking the part of John's anonymous "officer" and adding a rude retort to Jesus's comment. Similarly, the mocking of blindfolded Jesus at III.iv.25–27 builds on Luke 22:63–65, where a single taunter asks "who is it that struck you?" But multiple taunters speak and mention multiple offenses: face spitting, face slapping, kicking, and dragging by the hair. As in the Passion literature that mined the Hebrew Bible for violent passages to apply to the Passion, verbal and physical abuse proliferates well beyond direct Gospel models, heightening the general level of chaos and disturbance.

Apart from Malchus, the perpetrators of violence generally lack names. They are led by Leader (Teyacanqui), captain of the Jerusalem soldiers; in Princeton he retains the Spanish title Capitán, which he may have had in a Spanish model text. Centurion, a character in all plays except Penn, often acts in concert with Leader and, despite his Roman title, seems to have migrated from Pontius Pilate's service to the chief priests' retinue. However, he may have retained his Roman trappings. Edward Osowski (2010, 173–174) found that eighteenth-century Nahuas were fond of dressing up as Roman centurions to participate in Holy Week processions of *armados* 'armed men,' with breastplates, helmets, weapons, and sometimes horses. One of their activities was to accompany in procession and then stand guard over the statue of the dead Christ. Not surprisingly, these bands of armed Indigenous men parading through the streets made authorities nervous, and bans were attempted. In at least one instance, on Good Friday in 1799, some faux centurions did turn violent, rioting and attacking their local priest with their swords and lances.[16]

Beneath Leader and Centurion rank the *Judiomeh* or *Judiosmeh* 'Jews,' who may speak in unison or as individually numbered but interchangeable personae. In Tlatlauhquitepec, only First Jew has his own lines. Tepalcingo sends four individual Jews onto the stage, giving two of them a distinguishing costume element: First Jew, Second Jew, Jew with a Long Beard, and Second Jew with a Long Beard. Penn has First, Second, and Third Jew; while Amacuitlapilco, Axochiapan, and Princeton require Fourth Jew as well. Jews are, then, generic bad guys who need no further designation. These are their names in the script, but they are never addressed as such: that is, no one says "First Jew, come here" or the like. The words "Jew" and "Jews" thus appear much more frequently in the stage directions and character names than in the dialogue (ninety-five times compared to forty-eight times in the composite play).

Jews numbered one through six appear in the Nahuatl Epiphany play "The Star Sign" and in the play about Saint Helen and the discovery of the True Cross (Sell and Burkhart 2009, 87–103, 305). These cast members stand in for the portion of Jerusalem's populace not in Jesus's camp, proliferating as needed to provide enough individual speakers for any play's dialogue. Like Mary's companion women, their ranks could have been augmented by non-speaking extras. These numbered individuals are less of a feature in the Inquisition file's corpus of Spanish plays, where only one play, Cuaderno 1, splits Jesus's harassers into Jews numbered one through five. This playwright may be following the example of Nahua practice.

One named perpetrator of violence appears only in the Penn play (36v, 37v–38r, 39v). This nasty fellow is Flanquino, who enters the story just in time to help execute

Pilate's death sentence. He issues the order to have Christ dressed again in his own clothing and to carry the cross on his shoulder (V.ii.7), hurries him along with words appropriate to Leader or any numbered Jew (V.ii.24), and initiates the crucifixion process (V.iii.3). Flanquino stepped out of the L'Aquila death warrant and into at least this one line of Passion script transmission. None of the death sentences in the Nahuatl plays (IV.iv.28) includes the preamble that circulated along with Pilate's alleged declaration. This preamble lists Roman and Judean officials, some real and some imaginary, holding office at the time of Jesus's death. One of these is a Roman centurion called Joacchim Centurione in Judge Camillo Borello's 1588 Italian version (in Berliner 2003, 51), Tranquino Centurio in Hieronymite friar Rodrigo de Yepes's 1583 Spanish translation (87v), and Franchino Centurión in Archbishop Guerra's eighteenth-century Spanish version (n.d., 286r). The Spanish-language death sentence from Ozumba, preserved as a loose sheet in the Inquisition case, names Flanquino Centtulo, Nahuatlizing his name and garbling his title.[17] There is no Flanquino character in the Spanish plays. Nahua scriptwriters who adapted versions of the full-length death warrant into Nahuatl, such as those that survive in the Penn and Princeton Passions, must have had access to the preamble in some cases; one of them introduced Flanquino into his play, probably intending him to represent and be costumed as a Roman soldier.

When Jesus's enemies clamor for his crucifixion, refusing Pilate's suggestion that they grant clemency to Jesus and put the prisoner Barrabas to death instead, most of these demands are voiced by the various anonymous henchmen. But second-tier council members participate as well, most typically Simeon[18] and Samuel (e.g., IV.iii.4, IV.iii.8); in most of the plays, Samuel also joins the party that visits Herod (IV.ii.17, 19). One such figure always takes responsibility for the burden of guilt once Pilate has washed his hands to display his own innocence of Christ's blood. This is the passage in Matthew (27:25) when "all the people" say "His blood be on us and on our children"—a verse long deployed in anti-Jewish propaganda to promote collective guilt for Jesus's death. The three Spanish-language plays that include the line hew closely to Matthew: "they all" say, simply, "May his blood fall on us and on our children."[19] All five Nahuatl versions[20] are more elaborate, all predict future violence and punishment, and all feature at least one Nahuatl doublet or other traditional metaphor (IV.iv.24). In three cases the speaker is Simeon, in Tepalcingo he is Samuel, and in Princeton he is Joseph—in this play Joseph does not distinguish himself from the other leaders by supporting Jesus.[21] Four of the speakers begin with the polite acknowledgment "You have shown us favor, O ruler." In all cases the speaker invites "the wrath, the anger" (*zomalli cualantli*) to come onto us. In two cases he opts that "we bear [the sin] on our backs,"[22] turning to the present purpose an old image for the duties of leadership: rulers carry their subjects on their backs like a burden—a metaphor Simeon employs in II.i.17 (Sahagún 1950–1982, bk. 6, 242; Karttunen and Lockhart 1987, 54). Tepalcingo (106) and Penn (32r) predict future punishments by invoking the doublet "stones, sticks" (*tetl cuahuitl*), modified by "all" (*ixquich*) in Tepalcingo. All speakers appoint not just "us" and "our children" but also "our grandchildren" to pay the penalty, passing it down through the generations. The corresponding speech in the model Nahuatl play likely contained all of these elements, turning into elegant Nahuatl some Spanish text that played up this foundational anti-Semitic line and thus bequeathed to generations of future performers its invitation to hatred.

The violent henchmen have ethnographic analogs in the various ritual clowns that populate Carnival and Easter festivals in Mesoamerican communities. As Victoria Reiffler Bricker demonstrates (1973), these can represent monkeys, Pharisees, Jews, demons, Roman soldiers, Judases, French soldiers, conquistadors, contemporary non-Indigenous people (Ladinos), and other identities—often multiple ones at the same time. In part of Chamula's year-end Carnival festival, a group of the monkeys/ Jews/demons acts out an "orgy of drunkenness and violence, blindly quarreling with friend and enemy alike and beating them with their whips" (126). Inhibitions are abandoned; forces of disorder are let loose but only temporarily, until the new year begins and the order represented by the sun/Christ is reestablished (cf. Gossen 1998, chapter 5). For contemporary Sierra Nahuat as well, the sun creates moral order (Taggart 1983). The actors who played bad men in the Passion plays may have likewise seen their roles as both cathartic and necessary for the enactment of interstitial disorder, though the extent to which people found humor in their mayhem remains unclear.

The story of Huejotzingo's Judas actor don Bernabel Bustamante (see chapter 1) is not the only evidence that playing villains could be risky, if we include Nahua ethnographic data. The performers Luis Reyes García interviewed in Ixcatepec customarily took a number of palliative actions. Carnival dancers told him they had to perform the same role for either seven or fourteen consecutive years. Otherwise, they would suffer after death (Reyes García 1960, 52–53). They also depended on a ritual called *moixtomah* 'they untie themselves,' carried out at the end of the festivities, to free themselves from the evil they acquired by impersonating ancestors or demons (68–69). The "Jews" and "Pharisees" of Holy Week had their own purification rite: the burning of an effigy made of trash and called Xolcoch. This practice liberated them from the guilt of having played these characters while also representing the victory of the solar Christ over the ancestors, Jews, and devils (80–81, 84).[23]

THE FLAGELLATION

When the play began, the actor portraying Jesus signaled his identity with his costume (long robes and likely a long-haired wig and false beard) as well as his words and actions. As the play moves on, his body undergoes additional alterations that identify him with Christ. The stage blood he pretends to sweat in the Garden of Gethsemane scene may remain on his skin or clothing (III.i.12, 15; V.i.15). The chains used in the arrest may also continue to bind him or hang around his neck (III.ii.25; see figures 2.3, 5.2), and the slamming on the ground and other blows may dirty his robes and disarrange his hair and beard. But the flagellation begins a more brutal and intensive process of marking and investiture that will complete his conversion into an embodiment of Christ.

Speaking of the transformation of human beings into *teixiptlahuan*, the "localized embodiments" of gods in pre-Columbian Nahua rites such as the festival of Toxcatl, Molly Bassett (2014, 208) describes the "elaborate process of ritual manufacture and education that resulted in the localized embodiment looking and being (like) the god" (cf. Bassett 2015). Simply putting on the skin of an executed captive did not suffice to apotheosize the *teixiptlah* into, in the Toxcatl case, the deity Tezcatlipoca. By an analogous process, the Jesus actor comes increasingly to resemble familiar Passion-related images of Christ as his body attains, first, the marks of flagellation and, second, the material accouterments that—again following Bassett's (2015, 135–136) analysis of pre-Columbian gods—may partially constitute the god's identity as components in his "distributed personhood." That is, items such as the cross and the crown of thorns would be seen as parts of the assemblage that constituted Christ, containing his "personhood" even if separated from his human body.

Only one of the Gospels mentions the flagellation of Christ, and only in passing. John (19:1) says simply, "Then Pilate took Jesus and scourged (*flagellavit*) him"; the idea that he was tied to a column developed later, in the liturgy (Sticca 1970, 97). In Luke (23:16) Pilate, unpersuaded of Jesus's guilt, says, "I will therefore chastise (or, depending on the translation, punish) him and release him"; the Vulgate Bible here, however, uses not the verb *castigare* 'to punish' but rather *emendare* 'to emend, reform, correct,' which need not imply any act of violence. Yet the flagellation became one of the focal points in the Passion story. Late medieval Passion literature in Europe embroidered on this episode more than on any other one of Christ's ordeals (Marrow 1979, 134). It became a horrific ritual that could involve rotating teams of whip wielders, different kinds of whips, and the repositioning of Christ's body as many as seven times so it could be completely covered with lashings—which could continue after Christ was untied and collapsed on the ground (48–49; Marrow 2008, 45–47). This thoroughness was given biblical precedent through a literal application of, among other passages, Isaiah 1:6: "From the sole of the foot even to the head, there is no soundness in it, but bruises and sores and bleeding wounds" (Marrow 1979, 47; Marrow 2008, 46). Jesus seems to allude to this passage when speaking to his mother at I.viii.21. Even though Pilate often supervises, the torturers were almost always depicted as Jews rather than as Roman soldiers, diverting the blame into anti-Jewish channels (Hourihane 2009, 214).

As mentioned in chapter 1, Christ's torment under Pontius Pilate—that is, his flagellation—receives equal billing with the crucifixion in basic catechetical texts. Figure 5.1 shows the Roman prelate presiding over this event, its bloodiness made visible in the red stripes on Christ's body, in don Lucas Mateo's 1714 pictorial catechism from Tizayuca. Where the rosary devotion takes the flagellation as an object for prayer and contemplation, it attributes the action not to Pilate but to medieval Christians' usual suspects: "the Jews." In fray Domingo de la Anunciación's (1565, 77v–77r; Burkhart 2001, 125) Nahuatl rosary the line reads, "Then we will remember how the Jews seized our lord Jesus Christ, and they flogged him at the column." The devotee's prayer is to include: "It was very frightening, how they flogged you at the column." Nahuatl sermons could be very graphic, as where fray Juan de la Anunciación (1577, 60v) refers to Christ's body being "torn up everywhere" and his ribs being visible.

Lorenzo, the Nahua author of the "Passio domini nr̄i Jesu Christi," also assigns graphically violent orders to Pilate, although delivered with reverential forms. The floggers "are not to just flay him all over with ropes. They are to really tear him up all over his back, his delicate body, with thorny sticks, with chains." The procedure leaves Christ's bones exposed and his blood flowing so much that it was "like a spring of blood, like a lake of blood" ("Passio domini nr̄i Jesu Christi" 1617, 333v, 334v).[24]

The somatic sensations and effects of flogging were not alien to colonial Nahua experience. As this was the Passion ordeal with which Indigenous people could most readily identify, it is worthwhile to consider how flogging figured in *altepetl* life before we track it through the plays. The Christian practice of self-flagellation, widely propagated and practiced in early colonial Mexico (Larkin 2004, 498–499), spread to some Nahuas, who flogged themselves during Holy Week—whether in church or while marching in processions (Motolinia 1979, 55–56; Mendieta 1980, 436–437). Such activity was associated especially with Indigenous religious confraternities devoted to Holy Week topics (Webster 1997a, 10). In the murals at Huejotzingo, some of the robed confraternity members marching in the procession are flagellants (16; see Webster's figures 1 and 3). The Archdiocese of Mexico's Third Provincial Council, in 1585, banned women from flagellating themselves in processions, but it is unclear if Indigenous women's practices were part of what motivated this regulatory endeavor (*Concilio III provincial mexicano* 1870, 311). Paired with

Figure 5.1. Christ stands tied to the column, his body already whipped. The caption, from the Apostles' Creed, reads "for our sake he suffered, by command of Pontius Pilate"; the Roman prelate is seated to the right. Pictorial catechism made by don Lucas Mateo, notary of Tizayuca, Hidalgo, in 1714. British Museum, Egerton manuscript 2898, f. 15r. © The Trustees of the British Museum.

Lenten fasting, self-flagellation loosely adapted into an at least nominally Christian context practices of abstinence and bloodletting that had long been modes of achieving not atonement for sin but merit with the gods through manipulation of the body. Such acts were *tlamahcehualiztli* 'meriting things,' a term that was applied to Christian penitential practices in general but which may have retained something of its more transactional sense.

Apart from voluntary imitations of Christ's suffering, whipping—not a pre-Columbian sanction—was a punishment introduced by secular and religious authorities early in the colonial era. Thus, this was one way Indigenous people felt the force of colonial rule on their own bodies, whether the lashes were administered by priests, courts, or their own *altepetl* authorities.[25] Whipping was sometimes paired with head shaving, a punishment that did date to pre-Columbian times and which people apparently found particularly insulting (Pardo 2006, 86, 92–93).

A list of royal ordinances disseminated by Viceroy Antonio de Mendoza in 1546 and translated into Nahuatl reveals how flogging, as well as head shaving, was codified early on in the orders given to Indigenous *altepetl* officials (Sell and Kellogg 1997). While particularly serious or second offenses often entailed jailing the offender or taking them to court, many first offenses could be handled locally with whipping, sometimes supplemented by head shaving and/or confinement in stocks in the marketplace. Where the ordinances specify a number of lashes, it is always one hundred. To give a sense of how standard a practice this was and the many causes for which Nahuas might be obliged to involuntarily imitate Christ in this fashion, I list the offenses for which the punishment includes flogging: making offerings to the old gods, trying to hold office without being baptized, refusing to participate in sacramental confession, refusing to give up lovers or taking a lover when married, bigamy (both partners), non-attendance at Mass or catechism class, drunkenness, practicing divination or shamanic healing, obliging someone who is not sick to take a sweat bath, bathing naked in front of others, not kneeling when the church bells ring the Ave Maria, theft, playing the old gambling game (*patolli*) or ballgame (*ollamaliztli*), selling adulterated cacao, cross-dressing, sexual acts between women, singing songs of the old gods, or practicing certain old customs with one's children: giving them old-style names, body piercings, boys' hairstyles, or girls' face paint (352–363). It is doubtful that these regulations were followed to the letter.[26]

Osvaldo Pardo (2006, 83–84) discusses an interesting passage that appears in the "Description of the Archdiocese of Mexico," a report submitted to the Council of the Indies (García Pimentel 1897). Alonso Fernández de Sigura, the archdiocese's official in charge of Indigenous affairs (*provisor de los indios*), writing in 1569 about one of the Indigenous sectors of colonial Tenochtitlan, expressed an observation he claimed was backed up by trustworthy clergymen and by mestizos—who, he notes, have more communication with Indigenous people. He advised the council that "they no longer consider it an affront to be whipped or shorn as a penitence and punishment; rather, they are more highly esteemed and honored for it, and he who has been punished in this way the most times is held among them as the most valiant and courageous, and so as a punishment and correction for them it would be better to use some other punishment that they fear more" (279). Although we cannot assume that this counter-hegemonic attitude was widespread or long-lasting, it does accord with churchmen's general frustration over the limited impact of their preaching about sin, guilt, and damnation. And it is consistent with the admiration passional devotions accorded to Jesus for toughing out his own flogging.

Long a matter of controversy was priests' authority to deliver floggings and other castigations on Indigenous people with their own hands. Early on, the Franciscans condoned whipping even children for not knowing their catechism lessons (Hanks 2010, 64). A royal decree of 1560 forbade Mendicant friars from such acts, but priests were sometimes accused of violating this rule (Pardo 2006, 86–88). The standard instruction manual parish priests used during the late seventeenth and eighteenth centuries condoned the use of the whip for a series of offenses, regarding it as "key to Indian devotion, decency, and good order" (Taylor 1996, 216). William B. Taylor finds that Indigenous parishioners did not object strongly to whippings when applied in moderation and in response to actual lapses in such long-standing religious obligations as attending Mass, memorizing doctrine, or confessing; apparently, they had accepted that these were legitimate expectations. What they protested were unfounded, excessive, or demeaning floggings, especially if a woman was humiliated or the alleged offense was a matter of dispute—such as Indigenous peoples' obligation to pay clerical fees or provide priests with unpaid labor. In contrast to the hundred-lash prescriptions noted above, these clerical whippings ranged up to twenty-five lashes, with two or three administered for minor offenses (217–219).

This priestly prerogative came under dispute again in the 1760s, during the same era that the Passion plays were viewed with increased suspicion. We can see the same rationalizing discomfort with somatic excess at work in this shift, and the same archbishops—Rubio y Salinas and Lorenzana—were involved. They and their like-minded colleagues fomented an image of the parish priest as a refined, loving, and virtuous man who leads his flock with acts of kindness, good examples, and affection, not "the whip and the frown" (Taylor 1996, 216). Priests out in the Indigenous parishes were ill-disposed to change their behavior or their views of Indigenous people as recalcitrant cowards who required an occasional whipping to keep them in some semblance of Christian, civilized order (216–217).

As we might expect due to its somatic and performative nature, self-flagellation also earned the opprobrium of the reform-minded bishops. The Fourth Mexican Provincial Council, convened in 1771 under Lorenzana, banned self-flagellation— regardless of the devotee's gender—during Holy Week processions, choosing to see the practice as a mark of barbarity rather than devotion. Penitents could whip themselves in their own homes, but in public they could only suggest the practice by parading with a rope around their necks (Larkin 2004, 510–511). As the Passion play tradition passed into this era when all forms of public whipping were controversial, the flagellation of an Indigenous Christ resonated with the current context and with over two centuries of experience with whippings, memories of pain and humiliation, resentment of prejudiced priests, and disputes over religious and civil authority.

This crucial episode had to be included in Passion plays, but how would any particular cast carry it out? The stagings have two aspects: what Pilate says when he orders the flagellation (IV.iii.9) and how the stage directions indicate the actors are to represent it (IV.iii.11). Penn (30v) presents a mild version of Pilate's command: "Let me punish him so that you will be satisfied. I will flog him so that he will not ever lie to people, bewilder people, again. Come, my soldiers. Tie him to a stone column. Flog him. However, I see no sin in regard to him for which he should be sentenced to death."[27] The other five Pilates speak more harshly and similarly enough that the speeches may derive from the original play. At a minimum, Pilate demands something like the following, from Tepalcingo (101–102): "I won't admonish him. I will flog him. His blood will really flow, his body will be ripped to shreds, so that he'll never again bewilder people about anything."[28] In Amacuitlapilco (42r) and Axochiapan (32r), not only must Christ's blood flow *huel tlalpan* 'right onto the ground'; he must be whipped until he passes out and stops moving. In Princeton (37r), the stopping point is *intla ye miquiznequi* 'when he is about to die.'

Tlatlauhquitepec's Pilate speaks similarly to Tepalcingo's but goes on to issue a written "Sentence of Lashes": "Jesus of Nazareth, doer of bad things, because testimony has been made on his account to our chief priests that he does not want to obey the laws of Moses, unbind him and tie him to a very strong stone column. Flog him with thorny sticks. Let it be carried out in this way. President Pontius Pilate" (12v).[29] Pilate intends the flogging to set an example for others, as he does in the death sentence from L'Aquila.

Two of the scripts suggest a flogging that could have been at least partially concealed from the audience and thus easily feigned. Tepalcingo's scriptwriter, after having Leader protest that nothing short of Jesus's death will satisfy him and his fellow "Jews," instructs these players to "take him to the jail, where they will beat him. Then they will bring him out" (102).[30] Depending on how the stage set of the jail was constructed, the Jesus actor could have been partly or entirely out of view while the other actors pretended to whip him, with appropriate sound effects. Similarly, in Penn (30v), which, as we saw, has the mildest instructions from Pilate, the players are to bring Christ "inside"—meaning offstage—where they will strip him, tie him to the column, and beat him or at least make it sound as if they are doing so.

The Axochiapan scriptwriter left no specific instructions for the flogging. His stage direction here reads: "They will strip him. They will tie him to a tree. When they are ready, they will put him on a stone base. They will blindfold him. When they are ready, they will dress him in a red cape."[31] This "tree" could be a wooden pole made to look like a column. Those "when they are ready" (or "when they have prepared themselves") statements provide space for the flogging and perhaps, in the second case, additional mocking of the blindfolded Jesus as seen in IV.iii.12–16, only one line of which is then included in this script. The vagueness here allows actors to adjust their practice for any given performance and possibly for the script to pass any anticipated scrutiny regarding its level of violence.

Tlatlauhquitepec gives the explicit but terse "They will just beat him. He will fall on the ground."[32] Princeton gives the same instructions but adds the chanted antiphonal accompaniment "Miserere mei Deus" ("Have mercy on me, God") and further specifies that the actor should faint and his fall should be gentle or gradual (*yolictzin*). As usual, the Amacuitlapilco scriptwriter pens the most elaborate instructions and emphasizes that people must be able to see what is happening, however outlandish or offensive the actions may be. He specifies: "They will strip Christ right in front of people, on the stage. Inside he will have a loincloth (*maxtlatl*). It will be quite visible. They will tie him in front of people to a stone column. Then they will begin it. They will flog him. All the Jews will take turns.

In this way the judgment that Pontius Pilate issued will be carried out" (43r).[33] He makes sure to note that the Jesus actor will wear a loincloth and thus is not to appear completely naked. Nudity was one of the scandalous things Passion play critics complained about. A similar concern seems to have motivated the author of Cuaderno 1, who has Mary remove her headscarf and wrap it around Christ's middle when he is stripped before the crucifixion (219r); this motif dates back at least to the fourteenth-century *Meditations on the Life of Christ* (McNamer 2018, 141). Like the *tilmahtli* cloak, the *maxtlatl* is an Indigenous men's garment. While Jesus typically retains a loin covering, or *perizoma*, in Passion art, the script allows for the actor to wear an Indigenous-style item. Before Spaniards introduced shirts and trousers and different standards of decency, a man clad in only a *maxtlatl* was modestly dressed.

As a general practice, Jesus actors may indeed have been whipped, their performances becoming devotional acts of ritualized "meriting things" and even closer walks in Christ's footsteps, as well as demonstrations of fortitude and courage. None of the stage directions mentions blood, but the profuse blood flow certain Pilates demand may have been supplied through some artifice, to augment any that Christ's impersonator actually shed as he underwent this ordeal. When Jesus is to sweat blood in the Garden of Gethsemane—a feat that could only be feigned—the Princeton script instructs stagehands to "set down blood for Christ" (*quimotlalililizqueh eztli in Cristo*), which the actor will somehow use to give the appearance that it is his sweat (24v; III.i.12). Something similar could be done in this scene.

While the Nahuatl plays present a range of options including placing the flogging offstage or inside a stage-set jail, all four Spanish-language plays follow European conventions of cruelty to a higher degree—scripting a visible, violent, and drawn-out punishment. The perpetrators are generally identified as soldiers (*soldados*) or executioners (*sayones*). There is a fondness for having pairs of actors take turns beating their fellow cast member. Cuaderno 1 (216r) and the play from Amecameca (291r–291v) elaborate on this by having the actors tie Christ's hands first in front of his body, then behind, then in front again, as each pair of floggers replaces the previous one. They are to stop when Christ faints (perhaps giving the actor a chance to signal he had had enough). At that point an Amecameca executioner suggests stopping lest they kill Christ before a death sentence has been issued (291r). The Ozumba play provides hateful speeches for each of three pairs of executioners to recite while they whip (251r). In the Tenango play, Christ is to be whipped until he faints. One of the men then voices the same line about not killing Christ until he is sentenced, but after cutting him loose with a knife and letting him catch his breath, they resume flogging him (272r). In Cuaderno 1, they hang him upside down and whip him some more (216v). In a nice touch absent from the Nahuatl corpus, the

Ozumba (251r), Tenango (272r), and Amecameca (291v) plays have one or more angels then step in to help Jesus put his clothes back on.

The Spanish plays' unrestrained aggression highlights the relative hesitation, delicacy, and variable decisions with which the Nahua scriptwriters approached the scene. The situation here may parallel what we saw with the Last Supper scene: accustomed to scrutiny, some scriptwriters either minimize or leave vague certain elements of their play that might be seen as controversial. A degree of discomfort with this level of violence might also contribute to these decisions.

THE CROWN OF THORNS AND THE REED SCEPTER

Among the charges leveled against Christ is that he styles himself ruler of the Jews (*intlahtohcauh Judiosmeh*). Characters who recognize his divinity address him as "O my deity, O my ruler" (I.i.10, I.vi.12, III.i.15, III.v.4, V.ii.32) or "O my lord, O my ruler" (I.viii.18, II.v.9, V.iii.26, V.iii.67)—formulas of address that can be found throughout Nahuatl devotional literature. The equivalent in the Bible is the word "king" or, in the Vulgate, *rex. Tlahtoani* could be translated as "king," but it has a broader range of reference. Meaning "speaker" or "one who habitually says things," it denoted the dynastic ruler of an *altepetl* or, in the case of the *huei tlahtoani* 'great speaker,' the ruler of an *altepetl* that controlled other *altepetl*, as in the case of the Mexica emperor. Under Spanish colonialism, as dynastic rulership of the *altepetl* gave way to government by a council of elected officials, these officers became collectively called *tlahtohqueh* (plural of *tlahtoani*). Lockhart (1992, 48) found that in the late colonial period, *tlahtohqueh* "hardly goes beyond a courtesy title that could apply to any group of respectable citizens." Hence to translate this as "king" exaggerates its prestige and introduces an alien notion of rulership. However, I use the word "kingdom" for *tlahtohcayotl* and "royal" for the combining form *tlahtohca-*, which occur much less frequently than *tlahtoani*. These terms may have retained an association with higher levels of rulership. Alternatively, they could be rendered as "political domain" or "leaderish."

Reuben, the chief priests' porter, addresses Caiaphas as "O my ruler" on one occasion (II.vi.46), but these men, the Vulgate Bible's *principes sacerdotum* 'principal priests' or 'chief priests,' are generally designated *teopixcatlahtohqueh*. This title prefixes a term for a pre-Columbian or Catholic priest, *teopixqui* 'deity keeper,' onto *tlahtohqueh*. "Priest-rulers" or "priestly rulers" are alternatives to my "chief priests" (or, for Caiaphas, "high priest"). This was the Nahuatl neologism adopted for Roman Catholic bishops and higher officials, such as the pope. Since the Jerusalem officials were called *obispos* 'bishops' in some Spanish Passion texts (for instance, the *Gamaliel*), the author(s) of the model play could have been responding to the use of *obispos* in a source text. The Jerusalem "priest-rulers" act like a body of *tlahtohqueh*, meeting in an *altepetl* council that Tepalcingo's scriptwriter even calls a *cabildoh* (16; II.i.1), the borrowed Spanish word used for such governing bodies. However, the scripts almost always refer to them as priests or "priest-rulers," keeping them in a religious rather than a broader civic sphere.

After the flagellation, Christ is arrayed in mockeries of kingly accouterments: the scarlet (*coccineam*) or purple (*purperea*) cloak of an ordinary soldier rather than royal robes, a crown plaited of thorns (*plectentes coronam de spinis*) rather than of laurel leaves, and a reed in lieu of a royal scepter (Matthew 27:28–29; Mark 15:17; John 19:2; Gundry 2010, 128, 214). Tlatlauhquitepec (12v) substitutes a worn-out garment (*zoltic tlaquemitl*), consistent with the humiliation staged in this scene, but the others specify a red (*chichiltic* 'chili-colored') cloak. While Tepalcingo (102), Penn (30v), and Princeton (37v) make this the Indigenous *tilmahtli*, it is notable that Axochiapan (32r) and Amacuitlapilco (43r) borrow the Spanish term *capotillo* 'small [short] cape,' ethnically cross-dressing Jesus here in a Spanish garment (IV.iii.11).

The crown of thorns was one of the more important and familiar Passion implements. Indigenous sculptors carved it where the bars intersect on some of the sixteenth-century atrium crosses (see figure 1.3). The rosary prayer cycle commemorates it right after the flagellation. Here is the Nahuatl rendering of the rosary passage from Domingo de la Anunciación's *doctrina* (Anunciación 1565, 78r; Burkhart 2001, 125):

⁋ In the third marvel, there we will say another Our Father, and another ten Hail Marys. There we will remember how they laid a crown, a thorn circle, on his head. Then you will say this prayer.
⁋ O my lord, O ruler, because of your crown, the thorn circle that they laid on your head, I beseech you, may I obtain with others the kingdom of heaven when I die.

The passage employs the familiar device of coupling a Spanish or Latin word—here, *corona* 'crown'—with a Nahuatl neologism meant to explain it—here, *huitzyahualli* 'thorn circular thing.' Like *capotillo*, *corona* links the object to a Spanish or European frame of reference. Don Lucas Mateo included such a pairing when he illustrated the passage in his pictorial catechism (figure 5.2).

The plays use a variety of terms for this crown, drawing on the words *huitzyahualli* 'thorn circle,' *cuayahualli* 'head circle,' *huitztli* 'thorn,' and *xocohuitztli*. The latter term, seen in figure 5.2, compounds *xocotl* 'hog plum' (*Spondias purpurea*) or, by extension, 'sour,' with *huitztli* 'thorn.' *Xocohuitztli* was a specific type of spiky plant, a cardoon or bromeliad (Sahagún 1950–1982, bk. 4, 45).[34] John, speaking at the end of the Princeton play (49v), invokes another local thorny plant, *tlacatecolohuitztli*

Figure 5.2. The crown of thorns is forced onto Christ's head in this image from the rosary section of don Lucas Mateo's 1714 pictorial catechism. The images at left illustrate the pairing of the loan *coronah* with Nahuatl *xocohuitzyahualli* 'thistly circle.' British Museum, Egerton manuscript 2898, f. 22r. © The Trustees of the British Museum.

'human horned owl thorn' (V.iv.9).[35] Predicting his torments to Mary, in Tepalcingo (26), Jesus echoes the Gospels' reference to the circlet's plaited structure by calling it *tlamalintli* 'twisted cord' (I.viii.21). The loanword *coronah* occurs in every play but in dialogue is always compounded with a Nahuatl word: *tlahtohcacoronah* 'royal crown,' *huitzcoronah* 'thorn crown,' or *xocohuitzcoronah* 'sour-thorn crown' or 'thistly crown.'

According to the Gospels, the soldiers simply "placed" (*posuerunt* or *imposuerunt*) the crown on Christ's head, but this verb did not satisfy medieval Europeans' urge to amplify their savior's torments. In the thirteenth century, the thorns begin to be pressed into Christ's head, even piercing his eye or his brain, and the soldiers start using staves to force them through his cranium (Marrow 1979, 92–93, 141). Depictions of this scene typically show two men with staves on either side of Jesus, as in figure 5.2.[36] Thus, the scriptwriters could choose whether the actors would just "place" the crown on Christ or play up the painfulness of this action by having two actors brandish such tools (IV.iii.18). The six plays divide evenly on this issue, though all have some version of Matthew's mocking "Hail, King of the Jews" (27:29; Mark 15:18). On the lighter side, Tlatlauhquitepec (12v) has Malchus make a simple statement of mockery: "Be joyful! Here is a head-circle with which we will salute you as the ruler of the Jews." Even simpler, Second Jew in the Penn play (30v) says, "Here's your royal crown. Be joyful, O ruler!" And simpler yet, Tepalcingo's First Jew is to declare, "Here is your kingdom, O ruler!" (102), even though Jesus earlier predicted the use of metal (*tepoztica*) to place the crown (26; I.viii.21).[37]

The more vindictive versions include Second Jew's taunt in the Princeton Passion (37v): "O my ruler, here is your royal crown. Put it on. Let us make you wear it. It is very splendid, the way it is adorned. It was made as a precious golden garland. *(They will make him wear the crown.)* Pound it in all over, O our friends. Really wreck the scoundrel's skull."[38] The Princeton script's death sentence (40v) also embellishes the painfulness of the thorns: "and on his head will be laid a thorn circle, of very painful thorns."[39] Amacuitlapilco (43v) and Axochiapan (32v) share a variant that overlaps somewhat with Princeton and likely has a common origin. Fourth Jew recites: "Here is your royal crown, a thorn circle. Kiss it. It is very splendid, precious. Now we will put it on your head. It will really wreck your skull. Bend over. Come help me, O soldiers. We will put the deceiver's royal crown on him."[40]

Matthew (27:29–30) and Mark (15:19) have the soldiers give Jesus a reed as well—a mock scepter to complement the crown—and strike him on the head with it. In this case, the object corresponded to an accouterment of government familiar to Nahuas. Staffs of office, though introduced under Spanish rule, had pre-contact analogues, leading Nahuas to project the Spanish *vara* back into their representations of pre-Hispanic lords (Olko 2014, 292–295). Called *topilli* in Nahuatl, these staffs became markers of rank in colonial *altepetl*, with *topilehqueh* 'they of the staffs' (singular *topileh*) referring to intermediate-level officeholders in an *altepetl*'s civil or religious leadership (Lockhart 1992, 43, 217–218). In the stage directions, this object can be a reed, a reed stalk, or a reed *topilli*. But in every play, one of the numbered Jews presents Jesus with his *tlahtohcatopilli* 'royal staff of office' (IV.iii.20). In every play but Tepalcingo, Jesus is beaten with this staff.

Bloodied on body and head, accoutered with mock royal insignia, still tied with rope, Jesus is now ready for Pilate to put him on display in the *Ecce homo* ("behold the man") episode (John 19:5; IV.iv.1–4). Artists often portrayed Jesus in this humbled guise, flanked by Pilate, including in the sixteenth-century cloister murals at Epazoyucan, Hidalgo.[41] The imagery was familiar enough that the author of the 1692 Nahuatl morality play *The Life of Don Sebastián* has Christ come onstage outfitted *iuhqui Ecce homotzin* 'like the (revered) *Ecce homo*' (Sell and Burkhart 2004, 278).

THE CRUCIFIXION

Dragging a cross laid over his shoulder and perhaps shedding more stage blood along the way, the Jesus actor traversed some distance representing the *Via Crucis* or *Via Dolorosa*, beginning at the stage set for Pilate's residence and ending some distance from the stage, at the set for Calvary. All plays include the Spanish loanword Calvarioh, though in Penn it appears only in the death sentence, paired with Nahuatl Tzontepec 'Skull Hill' (33r). The actor could be tied between the two thieves as he walked (Amacuitlapilco, 37r) or dragged from horseback (Princeton, 43v). On the way, several of the Stations of the Cross were portrayed, as Jesus encountered his mother, Veronica, the "daughters of Jerusalem" (see chapter 3), and Simon of Cyrene, who is recruited to help him carry the cross (V.ii.26–31)—under the weight of which Christ may fall two or three times as he walks along.

Once the procession arrived at the Calvary set, the crew faced the most challenging special effect in the play: safely raising the actors playing Jesus and the two thieves up on wooden crosses. Scripts vary in how much instruction they provide, as well as how much step-by-step dialogue accompanies the attachment of the actors to the crosses.

The Princeton script has little dialogue here but gives useful details in the stage directions (44v–45r). The other actors make Jesus sit down while they make holes in the cross. They strip Jesus and the two thieves and tie the thieves to their crosses. Then they attach Christ to his cross. The stage directions say *mecatica quimotitich-ilizqueh* 'they will stretch him with ropes.' This statement suggests another torment: in some Passion texts Christ's arms and legs had to be stretched with ropes to reach the holes in the cross, to the point of dislocating his bones as if he had been tortured on the rack or by the strappado technique[42] (Bestul 1996, 155). John's recap of Christ's torments at the same play's end suggests that a simulation of this was intended, as John says, "His left hand did not reach, the way the crossed-wood device had holes made in it. They bound him tightly with ropes. Then his precious bones, his precious and royal man's body, came apart" (49v; V.iv.9).[43] Some painters, such as Matthias Grünewald in the well-known *Isenheim Altarpiece*, captured Christ's distorted and damaged arms and feet quite graphically (figure 5.3). Actors might feign such stretching and distortions as well as they could while at the same time ensuring that those being raised on crosses were tied securely and could hang safely.

Throughout Christian literature in Nahuatl, "to crucify" is expressed as *mahma-zohualtia* 'to cause (someone) to extend their arms,' from *maitl* 'hand, arm' and *zohua* 'stretch, extend, open,' with *itech cruz* 'on the (or a) cross' denoting where this stretching was done. Mario Sánchez Aguilera (2015, 291) proposes that this neologism was a cautious choice, for those who wished to discourage people from drawing connections between Christ's death and the ritual killing of pre-Columbian practice, as it drew attention to Christ's body position and not as directly to his execution. The use of nails in an execution had no pre-Columbian echoes,[44] and this act, especially on Christ's hands, receives graphic commentary in Penn and Amacuitlapilco and to a lesser degree in Axochiapan. See the composite rendering of this dialogue at V.iii.1–9.

As well as making hammering gestures, presumably the actors would also fasten or paint nails (or representations of nail heads) on Christ's hands and feet before

Figure 5.3. The crucifixion and entombment of Christ, from the *Isenheim Altarpiece.* Painting by Matthias Grünewald, ca. 1515 (cropped). Mary, John, and Mary Magdalene (with her jar) are on the left; John the Baptist stands to the right. Unterlinden Museum, Colmar, France. Photo credit: Jörgens.Mi. Courtesy of Wikimedia Commons (license: https://creativecommons.org/licenses/by-sa/3.0/de/legalcode).

they raised the three crosses up, with the thieves on either side of Christ. If the Nahua actors' hands were actually pierced by nails (or their limbs dislocated), I would expect this issue to come up in the complaints about the performances; as it does not, I assume that the nailing was feigned. This has not universally been the case in Mesoamerican Passion enactments, however. Allen J. Christenson, during his ethnographic research in Santiago Atitlán, Guatemala, during the 1970s, witnessed Passion performances in which men were tied to crosses; but he also met an elderly man who said that in his youth he had been nailed to a cross during several successive years of Passion plays, before this practice was banned. This former Jesus actor showed Christenson (2016, 66–67) the holes in his hands, which he still kept open by inserting small sticks, thinking God would be displeased if he allowed them to close.[45]

The three nails also number in another play. In the Nahua priest don Manuel de los Santos y Salazar's *Colloquy of How the Fortunate Saint Helen Found the Precious and Revered Wooden Cross*,[46] from 1714, Helen recovers not only the cross but the three nails on her excursion to Jerusalem (Sell and Burkhart 2009, 306–309). The stage directions call them by the Spanish *clavos*, as do the Passion plays, but Helen prefers to call them *tepozhuitzmeh* 'metal thorns' (pluralized as if they are animate) or *tepozmitl* 'metal arrows,' just as she, and the script in general, prefer the neologism *cuauhnepanolli* in place of *cruz*.

When the cross is raised, the Jews in the Tepalcingo play (113) are to beat their lips and cry out (*motenhuitequizqueh, tzahtzizqueh*; V.iii.9). Lisa Sousa (2017, 273) found this verb pair to be common in colonial Nahuatl descriptions of angry people. Tepalcingo (112) also stages the Jews dividing Christ's shirt (*icamisahtzin*) among themselves and gambling for it (V.iii.9)—informing us that this Jesus actor was to wear as part of his costume the long, tunic-like shirt standard to the Indigenous man's colonial wardrobe.[47] The play combines the passages in the Gospels where the soldiers either divvy up Jesus's garments (Matthew 27:35; Mark 15:24; Luke 23:34) or cast lots for his tunic, which they cannot easily divide as it is woven in a single piece (John 19:23–24).

This oddly seamless tunic had a later life in legends about Pilate and, like the nails, shows up elsewhere in Nahuatl theater. At the end of *The Destruction of Jerusalem*, Pilate—kept alive in legend to be punished for his role in Jesus's death—is put on trial after the Roman victory. An enslaved man offers to testify in return for his freedom. Claiming he was present at the crucifixion, he discusses the *tilmahtli* 'cloak' that was taken from the Holy Prophet, Jesus Christ; in the play's Spanish source, this was a *vestidura . . . sin costura alguna* 'garment . . . without any seam' (Molina 1536, 54r). Many marvels were witnessed in connection with this item, and then Pilate took it and wore it wherever he went. Pilate's clothing is then examined, and he is found to still be wearing it. When it is taken from him, he drops dead (Sell and Burkhart 2009, 274–275).

Most scripts leave it understood that the actors playing the two thieves are to be raised up alongside Jesus. His dialogue with the thieves, derived from Luke 23:39–43, appears in Penn (40r), Princeton (45v), and Amacuitlapilco (52r–52v), though only Penn gives them their legendary names, Dimas and Gestas. Amacuitlapilco calls them First Thief and Second Thief, using Nahuatl *ichtequi* 'thief,' while Princeton gives them titles from Spanish: *maladro* 'Bad Thief' (from *mal ladrón*) and *boen ladro* 'Good Thief' (from *buen ladrón*). In all three cases, the dialogue derives from a common model (V.iii.13–18).

The thieves play a further role in the Gospel of John (19:31–33) when, to finish the crucifixions in time for the "high day" Sabbath about to commence, the Jews ask Pilate for permission to break the victims' shins to hasten their deaths (by suffocation) and then remove the bodies.[48] The soldiers break the thieves' shins but then see that Jesus is already dead. Four plays include this act of violence, sometimes just in a stage direction and sometimes included in the dialogue (V.iii.48–50). In the Princeton play, Centurion echoes John's "and that they might be taken away" by calling on his companions to bury the thieves (47v; V.iii.51). Possibly, they were taken down and off the set at that point, but no stage directions call for that.

The actors proceed through Jesus's final moments. Except in Tepalcingo, he asks his father why he has abandoned him (V.iii.27–30). Matthew 27:46–47 and Mark 15:34–35 retain the Hebrew phrase *Eli, Eli, lama sabachthani*, from Psalm 22:1, to explain how bystanders could mishear his words as a call to Elijah (Elias in Spanish), the prophet believed to have been taken up bodily into heaven. In the Princeton play, which intersperses the Gospel passages of Jesus's last words, he calls to *noteouh* 'my deity' (46r), and all four Spanish-language plays have *dios mio*. But the other Nahuatl scriptwriters have him direct his lament not to God but to Elias. Some Nahua redactor did not distinguish Eli from Elijah, and this error was passed on along the Penn-Amacuitlapilco-Axochiapan lineage.

Christ then says he is thirsty and is given a bitter or sour drink (V.iii.43–47)—Princeton, in a kindly twist, providing plain water (46r). He declares his work finished and consigns his soul to his father (V.iii.52–55). In Tepalcingo this is simply his *animah*, but every other play pairs the loanword with the Nahuatl *noyoliya* 'my life force' or, in Princeton, *noyollohtzin* 'my heart' (46r). The Princeton script here instructs the actor to *hualmoquechpilotzinoz* 'he will neck-hang himself'—probably bend at the neck to suggest the moment of death and thus mirror the line in John (19:30) where Jesus "bowed his head and gave up his spirit."

All the complete plays stage the lancing of Christ's side, the final act of violence upon his body (V.iii.64–67). Although this piercing is a posthumous act in John (19:34), which cites the separation of blood and water as proof that Jesus was really dead, along the line of transmission to the cognate Amacuitlapilco (54v) and Axochiapan (42r) scenes the lancing became the finishing blow: Malchus says to the lamenting Mary, "Your child isn't dead yet." Only Penn (42r–42v), Princeton (48r), and Tepalcingo (115–116) give the lancer the name he acquired in medieval legend—Longinus (Longino in Spanish), from Greek *longche* 'lance'—but all include the motif, extant by the twelfth century, that this man was vision-impaired, had his sight miraculously restored, then immediately recognized Jesus's divinity and repented his deed (Farmer 1992, 302; Sticca 1970, 159). Indeed, his name in Amacuitlapilco (55r) and Axochiapan (42r) is Ixpopoyotl 'Blind Person.' Tepalcingo's scriptwriter chose to have the numbered Jews attempt to pierce Jesus, each in turn. Only as a last resort do they turn to the blind Longinus, thus heightening the suspense and the surprise that it is the blind man who is able to hit the target (114–115; V.iii.61–64).[49]

Accoutered with crown, cross, and nails and marked with blood and welts, hanging motionless with arms outstretched and head bowed, the Jesus actor has now completed the process that transformed him into a "localized embodiment," or *teixiptlah* (Bassett 2015), of Jesus Christ. He has been fictively or ritually, even if not literally, killed while he has been, at least in some sense, apotheosized. He looks like a crucifix, and his appearance might invoke more specifically any of the miracle-working crucifixes whose shrines dotted the landscape. He *is* a crucifix, a divine sign manufactured from human and material parts through a sequence of arduous steps. Yet it is still obvious that he is a Nahua man, known to his family and neighbors, who know he will come home later. It is in this moment that the categories "Indigenous" and "Christian" meld perhaps most completely. Christ is Indigenous. A Nahua is (like) a god. Those who would ban this practice sought to deprive Indigenous people of a particularly potent and meaningful route to connect, emotionally and materially, with the Christian sacred.

Christ hangs dead on the cross, while many of the actors assemble in a tableau that might resemble figure 5.4 (apart from the flying angels and small demon), an Indigenous artist's drawing of a Franciscan friar preaching to Nahua men, women, and children in front of a very vivid representation of the three crucified men and surrounding company. Indeed, the listeners enter right into the landscape, like an audience watching a reenactment. We see the INRI signboard above the cross, Roman soldiers with their SPQR (Senatus Populusque Romanus) banner, Longinus with his lance, Magdalene embracing the cross. At bottom left appears John, standing behind the Virgin Mary and the other Marys. Jerusalem lies in the background. A Passion cast might emulate such a scene as seen in a painting or a book.

According to Matthew (27:51–54), Jesus's death unleashed a series of ominous events: the temple curtain tore in two, the earth quaked, rocks split apart, many "bodies of the saints" returned to life and walked into Jerusalem. In response, the centurion and others watching over Jesus's body "were filled with awe, and said, 'Truly this was the Son of God.'" Princeton (46v; V.iii.68) places a similar line in Centurion's mouth, perhaps from the original play, but he is not responding to any such signs. After Christ drops his head, he says, "I believe indeed that he truly is

Figure 5.4. The crucifixion. Drawing for Gerónimo de Mendieta's *Historia ecclesiástica indiana*, 1590s. JGI 1120, Joaquín García Icazbalceta Manuscript Collection. Benson Latin American Collection, LLILAS Benson Latin American Studies and Collections, University of Texas at Austin.

the child of God who has died today"[50] and suggests that he and some numbered Jews should go to inform Pilate. Tepalcingo (114) moves Centurion's line back to where Jesus asked his father to pardon his tormentors, providing Centurion with a motivation in the absence of portents: "It's true that this one is the child of God, because he asks pardon for those who are tormenting him."[51] Back in the Princeton script, John in his final speech (49r) reels off a number of happenings that partially recapture Matthew's list (see V.iv.9). While some sort of sound or visual effects might have been used to dramatize John's account of weeping heavens, splitting crags, broken ground, and walking dead, the script presents no such stage directions. Hence the lancing and its resulting gush of blood seem to be the last bit of violence and disorder that is acted out.

STAGING ACTS OF *ILIHUIZ*

At the beginning of this chapter, I noted contemporary Nahuas' aversion to things that are *ilihuiz*. What did it mean to stage a drama in which so much hatred and abuse, ranting and raving, beating and bleeding are—even if partially feigned—nevertheless meant to be realistically represented? Or in which values are so inverted that Jesus is diabolized and the "deity-keeper" rulers put a deity to death? With Jesus and his followers labeled *macehualtin* and courtroom-like procedures that borrowed Spanish legal terminology, on one level Jesus is an Indigenous man unfairly tried and convicted in a colonial court. This is a betrayal of social order—one all too familiar to the colonized.

But on the cosmic level his divine status signals, this is the (temporary) death of a god. It comes at the end of the period of Lent, when the churches are filled with signs of mourning and priests have been pressuring their parishioners to review, report, and repent for whatever disorderly *tlahtlacolli* they have committed in the previous year. It is a time of decline and darkness, now reaching a violent climax.

With the plays enacted on Palm Sunday and omitting any resurrection, there is still all of Holy Week to go before Easter celebrates Christ's return to life. Christ's staged death placed the entire following week into an even more liminal state—holy and dangerous—while time caught up with its theatrical preview. Rites such as Thursday's Mandatum, or foot-washing ceremony, repeated some things the play has enacted. People who marched in Holy Week processions expressed collective identities in a peaceful and measured mode, tracing orderly patterns through *altepetl* streets with passional imagery and insignia while suspending their ordinary activities. Statues of Christ under torment or the sorrowing Mary froze those staged events in people's view.

Easter Sunday would come and spark its renewal and joy. The Easter songs from the 1583 *Psalmodia christiana* beautifully invoke this bursting back into life and celebration, as in these three brief excerpts (Sahagún 1583, 59v–60r, 62r–62v, 67v–68r):

> Let us sing together, let us be joyful together, let us praise together the great ruler Jesus, for he has revived!
>
> The ice, the chill, have left. The softness, the warmth, have come to arrive. The little insects, the various butterflies are now flying, are now rejoicing!
>
> Let there be singing, various spoonbills, various birds. Let the festival of the reviving be exalted. For a long time it was awaited. For a long time it was longed for.
>
> . . .
>
> May the golden drum, the jade log drum, the lordly flowers stand forth! May there be exaltation! May there be adornment!
>
> May the golden garland be taken, may it be worn! May the jade rattle be shaken!
>
> May the golden flute resound, may it ring out! May our song, our words resound everywhere!
>
> Happily, joyfully let us raise in song the marvelous deed of our deity, our ruler, Jesus!
>
> . . .
>
> You, our savior, Jesus Christ, accepted the cross death. Your precious blood became the price of our salvation.
>
> You, our savior, our creator, to you we pray: give your subjects what they rejoice for, your reviving!
>
> Let us adorn ourselves with pure adornments! Let us praise our great ruler Jesus Christ![52]

The songs evoke the increasing heat of spring's lengthening days. With Christ compared to the sun in the Christian liturgy and this identification avidly adopted by Nahuas (Burkhart 1988), the Passion also, on one level, enacts the death of the sun, which will return to life on Easter. This is not a winter solstice ceremony, but it does occur in early spring, when light is growing and the new planting season is approaching, when the coming rains will convert the sun's heat (*tonalli*) into food crops (*tonacayotl*). Jesus's conception on March 25 (the Feast of the Annunciation), near the vernal equinox, and his birth near the winter solstice—placed in accord with the Roman feast of the birth of the sun—also synchronize his annual cycle of festivals to the movements of the sun.

Obviously, some men were willing to play the roles of angry rulers and violent henchmen, even though they had to enact *ilihuiz* behaviors—regardless of whether they found any ludic or cathartic value in the license to act like bullies. The case of Huejotzingo's prematurely deceased Judas player shows that such behaviors were thought to carry some personal risk. How outrageous it was to speak of and to Jesus as these men do is highlighted by the fact that scriptwriters consistently employ the reverential register of Nahuatl in reference to Jesus even in their stage directions—another way the actor's close identification with the deity manifests itself. But apart from the solitary Judas, the inversion of proper social restraints and hierarchies of respect displayed in all the slapping and knocking around and verbal abuse (to say nothing of whips and crosses) was a collective enterprise, with responsibility for the disorder diffused across a chorus of "priest-rulers," numbered Jews, and other men—diluting any individual's responsibility for the chaos. They are participants in a collective ritual of reversal, turning the world temporarily upside down in the knowledge that renewal will follow—and may depend on the preceding inversion. In the meantime, in the midst of the carefully scripted disorder, there is space for some cultural critique as social elites and legal structures are revealed to be corrupt and the *macehualtin* reign morally supreme.[53] If the Indigenous Jesus embodies the *macehualtin* collectively, then the more he is ritually reviled, the more unjust colonial "order" is revealed to be, even though it cannot be escaped for long.

Conclusion

An Exemplary Passion

In chapter 1, I cited fray Agustín de Vetancurt's (1971, pt. 4, 42) view that Indigenous people "have no understanding except through their eyes." For priests, Passion plays and other *neixcuitilli* 'examples,' or Indigenous-language dramas, helped illuminate the faith for Indigenous people because of their appeal to the senses. If we accept that a performative and embodied theology is as valid as any other form, we can escape the colonial view of Indigenous people as *sin razón* 'without reason' and accept that they had perfectly rational reasons for preferring communal dramatic spectacle to rote recitation and passive listening. We can also cast off the contradiction between theology and theater that bothered European churchmen: faith concretized on a stage need not be a lesser form of religiosity than notions that live only in theological treatises or the contemplative imagination. Nahua *pasioneros* laid fair claim to their own forms of the Christian story, adopted from European models and adapted to the circumstances of their own lives as *macehualtin* in corporate communities—surviving in straitened circumstances under foreign occupation.

The Passion plays were indeed a feast for the eyes and for the ears. The pageantry depended on actors prepared to play more than fifty roles, singers prepared to sing in Latin, musicians ready at least to blow a horn and beat a drum now and then, the people who built and moved sets and props, and the people who sewed costumes and made wigs and feathery angel wings and everything else that turned actors into the characters they portrayed. When items were purchased or rented, those who provided the money and made the transactions supported the program in this

https://doi.org/10.5876/9781646424511.c006

manner. This entire collective effort that went into preparing things and rehearsing scenes can be considered part of the show; Palm Sunday afternoon was merely the culmination of this preparatory process. Regarding sixteenth-century Nahua ritual, Inga Clendinnen (1990) argued that what outsiders might view as preparations for a religious event were experienced as integral parts of the ritual process, acts of service and sacralization. The same may have held true for later colonial Nahuas. The old man who lent his donkey, the woman who toasted the tortillas for the Last Supper, the carpenters who put up the stage or made the crosses, the mother who sewed her child's angel costume: all participated in this process. Audience members too may have been less passive observers than participants in a communal event.

The Passion performances assert compliance with the colonial imposition of Christianity, just like the building of churches, attendance at Mass and catechism classes, participation in baptism and other sacraments, and the other modalities by which colonial Nahuas appeased their colonial overlords by participating in expected manifestations of a Christian identity. In this sense, the performances can be seen as a survival strategy. But they go far beyond any simple and obligatory demonstration of Christian conformity meant to gratify Roman Catholic priests. In that surplus of words and action, we can see that the plays became an active, artistic assertion of survivance—with Nahuas engaging intentionally and meaningfully with the sacred story, asserting ownership of the scripts and altering them to their tastes, and embodying the story in a complex, synesthetic fusion of word, song, costume, prop, and body. This assertiveness is apparent especially after about 1700, when priests began to prefer tamer Holy Week observations, such as processions with silent statues, and the Bourbon Reforms inspired more suspicion of materialized devotions. The play Vetancurt observed, approvingly, at San José de los Naturales was also a tamer affair, as were the priest-mediated descent from the cross ceremonies carried out at some churches. For people who had lost so much, suppression and surveillance of this vibrant tradition dealt yet another sad blow to their autonomy.

Given the sophistication of the plays' language and content plus their tie to fray Juan Navarro's 1604 choral book, the first Nahuatl redaction most likely engaged the talents of one or more of the educated Nahua scholars and writers associated with the College of Santa Cruz in Tlatelolco—in collaboration with or under the auspices of one or more friars—in the very early seventeenth century, though other composition scenarios are possible. Hence, the original composition was probably at least priest-approved. But the decision to compose this play occurred at a moment when other particularly erudite Nahuatl texts, including contemplative works in the *Devotio moderna* mode, were also being produced, their authors envisioning an educated Nahua readership quite different from the eighteenth-century audiences the play would later reach. If the model Passion play was intended for performance—which seems a safe assumption—it may have been directed at a relatively well-indoctrinated or at least an urban audience. Yet provincial *altepetl* rose to its standards of elegant language and narrative detail.

However and for whomever the model play was written, it was a masterwork of Nahuatl Christian theater in its scale, its topic, and its writing. Among the Nahuatl plays I have translated, or co-translated with Barry D. Sell, I have held a particular fondness for don Bartolomé de Alva's *The Animal Prophet and the Fortunate Patricide*. This *comedia* in three acts—enlivened by an inadvertent parent murder, a rape-scheming villain, and the antics of the hero's comic sidekick—was adapted and creatively Mexicanized from a Baroque Spanish work by Antonio Mira de Amescua (see Sell, Burkhart, and Wright 2008). Alva designed his plays with performance in mind, but whether and how often this occurred is unknown. For significance in both subject matter and influence, Alva's work offers the Passion play no competition. For, as this volume has shown, that model play circulated widely, performed and recopied and updated for—if my guess about its origin is correct—at least 150 years before the mid-eighteenth-century suppression efforts, remaining in some local archives beyond that point even if fewer productions were staged. It is, judging by the records we have, not only the most elaborate but the most widely performed Nahuatl play and one that, in telling the Passion story, encased the essence of Christian faith inside the words and gestures of Nahua actors. My journey through the six scripts has made me an avid admirer of this exemplary play.

This Passion play is also the most significant work of Passion literature in Nahuatl or any other Mesoamerican language. The "Historia de la Pasión de Nuestro Señor Jesu Christo en lengua mexicana" (León-Portilla 1994) is a masterwork as well, even longer and even more sophisticated in its adaptation of the contemplative Passion tradition into Nahuatl. However, one manuscript copy is known. Others may have existed, but probably only a handful of elite, literate Nahuas ever read this never published work. Compare that to the thousands of people who saw, acted in, or helped out with Passion plays just in the communities that used these six scripts or their earlier or later copies—including women, children, non-literate men, speakers of other Indigenous languages, and non-Indigenous spectators. Not only that: this play gave rise to what I have described as a tradition. It is not a single text but a collective one, augmented and adjusted by different stakeholders as it roamed from *altepetl* to *altepetl*, scriptwriter to scriptwriter, choirmaster to choirmaster. For that reason, I have treated each redaction as a valuable participant in this process and a worthy constituent of the paper trail through which we can partially chart the tradition's variants. Some other unpublished Nahuatl Christian texts exist in multiple copies, but nothing on this scale or with this level of active reinterpretation.

The Passion play would not have become a tradition, passing through space and time, if Nahuas had not continued to value its increasingly archaic words and pass them on substantially intact while at the same time feeling authorized to make some additions and other changes. The play lost its connection to whoever first wrote it based on whatever Spanish source and became something handed down, something that spoke in authoritative tones not only because so much of it came from the sacred book or corresponded with familiar art and ritual but because of its inscription in Nahuatl. Fray Miguel Camacho Villavicencio of Tlatelolco opined that plays in Nahuatl were unnecessary because nearly everyone understood Spanish by the end of the seventeenth century. While this flippant assertion would have been less true of provincial *altepetl*, there were other good reasons to retain the Nahuatl scripts. In putting these plays onstage from year to year, Nahuas spoke again the words previous generations of *pasioneros* had uttered before them. These are *huehuehtlahtolli* 'words of the elders' not only in the stylistic sense, with the parallel constructions and reverential formalities retained in so many speeches, but in the literal sense. It is not just Jesus Christ, the Bible, or the Roman Catholic Church that blesses these words but the preceding generations who had uttered them in other years. If the play is something that belonged to the ancestors, it becomes less alien, less Spanish, less a thing imposed by priests who never thought Nahuas were good enough. At least in some cases, this history of Passion performance was remembered as dating back to the establishment of the colonial *altepetl*, with its new church and its newly affirmed rights to local autonomy. To lose the language would break that bond with the elders and the past. And given how much meaning is encoded in the Nahuatl words and grammatical and syntactic structures that does not quite correspond to the Spanish lines that would have replaced them (and did, in a sense, in the four Spanish scripts), a great deal of the nuanced interpretation and critique of European Christianity and colonial rule would have been lost.

It was not only this textual heritage from the ancestors that Nahuatl Passion performances legitimized. We must also include the prestige that flowed to the *altepetl* as a whole, to the sponsoring religious confraternity or other community leaders who provided funds and organization, and to the actors, singers, and other participants. While local noblemen and noblewomen might monopolize major roles, enhancing their prestige relative to those of less elite lineage, there were plenty of smaller roles and auxiliary activities through which less well-connected folks could publicly show their devotion and their community support. The performance inserts this place and these people into a bigger story, the cosmic drama of Holy Week, including the unstaged but imminent resurrection. It takes the story out of the church buildings and out of the dry catechisms and sermons or even the rote prayers of the rosary and into the semi-sacred community space of the cemetery, where *pasioneros* of earlier generations might lie near their current replacements. There is room for license, such as the drunkenness that so appalled fray Miguel and the acts of beating and bullying that would get a person in trouble outside of this sanctioned inversion of the rules. There is room as well for profit, as visitors could be solicited for donations to shrines or confraternities and vendors could hawk their wares to all comers.

Many roles in the play were essential to the story. I have paid some particular attention to the women's roles because Marian devotion figured so prominently in European Passion practice, while the Nahuatl plays read gendered roles in a different, more complementary manner. However, Jesus Christ is the main role and a unique one because only don Antonio de Guevara and all the other Nahua Jesus players through all the years played a person who is both human and god—indeed, the only god Nahuas were now permitted to openly avow. And only in Passion plays did Jesus players have more than minor roles on the Nahuatl stage. Only here were they subjected to bullying and abuse. Only here did they go through the process of material investiture and bodily marking that gradually increased their identification with and as the deity, until they hung bloodied on a cross feigning Jesus's transformational death.

Very few Indigenous men became Roman Catholic priests during the colonial era, especially in its early days. Without belittling the attainment of so guarded a status by such men as the Tlaxcalan priest and playwright don Manuel de los Santos y Salazar or the deathbed-ordained Lorenzo, I would note here that there were many more Indigenous Christs than Indigenous priests. Even while men like Santos y Salazar brought some degree of an Indigenous sensibility or at least local ethnic pride to their positions in the Church hierarchy, they were not the counter-hegemonic force that Jesus players were. Only one day a year did actors play this role, yet each show would live in memory and in anticipation of the next enactment.

The verisimilitude that bothered churchmen about theater—the precept that Christianity's core beliefs must be accepted with blind faith, not because a person could see them unfolding before their eyes upon a stage—granted these actors a legitimacy and an at least partial and temporary divinity that other Indigenous people, keyed to an embodied and performative faith, would recognize even as priests fretted about raised tortillas and sopped-up blood. An ordained priest was carefully educated and under his bishop's authority. Scripts could be reviewed and even confiscated, but exactly what the actor—whom everyone recognized as a local man—would do and say as he played this part, and what other people would make of that, was not so easily controlled. The mediating voice of the priest, explaining what everything means and how people should think about it, is, for once, silenced, while the sacred story unfolds before one's very eyes and, for all the actors, through their own bodies.

As we have seen, that sacred story draws much from the four Gospel accounts, but holy writ intertwines with many later accretions. These additions draw from apocryphal gospels of the fourth century or later, composite legends like the story of Veronica, influential Passion tracts like the *Meditations on the Life of Christ*, interpretations of the Hebrew Bible made by Jew-hating Passion writers, the Stations of the Cross devotion, the *Gamaliel* of Catalan and Castilian popularity, the 1580 death warrant hoax from L'Aquila, and other sources. A veritable archive of Passion lore, from the Gospels to the sixteenth century, is packed inside this Nahuatl play. Most of this lay perhaps in a single text used by the author(s) of the model play, but some parts appear to have been added to the tradition on the way to these six variants: the farewell scene derived from the *Meditations*, the Veronica story, the L'Aquila warrant. To a lesser degree, conventional formulas of Nahuatl preaching and theatrical practice found their way into the mix: Magdalene's burning adornments, bits of preaching about sexual and other sins.

Like all works of art, the Nahuatl Passion play, in its six manifestations reviewed here, can support many different interpretations. It can be read as Christian literature or as Native American ritual performance. It can be read as a collection of late medieval European Passion lore or as a Mesoamerican enactment of world destruction and the temporary death of a maize-embodied solar deity. It can be read as an anti-Jewish tract or as a critique of colonial rule. It can be read as a prestige exercise for its elite sponsors and lead actors or as an assertion of *macehualli* solidarity. It can be read as a statement of gender complementarity and female power or of women's weakness against masculinized violence. It can be read as a model for formal social interaction and wise teaching or as a free-for-all inversion of polite norms by a raging mob. It is all these things, and it is everything else that it meant to each participant in each *altepetl* that staged it over the years and to each reader who encounters it today.

The scripts are only paper transcripts of a multimedia performance, yet they have much to say. In this book I have pursued topics and lines of interpretation that stood out in my own reading and comparison of these six manuscripts. And I have endeavored to represent the collective creativity of the tradition's originators and modifiers by merging these six manifestations of their work into a composite version. Many more veins could be mined in this rich deposit of colonial Nahua treasure. I hope the material presented here and on the digital project that houses the individual plays and related documents will suggest additional studies from various disciplinary and interdisciplinary perspectives and that new evidence from the archives will expand the documented Nahuatl Passion play tradition beyond the texts currently at my disposal.

The Nahuatl Passion Play

A Composite Translation

ACT I: JESUS AND THE APOSTLES TRAVEL TO
JERUSALEM. JESUS PREACHES THERE.

Scene i: Christ and the apostles prepare to set out for Jerusalem.

I.i.1   *Christ will come out, with all of the apostles. They will all be in a line.*

I.i.2   CHRIST: Please come here, you who are my dear students, you who are
my chosen ones in the world. My beloved father, God, has blessed you.
Now please listen. It is time now, the time has come, for what the prophets, those who said things first, established to come true, to happen. All
the things will happen to the maiden's child. And you, Simon Peter, do
not grow faint in your faith, as I take you (all)[1] over into the *altepetl* of
Jerusalem. You are to fortify your hearts well, as you will see, you will
marvel at all the torments, which are many. I will be stoned. I will be
dishonored. I will be hated, just because of my love for others.

I.i.3   SAINT PETER: What are you saying to us, O our teacher? Do not
desire to go into the *altepetl* of Jerusalem, because the Jews hate you very
much! Don't go fall into their hands. Where will you go off to and leave
us, we who are your children?

I.i.4   CHRIST: That is how my beloved father, God, wants it to be. So I will now take you along to where the Jews gather together so that I will there explain, declare, the breath, the words, of my beloved father, God. And for my teachings, my love of others, I will just be stoned. With their misdeeds, the scoundrels, the sinners in the world, will just throw stones at me. And they have pronounced death on me there, since they will make the maiden's child stretch his arms on the cross there. But, O my children, do not be faint. Be very strong. You are firmly in the faith.

I.i.5   SAINT JOHN: How very saddening, how heart-crushing, are your precious words, everything you mention that will happen to you, O my beloved teacher. Why, for what reason, will this happen to you? Aren't you a deity, a ruler? Let us be the ones whom the suffering happens to, because you are our benefactor. That is how our hearts feel. You will be doing us a favor, you will be showing us compassion.

I.i.6   CHRIST: That is what my beloved father, God, wants: that I will save the people of earth, the sinners, so that the wolf in the place of the dead, Lucifer, won't eat them, won't swallow them. And since they are my creations, I am also the one who will save their life forces, their souls. But they do not think of me, so now for their sake I am about to die.

I.i.7   SAINT PHILIP: O my beloved teacher, where will you go? Now you are bidding us farewell, we who are your children. All the time that you brought us up, you never left us. And now you want to leave us? Do not think such a thing, O my beloved teacher.

I.i.8   CHRIST: Listen, O my beloved students. What will come true first are the precious and revered words, the will, of my beloved father, God. Now it will come true, how I came to become a person here on earth. Everything that lies written about me in the sacred book I will now show to you. Even though I will go, I will abandon you, I will not leave you. When I am on the verge of death, when my enemies the Jews arrest[2] me, I will pray to my beloved father for your sake. He will take care of you. Do not grow faint. Fortify your hearts.

I.i.9   SAINT JAMES: We thank you very much for all your precious and revered words that you are bequeathing to us. We strongly beseech you, all of us, O our beloved teacher, do not desire to abandon your beloved mother. Do not desire to go over into the *altepetl* of Jerusalem, because the Jews hate you very much.

I.i.10   SAINT PETER: I throw myself facedown in front of you, O my deity, O my ruler! May you not abandon us. We will perish, we your creations.

I.i.11   CHRIST: You have heard all my words with which I commanded you. It is just a few days that I will live here with you. You are not to forget my words. I leave you tied, I leave you tightly bound, by my words.

I.i.12   *The apostles will line up.*

I.i.13   CHRIST: Now we will go up to Jerusalem. And everything that the prophets left said will be done to the maiden's child. He will be betrayed, he will be mocked, he will be spit at in the face. And when they have whipped him, afterward they will kill him. After three days he will revive.

Scene ii: The journey to Jerusalem begins; the donkey is secured.

I.ii.1   *Everyone will walk along and Poor Person will run up. He will cry out.*[3]

I.ii.2   POOR PERSON: What's this? Who are crossing here? It seems like I am hearing a lot of rumbling.

I.ii.3   SAINT PETER: The savior, God's beloved child, Jesus of Nazareth, is passing by here.

I.ii.4   POOR PERSON: You great ruler, you child of God, please have compassion for me, by your leave.

I.ii.5   CHRIST: What do you want? It will be done to you, my child.

I.ii.6   POOR PERSON: O our lord, I want to see! Have compassion for me, you merciful one.

I.ii.7   CHRIST: See, by means of your faith!

I.ii.8   *He will bless the sick person, who will kneel. He will kiss Christ's feet.*

I.ii.9   CHRIST: I have saved you. *(To the apostles:)* Go into the *altepetl* toward which we are looking. You are hated there, you will be met with contention there. And when you get there, you will see a little house. In the doorway is a female donkey, standing tied up, with her child standing beside her. Untie her, then bring her to me with a bridle. And if someone says something to you, tell them, "We came to take her on behalf of the ruler. He has need of her. He's the one who sent us. He will come in on her, here on his land." And then they will leave you alone. Go with great haste.

I.ii.10   SAINT JOHN: Very well, O our lord, O our teacher. Let us go and do what you desire. We are just waiting for your precious and revered words. Let us go get her.

I.ii.11   SAINT JAMES: O our beloved teacher, may it be done as you wish. We will carry out what you command us right away.

I.ii.12 *Christ will go inside, with all the apostles. Saint John and Saint James will remain on the stage.*

I.ii.13 SAINT JOHN: O my beloved elder brother, here now I am marveling at his precious words, for what he is always teaching us will now come true, it will happen. For he says, "O my children, you will see it, you will marvel at it, for it will come true, it will happen, as it lies written in the sacred book of the prophet Zechariah. For he said, 'go and tell the daughter of Zion, behold, here comes your lord, your ruler, a very humble person, a very humane person, he comes riding on a donkey, and her child comes along. He comes passing you, he comes humbly, he comes downcast. He will go into Jerusalem.'"[4] That's how he said it then.

I.ii.14 SAINT JAMES: What you say is quite right. All of his precious arrangements will come true, will happen, since he is all-powerful. Let us just put our trust in him, we his creations.

I.ii.15 SAINT JOHN: O my beloved elder brother, we are taking a very long time. Let's hurry up.

I.ii.16 SAINT JAMES: So be it. Let us hurry to where our beloved teacher sends us.

I.ii.17 *They will go to where a donkey will be tied up. When they have arrived, they will seize her. They will speak.*

I.ii.18 SAINT JOHN: We have arrived here where we were sent. The donkey is standing there.

I.ii.19 SAINT JAMES: It's not that one. Our beloved teacher told us that the donkey is standing beside her child.

I.ii.20 SAINT JOHN: She's looking out the door of that little house. That's the one! Untie her. Let's take her, quickly. Now we have come and carried out the command of our beloved teacher. And now, let's go, quickly!

I.ii.21 *Then they will untie the donkey. While they are untying her, First Jew will speak on the edge of the stage.*

I.ii.22 FIRST JEW: Why are you untying the donkey? Don't you know that she belongs here?

I.ii.23 SAINT JOHN: The teacher sent us. He has need of her. We came to take her for him.

I.ii.24 FIRST JEW: We have heard your words. Take her.

I.ii.25 CENTURION: What teacher, deranged ones? Move aside. Maybe you are bewildered.

I.ii.26   *Then they will take the donkey in front of Christ and all the apostles. First Jew and Centurion will go inside.*

I.ii.27   SAINT JOHN: O our lord, O ruler, we have gone and carried out your sacred command. O our beloved teacher, we have brought the donkey. Here she is.

I.ii.28   CHRIST: I exalt your obedience. Come here, O my beloved children. Keep the donkey over there.

I.ii.29   SAINT JAMES: Everything that you will command us we will carry out, because our hearts know well that you will have mercy on us, tomorrow, the day after tomorrow.

I.ii.30   CHRIST: O my beloved children, today we are going into the *altepetl* of Jerusalem so that the maiden's beloved child will be killed, will be tormented there. Now, each of you take an olive branch and a palm frond, which will go in your hands as we enter into Jerusalem. By that the Jews will recognize you as my children, my students.

I.ii.31   SAINT PHILIP: Let us carry out your precious wishes, O our beloved teacher.

I.ii.32   *Christ will go and sit on the Mount of Olives. And the apostles will go and take palm fronds and branches from the mountain of olives.⁵ Saint Peter, along with Saint John and Saint Philip, will distribute them to the others. Saint Philip will kiss them and bow. Each apostle will grasp a palm frond and a branch.*

I.ii.33   SAINT ANDREW: How will you go on the donkey like this? She doesn't have a saddle. You are all-powerful and you are revered inside heaven and you are ruler everywhere in the world. Let us take off our cloaks. Let us saddle the donkey on which you will go. *(To the audience:)* Oh! O people of the world, whoever you are, you who are seated there, doesn't anything happen to your heart as you see in what a very saddening way your deity, your ruler, is going to Jerusalem in order to save your life forces, your souls, for you? He is going, he is going to die for your sakes. Let that be all, stop, because it is an offense to our lord God.

I.ii.34   *Then they will saddle the donkey. Saint John will bring a white cloak and Saint Andrew will bring a piece of taffeta.*

I.ii.35   SAINT PETER: We have saddled the donkey. Let us lift you up, O our beloved teacher.

I.ii.36   CHRIST: O my children, take hold of her for me. Let me sit on her. Let us go to Jerusalem. Right now, I will begin my teaching, with which I will instruct the Jews.

I.ii.37   *Then all the apostles will lift Christ up onto the donkey.*

Scene iii: The triumphal entry into Jerusalem

I.iii.1   *Then everyone will go to Jerusalem. The apostles will clutch palm fronds in their hands. Some will go following Jesus and some will go in front. They will be spread out. They will walk a little way. The children of the Jews will go to meet them. Some will wave flowers and others palm fronds. Simeon and Centurion will go with them.*

I.iii.2   ISRAELITE CHILDREN: *Hosanna, filium David. Benedictus qui venit in nomine domine, O rex Israel, miserere nobis.* You ruler, you are the child of David. May you have compassion for us. Fortunate is he who has come by the command of God. May he be praised, Israel, may he be utterly praised, he who has come by the command of God.

I.iii.3   FIRST LITTLE CHILD: You completely good one, you ruler, you have endured fatigue⁶ as you came to save me. How is it possible that we, your creations, deserve, that we merit, that you have come to your home, Jerusalem, where we are waiting upon your words? Let us go along with you!

I.iii.4   SECOND SMALL CHILD: You great ruler, have compassion for us, we children of David. How can it be that you have followed us, by God the father's command?

I.iii.5   THIRD SMALL CHILD: You are the deity of the world, you are the ruler of Israel. Save our life forces, our souls, for us.

I.iii.6   FOURTH SMALL CHILD: It is true that you are a man and you are a deity and you are the savior, you are the child of David. May you show us favor so that we will go to heaven.

I.iii.7   SIMEON: O teacher, don't you hear the little children? What are they saying to you? Make them stop. Let them not speak in this way. Won't you be spoken ill of? Won't you be laughed at? They praise you as a deity everywhere.

I.iii.8   CHRIST: Why should I stop them? Truly I say to you, if the little children stop, the rocks and trees themselves will utter praises. But as for you, you can see, you can hear, but you do not want to acknowledge me, you will not recognize me. Have you never read what is said in the sacred words, in the book of David: that the little children, with their praise, with their reverence, will be the first to believe, because they are not yet two-hearted? The unweaned children are devoted to me. They cannot yet speak well, but today they uttered praises, just by the will of my beloved father, God.

I.iii.8
(*cont.*)   Don't your priests teach you that I will reach beyond the earth, even though now you see me as a *macehualli*? It is as a man that I have come, that I have come to enter upon you. But as a deity, as a ruler, everything belongs to me, everything is my creation, heaven and earth and the place of the dead. I will pass judgment on all of you when it is the day of passing judgment on people.

I.iii.9   CENTURION: We do not recognize you. What did you come here to say? Will you overcome the chief priests who are in charge here in Jerusalem?

I.iii.10   SIMEON: And who are you, coming from over there, pretending to be such a very great personage, with so many *macehualtin* leading you here? Where are you a ruler of, if that is so? And in Jerusalem, aren't there nobles and rulers who govern the *altepetl*? Where is your home? What did you come here to say, O teacher?

I.iii.11   *Everyone will walk on. The little children will go inside, along with Simeon and Centurion. The Jews will come out. They will go looking. They will see Christ. They will really stare.*

I.iii.12   TOWN CRIER: Who comes there? A great many *macehualtin* come leading him this way. What is happening? The ground is reverberating.

I.iii.13   REUBEN: I think it is the one they call Jesus of Nazareth.

Scene iv: Christ teaches in Jerusalem.

I.iv.1   *When Christ has reached the edge of the stage, he will get down from the donkey. The apostles will line up. They will kneel. And Christ will speak there on the ground. He will weep a lot as he addresses the altepetl of Jerusalem.*

I.iv.2   CHRIST: O Jerusalem, you *altepetl* of Jerusalem, you did not show favor as I came to enter into you. You were just especially proud and presumptuous. You were not grateful to your creator, God. Truly I say to you, if you knew what is going to happen to you, you would weep like I am weeping. Today you are still happy, you are still content, because you do not yet know, you do not yet see what will happen to you. It is going to happen. Your enemies, the people of Rome, will come. In just forty years they will come to encircle you and they will surround you, they will destroy your kingdom. They will knock you down, they will leave you on the ground. And you will starve, and your children will eat one another. They will kill you. Truly you will weep, you will be sad.

I.iv.3   *Everyone will go into the temple. And the Jews will speak on the stage. They will converse with one another, and some will sell merchandise. All the Jewish priests will go there.*

I.iv.4   SAMUEL: Here in the supremely good *altepetl* of Jerusalem, very great is the lordship, the rulership, the mat, the seat, the royal place. It cannot yield its place in the world. There is our own honor and the honor of the ruler President Pontius Pilate. Nothing lies destroyed. And now it is as if something worrisome is about to go into the royal *altepetl* of Jerusalem. Maybe it cannot happen thus. The chief priests are seated in honor, and the great ruler, the president, will be strong. And as for us, we will be strong so that no one will overcome us.

I.iv.5   *Then Centurion will go strolling by. When Samuel has spoken, then Centurion will speak.*

I.iv.6   CENTURION: And you, you vendors, hurry up! Don't move away everything you are selling. This market is the temple of our father Moses.

I.iv.7   *Then Christ will enter the temple with all the apostles. He will admonish them.*

I.iv.8   CHRIST: As for you, you scoundrels, you Jews, what are you doing here in the temple? Why, for what reason, do you sell here indoors, in the home of my beloved father, God? People are to enter with weeping, with sadness. But you all act like you think it's just a marketplace where you go to buy and sell, where you lie around selling things, where you lie around making sport of people. You are deceivers, you are cheaters. You say that you are sages, that you teach people what is good, what is proper. And that you cause people to stop what is bad. But you just go around tasking people with these various depravities, offenses to God. Get out! Go out the door! Leave the house of my beloved father, God!

I.iv.9   *Then he will beat the vendors, some of whom will be playing games. A Pharisee will stand up. He will slap Christ in the face.*

I.iv.10   PHARISEE: Why, for what reason do you speak in this way, O teacher? Is this not the command of Moses, that we will do it in this way? Will you break the commands of the prophet?

I.iv.11   CHRIST: There are no prophets anymore. That was before there was me. But now, thus have I come: I came to destroy the old testament.[7] For I came to renew it, as my beloved father, God, desires.

I.iv.12   *They will slap Christ in the face again.*

I.iv.13   PHARISEE: Who will believe you, O scoundrel, O bewilderer?

I.iv.14 CHRIST: Come here. Listen, you scoundrels, you false priests, you be-wilderers. Tell me, how well do you carry out the ten commands of God the way Moses, who declared them to you, commanded you?

I.iv.15 PHARISEE: Please listen, O teacher. If it is true that you are the awaited one, you are the child of God, our faces, our hearts, are not in agreement. He that is awaited is really the child of God. And as to how we carry out God's commands that he gave to Moses there on the mountaintop, Mount Zion,[8] when a person sins against one of the sacred commands, then they are arrested in the marketplace, the place where people are stoned alive so that they will die. Or perhaps they are dragged or tor-tured, according to how they broke the command of God.

I.iv.16 CHRIST: And as for you, you scoundrels, you judges, you viceroys, you governors, you magistrates, you who pass judgment on people, all the bad and wrong things that you do, give them as his tribute to the emperor, Caesar. For they are his possessions, his goods. And your deeds that are good, that are proper, give them to my beloved father, God. For they are his possessions, his goods. And indeed, now for this have I come: I came to cure the life forces, the souls, of the sinners, as my beloved father, God, the all-powerful, commanded me. And as for you, you who pass sentence on people, for a great many things do the daughters of Jerusalem mock you. And very great is your pride. You think that perhaps you have surpassed your creator. Truly I say to you, a much graver sentence will I pass on you there in the place of the dead. I am going to cast you into the hands of the scoundrel Lucifer.

I.iv.17 PHARISEE: Who believes you? Will you overcome others? Are we priests not here?

I.iv.18 *Samuel will get up. He will slap Christ in the face.*

I.iv.19 SAMUEL: Maybe you're crazy! Who are you? Get out of here!

I.iv.20 *Christ will sit down. He will teach the Jews. And Magdalene will be in the back.*

I.iv.21 CHRIST: Listen, you nobles of Jerusalem. Although I have entered here into your *altepetl*, I am very angry with you here. Many of your children led me here. They will all be my beloved ones, for that is what my be-loved father, God, who is seated in honor in heaven, desires. He sent me from there, such that I came to appear as a *macehualli* on earth. As for me, I will begin, I will start, the destruction. I will die. With my death I will open heaven so that my beloved ones will go there, those who serve me, who follow my commands. But those who will see nothing in

I.iv.21
(*cont.*)
my words, my teachings, O how wretched they are. They will go to be imprisoned in the place of the dead, where they will burn forever. And those who are big hypocrites, who are proud, who are haughty, O how wretched they are. At that time, they will say, "Would that we had not been born! O how wretched we are!" Especially you who have entered here into the home of my beloved father, who is seated in honor in heaven, just with your bragging, just with your pleasures on earth, you begin and end your day. You no longer think of your deity, your ruler. It is indeed you for whose sake I'll be made to stretch my arms on the cross. What's become of you? You no longer see. It would be better if you had not been born. Listen well to what I am saying now. If you do not turn your life around, cut off your sins, and if your dirty life does not make you weep, make you sad, you will never go to my home inside heaven. You'll never see my face again, for I will abandon you in the big houses in the place of the dead. You'll be locked up there. Forever will you pay the penalty for your pleasures on earth. Your beauty, your good looks that you fit on yourself will all turn into red-hot coals in the place of the dead. How wretched you are, you woman!

I.iv.22
MAGDALENE: Ah! Ah! O my God! That's all! I am dying now. My adornments are burning me very much. How much more will it be in the place of the dead, for they will torture me with burning pain. Right now, I scorn you, you adornments of mine, for you are no longer of use to me. You really burned people. Flop down over there! You afflicted me indeed. Ah! O my God, how wretched I am!

I.iv.23
She will fall. She will lie facedown. And two women—Martha and an adulterous woman—will come to take hold of her.

I.iv.24
WOMAN: Get up, O my friend.

I.iv.25
All the Jews will go inside. Christ and the apostles will remain.

Scene v: Three angels visit Christ.

I.v.1
Then three angels will appear. They will speak.

I.v.2
FIRST ANGEL: You utterly great one, you utterly exalted one, your beloved father, God, sent us to you. He says, "Go and tell my beloved child, Jesus Christ, though he already knows, that the time has come when he will suffer pain, when he will hurt, because of his creations, the people of the world." And my beloved and revered father, God, says for you to be strong, as you will revive again in front of your enemies the sinners.

I.v.2
(*cont.*)
How your chest, your head will be broken, as you will cause them to hear your breath, your precious and revered words, which are very pleasing. And since you are all-powerful, may you fortify yourself, O our lord. May you not feel faint, O Jesus Christ!

I.v.3
SECOND ANGEL: O my beloved father in heaven, you who are our consoler, you who are our life, your beloved and revered father, God, says, "My beloved child, so that his creations will be saved with all of his beloved and precious words, his beloved and precious teachings, will be cast into the hands of others in front of the most holy cross. The obstinate-hearted ones will be especially enraged by [his teachings], those who do not see, who do not hear, who do not know that you will judge them, tomorrow or the next day." What do you think, O my beloved father? Be strong. You will endure everything, O my beloved father. Exert all your effort, O Jesus Christ!

I.v.4
THIRD ANGEL: Exert all your breath, all your effort, O Jesus Christ! Already you are entering into some of your pain, your agony, on account of the sinners. And now, O my beloved father, you will bring your breath, your words, to an end. The sinners are coming now to dishonor you and to speak of your death. It is just for your love for people that you will suffer, that you will endure pain. And when death has passed, then you will draw near to happiness in the world, complete delight, glory.

I.v.5
CHRIST: What I greatly desire is the loving words of my beloved father, God, the all-powerful. That which he wants is what will be done. My will is not to be done. And now, may the will of my beloved father, God, be done.

I.v.6
The angels will go singing. They will say the Sanctus.

I.v.7
ANGELS: *Sanctus sanctus sanctus. Dominus Deus Sabaoth. Pleni sunt caeli et terra gloria tua. Hosana in excelsis.*[9]

Scene vi: Christ teaches his followers. He and the apostles visit the home of Simon the Pharisee. Christ spreads a precious unguent on Mary Magdalene's head.

I.vi.1
CHRIST: Please come, you students of my beloved father, God. Listen. Be very prudent, and be looking under your underarm hair. Let your pine torch, your lamp, be burning in your hands so that you do not let your life forces, your souls, fall asleep, because it is not just anything that you would be neglecting. It is eternal life in heaven, there in the home

I.vi.1 (cont.) of my beloved father, God. There are more thrones, seats, there than anyone can say, which my beloved father, God, is keeping for you. If you will do good, do not copy the person whose heart is not good, who has pride and desire for things on earth, the thief, the adulterer, who just go about neglecting the dirtiness of their life forces, their souls, so that they gain eternal pain, agony, there in the abyss, the place of the dead. For that is why I came. I came to save you. I came to cure your depravity so that you will merit the eternal happiness, the delight, that my beloved father, God, is keeping for you.

I.vi.2 SIMON [THE PHARISEE]: O ruler, O teacher, I am very grateful for what you have taught all of us. You have tired yourself. Rest a bit. Come into your humble home. You will have a bite to eat, along with your students.

I.vi.3 CHRIST: O Simon, I am very grateful to you for taking us to your home. May it so be done. Let us go.

I.vi.4 *Simon will set down a table. Then Christ will sit down, along with the apostles. Christ will teach. Then Magdalene will come out. She will speak.*

I.vi.5 MAGDALENE: O my beloved young man, which one is the ruler, the teacher?

I.vi.6 SIMON: O noblewoman, it is the one who is here in the middle.

I.vi.7 MAGDALENE: I implore you, tell him for me that I want to see him.

I.vi.8 SIMON: Very well, O noblewoman, let me see him. *(To Christ:)* O our teacher, a dear woman has come. She wants to see you.

I.vi.9 *Christ will stand up. He will walk around a bit.*

I.vi.10 CHRIST: O dear woman, why do you want to see me?

I.vi.11 *Magdalene will walk on her knees. She will go to stand [on her knees] at Christ's feet.*

I.vi.12 MAGDALENE: Oh! O my deity, O my ruler, just you alone are worthy of utter exaltation. Here is a cross. At your feet I humbly bow and I humbly beseech you, have compassion for me, pardon my sins for me, because I am a very great sinner. Do not despise me. Pardon me, your creation, for I have come here before you to weep, to kiss your precious princely feet. Let me sprinkle my tears on your feet. And let me also clean them for you with my hair. O my deity, may your heart be compassionate, O my ruler.

I.vi.13 CHRIST: You, Magdalene, I have seen your weeping, your sadness, how you are resolved. You have washed my feet with your tears. *(To John:)* O dear John, bring here the precious unguent you have in your hands.

I.vi.14   SAINT JOHN: O my beloved teacher, here it is.

I.vi.15   CHRIST: O dear woman, you have said you are assigning yourself to me and that you scorn the pleasures on earth. And for as long as you live here on earth, you are to always give torment to your earthly body. And now I will give you a precious liquid. It is not a liquid from here on earth. Bend down. Let me spread the precious unguent on your head. O dear woman, with that you are going to be happy. It will become your good fortune in heaven. Stand up, and go to your home.

I.vi.16   *Then he will bless Magdalene. Magdalene will stand up. She will go inside. Christ will sit down again. Judas will stand up. He will speak.*

I.vi.17   JUDAS: God knows, but why is Christ wasting what he spread on this woman's head? Isn't it just going to waste? And why does he do this? Truly, if the unguent had been sold, maybe 300 pesos could have been obtained for it. That would have proven useful to us for a long time. Or maybe poor people could have been shown compassion, who are trying to extricate themselves from danger.

I.vi.18   CHRIST: What are you saying? Although I spread the precious unguent on the head of the noblewoman, what she did is very good. She washed my feet for me with her tears. But you, you say you would have had compassion for the miserable, the poor. But I am about to abandon you; I am about to go away. The poor will live here with you; when I am gone you are to show them compassion. But it is not much longer that I will be living with you. Why do you say such things? Truly I say to you that this noblewoman will be praised for what she did. The Christians of the world will hear of it.

I.vi.19   *Christ will go inside along with all the apostles. Judas will just turn around at the edge of the doorway. He will speak.*

I.vi.20   JUDAS: O teacher, why did you want the very good unguent to be wasted? I think you'll just give me problems. But you'll pay the price of it. And if not, may my name not be Judas Iscariot!

I.vi.21   *Judas will go inside.*

Scene vii: Jesus continues teaching. The high priest, Caiaphas, has him pass judgment on the adulterous woman.

I.vii.1   *Christ will come out, along with the apostles and the Jews. They will sit down. He will teach.*

I.vii.2   CHRIST: Now listen, you nobles of Jerusalem and you *macehualtin*. Do not be bewildered about me. I am the one you have been awaiting for a long time. Now I have come to tell you my breath, my words. Turn your lives around! You need not go to the place of great affliction, the place of the dead. It is better that you go to my home in heaven, which makes people very happy.

I.vii.3   CAIAPHAS: O rulers, what is the bewilderer saying? He really shames people and he's really about to crack my skull. Let him admonish the woman who's in jail, for she is sinful. Let them go get her, let them bring her here in front of me.

I.vii.4   JEWS: What you are thinking is very splendid, O high priest. Let him admonish her, for what she has done is worthy of death. Let us go and get the wretched little woman. *(To Woman:)* Come out here, O despicable woman! Now you'll see! We'll take you in front of the bewilderer, your lover. He'll pass judgment on you. Get moving, O despicable woman! *(They all will speak in front of Christ.)* O rulers, we have brought this woman here.

I.vii.5   CAIAPHAS: O my noble, how do you want it? This wretched little woman here sinned, committed mortal sins. She practiced adultery, she took a lover. Our grandfathers, our grandmothers, left it commanded that, as to one who takes a lover, they will stone them. Now then, how do you want it? Pass judgment on her.

I.vii.6   *Christ will come down. He will write something on the ground. Caiaphas [and the Jews] will all stand up and read what is written on the ground. They will all go out quickly, they will run. Only Woman will remain.*

I.vii.7   CHRIST: O dear woman, who are the ones who brought you here before me, those nobles who were here?

I.vii.8   WOMAN: O ruler, O teacher, they've already gone. They fled after they saw that you wrote something on the ground.

I.vii.9   CHRIST: O dear woman, go to your home. Be consoled, for you will be one of my beloved ones. At no time are you to commit sins anymore. Go.

I.vii.10   *Then Woman will go out. All the Jews will come out, along with the priests. Then Christ will teach.*

I.vii.11   CHRIST: Now listen, you nobles of Jerusalem and you *macehualtin*, you Jews. Do not be bewildered. I have come down from heaven. My beloved father, God, sent me here from there, so I came to become flesh inside my beloved mother. I'm the one who will save people. I will die. But even though I will die, I will revive in just three days. I will go up to heaven. I

I.vii.11
(*cont.*)
will go to sit at the right hand of my beloved father, God. And afterward I will come from there, I will come to judge the lives of the living and the dead. But as for you: how wretched you are! Even though you are about to knock me down as if I were a house, it won't be long until I arise, I revive. In just three days I will take my body, which will be very clean, which will be very good. And at that time you will say, "It is the maiden's child." For it is I who made heaven and earth and the place of the dead. Everything is my creation, all that you see and that you do not see.

I.vii.12
MALCHUS: Now we are questioning you. How many more years will you treat us like this, will you keep going around beating on us, tormenting us so? Now what do you say to us? Who are you? Where did you come from? Who sent you here? What are you saying to us? What we are hearing: who told it to you? Who instructed you, you bewilderer? Don't crack our skulls on us. Don't you know that we are nobles?

I.vii.13
CHRIST: You are not prudent. You do not see. You do not believe. Truly I say to you, afterward you will believe, when I, the maiden's child, revive, arise. And it will be me.

I.vii.14
MALCHUS: O rulers, he's really cracking your skulls. Leave. Let the bewilderer cry out over there. Let's go.

I.vii.15
All the Jews will go out.

I.vii.16
CHRIST: O my beloved children, come, listen. I know well that in just two days Passover will take place. That is when the maiden's child will be made known to people, will be betrayed, so that I will save people on the cross. I will suffer pain, torment, so that I will open up heaven for those whom I will take there, my subjects, the good, the proper.

I.vii.17
Christ and the apostles will go out.

Scene viii: The leave-taking: Christ goes to Bethany and bids farewell to his mother.

I.viii.1
Saint Mary will come out, with Magdalene and Martha.

I.viii.2
CHRIST: You who are supreme, you beloved noblewoman, you the Most Holy Trinity's chosen one, you beloved daughter of God the father, you who surpass all women, you who are very humble, you consummately good maiden whom no one can equal, may the peace of the deity Holy Spirit be with you. But may you know now, O my beloved mother, that it is time, the time has come, we have now reached the time when I am to die and, with my suffering, all the people of the world, who are my creations, will be saved, those proper, good ones who are in the great

I.viii.2
(cont.)
sacred commands and those who are bad. It is just for this reason that I came down from heaven, that I came to be born of your belly, so that I would die on behalf of my subjects, the people of the world, so that they would be saved. And now, O my beloved mother, be consoled. Let your precious soul be undisturbed. Do not be sad. It is essential that I die. And it is essential that what those who say things first, my beloved prophets, left said about me will come to pass, that I will die so that I will purify the world. O my beloved and revered mother, rejoice, be consoled. My suffering, my death, will become the joy of the good people of the world. But now it is time for me to take leave of you so that I will go into the *altepetl* of Jerusalem, O my beloved mother.

I.viii.3
SAINT MARY: You, my consolation and beloved child, you who emerged from my womb, as you came to become a man, what are you saying to me? Where do you want to go? Why, for what reason, do you want to abandon me, I who am your mother? I couldn't abandon you. I will be forever at your side. I can see that your beloved, revered, and completely good face has become quite pale, has gone white, with worry, with sadness, And I fervently beseech you, O my beloved child, may your heart be so compassionate that you spend Passover here. Do it just because I raised you, because you love me so dearly. Let it be for my milk that you obey me. Please listen well, you my jade only child. If you go into the *altepetl* of Jerusalem, you will be taken into custody. You know they hate you there.

I.viii.4
CHRIST: O you who are my beloved and revered mother, what you are saying can no longer be done. It is essential that I die, because of the sins in the world.

I.viii.5
SAINT MARY: You are my one and only beloved child. And I know well that it was for your torment, your death, that you came here to earth, by which you came to save us. But now, O my beloved child, with all your power, even if you didn't die it would be possible for you to save people. Let the price for destroying the sins of the world be your health, and let it also be your blood that was spilled when you were still a little child, when they cut your male flesh from you. Let the price also be the way you fasted everywhere in the forest, how you went without sleep. Let this too become the payment: how your heart ached, hurt, when you taught people in the *altepetl*. Let that be the price paid for the sins of the world. It will be possible if you want it to be like this, you my beloved child.

I.viii.6
CHRIST: May you know, O my beloved mother, that everything the prophets predicted, all the prophecies that lie written in the sacred book,

I.viii.6
(*cont.*)
that lie spoken about me, will come true, will happen. Do not be sad, O my beloved mother. I will make the words of my beloved father, God, come true.

I.viii.7
SAINT MARY: How very tear-inducing, how saddening, is the way you answer me, you my beloved child. Don't you know, don't you remember, how I brought you up, how I carried you in my arms? And don't you remember when I went to hide you in Egypt, when Herod was searching for you? He forcefully commanded that his warriors kill you if they had found you! And don't you remember when I lost you for three days in the temple in Jerusalem? Very great was the worry that I endured for your sake. Because of that, obey me. And so that the world will be purified, desire some other thing with which you may pacify your beloved father. I implore you, you my beloved child.

I.viii.8
CHRIST: May you know well, O my beloved mother, that what is written in the sacred book, all the torments, will be done to me. The Jews will tie me to a stone column. They will flog me. And they will make me carry on my shoulder a very large crossed-wood device, a cross, on which I will be made to stretch my arms so that I will die. That is how all my creations in the world will be saved. Everything will come true in front of you, all my torments.

I.viii.9
SAINT MARY: O my lord, O my child, by your leave, have compassion for me. If that's what you want, may it so be done. But my heart suffers great pain and torment.

I.viii.10
CHRIST: O my beloved mother, truly indeed I must obey you, for you are my beloved mother. But even more must I obey my beloved father, God. What he wants is that I go to Jerusalem.

I.viii.11
SAINT MARY: O my beloved child, remember for me how you ordered, you admonished, children to obey their fathers, their mothers. And now, O my beloved child, I fervently implore you, do not go to Jerusalem.

I.viii.12
CHRIST: O my beloved and revered mother, I really must die, for I'm about to be late for my death. And the first parents,[10] our relatives, the prophets, who are in limbo, are very discontented. They've been waiting for me a long time, as has my predecessor, Saint John the Baptist, who went to console them, went to tell them that I would soon go to save them. And now I really must go to die in Jerusalem.

I.viii.13
SAINT MARY: O my beloved and revered child, such is the will of the one to whom you must be very obedient, your beloved father, God. But may it be when you are old, great [in years], that you die, you who are my only child.

I.viii.14   CHRIST: O my beloved and revered mother, we have already reached the time when I shall die. It also says in the holy words that I am to die now. Even if the earth were to be destroyed, that would not delay my dying. And now, O my beloved mother, remember that when you went to make an offering of me before Saint Simeon, he told you of your suffering, that your face, your heart, would suffer great pain.

I.viii.15   SAINT MARY: O my beloved and revered child, wait for me until I die. Don't let me witness your death. Don't let it happen in front of me.

I.viii.16   CHRIST: Ah, O my beloved and revered mother, it's no longer possible for what you are saying to be done. The people of the world would perish, just from the sins that have been done. And now, I will pay for them so that they will revive. Because when they sinned, they sinned in public, therefore I will die in public. That will be the price. It is necessary that someone die and that it be very painful, that it be shameful. And Adam and Eve stretched out their arms to the fruit tree as they sinned. Thus, they betrayed their children. And I must be made to stretch my arms on the cross so that I may save the children of Adam and Eve from the hands of the human horned owl.[11]

I.viii.17   *Then Saint Mary will faint, and Magdalene will grab hold of her.*

I.viii.18   MAGDALENE: O my lord, O my ruler, do not say such things! Don't you see that your beloved mother has fainted? Why won't you help her? O my beloved savior, O my ruler, have compassion for her. Obey your beloved mother. Spend Passover here with us! Do not go to Jerusalem. *(To Mary:)* O noblewoman, O my child, O my daughter, how are you doing? What is happening to you, O you utterly humble one? Take heart! *(To Martha:)* O noblewoman, O my older sister, bring a little something to drink. Let us give it to the noblewoman. Perhaps she'll be revived a bit with it. Hurry!

I.viii.19   *Then Martha will come out. She will bring a little water. They will give it to Saint Mary to drink.*

I.viii.20   MARTHA: You utterly great noblewoman, Saint Mary, you who are the mother of God, what is happening to you? Be strong! Drink a little bit of water, O noblewoman, O my child.

I.viii.21   CHRIST: O my beloved and revered mother, revive, don't die of sadness. O my beloved and revered mother, console yourself, be strong, for truly I say to you that no one at all will die the way I am to die. It will be very painful, it will be shameful, because my suffering will last a long time. My heart, my body, my face will suffer great pain, torment. My enemies

I.viii.21 (cont.)   the Jews will mockingly dress me in a cloak. They will spit on me. Their fingers will be full of my hair and they will lay on top of my head, with metal [staves], a twisted cord, a circlet of thorns. And they will strike my hands, my feet with metal [nails]. And they will stab my heart with a metal staff. And they will beat my body everywhere, 6,606 times, so that what the various prophets left said will come true. They left it said that his body would suffer everywhere: on his head, his face, his hands, and his feet. And now, O my beloved mother, be comforted, be strong, exert all your effort so that you won't be sad. Pay close attention. You have no child, you are alone, you are just a poor little thing. What is to be done? Pay close attention, O noblewoman, O my mother.

I.viii.22   SAINT MARY: Ah, O my beloved child, you speak in such a way that my heart suffers greatly. I can no longer endure it, O my child, for the time has come when I am about to die.

I.viii.23   MAGDALENE: O my beloved teacher, by your favor, remain here with us until Passover is observed. Do not go over to Jerusalem.

I.viii.24   *Then the twelve apostles will come out. They will kneel in front of Christ. They will all be sad.*

I.viii.25   SAINT PETER: O our lord, O our teacher, why are the dear women weeping, as if you are giving them worry? They are very sad. Don't you hear them? Comfort them.

I.viii.26   *Then Magdalene will go to meet him, joining her hands together.*

I.viii.27   MAGDALENE: May you (all) implore him also, for we've been beseeching him all this time but he no longer wants, he no longer accepts, our words, our entreaties. Now then, you beseech him too. Maybe he will obey, maybe he will receive, your words.

I.viii.28   SAINT JOHN: O our beloved and revered teacher, stay here with us. Do not go to Jerusalem. You already know that the Jews hate you indeed. Don't desire to go over there.

I.viii.29   SAINT PETER: O our lord, by your favor, have compassion for us so that you will not go over to Jerusalem. The people there want very much to kill you. Spend Passover right here. Go to Jerusalem later. Let your heart desire it.

I.viii.30   CHRIST: O my beloved children, it is absolutely no longer possible, it no longer can be done, for my beloved father, God, wants me to go to Jerusalem. I will spend Passover there.

I.viii.31   *Then he will embrace his mother.*

I.viii.32 CHRIST: O my beloved and revered mother, that is all. Let me take leave of you. But let it be with your authorization. Give me your blessing, because you are my beloved mother. You gave birth to me on earth. It is you who will bless me, O my beloved and revered mother, O noblewoman.

I.viii.33 *Then Saint Mary will bless Christ.*

I.viii.34 SAINT MARY: May he who always and forever sheds light for people, our lord God, go leading you, as you are a man. But before you go and lay down a foot, first embrace me with goodness, with propriety, and give me your blessing, I who am your mother.

I.viii.35 *Then Christ will embrace his beloved mother. Blessing.*

I.viii.36 CHRIST: O my beloved and revered mother, let me bless you. In the beloved and revered name of my beloved and revered father, God, and me, and the Holy Spirit, may you be blessed always, forever. May you be praised, for I was in your belly for nine months. May your beloved soul also be praised, which will always, forever, be filled with the Holy Spirit, grace. Don't be anxious because I am to die, for that is how my beloved father, God, desires it. Everyone in the world has been pushed around by death, but my death [will save them]. And now, O my beloved mother, I say to you that even though I will die, I will revive once again in three days. You will see me once again. My body will be pure through and through. I will never die again. Finally, you will be happy, O beloved noblewoman, O my mother. Now I am going to go, O my beloved mother.

I.viii.37 SAINT MARY: O my beloved child, O my consolation, O my joy, what your beloved father, God, wants, if it is what you want, may it so be done, you who are my only child.

I.viii.38 CHRIST: O my blessed mother, how very much you suffer from sadness on my account. You are not to fall down, O my beloved mother. O Magdalene, take hold of her, and may she not fall down somewhere.

I.viii.39 *Then Saint Mary will go inside, along with Magdalene and Martha.*

ACT II. THE PLOT AGAINST JESUS UNFOLDS. THE LAST SUPPER. JUDAS'S BETRAYAL.

Scene i: The leaders of Jerusalem conspire to arrest and kill Jesus. Joseph (of Arimathea) and Nicodemus defend him.

II.i.1   *Then Caiaphas and all the Jews will come out. They will hold a town coun-*
          cil meeting. Drums will be beaten, trumpets will be played. All the chief
          priests will sit on a bench. And the Jews will be spread out. They will be in a
          row. The chief priests will consult with one another about Christ.

II.i.2   CAIAPHAS: Now that I have gathered you together, you very honored
          people, you rulers: you already know that Christ, the child of Mary, is
          stirring people up, is going around lying to people and bewildering the
          macehualtin. They all follow behind him now. They go around saying
          and telling other people that he is the Messiah. But we know that he is
          just a wretched little person, a wretched little *macehualli.* And our very
          splendid *altepetl* he considers as nothing. He is spoken of as if he's really
          great, because he bewilders people. And he indeed deserves death. Tell
          me, what are we up to? What are we doing? If we just leave him like this,
          he will seat himself as ruler. He will make all our subjects his subjects.
          And as for the people of Rome, won't they come to destroy us? They will
          say, "Maybe this is another time that we take their rulership from them."
          Won't they come to lay siege to our *altepetl*? And our very splendid
          temple and the commands of God, won't they all be destroyed if Christ
          makes them all his subjects, if they obey his teachings? You see that our
          fathers took great care of the commands because Moses left them to
          us as a gift. Even though we may perhaps destroy it ourselves, aren't we
          also very wise? If he truly were the Messiah whom we are waiting for,
          wouldn't he be afraid of death? You see how no one appears here inside
          our *altepetl* today because we would have stoned this one on Sunday.
          That's why he went to hide.[12]

II.i.3   ANNAS: O rulers, O my nobles, you who are seated in honor, you the
          great high priest, the pontiff Caiaphas, and you who are present here, you
          elders, you chief priests, you Jews. I say what, what, what do we do? For
          he who is called Christ, he performs a great many marvels, and so he is
          obeyed, he is loved, he is honored. And our lordship, our honor, our rul-
          ership is thus being destroyed. And here is what I say: if we just leave him
          like this, if we don't do something to him, truly every person will believe
          in him, every person will take him as a ruler. The ruler President Pontius
          Pilate will no longer count for anything. And so, may you give commands,
          may your breath, your words, be issued as to what can be done.

II.i.4   CAIAPHAS: It is correct, what you say, what you think, you great priest
          Annas, you ruler. But you, you elders, you chief priests, you Jews: it
          seems to me that you are fools, that you are careless. Listen! Here's what
          I say. It is necessary that one person die for the sake of the *macehualtin*

II.i.4
(cont.)

so that all do not perish, they of the water, they of the hill, the people of Jerusalem. Please listen. Don't you already know that our fathers long ago kept their commands well? But as for us, now they are about to be destroyed in our hands. And it won't happen like this. Why? What for? Will one wretched little person overcome us? I know for sure that he is just a wretched little *macehualli*. His father's name is Joseph. He's a carpenter. And why does he go around saying that he is a great ruler? Where were we when he came into the temple, when he knocked at the door? We should have seized him then! And so, let it not just be left like this. Do not let your hearts be at rest, O rulers, O my nobles.

II.i.5

ELEAZAR: O ruler, what you say is very splendid, that Christ will die, for there it shows that you love your subjects very much and you do your job correctly.

II.i.6

PHARISEE: You who are seated in honor, you our lords, you rulers, you pontiffs, you priests: I say in front of you, what are you doing, you our lords, you rulers, in regard to that Jesus, whom the *macehualtin* call Christ? How did he dare to come into the great temple? He beat all the vendors, such that he really threw them all down as he scattered their merchandise. He said, "Get out! This here is not a house of pleasure. This here is the home of my beloved father, God." And he said that we priests are wrong, that we are just deceivers!

II.i.7

CAIAPHAS: What are you saying? Has Christ not heard the law of Moses? Will he break, will he destroy, that which Moses set in order?

II.i.8

SAMUEL: This is what we told him. And he just said, "There's no Moses anymore. That was before there was me. I am all-powerful. I am the child of God."

II.i.9

ANNAS: And why won't you ask the deceiver, the bewilderer, what sort he is, who he is, where he is from? And furthermore, you Jews, you Pharisees, how will you get hold of him so that he can be questioned as to who he is, what sort he is?

II.i.10

FIRST JEW: O rulers, he is from Galilee. He is a subject of the ruler Herod, he is under his rule. And he was so daring as to come into Jerusalem. He rode on a donkey. As he came here into the *altepetl* of Jerusalem, he was greatly honored, he was considered as a deity. And a great many *macehualtin* came with him, people from over in Israel. The *macehualtin* scattered many flowers as they led him this way, and there were palm fronds in their hands as he came to enter. And the little Hebrew children behaved ominously to people. They all praised him. And many people of wealth, people of property, came with him. And many

II.i.10
(*cont.*)

rulers and nobles of the Hebrew people. And many soldiers went spread around him. That is why we did not say anything.

II.i.11

SECOND JEW: We were very astonished that the little children of the Hebrews and those from Jerusalem, those old enough to crawl and those who are newborns, all praised him. Everyone came into Jerusalem there. That is why we did not say anything.

II.i.12

SAMUEL: You who are seated in honor, you chief priests, and here are the Pharisees: I say in front of your rulerships, what are we up to? What are we doing? It is as if I see something worrisome that will come upon the royal *altepetl* of Jerusalem in regard to Jesus, whom the *macehualtin* call Christ. How did he dare to come and enter here? He sees you as nothing and he sees your honor as nothing. Your fame, your honor, are about to perish, here in the *altepetl* of Jerusalem. And who has any regard for the ruler President Pontius Pilate? His fame, his honor, are about to perish. Fortify yourselves, O our lords, O our rulers!

II.i.13

CAIAPHAS: What are you saying? It's as if you are deranged. As long as we will live, our fame, our honor, will forever be exalted. One person must die for the sake of the *macehualtin* so that everyone does not become bewildered, those of the water, those of the hill, the people here in Jerusalem, lest what Moses put in order, what he prophesied, be ruined. No one whatsoever will overcome us.

II.i.14

ANNAS: If our lords, our rulers, the people of Rome find out, won't they be angry with us? They will come to take from us our lordship, our royal seat. Won't they shame us very much? And won't they carry out a great war? Won't some of the other nobles and rulers thus overcome us? Let us deliberate carefully as to how it can be done in regard to Christ. He sees rulership as nothing, he counts it as nothing. Will Christ overcome us? Let me hear your words as to how it can be done. Let us be united.

II.i.15

CAIAPHAS: What you say is correct, you great priest Annas. Now come, you elders, you Jews. It is as if you do not know, as if you are deranged. Let us take counsel as to how the deceiver can fall into our hands.

II.i.16

CENTURION: We are just waiting on your priestly command. The liar, the deceiver, worries us a great deal. If you want, we will go to look for him right away, where he is housing himself, the bewilderer Christ. Then we will destroy him.

II.i.17

SIMEON: Your words are very good, the way you say that he is to die, the bewilderer, the deceiver, this Christ. That indeed is what we long for, what we thirst for, what we hunger for. For he really stirs up the *macehualtin*, they who must be carried, who must be borne on the back. We

II.i.17
(*cont.*)

must arrest him, seize him. Likewise we say that we really must sentence him to death so that he will die, he will perish. Quickly, say how we will arrest the scoundrel.

II.i.18

When Samuel speaks, "Non in festo ne forte tumulus fieret in populo"[13] *will be sung.*

II.i.19

SAMUEL: O lords, O honorable chief priests, here is what I say abut this meeting, how I assist you. I say, your order that Christ die is very good. However, you see that something that is done quickly can have bad results. I'm not saying that the rotten scoundrel shouldn't die. But we are already in Passover, and all sorts of people are coming to gather together everywhere. We should not consider seizing him on the festival. You know well that this person is loved, he is honored, by all the people here in Jerusalem. Let's not inflame the *macehualtin.* If we seize him on the festival, they'll think about making war, and they'll kill us. Let it be on an ordinary day that the bewilderer is taken into custody, is arrested.

II.i.20

MALCHUS: O rulers, what you are thinking is very splendid. It must indeed be on an ordinary day that we go arrest, that we seize, the bewilderer so that the *macehualtin* won't know it, so that we don't stir up those of the *altepetl.*

II.i.21

JOSEPH: You royal nobles, you who are seated in honor, let it not be in vain that I try to calm you down. Do not let me anger you as I raise to your ears, as I speak, a word or two in front of you. Why do you say that Christ stirs people up and mocks them? Whoever says that just speaks from envy. Don't you know that he is a person of proper life, a humble person? Doesn't everyone esteem him for his humility? Please tell me: is there anyone like him anywhere? In all the time that you have lived, have you seen a prophet perform marvelous things like we see now, the marvels that the teacher Christ performs now? Do not think that you want to sentence him to death. What Jesus goes about doing is all very good, very splendid. He helps our subjects. He cures our sick. He makes the lame walk. He makes the blind see. He makes the deaf hear. He brings the dead to life. He loves our subjects very much. And many are his merciful and loving acts. And the people of wealth, the soldiers, the warriors, they are all fond of him already. Don't you know that not long ago he revived the highborn noble Lazarus when he was dead? They'd already buried his body. He lay festering in a tomb for four days. But when the teacher found out, then he went there where they buried his body. He cried out for him to come out from under the ground. It was Christ who revived Lazarus. And the marvel happened right in front of

II.i.21
(*cont.*)

me. Many people saw it. It didn't happen in secret. And you also know what God's spokesman the prophet Isaiah left said: that the beloved son of God will come, he will come to perform many marvels, the savior of the world. He will come to cure those who are sick with various illnesses and pestilences, those who have leprosy. That is how it will be evident that he is the teacher who has been awaited for a long time. If the prophecies are genuinely true, that the Messiah will come to the *altepetl*, then he has already reached us. If, perhaps, he is not the savior, what harm has he done that you want to sentence him to death? Consider carefully what you shall do. My heart is not this way. If you will sentence him to death, I withdraw myself before God and before you.

II.i.22   CAIAPHAS: I know well and I see well your words. You are a person of great prudence and you are a keeper of the five temples, you, Joseph. You used to think that you should lead us, that we'd take you and your white beard as our mirror, our sign. You could have directed us, you could have deliberated with us as to what we will do. But everything you are saying is very bad. You advocate for, you turn yourself over to, Christ, the bewilderer. Do you have no regard for all the elders? We will not desist for that. Our royal agreement will be carried out, will be done. We will destroy Christ.

II.i.23   NICODEMUS: But why are you responding to Joseph with anger, O ruler? Everything in what we say is true. Truly indeed, Christ is the Messiah himself, who has come. You all see all the sacred marvels he performs. He cures your sick and revives your dead. But you pay him back by hating him and slandering him.

II.i.24   JOSEPH: Even though you hate the teacher, he goes about helping our subjects very much. He has mercy on all the poor people. As for me, I have not seen any one of our subjects whom he bewildered. I saw only the great many dear sick people whom he has cured and the many dear dead ones whom he has revived.

II.i.25   CAIAPHAS: With your words, it is obvious indeed that you are truly changing over to his side. Are you his students? We will not let him go. Not thus will our royal decision be destroyed. We will carry it out, we will put it into effect. Move them over to the door this instant! They must not sit where the rulers are gathered together. Let them go immediately!

II.i.26   *Right then Caiaphas will strike the table. They will make Joseph and Nicodemus go out the door.*

Scene ii. The orders against Jesus are announced to the public.

II.ii.1   CAIAPHAS: Listen, O you honored people, to the true words I say on the festival. One person must die so that the whole world won't be destroyed. Come, notary. Put down our royal command, write the document quickly. Let the town crier call out in this way everywhere in the four corners of the *altepetl*. We chief priests all command, in regard to the so-called Christ of Nazareth, that no one whatsoever is to pay heed to his teachings. And no one is to bring him into their home, no one is to befriend him. We command that anyone who brings him into their home or befriends him, they too will be arrested, seized, sentenced to death. So that our royal command can be carried out, we command that anyone who sees where he is housing himself will then come to tell the chief priests. They will pay them a lot of silver,[14] and they will be greatly loved.

II.ii.2   *All the Jews will be very happy.*

II.ii.3   JEWS: May your will be done in this way, O high priest!

II.ii.4   NOTARY: O our lords, O rulers, let me put down your royal command right away.

II.ii.5   *Then he will sit at a table. He will write something. They will give the document to the town crier.*

II.ii.6   NOTARY: I have carried out your priestly command. Let the town crier call out everywhere in the streets. Play trumpets. Let him make it known to all the *macehualtin* so that they will all know it, those of the water, those of the hill, here in the *altepetl* of Jerusalem.

II.ii.7   *Notary will lay the document on the table.*

II.ii.8   ANNAS: Come, town crier. Here is the document, our royal command. Cry out everywhere in the streets. Make the *macehualtin* hear it.

II.ii.9   TOWN CRIER: Very well, O our lords, O rulers. Let me carry out your words, your command. Let me make all the *macehualtin* hear it.

II.ii.10   *Drums will be beaten and trumpets will be played. Town Crier will call out in four directions, on the stage.*

II.ii.11   TOWN CRIER: The chief priests issue a command. They say, in regard to the so-called Christ of Nazareth, who bewilders the *macehualtin* with a great many things, anyone who knows where he is will come to inform the rulers so that he will be arrested, he will be seized, he will be taken prisoner. And anyone who listens to his teachings and befriends him or brings him into their home, who gives him something to eat, will also

II.ii.11
(*cont.*)

be arrested, seized, punished with stones and sticks, then sentenced to death so that the royal command will be carried out, so that it will not be ruined. And anyone who sees where Christ is housing himself will then come in good manner, will come to tell the chief priests. They will pay them a lot of silver and they will be greatly loved. (*Returning to the priests:*) I have gone and carried out your royal command. I went to make all the *macehualtin* hear it everywhere in the streets.

II.ii.12

CAIAPHAS: Now let us go. And you, Leader, you, war leader, I firmly command you, look for Christ. All of you who are here, you elders, you Pharisees, I firmly command you, look for him, all of you, and consider well how you will be able to arrest him, to seize him. Be cautious. If someone comes to tell you where he is housing himself, then you will tell us.

II.ii.13

LEADER: Don't let it worry you. We will now consult with one another on how we will do it. He goes around making all of us very angry. We have been waiting for your royal command for a long time. We are very happy and delighted with it. He will be arrested, he will be seized.

II.ii.14

Then the priests will embrace one another. Trumpets will be played. All the Jews will go inside. The chief priests will go in front.

Scene iii. Preparations for the Last Supper.

II.iii.1

Christ will come out, along with all the apostles. "Scitis quia post vidum pascha [et Filius hominis tradetur ut crucifigatur]"[15] *will be sung.*

II.iii.2

CHRIST: O my beloved children, your faces and hearts are already aware, you already know, that the very day after tomorrow will be Passover, at which time the Jews in the great *altepetl* of Jerusalem will celebrate a festival. And the maiden's beloved child will be arrested there, will be seized, will be betrayed to the sinners. They will make him stretch his arms upon the cross. And now, O my beloved children, you, John, and you, James, I am going to send you as messengers. Go and prepare my festival food for me, now that it is Passover.

II.iii.3

SAINT JOHN: O my beloved teacher, where does your heart concede that we should go to make preparations?

II.iii.4

CHRIST: Listen, O my students. Go directly over into the great *altepetl* of Jerusalem. When you have arrived, you will see a little water carrier, going carrying his water jug on his back. When you have seen him, go follow him to where he goes indoors. You will go inside there as well. You will say to the householder, "The teacher says, 'It is time, the time

II.iii.4
(cont.)   has come for my work to come to an end, so that I will rest. I will spend Passover there in his home. And today I will feed my students there, I will give them refreshment there.'" Then he will show you a large house. And when he has shown it to you, then make preparations there so that it will be my place of waiting, so that I will rest there.

II.iii.5   SAINT JAMES: Very well, O our teacher. Let us carry out your precious words. Let us go.

II.iii.6   *Christ will go inside, along with the apostles. And Saint John and Saint James will remain on the stage.*

II.iii.7   SAINT JAMES: Let's go and carry out very quickly whatever he commands us, because he is our savior.

II.iii.8   SAINT JOHN: Let's go where our beloved teacher is sending us. Let's hurry so we can return quickly.

II.iii.9   *Saint John and Saint James will go inside. Gamaliel will come out. He will be very worried. As he speaks, he will spread his turban on the ground.*

II.iii.10   GAMALIEL: Now where is the teacher, the Messiah, God's beloved child, my great benefactor? Where will he spend Passover? I am very worried about it, I go about distressed over it, because our rulers, the chief priests, have commanded that anyone whose home he enters or who befriends him will also be arrested and sentenced to death along with him. But I say, let me be so fortunate, so favored, that he may come into my home today on Passover. I am very willing to receive him. I desire wholeheartedly that my great benefactor will come and rest here in my home, in my humble shack.

II.iii.11   *Water Carrier will come out. Gamaliel will call to him.*

II.iii.12   GAMALIEL: Come, O my younger brother. Run off quickly, hurry up and fetch a little clean water. Maybe it will be our good fortune that the great teacher, God's beloved child, will come into our home.

II.iii.13   WATER CARRIER: Very well. Let me hurry up and fetch some clean water.

II.iii.14   *Gamaliel will go inside. Water Carrier will go. He will carry his jug on his back. He will go where water will be lying. When he has arrived where the water is laid, he will take down his jug. He will collect water with a gourd vessel that is inside of it. He will keep pouring it into his jug. When he has filled it, afterward he will speak.*

II.iii.15   WATER CARRIER: I am tarrying a long time since I came to get water. Maybe the people of my household will scold me. Let me go. How is it possible that it took me so long?

II.iii.16   *Water Carrier will grasp his jug. He will go. When he has gone a ways, he will turn around. He will see the two apostles, Christ's messengers.*

II.iii.17   WATER CARRIER: Hey! Who are they who are coming here? It seems like they're following right behind me! It seems like they're going directly to my home. I'd better get going!

II.iii.18   *Water Carrier will walk on a little bit. Saint John and Saint James will come out in a gentle manner.*

II.iii.19   SAINT JOHN: O our lord, O God, it seems that we've been so favored as to have found the water carrier of whom you told us. He is carrying his jug. Let's go and follow him. Where will he go inside?

II.iii.20   SAINT JAMES: May our great teacher be exultantly praised! We've now been so favored as to have come upon the water carrier of whom he told us. Let's follow behind him.

II.iii.21   *Water Carrier will go inside. And when Saint James and Saint John have arrived there, Saint John will knock on the door. Then Gamaliel will show himself in the doorway. He will speak.*

II.iii.22   GAMALIEL: Who are you who are knocking on the door?

II.iii.23   SAINT JOHN: O my noble, O ruler, be joyful.[16] Our teacher sent us here to you. He says, "I have now come near to it, it is now time, the time has come, for me to rest, for my work as a teacher to come to an end, and my salvation of people is going to begin. Tell the noble householder that, by his leave, I will rest there, I will spend Passover in his home. And I will feed my students there, I will give them refreshment there. And he will show you a large and splendid house, which will be my waiting place. Make preparations there." Those are all the precious and revered words of our benefactor that we have brought, O beloved and revered noble, O ruler.

II.iii.24   GAMALIEL: You have endured fatigue, you have wearied yourselves, you honored ones, you personages. Come here. My teacher, the Messiah, God's beloved child, has been generous, has thought of me. I am greatly favored. I am delighted to hear his precious words, with which he honors me with his favor. Come inside! I will wait here for the words of our great teacher. I have already prepared his house so that he will come to rest there. I will do what is of service to him. Make the preparations right away. I will give you whatever is needed. O my servants, come! Let us all make preparations for him, for we have been so favored that God's beloved child, Jesus, will spend Passover here with us.

II.iii.25   *Then a table will be set out with tablecloths, a salt cellar, pewter tankards, vases, and four candleholders with wax candles. Many flowers will be scattered. Gamaliel, his servant, Water Carrier, and the two apostles will place things on it. Tortillas will be set down and a flask of wine, oranges, bananas, lettuce, watermelon, radishes, mameys, table knives, and silver plates, on which will be lain one white tortilla and twelve small hosts. And a chalice will be placed on the table, in which the wine will go, and the candles will be lighted. When the preparations have been made, then Saint John will speak.*

II.iii.26   SAINT JOHN: Now we are going to go. We will go and explain to our beloved teacher how we have obtained your favor, how we have made preparations, O revered personage.

II.iii.27   GAMALIEL: Tell him that I am waiting for my revered lord. I do not deserve, I do not merit, that he has remembered me in this way. But I am wholeheartedly willing to receive him, to be deserving of his favor. His precious heart has granted a favor.

II.iii.28   *Gamaliel will go inside. Christ will come out, and all the apostles. Saint John and Saint James will go to meet the others.*

II.iii.29   SAINT JOHN: O our beloved teacher, we went and made preparations where you sent us. The householder, dear Gamaliel, says, "Tell him that I am here awaiting my revered lord. I do not deserve, I do not merit, that he has remembered me in this way. I am wholeheartedly willing to be deserving of his favor." That is how the dear[17] householder humbly beseeches you.

II.iii.30   CHRIST: His heart has granted a favor. Let us go, O my children. It is high time. My beloved servant has made preparations for us. Let us go.

II.iii.31   SAINT PETER: Very well, O my beloved teacher. May you take to your feet. Let us go.

II.iii.32   SAINT JAMES: Let us all go leading you, you who are our benefactor.

II.iii.33   *Christ will walk along, and all the apostles. Then Gamaliel will come out. He will go to meet Christ. He will kneel in front of him. He will join his hands together. He will kiss Christ's feet. He will still be on his knees as he speaks.*

II.iii.34   GAMALIEL: O my lord, O my beloved teacher, I am so fortunate, I am so favored, that you have come here to my humble shack, where I am awaiting your words. You have endured fatigue. Come inside. Please rest, O beloved ruler. I have made preparations, I your creation.

II.iii.35   *Christ will greet him.*

II.iii.36   CHRIST: You have shown me favor, you have been generous, dear Gamaliel. May we be deserving of your love. Let us rest with you.

II.iii.37   GAMALIEL: I humbly beseech you, may you bless me, along with all your servants here, so that they will work rightfully for you here on earth and afterward attain your kingdom in heaven.

II.iii.38   *Christ will bless Gamaliel. Gamaliel will stand up. They will go to the table. Gamaliel will lead Christ by the hand to where the table is.*

Scene iv: The Last Supper.

II.iv.1   CHRIST: O my beloved children, be seated now. Rest. Eat.

II.iv.2   SAINT PETER: Very well, O our beloved teacher.

II.iv.3   *All the apostles will sit down. Six will be on each side. Christ will sit in the middle. Saint Peter will be at his right hand. And Saint John will be at his left hand. And Judas will just be at the end. "Cenantibus autem eis [accepit Jesus panem, benedixit ac fregit, dedit discipulis suis]"[18] will be sung.*

II.iv.4   CHRIST: All this time I have wanted, I have desired, to spend Passover with you before the torment is done to me. Truly I say to you, I will not eat beside you again now until it is on the seat, on the mat, in the kingdom of my beloved and revered father, God. Listen, O my beloved children. This is my final wish. I want to bequeath to you, you will merit, my supplication. I am going to establish a sign, a model, for all of you and the people on earth, so that you will always do as you will see now. It is a new jade temple where my beloved and revered body will always be kept and my blood that will be spilled as I am made to suffer. And they who can receive it correctly and purely, their sicknesses will abate and they will thereby merit heavenliness. Since my beloved father, God, made me as the *macehualli* that I am, I will become the head of the people on earth, now and when the world comes to an end. And now I bequeath to them my precious body and my blood. It is by them that they will go about remembering me all the time that they go on living. Now I will bless this tortilla and wine. I myself extend into it. I will remain here with you. This will become my localized embodiment forever.

II.iv.5   *Then he will bless the tortilla and lift it up. He will say:*

II.iv.6   CHRIST: O my children, look at this tortilla. It is my precious body; the tortilla is filled up with it, which for your sakes will be made to stretch its arms upon the cross. And now, receive it, eat it, O my children.

II.iv.7   *"Pange lingua gloriosi"[19] will be sung. Then he will have each one receive [the host], Judas the same as the others. When Christ is about to give him the host, an angel will be watching him and will take it out of his mouth with*

II.iv.7 (cont.)   *a napkin and show it to people. Likewise with the wine: Christ will drink some and bless it.*

II.iv.8   CHRIST: O my beloved children, look at this wine that I drink. It is my precious blood that will be spilled on the cross for your sakes, so that the new life will be strong. The wine is filled up with it. Receive it, drink it, O my children.

II.iv.9   *"Tantum ergo sacramentum"* [20] *will be sung. He will have each one drink. All the apostles will be spread about kneeling. When they have received it, then Christ will sit down, as well as the apostles. Judas will be the very first one to eat.*

II.iv.10   CHRIST: And now, eat, O my beloved children. Even though you are eating here with me, you are enjoying yourselves, truly I say to you that here at the table the one who will sell me, who will betray me, to those scoundrels the Jews eats with me and drinks with me. And moreover, I say, wretched is he! It would have been much better if he had never been born. But as for the maiden's child, everything that lies written in the sacred words, in the books of the prophets, must happen to him.

II.iv.11   SAINT JOHN: O my teacher, by your leave, tell me who has done such a thing.

II.iv.12   CHRIST: O John, yes, I will tell you. You'll see in just this way: it's the one to whom I'll give the wet tortilla. That is the one who has done this thing.

II.iv.13   *Each of the apostles will ask a question. The very last who will ask a question will be Judas.*

II.iv.14   SAINT PETER: Is it me, O my dear teacher?

II.iv.15   CHRIST: No. Be at rest.

II.iv.16   SAINT JOHN: Is it me, O my dear teacher?

II.iv.17   CHRIST: No. Be at rest.

II.iv.18   SAINT JAMES: Is it me, O my dear teacher?

II.iv.19   CHRIST: No. Be at rest.

II.iv.20   SAINT BARTHOLOMEW: Is it me, O my dear teacher?

II.iv.21   CHRIST: No. Be at rest. [21]

II.iv.22   JUDAS: Is it me, O teacher?

II.iv.23   CHRIST: It is you who said it. You've admitted it. Bring it to an end.

II.iv.24   *When all have eaten, the table will be moved aside. And Judas will collect everything that will be left on the table. He will wrap it in his cloak.*

Scene v: Christ washes the apostles' feet.

II.v.1   CHRIST: O my beloved children, now you have eaten, but another thing is lacking. I want to wash your feet. Give me water and an earthenware tub. I will wash my students' feet.

II.v.2   *"Dominus Jesus postquam cenabit [cum discipulis suis lavit pedes eorum et ait illis scitis quid fecerim vobis ego dominus et magister exemplum dedi vobis ut et vos ita faciatis]"*[22] *will be sung. They will move aside the benches on which everyone ate. A large towel will be brought out, which Christ will tie at his side, along with a washbasin, and a cloak with which Christ will dress himself, and a large earthenware tub with which people's feet will be washed. Then he will wash each person's feet, lastly Judas. He will embrace both his feet. He will bring them very close to himself. Gamaliel will go following; he will go kissing the feet of the apostles. Saint Peter will be very astonished as he speaks. "Domine tu mihi lavas pedes? [Respondit Jesus et dixit ei: si non lavero tibi pedes, non habebis partum mecum]"*[23] *will be sung.*

II.v.3   GAMALIEL: Here is the water you are asking for, O our teacher.

II.v.4   CHRIST: Uncover your feet, O my beloved child, O Peter. I will wash your feet.

II.v.5   SAINT PETER: Me? You will wash my feet? You are my deity, you are my ruler. I cannot possibly permit you to wash my feet.

II.v.6   CHRIST: Please listen, Peter. What I do today you do not yet understand. You will understand it at some later time.

II.v.7   SAINT PETER: In all the time that is still in our future, I cannot possibly allow you to wash my feet. For you are my deity, you are my ruler.

II.v.8   CHRIST: Please listen, Peter. If I do not wash your feet, you will not rejoice with me in heaven.

II.v.9   SAINT PETER: O my lord, O my ruler, may I be deserving of your mercy. Don't wash only my feet. Wash my hands and my head as well!

II.v.10   CHRIST: One who is clean does not need to bathe but only to wash their feet. Moreover, you are not dirty, you are not muddy. And you others, you are clean. But, it appears, not all of you. *(To Judas:)* O, you my student, you, Judas, come give me those feet of yours. I will wet them for you and I will wash them for you, while the time has not yet arrived for [mine] to be pierced with nails and for my possessions to be wetted with my precious and revered blood. And if I make you angry about something, you have me here at your feet. And do what you want with me, so that you do not destroy yourself in vain forever and so that you do not offend me.

II.v.11   *When everyone's feet have been washed, then Christ will sit down. And Gamaliel will kneel. Saint Peter will lay his head on the table.*

II.v.12   CHRIST: O my beloved children, you have seen what I did to you, how I washed your feet. By that I showed you my love. Please listen. You call me your teacher, your ruler. What you are saying is correct. It is the truth. I am your teacher, I am your ruler. Even though I am your teacher, I bowed down at your feet as I washed your feet for you. In just the same way you are to do it, you are to wash one another's feet. It is a sign, a model, that I have set down for you. You are to do it in just the same way that I have done it. Truly I say to you, someone's subject cannot surpass their lord, their ruler. Likewise, someone's student cannot surpass their teacher. If you will do this like I command you, you will be rewarded very greatly. However, I do not address all of you: I know whom I have chosen, who are my chosen ones, because what lies written in the sacred words, in the sacred book of the prophet David, must come true. He says that one who eats with me, who drinks with me, that same one will kick me, will offend me. And you all, do not forget my words, for I am about to leave you. Here is a new command that I order you to carry out: love one another like I was loving you all the time that I was living here among you. And if you indeed love one another, that is how the people on earth will recognize you, that you truly are my students. But if the people on earth scorn you, you are not to be discouraged by it. Remember that first it was me whom they hated, whom they scorned, I who am your teacher. Pain, affliction, must befall you as well. Truly I say to you that you will weep, you will be sad. And the people on earth will go around enjoying themselves, will go around having a good time. But your tears, your sadness, will turn into very great happiness, which will never end, which will never be finished. And as for you, Simon Peter, do not be discouraged, do not grow faint. Truly I say to you (all) that the human horned owl has asked for you in order to scatter you like dried maize, like wheat, is scattered, is sown. But I will pray to my beloved father, God, on your behalf so that your faith will not perish. You, Simon Peter, may it be that you have taken heed of these good words of mine. You are not to be discouraged, you are not to abandon your younger brothers. Take care of them, encourage them.

II.v.13   SAINT PETER: O my beloved teacher, you have shown me favor. I, Peter, a little old man, am very grateful for all your words, with which you strengthen my heart for me, and the love that you are bequeathing to us. The only thing that worries me is: where are you going, that you are about to leave us behind?

II.v.14   CHRIST: Where I am going you cannot go yet. Someday you will go there.

II.v.15   SAINT PETER: Why can't I go with you, you who are my deity, you who are my ruler?

II.v.16   CHRIST: O my beloved students, please listen. It is high time, it is the time when all of you will disperse, you will go off and leave me all by myself. But I will not be all alone. My beloved father, God, will remain by my side. Moreover, you will endure suffering on earth. You will not become faint from it. Let your faces, your hearts, be thus assured. As for me, I will reach and pass beyond the earth. But tonight all of you will be bewildered in regard to me. As it is written about me in the sacred words, I will beat, I will afflict the shepherd so that the sheep will be scattered. But on the third day I will revive. I will lead you to Galilee, where you will see me.

II.v.17   SAINT PETER: O my teacher, even if it is true that my younger brothers will become bewildered, as for me, I will not be bewildered. I will be strong.

II.v.18   CHRIST: O Peter, truly I say to you, tonight before the rooster cries out, three times you will not acknowledge me, you will deny me.

II.v.19   SAINT PETER: Truly I say to you, O my teacher, I will not abandon you. If you are imprisoned, whatever happens to you, let me suffer along with you. And if need be, I will die with you. It is not possible that I will abandon you.

II.v.20   CHRIST: Let us go, O my children. Get up. Let us go to the garden of my grandfather the prophet David. Go ahead of me. Let us go.

II.v.21   *Wind instruments will be played. All the apostles will stand up. They will lead the others. They will go inside. Judas will turn around at the edge of the house and remain on the stage. He will look at the others three times.*

*Scene vi: Judas decides to betray Christ
and meets with the chief priests.*

II.vi.1   *When Christ and the apostles have all gone inside, Judas will sit on a bench. He will leap up to speak. He will speak as he walks around.*

II.vi.2   JUDAS: Now I am mulling it over, inside my heart I am thinking, I am saying, how I ate a little bit apart, and the teacher singles me out as if he no longer wants to acknowledge me, as if he no longer wants to recognize me. Truly I say that my face, my heart, are in great pain. And

II.vi.2
(cont.)

what's to become of me? O how wretched I am! He really tosses in my face that I am to carry out something that for a long time has gone about in the chambers of my heart. He pressured me to bring it to an end, to do it. Alas! What's to become of me? Now I say truly that I must sell him in secret, that I truly will carry it out. *(He will sit down. He will hold his head.)* What in the world is this foolishness of mine that I am about to do? And if I carry out my task in this way, it is true that I am a wretch. My reward is really the scoundrel.[24] I am a big, wretched sinner on earth. Moreover, how will I be able to do it? My teacher's head, his chest, have grown stiff[25] as he has taught me a word of his teachings, which are very agreeable. And besides, he is my benefactor. He loved me, he brought me up, he showed me his love. I used to live right beside him, with him. He used to love me like he loved no other person. He used to treat me as his youngest child. And now I want to sell my teacher, who loves me? What has he taken from me, what has he afflicted me with? He favored me in many ways. Oh, what task am I about to carry out? It is not just a joke, not just a boast. No one has undertaken such a thing, no one has contemplated what I am about to do. Will I carry it out like this? What's to become of me? Maybe I'll just quit this. But what will I get if I sell him? Truly, I say that eternal suffering in the place of the dead will be my reward, my recompense. But let me still think things over calmly. What might become of me? Will I perhaps just leave it like this? Or will it be like this? Why am I just uselessly afflicting my face, my heart? What is scaring me, what is bothering me? He is a great teacher. He is a benefactor of the Jews. He cured the sick. He revived the dead. And the chief priests, won't they just rescue him? And won't the *macehualtin* all speak up for him? What will the rulers do to him? Won't it be just for a few days that he will be imprisoned? Won't they just release him? And he is all-powerful. God will save him. Or maybe they won't be able to arrest him. Let me give it a try after all. Let it be that I will betray him, especially since I'm delaying so much. What in the world am I thinking? I'm stalling now. Maybe my heart will be content, maybe I will be satisfied. For all this time I am suffering pain, hurt, and affliction. I serve him. All he does is send me on errands. I don't cast aside any of his words. I obey all of them. I don't earn anything from it. I just go around naked, I just go around in my rags. The iciness, the cold, rise up right against me and rampage over the earth. And my wife and my children have nothing coming to them. They go around in tattered clothes. I can't provide their dinner, their breakfast. And the people of my household likewise lack what they need. They have no rest, no happiness. Poverty is always near them. I support myself with great affliction and trouble.

II.vi.2
(*cont.*)
I have no house. I have no fields. Who will offer me relief? Who will feel compassion for me? For I go thinking, who am I waiting for on earth? Will I perhaps still just stop it? What's intimidating me? What's holding me back? I think that if I betray him to the lords, the rulers, the Jews, the chief priests, they will love me very much for it. They will favor me with lots of silver. They will pay me. But as for him, what does he give me? What do I gain from him? He gives me nothing at all, I get nothing from him. He just keeps me forever in poverty so that I will suffer. But is that how I serve him? What in the world am I saying? My teacher, my ruler, will show me favor and with his help I will rest. But he favors me with nothing! Here is what is very painful, very distressing: that he spread the precious unguent on a wretched little woman's head. It was just wasted. It spilled on the ground. If it had just been sold, its price would have been more than 300 pesos. He should have said, "My children are poor. I will buy them something with it. Let it be sold." I have no confidence at all in him on earth. How will the teacher have compassion for me? But now, maybe nothing will happen to me. However I am to perish, today I will sell my teacher. I can't wait any longer. Now I am leaving him. Now I will approach them. Let me go. Let me go to see the chief priests, the Jews, the rulers, the pontiffs, the priests. Let me give it a try in front of them. Let me go notify the elders, the soldiers. Where will I be able to see them? Let me go.

II.vi.3
Then all the chief priests will come out, and the Jews. Wind instruments will be played. Drums will be beaten. The chief priests will sit on a bench. And the Jews will just be spread out. Some will be playing with oranges. And Reuben will walk back and forth in front of the Pharisees. Judas will go to meet him.

II.vi.4
JUDAS: O my noble, O ruler, let me ask you, where are the chief priests? Will it be possible for me to see them?

II.vi.5
REUBEN: O young man, what have you come to do? What are you looking for, that you have come here? You look to me like you have come very worried. It is obvious from your face that your problem is very great. Say what it is.

II.vi.6
JUDAS: O my noble, it is as you say. What you say to me is correct. But it is not to you that I will speak of my problem. All I ask of you is, where are the rulers, the pontiffs, the chief priests? I have come to see them. It is to them that I will tell, that I will explain, the painful matter about which I have come.

II.vi.7
REUBEN: You have endured fatigue. Very well. You have come to the right place. Many of our lords, the rulers, the pontiffs are here. Let me tell them. Wait for me here.

II.vi.8   *Reuben will go in front of the rulers.*

II.vi.9   REUBEN: May you be seated in honor, O rulers, O our lords. I have
            come here before you. I have come to tell you that a certain person has
            come here. A certain young man wants to come in, wants to see you. As
            he says, "I have come to present a humble word of mine to the rulers."
            And so, shall he come in?

II.vi.10   ANNAS: Find out who that is. Maybe he is just a wastrel or just an im-
            poster or just a servant. And find out why he has come.

II.vi.11   REUBEN: Very well, O ruler. May your command be carried out in this
            way. Let me ask him why he has come.

II.vi.12   *Reuben will go near Judas.*

II.vi.13   REUBEN: Please come. Please listen. The lords, the rulers listened. They
            say, "Maybe he came for something bad. Maybe his heart is not good.
            Maybe he's somebody's servant or an imposter." I am to find out who
            you really are. Tell me honestly.

II.vi.14   JUDAS: Let the rulers know that I am a student of Christ's. But today I
            have abandoned him. I have come away from him. As to why I came to
            them, it is because I found out what is worrying them. And I know how
            to comfort them. I will tell them how it can be done.

II.vi.15   REUBEN: Very well. Wait for me here. Let me tell the chief priests. Rest
            for a little while.

II.vi.16   *He will go near the rulers.*

II.vi.17   REUBEN: O rulers, he says, "I am a student of Christ's. But today I have
            abandoned him. And that which worries the rulers, I know how it can
            be done. I will tell them."

II.vi.18   CAIAPHAS: Very good. Summon him. Let him come in here.

II.vi.19   *He will go. He will summon Judas.*

II.vi.20   REUBEN: May your words be carried out. Let me summon him. *(To
            Judas:)* Come inside, young man. The rulers are summoning you.

II.vi.21   JUDAS: Very well, O my noble, O ruler.

II.vi.22   *Judas will go in front of the priests. He will bow quite low as he approaches
            them. And Reuben will then go among the Jews. "Quid vultis mihi dare [et
            ego vobis eum tradam?]"[26] will be sung.*

II.vi.23   JUDAS: O our lords, O rulers, I have come to greet your royal honors,
            you who govern the royal and honored *altepetl* of Jerusalem. May you be
            seated in honor. It is just for a word that I have come here before

II.vi.23 you. They told me some days ago about the little problem you have
(*cont.*) concerning Christ. You go about seeking him, wanting to arrest him.
You attempt it many times, but it cannot be done. But he is my teacher;
I am his student. Today I have abandoned him. The reason I have come
before you today is that I have come to deliver him into your hands.

II.vi.24 CAIAPHAS: Come here, O wonderful person! May our lord keep you.
Take a good look at what you say. Consider how the saying goes: "one
who says a great many things to people is giving them nothing." And it
is the same now with you. Don't make fun of us.

II.vi.25 JUDAS: O my noble, is what I am saying so difficult? He will be brought
before all of you in custody. I will give you Christ. Know that I didn't
come here just to be spying. For right now I say that I despise Christ
and all his teachings. May I not die a good death if I ever go back to
him. You said that once Passover is finished, you will have him in custody. Better that it be right now. Don't put off the death sentence to be
imposed on him. If he finds out that you do not dare to take him into
custody here, it will be postponed for a long time. If you kill him now,
then all his students will forget him. Let it not be God's will that I have
two faces concerning the *altepetl* and before the justices. Therefore I will
kill Christ. Give the orders quickly. You already see that a great many of
the *macehualtin* love him. Nevertheless, I know that I will bring all your
problems to an end. Don't be afraid because all the people worship him
and his power is very great. But if you arrest him, what will you pay me?
I myself will betray him to you. I will make him known to you.

II.vi.26 SIMEON: O our lords, O rulers, the words that have come to reach you
are very good. We are very happy about it. But now, deliberate quickly!
Let the young man be given whatever payment he asks for, whether it is
silver or some other kind of goods. Let it be given.

II.vi.27 ANNAS: May it so be done. But rest a bit, wait a bit, young man. Let us
consult with one another. Wait in the doorway.

II.vi.28 JUDAS: May it so be done, O rulers.

II.vi.29 *Judas will go to the edge of the stage while the chief priests consult with one
another. He will speak, aside.*

II.vi.30 JUDAS: Now it is very good, what has happened, that I went and put my
problem in front of the chief priests. It was like a burden that no longer
weighs on me. It is like I have become tranquil. It is like I am rejoicing. I
am no longer heavy. What was perturbing me has now departed from
me; I have cast it down. And now, let me wait for their words. It is good,

II.vi.30 (cont.)	how they replied to me. And my heart knows that I will be fortunate. I will no longer go about worrying about tomorrow or the day after. I will have everything to eat and drink. I will be happy, I will be content, I will be prosperous now.
II.vi.31	ANNAS: Come, all of you Pharisees, you prudent ones. We will consult with one another. We say, let us give twenty pieces of silver to our young man. Summon him.
II.vi.32	SAMUEL: Maybe he will not be satisfied with that.²⁷ Let us summon the young man. Call him, O porter.
II.vi.33	*Reuben will go to call Judas.*
II.vi.34	REUBEN: Come here, O young man.
II.vi.35	JUDAS: I have come, O my noble.
II.vi.36	*Then Judas will go in front of the chief priests. Reuben will lead him. When he has arrived in front of the chief priests, then Simeon will address him.*
II.vi.37	SIMEON: The chief priests say that they are giving you twenty pieces of silver. Will that not satisfy you? How do you see it, O young man?
II.vi.38	JUDAS: O my lords, I deserve a great deal for what I am doing before your rulerships, you beloved nobles. What will I do with twenty pieces of silver? That is not his price. Did I come in front of your rulerships for just anything? It is the honor of your *altepetl*. It is your reputation. And if you do not want me to be given anything more, let me take leave of you, let me go.
II.vi.39	SAMUEL: Don't worry! They will give you whatever you ask for, O young man. Go outside the door.
II.vi.40	*Judas will go out on one side. Samuel will jump up. He will be angry. He will strike the table.*
II.vi.41	SAMUEL: You who are seated in honor, you our lords, you rulers, what are you doing? What will the silver be? Give him some more, whatever he wants, for turning the bewilderer in. Did he come for just anything? It is your honor and the honor of the *altepetl*.
II.vi.42	ANNAS: Come here, all you Pharisees, you sages. Let Christ's student be given thirty pieces of silver. Give them to him.
II.vi.43	SAMUEL: Come, O young man. Our rulers have decided to give you thirty pieces of silver for your fatigue and loss of sleep.
II.vi.44	JUDAS: Thank you very much, your honors. I'm well satisfied. So be it.
II.vi.45	ANNAS: Call the majordomo here. Let him appear here before us.
II.vi.46	REUBEN: Very well, O my ruler. Let me go summon him. *(To Majordomo:)* Come here, you, majordomo. The chief priests are summoning you.

II.vi.47 CAIAPHAS: Majordomo, take silver out of the wooden vessel that belongs to the *altepetl*. Count out thirty pieces here in front of us for the young man.

II.vi.48 MAJORDOMO: Very well, O our lords, O rulers. I am just waiting for your command. If some more silver is needed, I have it here. *(To Judas:)* Come here, O young man. Here is your payment. Receive it.

II.vi.49 JUDAS: May I be worthy of it, O young man.

II.vi.50 *Then they will count the money for Judas. Majordomo will count thirty pieces.*

II.vi.51 MAJORDOMO: O young man, I have counted the money for you. May you be comforted by it. Don't be careless with it. Take it. Wrap it up in your cloak.

II.vi.52 *Then in front of the others Judas will lift up the money with a sack.*

II.vi.53 JUDAS: O our lords, O rulers, you have been generous. Now it is good, it is enough. I am satisfied. And now, give the commands to all the soldiers, the mighty ones, whom I will bring with me, so that they will be able to arrest him, to seize him. Let them prepare themselves well for war, with metal [weapons], and order them not to let the very great scoundrel get away. And I will lead them myself. I will take them, I will show him to them. I will leave him in their hands. I know where he is.

II.vi.54 CAIAPHAS: Please come here, you, war captain, Leader, Quinto Cornelio. Give orders to the Jews. I command you to select mighty warriors to go with our young man so that you will be able to arrest him. You're not to let the scoundrel get away. Exert all your effort so that the deceiver does not escape. Prepare yourselves well for war. Bring chains to tie him up with right away.

II.vi.55 LEADER: Very well. May it so be done, O rulers. Don't worry. I am going now. I will choose the warriors. You can be sure that the bewilderer will be sought alive to be brought here today, in front of all of you.

II.vi.56 *All the chief priests will go inside. The Jews will go playing wind instruments. They will go in the lead. And Judas will remain on the stage. He will speak.*

II.vi.57 JUDAS: Oh, it's thirty pieces of silver that the chief priests have given me because I sold Christ! Let me be satisfied with that. Now I will go about happy. I have been comforted. Now I will devote myself to drinking and eating, and I will buy a great many goods, many possessions. My house, my fields, my horses, and a great many other things will I have! Now the people of my household will prosper, will go about happy. Let me go home.

II.vi.58 *Judas will go inside.*

**ACT III: CHRIST VISITS THE GARDEN OF GETHSEMANE
AND IS TAKEN INTO CUSTODY. PETER'S DENIAL.**

Scene i: Christ in the Garden of Gethsemane

III.i.1 *Then Christ will come out. Saint Peter will lead the way, and Saint John
and Saint James. "Tristis est anima mea [usque ad mortem, Sustinete hic
et vigilate mecum]"[28] will be sung. Then Christ will tremble. He will slowly
fall onto the ground.*

III.i.2 SAINT PETER: Whatever are you doing?

III.i.3 CHRIST: The way my heart aches, it's as if I am already about to die. I
am so sad, sadness already reaches my heart. How is my heart going to
be able to rest?

III.i.4 *They will raise Christ up.*

III.i.5 CHRIST: O my beloved children, my heart, my soul, is very troubled.
And now for a little while I will pray to my beloved father, God. Wait
for me here. Settle down. Stay awake with me. You pray to him as well so
that you will not fall into temptation.

III.i.6 *Then the apostles will sit down at the edge of the stage. They will sleep. And
Christ will go into the garden. He will pray.*

III.i.7 CHRIST: O my beloved and revered father, O merciful one, will it be
possible that I not die, that the suffering just pass me by? But it is not for
me to say. It is not what I ask for, what I want, that will be done. Rather,
it is your will that will be done, for you are my beloved father.

III.i.8 *Christ will go down. He will go to wake up the apostles, who lie about sleeping.*

III.i.9 CHRIST: O Simon, you're asleep. Can't you stay awake with me for even
a little time? Wake up, you (all). Pray to my beloved father, God, so that
you do not fall into what is bad, what is improper. Don't let the human
horned owl lead you into sin. Look, my enemies and your enemies do
not sleep like you are sleeping. Wake up!

III.i.10 *They will not answer him. They will just sleep in the same way. Christ will
go into the garden again. He will pray.*

III.i.11 CHRIST: O my beloved father, O merciful one, you do not want to take
this chalice away. But what I want is not what will be done. Rather, it is
your will that will be done.

III.i.12 *They will set down blood for Christ. He will go to see the apostles again. He
will not call to them anymore. He will look at them and he will weep. He
will go into the garden again. He will pray. He will sweat with his blood.*

III.i.13   CHRIST: O my beloved father, O merciful one, will it be possible for me
not to die, for the suffering to just pass me by? But it is not for me to say.
What I want is not what will be done. What will be done is your will, for
you are my beloved father. I entrust my beloved mother and my students
to you. Look after them. May nothing happen to them.

III.i.14   *Then an angel will appear on high. He will speak.*

III.i.15   SAINT MICHAEL: Exert all your breath, all your effort, O my deity, O
my ruler! You have endured fatigue, O Jesus Christ. Now, please listen. I
have bowed down in front of your beloved father, the great ruler of the
world, God. I have placed before him your prayer, with which you have
beseeched him. I have placed before him your precious blood, your red
dye, with which you have sweated for the sake of the people of the world,
your creations. And moreover, all of us who live in heaven humbly
beseeched him that you not suffer, that you not die, that he just save you.
But he said to us, "My beloved child, Jesus Christ, knows well how the
people of earth will be saved. It is with my beloved child's blood, with
his red dye, his death. Later, my beloved child will be saved. That is how
he wants it. He will die for the sake of the people of earth, so that their
souls will be saved." And now, what do you say? How do you want it to
be, O my beloved lord?

III.i.16   CHRIST: I do indeed desire, I yearn for, the salvation of all the people
of the world. For the sake of their souls, death is what I strive for, what I
surrender to, so that with my death I will save all the people of earth. Let
my beloved father's will be done, here on earth and in heaven.

III.i.17   SAINT MICHAEL: O my beloved father, be strong! Exert all your effort!
You are great, you are very valiant. The pain, the torment, that you are
about to suffer is also great. Here are the chalice, so that you will drink
bitter water from it; the crossed-wood device, so that you will be made
to stretch your arms on it; and the nails, so that you will be pierced by
nails on it; the rope with which you will be flogged; the thistly crown,
so that it will be placed on your precious and revered head. And here is
the lance, so that it will be the key with which you will open happiness
in heaven for the chosen ones of your beloved and revered father, God,
and all the people of the world. Be strong of heart, for it will not last
long. The torment will pass quickly. And when it has passed, then you
will achieve eternal happiness. And your beloved father will never leave
you. He will always be seated in honor at your side; he has said so. And
your beloved and revered mother will endure all of your suffering. She
will not leave you either. And as for your students, nothing will happen
to them. You will see them just as they are.

III.i.18   *The angel will disappear.*

Scene ii. The arrest.

III.ii.1   *Then all the Jews will come out. Judas will go in front. He will lead the Pharisees, with torches and lanterns. They will come arrayed for war. They will bring chains, ropes, lances, and halberds. When all the Jews are on the stage, then Judas will speak. He will encourage them.*

III.ii.2   JUDAS: We're taking a long time, O our lords, O rulers. Come on! Let's go quickly! Let's arrest him!

III.ii.3   SAMUEL: Here are the soldiers, the warriors, the mighty ones. Go with them, young man. Don't be careless, you soldiers. And you Jews, go and follow him. You're not to forget anything. Are you bringing the metal ropes, the chains, with which he will be tied up? Listen well to what our young man will tell you. Whatever he says, you are to do it. You're not to let the bewilderer get away.

III.ii.4   LEADER: We hear your breath, your words. Don't worry. As for us, we know how we will seize the bewilderer.

III.ii.5   CENTURION: Now you will see what we'll do to the deceiver, Christ. We've been going around looking for him for a long time.

III.ii.6   JUDAS: Please listen. Here is what I command you. You're not to get bewildered. You're not to arrest a student of his who looks just like him, who is very like him. Listen. The one I will embrace, whose face I will kiss, is the one you are to arrest, you are to seize. Have you paid close attention? You know that if you let him get away, it is no longer any fault of mine. It is in your hands now. It's not my responsibility any more. I take leave of you.

III.ii.7   *All the Jews will go little by little to where Christ is. They will not make rustling sounds. Judas will go in the lead. And Christ will address the apostles.*

III.ii.8   CHRIST: O my beloved children, let that be all that you sleep. You really fell fast asleep. Get up, stand up. The time has now arrived for the maiden's beloved child to be betrayed to the sinners. Here comes the one who will betray me, because he has already sold me. But everything painful, afflicting, and insulting must be done to me. Bow down here quickly, you death of mine, so that the people of the world will be strengthened. And as for you, blind ones, draw near to the sacred lamb so that you will kill him. It is with my death that I will overcome people's enemy, that I will win the salvation of my creations. Come quickly.

III.ii.9   *The apostles who were sleeping will stand up. Then Judas will go next to Christ. He will embrace him. He will kiss his face.*

III.ii.10 JUDAS: *Ave rabbi.*[29] Be joyful, O teacher. Go on and say whether I come with scoundrels.

III.ii.11 CHRIST: O my friend, why have you come here? Why is it with a kiss that you betray the maiden's child?

III.ii.12 *Then Judas will go inside. The Jews will just remain standing around.*

III.ii.13 CHRIST: And as for you all, who are you looking for?

III.ii.14 JEWS: He who is Jesus of Nazareth.

III.ii.15 *Then all the Jews will fall on the ground. They will get up again.*

III.ii.16 CHRIST: I am Jesus of Nazareth. Get up. Who are you looking for?

III.ii.17 JEWS: He who is Jesus of Nazareth.

III.ii.18 *Then all the Jews will fall on the ground. They will get up again.*

III.ii.19 CHRIST: I am Jesus of Nazareth. Get up. Who are you looking for?

III.ii.20 JEWS: He who is Jesus of Nazareth.

III.ii.21 *Then all the Jews will fall on the ground. They will get up again.*

III.ii.22 CHRIST: I already told you that I am him. Get up. If I'm the one you are looking for, if you have come to arrest me, arrest me, seize me. Just leave my students be. You are not to harm them.

III.ii.23 *The Jews will really run in order to arrest him. They will throw him down.*

III.ii.24 LEADER: Arrest him, seize him, O our friends! He's the one we're searching all over for. Bring the chains. Tie the bewilderer up with them. He is our purchase.

III.ii.25 *They will arrest Christ. They will tie Christ's neck with chains, and they will tie his hands. The Jews will beat drums, cry out, and play trumpets.*

III.ii.26 SAINT PETER: O our teacher, shall we fight? We are beating up the scoundrels!

III.ii.27 *Saint Peter will draw out his metal hand stick.*[30] *He will cut off Malchus's ear with it. Then it will fall on the ground.*

III.ii.28 MALCHUS: Ay! Ay! Who was that? Find out who the scoundrel is who threw down my ear, O soldiers!

III.ii.29 CHRIST: O Peter, put your knife, your metal hand stick, in its place. Don't you want me to suffer, like my beloved father, God, wants? How will everything that lies written in the sacred words come true? If I wanted to help myself, wouldn't I beseech my beloved father, God?

III.ii.29 Wouldn't he send me all the angels, the warriors who fill up heaven, who
(cont.)   are more than 2 million, who would come to help me so that I would
           not be betrayed to the Jews? Bring the poor man's ear. I will stick it on
           for him. Truly I say to you, one who kills others with cutting instru-
           ments will be killed the same way.

III.ii.30 *Saint Peter will pick up Malchus's ear from the ground. He will give it to
           Christ. Then he will stick his ear on for him. And this Malchus will get
           right up and go slap Christ in the face just like that.*

III.ii.31 MALCHUS: Will we let you go because of that marvel, O scoundrel?
           Seize the bewilderer, O soldiers! You're not to let him go. Get a tight
           grip on his hands. Bring some more ropes.

III.ii.32 CHRIST: You have come here to arrest me as though I were a thief,
           bringing your metal hand sticks. Haven't I gone about among you every
           day? I used to teach you, I used to counsel you, in the great temple. You
           could have arrested me then. But the time has come, and you will carry
           out your folly. But I will leave to you, I will bequeath to you, teachings
           in sign words.

III.ii.33 LEADER: Shut up! Seize him, O soldiers. Don't let the bewilderer go!
           He is our purchase, the deceiver. Come on out. Let's take him into the
           altepetl of Jerusalem, straight to the high priest Annas's house.

III.ii.34 SAMUEL: Drag him, kick him. Let him die right in our hands.

III.ii.35 *They will beat him against the ground.*

III.ii.36 MALCHUS: Run along, O scoundrel. If you don't run along, we'll
           destroy you right here.

III.ii.37 FIRST JEW: Make him run!

III.ii.38 SECOND JEW: Beat him up, beat him up!

III.ii.39 THIRD JEW: Destroy him, destroy him!

III.ii.40 FOURTH JEW: He is taking our way of life, our protection, our estab-
           lished order. Let him die right here in our hands.

III.ii.41 *Then they will throw him on the ground.*

III.ii.42 SAMUEL: Do stand up. Do get up, O scoundrel. If you don't get up
           quickly, we will interrogate you right now. We might annihilate you
           right here.

III.ii.43 *Then they will take Christ to Annas's home. They will all go dragging him.
           The Jews will beat their lips. They will whistle through their fingers. Saint
           Peter, Saint John, and Saint James will follow the others from a distance.
           Saint James will go inside with them.*

Scene iii. Christ before Annas.

III.iii.1   *Annas will come out. He will sit on his seat.*

III.iii.2   CENTURION: Be joyful, you great high priest and pontiff Annas!

III.iii.3   ANNAS: Come here. You have endured fatigue.

III.iii.4   CENTURION: O ruler, we went to carry out your royal command. Here is the one you are looking for. We bring this bewilderer here, who with his bad deeds, his bewilderings, goes around stirring things up here in the *altepetl* of Jerusalem and everywhere in Judea. He used to tell people that he was performing great marvels. But how is it that he cannot help himself get out of our hands? Take a look at him.

III.iii.5   ANNAS: Please come here, O scoundrel, O mocker, O liar. Are you the one who calls yourself a teacher? What do you go around teaching the *macehualtin*? Who are your students who go around with you? Tell me who they are. Let me see them. Who ordered you to do what you go around doing? Will you overcome the established order set up by our father, Moses? Are you so much better than him? Aren't you satisfied with his teaching, his counsel? You want to reveal something else, something new, so you are known as a great saint. Speak.

III.iii.6   CHRIST: As for me, it is in public, in front of everyone, that I used to teach, that I used to gather together all the *macehualtin*. There was nothing secret, nothing in corners. It wasn't in darkness that I would speak to people. Why are you questioning me about it? Question those who heard me. They know well what I used to teach.

III.iii.7   *Malchus will get up. He will slap Christ in the face.*

III.iii.8   MALCHUS: What are you doing? Who are you, that you answer the chief priest Annas in this way, O scoundrel?

III.iii.9   CHRIST: If what I said is not correct, you explain it, you say if what I said is not good. And if what I said is good, why do you slap me in the face?

III.iii.10 MALCHUS: Will we only slap you in the face, fool? We'll kill you! We'll destroy you! You'll die in our hands, O scoundrel!

III.iii.11 ANNAS: Now take him to the home of the great high priest Caiaphas. Let him take a look at this deceiver who goes around confusing our subjects. Let him chastise him.

III.iii.12 LEADER: Very well, O ruler, O chief priest. Now we'll see about you, you bewilderer. Will you answer the great high priest, the pontiff Caiaphas, the same way, as if you have no respect? Hurry up, get moving, O scoundrel. O soldiers, haul him along, bring him.

III.iii.13   *They will beat him on the ground along the way.*

III.iii.14   CENTURION: Kick him. He is our purchase now. He will die in our hands. We won't let him get away.

Scene iv: Christ before Caiaphas.

III.iv.1   *Caiaphas will come out. He will sit on his seat. A table will be placed there, and Notary will sit down by it.*

III.iv.2   LEADER: Be joyful, O ruler, O my noble, you great high priest Caiaphas.

III.iv.3   CAIAPHAS: Come here. You have endured fatigue.

III.iv.4   SAMUEL: O ruler, that one who comes tied up here is a bewilderer, a wretched deceiver. He goes around bewildering our subjects. He considers your honor as nothing. He goes around destroying it, here in the *altepetl* of Jerusalem. Pass judgment on him, as he must die.

III.iv.5   CENTURION: O ruler, he goes about lying to people about a great many things. He just goes about bewildering the *macehualtin*. You are not to let him go. See well to how you will pass judgment on this liar who is standing here.

III.iv.6   CAIAPHAS: Very well. We hear a great many things about this one, all of them bad, improper. He must indeed be sentenced to death. And now, let an investigation[31] be done. Have the testifiers, the witnesses,[32] appear here. Let them tell all the bad reports that they have heard about him.

III.iv.7   LEADER: O ruler, here are the witnesses. There are lots of them. Let them explain everything that Christ used to go around doing.

III.iv.8   CAIAPHAS: Come here. You all are to testify. Do not make any false declarations here. State only what he did.

III.iv.9   LEADER: Here is the first witness, O ruler.

III.iv.10   FIRST WITNESS: O ruler, as to this bewilderer, here is how he bewilders people. He makes people stop the tribute of the ruler Tiberius Caesar, who is seated in honor in Rome, our ruler. That is what he goes around telling the *macehualtin*. We hear him say it all the time, O ruler.

III.iv.11   CAIAPHAS: I have heard it. Put it down in this way, notary.

III.iv.12   NOTARY: Very well, O ruler. Let me put it down in this way.

III.iv.13   LEADER: Here is the second witness, O ruler.

III.iv.14   SECOND WITNESS: Listen, O ruler. Here is what we know in regard to the deceiver who stands here tied up. We indeed heard about him that he goes around saying, "I could knock down your temple, which you made

III.iv.14   with your own hands. I will put it on the ground. I will put up another one
(*cont.*)   in just three days, by means of a marvel, which will be much more splendid,
            which will be surpassingly good." This is what we hear about how he goes
            around deceiving people. You have heard it, you great high priest.

III.iv.15   CAIAPHAS: Put it down like so, write it like so, notary.

III.iv.16   *Notary will write something.*

III.iv.17   NOTARY: I am putting it down like so, all of Christ's deeds, with which
            he goes around lying to people.

III.iv.18   CAIAPHAS: Why do you make no reply to all that they say about you
            here, with which you are accused? I command you, by God's authority,
            tell me: is it true? Are you Christ, are you the child of God? Or are you
            just a deceiver? Tell me, who are you? Where is your home?

III.iv.19   CHRIST: It is you who said it. You stated that I am the child of God. It
            is true, it is correct. All I have to say to you is that it won't be long until
            you (all) will see the maiden's child seated in honor at the right hand
            of his beloved father, God, in heaven. From there he will arise, he will
            come out on the clouds when he comes to pass judgment on the living
            and the dead.

III.iv.20   *"Blasphemavit: [quid adhuc egemus testibus? Ecce nunc audistis blasphe-
            miam. Quid vobis videtur?]"[33] will be sung. Caiaphas will leap up. He will
            tear his cloak in rage. He will strike Christ in the face with it.*

III.iv.21   CAIAPHAS: Whatever for do we look for witnesses? You all have now
            heard Christ's blasphemies, the belittling, the slandering, of God. And
            so, you see how he pretends to be a deity. How do you see the way he
            has spoken, you Pharisees?

III.iv.22   CENTURION: He must be sentenced to death because he sees your
            honor as nothing, he counts it as nothing. He deserves death. Pass judg-
            ment on him so that he will perish for his lies!

III.iv.23   CAIAPHAS: It will not be possible for us to sentence him to death. It is
            not our responsibility. Tomorrow, you're to take him before the ruler
            President Pontius Pilate so that he will be the one who will pass judg-
            ment on him. And now, keep guarding him for a while in the jail. Keep
            watch on him, all of you. Let him be tied up tightly. You are not to let
            him run away. The witnesses are to appear early in the morning to go in
            front of President Pontius Pilate.

III.iv.24   LEADER: Very well, O ruler. Let us carry out your command. O soldiers,
            take him straight to the jail. Tie him up tightly there. You're not to let
            the wretched deceiver get away. *(To Christ:)* It will be now, O scoundrel,

III.iv.24
(cont.)
now that you'll pay the penalty for your depravity. We'll take you in front of the great ruler Pilate, the great judge. Run along, get moving.

III.iv.25   *Then they will take Christ to the jail. All the Jews will be on guard. They will blindfold Christ, and the Jews will make sport of him.*

III.iv.26   FIRST JEW: If it's true that you are the child of God, please tell me who spit in your face and who slapped you in the face?

III.iv.27   SECOND JEW: If it's true that you are the child of God, please tell me who kicked you and who dragged you by the hair?

Scene v: Two angels visit Christ in jail.

III.v.1   *At a little distance, First Angel and Second Angel will come out at the edge of the stage. They will go over to the jail where Christ will be tied up. When they have arrived, they will kneel. Then they will throw themselves facedown. They will kiss the ground. Then they will speak.*

III.v.2   FIRST ANGEL: You who are worthy of utter exaltation, you great ruler, all-powerful one, your royal name is exalted inside heaven and here on earth. We beseech you, you sacred lamb, give us your royal power so that we can destroy your enemies. Say it! Let us drop a rain of fire on them so that they will be completely destroyed, so that they will do no more dishonor to your face of sacred goodness. And we beseech you, give us your power so that we may untie you and take you to your royal home, the home of your beloved father, God. Very great is your mercy, O my deity, O Jesus Christ. May your creations obtain it, all the people in the world. May your will be done.

III.v.3   CHRIST: My heavenly spirits, praise singers of my beloved father, God, it is not my will that I receive your help now, in my suffering, because I want to bequeath to my chosen ones, my beloved ones, a model, a sign, so that they will remember me all the time that the world remains. But keep my beloved mother company, stay with her.

III.v.4   SECOND ANGEL: O my deity, O my ruler, it was just by your will, how you came to take flesh in the womb of the noblewoman Saint Mary, by means of a sacred marvel, just for the sake of your creations, all the people on earth. Very great is the suffering that you will endure for the sake of your creations. You came to save their life forces, their souls. Exert all your breath, your effort! You are placing yourself into everything that will happen to you, the pain, the affliction. You are without sin. They will tie you to a stone column. They will flog you. Your precious and sacred blood will spill on the ground, and they will make you carry a

III.v.4   very large crossed-wood device, a cross, on your shoulder. Your enemies,
(*cont.*)   the Jews, the stubborn-hearted ones, will make you stretch your arms on
it, so that everything that is written in the sacred words will come true,
will happen, that all the prophets left said.

III.v.5   *The angels will go inside.*

Scene vi. Peter's denial.

III.vi.1   *Saint Peter will come out. He will go to where a brazier will be laid. He
will be warming himself. A woman will go out. She will speak to him.*

III.vi.2   WOMAN: You who are warming yourself here, aren't you a student of
Christ's, who's tied up here?

III.vi.3   SAINT PETER: Maybe you're mistaken, O my friend. I don't know the
one you're talking about. Maybe you are just confusing me with someone else. (*Aside:*) Please, let me just go somewhere else peacefully. Don't
let anything happen to me here.

III.vi.4   *Saint Peter will move some distance away. Malchus will rush in. First, he
will shove Saint Peter in the chest. Afterward, he will address him.*

III.vi.5   MALCHUS: Why don't you acknowledge him? Didn't we see you too
over in the garden? Weren't you going around with the deceiver when he
was arrested? You are his student too.

III.vi.6   SAINT PETER: Garden where? O my noble, I don't know the one
you are talking about. You all are just making false accusations against
people. Leave me alone. It wasn't me.

III.vi.7   REUBEN: We're not making up our words for pleasure, O scoundrel.
Are you lying? Isn't it true that you also are a student of the one who was
arrested, who was seized today? Don't you also speak the Galilee speech?
You look like you're from Galilee.

III.vi.8   SAINT PETER: Truly indeed, God knows that I don't know the one you
all are talking about. If I know him, then may God pass judgment on
me right here. Let him destroy me, let him kill me, if I know that person.
What I am telling you is correct. I'm not lying.

III.vi.9   *Then the rooster will cry out three times. "Et recordatus est Petrus [verbi
Jesu, quod dixerat: priusquam gallus cantet: ter me negabis. Et egressus
foras: fleuit amare]"*[34] *will be sung. Then the Jews will move away. They
will leave Saint Peter alone. He will kneel next to Christ [where he is in
jail]. Then Saint Peter will weep.*

III.vi.10   SAINT PETER: Alas! O our lord, O God, O my beloved teacher, O how wretched I am! I am a rotten sinner! I have offended you, I have done what is bad and wrong. Three times I did not acknowledge you, I denied you. Do not despise me for it, rotten sinner that I am. Pardon me, O my deity, O my creator!

III.vi.11   *Saint Peter will go inside.*

Scene vii: Judas repents.

III.vii.1   CAIAPHAS: Bring out the one you are guarding in the jail. Take him to the home of the great ruler President Pontius Pilate, so that he will be the one to pass judgment on him, since it is his responsibility. Let the witnesses go there so that they will testify. Take him away.

III.vii.2   LEADER: Very well, O my noble, O ruler. Let us take him away. O soldiers, bring out the bewilderer, Christ.

III.viii.3   *Then all of the Jews will go to the jail. They will go to grab Christ. They will bring Christ out.*

III.viii.4   SECOND JEW: Jesus of Nazareth, your marvel working does not help you with anything. It would have been good: today you could have helped yourself in that way. You go around saying that you will erect the temple in just three days. Now you will pay for all the ways you consider yourself a deity.

III.viii.5   LEADER: Untie him. *(To Christ:)* It will be today, O scoundrel, today that you'll pay the penalty for your depravity, your lies. Today we will take you in front of the great judge, President Pontius Pilate. Come on, get moving.

III.viii.6   *All the Jews will untie Christ. They will bring him out of the jail. They will go along shoving him. Judas will come out. He will come to stand at the edge of the stage. He will look over at Christ when they bring him out.*

III.viii.7   JUDAS: Let me wait for him a bit, let me watch from here. Let me be satisfied as to how they are treating the one I betrayed. Maybe they're doing something to him. Is he all right? Is that him they are bringing out here now?

III.viii.8   *He will stare at him.*

III.viii.9   JUDAS: Alas! O how wretched I am! What will I do? I have sinned very greatly. I think they will kill him. No one cares about him. Alas, O our lord, truly I have sinned greatly. My heart knows it well. I have offended you. There's no way you'll be able to have mercy on me, to show me

III.viii.9   favor. I no longer deserve to live on earth. I must throw my depraved self
(*cont.*)   off a cliff somewhere or go hang myself somewhere. I am a great scoundrel.

III.viii.10   *Judas will go to meet the others where they are conveying Christ. He will*
   throw the purse on the ground. He will scatter the coins. He will go weeping.

III.viii.11   JUDAS: O my lords, O rulers, I have sinned in that I sold to you, I
   betrayed to you, God's own blood, his red dye.[35] Here is the silver that
   you gave me. Take it! And let my teacher go, God's beloved child. I have
   sinned very greatly, as I betrayed him to you.

III.viii.12   *First Jew will go and push Judas with his hands.*

III.viii.13   FIRST JEW: What business are you of ours, you scoundrel? Did we go
   to arrest you? Did we oblige you to come here on our account, to come
   betray him to us? You just came here on your own and left him in our
   hands. Do we know whether you sinned in some way, you scoundrel? Is
   it our responsibility? Get out of the way. And hurl yourself down over
   there, O scoundrel.

III.viii.14   SAMUEL: Come, you steward, majordomo. Go get, go pick up, the
   silver. Keep it separate. Don't put it back in the *altepetl*'s coffer, because
   it has become a death payment. Put it somewhere else. It has become our
   means of making a purchase. We will buy a field with it, where travelers
   who die here in Jerusalem will be laid to rest, will be buried.

III.viii.15   MAJORDOMO: May it so be done, O ruler. I will put it away separately,
   for it has become a death payment.

III.viii.16   *Then Judas will go by a tree. He will be weeping. He will hang himself with*
   a rope.

ACT IV: JESUS BEFORE PONTIUS PILATE AND
KING HEROD. JESUS SENTENCED TO DEATH.

Scene i: Jesus is taken before Pilate for the first time.

IV.i.1   *They will take Christ to Pilate's home. Caiaphas will lead the way; the*
   other chief priests will follow him. They will chatter a lot as they go. They
   will beat Christ against the ground. And while they are on their way,
   Pilate will come out. He will sit on his seat. And Notary will go in the lead
   to a big table where he will write.

IV.i.2   CAIAPHAS: O my noble, O ruler, be seated in honor, you ruler, you,
   Pontius Pilate. All your subjects, the Jews, the people of Jerusalem, have
   come to appear before you. They have brought a certain wrongdoer here,

IV.i.2
(*cont.*)
by order of all the great chief priests, the teachers, here in Jerusalem, so that you will pass judgment on him, as he must die. Listen to what they say. We beseech you as well.

IV.i.3 PILATE: Please come here. You have endured fatigue. Let me hear your problem.

IV.i.4 SIMEON: O our lord, O ruler, this one whom we have brought here today, whom you see tied up here, is a very great bewilderer, a wretched deceiver. He pretends to be a ruler. He goes around saying he's the ruler of the Jews. He has bewildered all those of the water, those of the hill, the people of Jerusalem. Pass judgment on him so that he will die, he will perish.

IV.i.5 PILATE: Which one do you accuse in this way? What harm has he done? Is there proof?[36] Or are there witnesses who will testify as to what he did, what harm he has done?

IV.i.6 LEADER: There are, O my noble, O ruler, the witnesses whom you seek. There are a great many. Look at them. Listen to them. They will testify honestly as to what he has done.

IV.i.7 PILATE: You who are witnesses, do not say anything that is a lie in front of me. Do not utter anything with hatred, with envy, but rather speak very honestly. And observe well that the way you measure other people now, someday they will measure you in just the same way. It seems to me that he is without sin. Now then, say only what you know.

IV.i.8 LEADER: Here is the first witness, O ruler.

IV.i.9 FIRST WITNESS: Listen, O my noble, O ruler. We could not lie to you. Here is what we indeed heard about him, which is very painful. With his own mouth he says to the Jews, "I am the one who is the ruler of the world. You must not give the emperor Caesar, who is ruler in Rome, his tribute, his service, anymore." Now you have heard it, O ruler.

IV.i.10 PILATE: O notary, write it down like so, put it down like so.

IV.i.11 NOTARY: Let me write it down like so, O my noble, O ruler.

IV.i.12 LEADER: Here is the second witness. Let him say what he did. They are correct words, O ruler.

IV.i.13 SECOND WITNESS: Here, O ruler, is what we know about how he bewilders people. He pretends to be a ruler. He goes around telling people, "I am great, I am a ruler, I am the ruler of the Jews." And he no longer thinks anything of the lordship, the rulership, here in Jerusalem. Nor does he have any respect for you, nor does he have any respect for the priestly elders, the pontiffs. Oh, this indeed is what I know he said.

IV.i.14   PILATE: Write it down like so, the accusations against Christ, O notary.

IV.i.15   *Notary will write something.*

IV.i.16   NOTARY: May it so be done, whatever words the witnesses say, as they testify.

IV.i.17   LEADER: Here is the third witness, O ruler.

IV.i.18   THIRD WITNESS: O ruler, may you know, in regard to the bewilderer who is standing here, as to how he goes around bewildering people, that he goes around saying, "I am the child of God. And your temple that you made with your own hands, I could knock it down. And in just three days I will raise it right up again. It will be even more splendid." That is how he goes around lying to people everywhere. We aren't just accusing him falsely, O my noble. It's correct. That's what he said.

IV.i.19   PILATE: O notary, write it down like so, put it down like so.

IV.i.20   NOTARY: Very well, O my noble, O ruler.

IV.i.21   LEADER: O ruler, now you are satisfied, for you have heard all that he did, how he bewilders people. And so we beseech you, pass judgment on him. He must indeed die.

IV.i.22   PILATE: Please come here, you poor wretch. Please tell me, is it true that you are the ruler of the Jews?

IV.i.23   CHRIST: It is you who say that I am the ruler of the Jews. All that I say to you (all) is that it will not be long before you will see the maiden's child coming to appear in the clouds.

IV.i.24   PILATE: Please listen, you (all). I am not a Jew. I do not belong to them. Tell me what is correct.

IV.i.25   CHRIST: O Pilate, my kingdom is not here on earth. If my servants were here, they would do battle for me, they would help me so that I would not be betrayed to the Jews. I say to you, my kingdom is not here on earth.

IV.i.26   PILATE: It is true that you are a ruler.

IV.i.27   CHRIST: It is you who say that I am a ruler. May you know well, O Pilate, that as to how I came to be born on earth, I came to advocate for the truth.

IV.i.28   *Then Leader will shove Christ in the chest.*

IV.i.29   LEADER: Take careful note of how, with his depravity, he admits everything. Right in front of you he has acknowledged his bewilderings, that he goes around saying, "I am the ruler of the Jews." He's admitted that he considers himself a deity. You must indeed pass judgment on him so that he will die, so that he will not go around pretending to be a deity.

IV.i.30   PILATE: Respond to everything that's been said about you here. They accuse you of very grave things. It is your priests who have come to throw you into my hands, along with the *macehualtin*. Make things right for yourself. Don't you know that it is in my power to let you go, and it is also in my power to pass judgment on you? Say what you have done.

IV.i.31   CHRIST: O Pilate, it is not for you to say. It will just come upon you, it will just be given to you, that I will pass judgment on you in just a little while.

IV.i.32   PILATE: I see no sin in regard to this person that deserves punishment. But what am I to do to him? You all, say it.

IV.i.33   SAMUEL: O ruler, how is it that he is without sin? He has indeed bewildered, deceived, all the *macehualtin*, and he goes around making them abandon what Moses put in order. He started over in Galilee, and now he's gotten here to the great *altepetl* of Jerusalem with these frivolous words and bad deeds of his. If he is without sin, would we have brought him here? Pass judgment on him, so that he will die.

IV.i.34   PILATE: As I understand it, he's from Galilee, which is governed by the ruler Herod, who is seated in honor there. Take him in front of Herod. You are to tell him that I beseech him, let him admonish his subject, his governed one. Let him be the one to pass judgment on him. It would be better if he is under his governance.

IV.i.35   LEADER: Very well, O my noble, O ruler. Let us take the liar, the deceiver, Christ, over there.

IV.i.36   CENTURION: Get moving, deranged person. Now we will take you in front of the great ruler Herod.

IV.i.37   REUBEN: Seems like you can't walk anymore, O scoundrel. Now you'll pay the penalty for your depravity. Hurry up. Get moving. If you don't walk quickly, we'll destroy you here.

Scene ii: Jesus is taken before King Herod.

IV.ii.1   *They will take Christ to Herod's home. Then Herod will come out. He will sit on a little chair. When they have reached Herod's home, Centurion will speak.*

IV.ii.2   CENTURION: Be joyful, O ruler. We have come here before you. Hear our words.

IV.ii.3   LEADER: O my noble, here in front of you we have brought this deceiver, Christ, who comes tied up here. The great ruler Pontius Pilate beseeches you. He says, in regard to this scoundrel standing here, "I beseech him, let him admonish his subject, his governed one, who was brought in front of me. Why does he go around bewildering people here in Jerusalem? Let him admonish him, let him pass judgment on him. Let him make him stop. Let him be the one to say what will be done to Christ." That is why we brought him before you.

IV.ii.4   HEROD: The ruler Pontius Pilate has shown me favor. Please come here. Are you the one who calls yourself Christ? My late father, whose name was Archelaus, who used to be ruler, was searching high and low for you in Egypt. You could not be found. He used to talk about you a lot. Because of you he ordered them to cut the throats of a great many little children over in Bethlehem, when you were born.

IV.ii.5   *Christ will not speak.*

IV.ii.6   HEROD: Tell me, are you the one whom the Baptist was always exalting in all his speeches?

IV.ii.7   *Christ will not speak.*

IV.ii.8   HEROD: And aren't you also the one who revived Lazarus when he'd been dead for four days and turned water into wine over in Galilee? Answer me.

IV.ii.9   *Christ will not speak.*

IV.ii.10   MALCHUS: O scoundrel, answer the great ruler Herod. Where did your words go? Aren't you being addressed? You are being questioned. Are you mute? It seems that you can no longer speak.

IV.ii.11   HEROD: Or would you please perform some marvel in front of me? I have been hearing about your renown for a long time. I'll have compassion for you, I'll save you from the hands of those who hate you, if you will perform some marvel in front of me. I'll be satisfied with that.

IV.ii.12   *Christ will not speak.*

IV.ii.13   HEROD: Hey! I think you brought a deranged person here in front of me. It's like he's a little dimwit. Throw him down over there. He's giving me a headache here. Take him out, take him away.

IV.ii.14   *Herod will give the others a white cloak.*

IV.ii.15   HEROD: Here's a raggedy little white cloak. Go wrap him in it. Make sport of the deranged wretch over there. He really disgusts me.

IV.ii.16   *Then they will shove Christ around.*

IV.ii.17   SAMUEL: It seems you've gone mute, O scoundrel. Wasn't it you who used to go around teaching people everywhere? You frequented the temple, you went out and about in the streets. And now you can't speak, you've turned mute. Here's how you can't speak!

IV.ii.18   *Samuel will slap Christ in the face.*

IV.ii.19   SAMUEL: Take him out on the patio. Wrap him in this raggedy little white cloak here. Make sport of him.

IV.ii.20   *They will take the white cloak. They will wrap Christ in it. They will make sport of him.*

IV.ii.21   HEROD: And now, take him before the ruler Pontius Pilate once again. Tell him that he has shown me favor, in that he sent him to me. But he just turned mute in front of me. He doesn't answer me. But the ruler knows what to do to him. Let him see to him. Let him pass judgment on him there, as he has the power. He is just a deranged person. Take him away.

IV.ii.22   LEADER: Very well, O my noble, O ruler. Let us take him in front of him once again. It will be obvious there that he is just a liar and not to be believed.

IV.ii.23   FIRST JEW: Now you'll be in for it. Now you'll perish once and for all. Now they will pass judgment on you. You don't speak. Why don't you speak? Now you'll be in for it. Where did your words go? There you make it clear that you are just a mocker of people. Run along, get moving.

IV.ii.24   SECOND JEW: Get moving, O scoundrel! It seems like you can't walk anymore. What of your students, you deceiver? Walk quickly. Don't delay us and we won't destroy you here.

Scene iii: Jesus is taken before Pontius Pilate for the second time. Jesus is flogged and mocked.

IV.iii.1   *They will take Christ to Pilate's home.*

IV.iii.2   CENTURION: O ruler, we have brought this bewilderer in front of you again. The ruler King Herod says, "Take him before the ruler Pilate once again. He showed me favor. But he answered me with nothing. He turned mute in front of me. Let him be the one to pass judgment on him."

IV.iii.3   PILATE: What am I to do? You brought him here to me as if he were a scoundrel whom you accuse here. Of everything you accuse him with, I see nothing in regard to him that is worthy of death, that is worthy of punishment. I have questioned him in front of you. And Herod,

IV.iii.3   likewise, does not see any sin in regard to him. Why would I pass
(*cont.*)   judgment on him? Would I do something that is without purpose? You
seize him and pass judgment on him according to your laws.

IV.iii.4   SIMEON: We brought him in front of you. He's in your hands now.
Work your justice[37] on him. He must die.

IV.iii.5   PILATE: Please come, you, Christ. What is it that you used to go about
teaching people? If only you would have desisted. Tell me honestly, what
did you do, what harm have you done, that you are accused in this way?
Answer me.

IV.iii.6   *Christ will not speak. Pilate will leap up.*

IV.iii.7   PILATE: Listen, you Jews. I see no sin in regard to him. And I cannot
sentence him to die. And now, what do you say? Let Christ go, have
compassion for him. His sins are not at all evident.

IV.iii.8   SAMUEL: It won't be possible for us to let him go, for he bewilders the
macehualtin with a great many things. Christ must die.

IV.iii.9   PILATE: Very well. Now I will do something else to him. I will punish
him well, so that you Jews will be satisfied, so that he will never again
lie to people, deceive people, here in Jerusalem. I won't admonish him.
I will flog him. Now come, you soldiers, you mighty ones. I command
you: seize him, grab hold of him. Tie him to a stone column. Beat him.
His body is to be ripped to shreds, and his blood is to flow from his
whole body, right onto the ground. All of you, flog him. Right when he
is on the verge of death, when he is no longer moving, then you are to
stop. There is no reason for me to pass judgment on this one, for me to
punish him. He is without sin.

IV.iii.10   LEADER: Very well, O ruler. May your royal command so be done.
Come, O soldiers. Quickly, strip him, take off his clothing. Tie him to
a stone column so that we can flog him there. *(To Christ:)* Come, my
friend. Now you will see, you will know, something the like of which no
one has ever seen. Now you will die in our hands.

IV.iii.11   *They will strip Christ right in front of people, on the stage. He will have a
loincloth inside [his clothes]. They will tie his hands to the stone column.
They will blindfold him. Then they will begin to flog him. All the Jews will
take turns. "Miserere mei Deus"[38] will be sung. Christ will faint. He will
gradually go and fall on the ground. Afterward, they will take him down.
They will put him on a wooden seat. Then the Jews will mock him. They
will dress him in a red cloak. Some will, using a sword, amuse themselves
with his shirt. Some of the others will make sport of him. They will slap him*

IV.iii.11   *in the face, they will pull out his hair, they will blow things*[39] *in his ears.*
(cont.)   *First Jew will first spit in Christ's face, then he will speak.*

IV.iii.12   FIRST JEW: If it's true that you are the child of God, who spit on you, O
             deceiver?

IV.iii.13   *Second Jew will first slap Christ in the face, then he will speak.*

IV.iii.14   SECOND JEW: It's true that you are Christ, who slapped you in the
             face, liar? You went around pretending to be a deity. Who will believe
             you, deranged person?

IV.iii.15   THIRD JEW: If it's true that you are the child of God, who pulled out
             your hair?

IV.iii.16   FOURTH JEW: If it's true that you are the child of God, who blew some-
             thing in your ears?

IV.iii.17   *And Malchus will bring the crown of thorns.*

IV.iii.18   MALCHUS: O my ruler, be joyful. Here is your royal crown, a thorn
             circle, with which we will salute you as ruler of the Jews. Kiss it. It is very
             splendid and precious, like a precious golden garland. Now we will put
             it on your head. (*They will put the crown of thorns on him.*) Pound it in
             all over, O our friends. Really wreck the scoundrel's skull.

IV.iii.19   *And First Jew will bring a reed. First he will beat him with it. Then he will
             give it to him.*

IV.iii.20   FIRST JEW: Be joyful, you ruler of the Jews. Here is your royal staff of
             office, the sign that you are ruler of the Jews. It will be broken to bits
             against you.

IV.iii.21   CENTURION: Oh, do see that if it were true, if he had the power, he
             would have said something, he would have made some response to us.
             Now it is clear that he is powerless. He just goes around making fun of
             people. Have we not likewise made mockery of him? And let us take
             him to Pilate, so that he will be satisfied that we have carried out his
             command.

IV.iii.22   SECOND JEW: May it so be done. Let's go show him how we did it, we
             carried out his command. (*To Christ:*) Get up, my friend, little dimwit,
             mocker.

IV.iii.23   *Christ will stand up. He will go.*

             Scene iv: Pilate sentences Jesus to death.

IV.iv.1   *Then they will take Christ to Pilate's home. "Ecce homo"*[40] *will be sung.*

IV.iv.2   CENTURION: O ruler, O my noble, we have carried it out in accordance with your command. We have flogged him. Look at Christ. Here he is.

IV.iv.3   *Pilate will leap up. He will grab hold of Christ. He will go down to his praetorium. He will display him in front of everyone.*

IV.iv.4   PILATE: *Ecce homo, ecce homo.*[41] Here is the person. Now I'm bringing out before you the one whom I flogged so that you will be satisfied that he is without sin. It is a very great punishment, what I did to him. Take a good look at him. Here is the one whom you accuse. What more do you want me to do in regard to him? I have punished him very severely. You haven't told me anything more about him. Moreover, I see no sin in regard to him for which he should die.

IV.iv.5   ALL THE JEWS: Seize him! *Tolle, tolle!*[42] Make him stretch his arms on the cross!

IV.iv.6   CENTURION: O ruler, O my noble, we implore you, pass judgment on him. Make Christ stretch his arms on the cross so that he will die, he will perish, because he has no regard for the chief priests, the pontiffs.

IV.iv.7   PILATE: It is not in my power to make God's beloved stretch his arms. You (all), you seize him, you make him stretch his arms. As for me, I see no sin in regard to him for which he should die. But I know well that he is God's beloved.

IV.iv.8   SAMUEL: How is he without sin? His sins are very great! And as it is written in our laws, he must die because he says that he is the child of God.

IV.iv.9   *Pilate will sit on his chair.*

IV.iv.10   PILATE: Please come here. Please tell me, where is your home? Where do you come from? And what harm could you have done that you are accused in this way?

IV.iv.11   *Christ will not speak.*

IV.iv.12   PILATE: Why don't you answer me? You make no return to me for my words? Don't you know that I could make you stretch your arms? It is also in my power to have compassion for you.

IV.iv.13   CHRIST: As for you, you do not know that it will not be by your command that I will die. It will just be given to you, it will just fall to you, that you will sentence me to death. You would not be able to do anything to me if it were not by order of our lord, who is seated in honor in heaven. Truly I say to you, the sin is not yours. Much more sinful is the one who came to leave me in your hands.

IV.iv.14   FIRST JEW: O Pilate, if you just let him go, you will no longer be the great emperor's friend. He will no longer have confidence in you. He will hear about it. One who claims to be a ruler is his enemy, is offensive to him. The great emperor's commands will be carried out.

IV.iv.15   PILATE: I don't know what to do. I have already punished him. You are not satisfied with that. But please listen, you Jews. You always pardon one person on your great festival Passover. And the murderous thief Barrabas is tied up here. His sins are notorious. And he has destroyed a great many people. Let him be the one whom we sentence to death. And as for God's beloved, Christ, let him be the one for whom we have compassion. What do you want?

IV.iv.16   FOURTH JEW: It will not be possible that we have compassion for Christ. Barrabas is the one for whom we will have mercy, we will have compassion. We demand him!

IV.iv.17   PILATE: But as for Jesus, who is called Christ, what am I to do to him? All of you, say it.

IV.iv.18   ALL THE JEWS: Make him stretch his arms on the cross! Make him stretch his arms on the cross!

IV.iv.19   *They will place Christ up high in Pilate's home. Pilate will put him on display. "Ecce rex vester" will be sung.*[43] *Pilate will be gripping Christ on his shoulders. Then he will speak.*

IV.iv.20   PILATE: Here is your ruler. It will not become my shame that I stretch your ruler by the arms.

IV.iv.21   SIMEON: Is he our ruler? We have no other ruler. Our only ruler is the great ruler Tiberius Caesar. And he will hear about how the deceiver, Christ, goes around pretending to be a ruler.

IV.iv.22   *They will give Pilate water. He will wet his hands.*

IV.iv.23   PILATE: Very well. Hear, O Jews, that it is not my sin that God's beloved one, called Christ, will die. Look. I wash my hands in front of you. I cleanse myself. It is no sin of mine, there will be no consequence for me, in that your ruler will die. It is all of you who demand that he die, that he be made to stretch his arms on the cross.

IV.iv.24   SIMEON: You have shown us favor, O ruler. Let it not worry you. It will become our own sin. It is onto us that the wrath, the anger, will come. It is to us that all sorts of sticks, stones, will happen. Let it also be with our children, our grandchildren, that we bear it on our backs. It is to us that the affliction will happen as to how Christ will die, will perish. We offer

IV.iv.24 (*cont.*)	ourselves, and our children and our grandchildren offer themselves. We all will go paying the penalty for Christ's death.
IV.iv.25	PILATE: And now, notary, read them the sentence, as I have ordered things, as the legal actions[44] have been set in order. Let every person hear it so that they will be satisfied as to how I passed judgment on Christ.
IV.iv.26	NOTARY: Very well, O my noble, O ruler. Here is the document. Let me read it.
IV.iv.27	*Notary will read the sentence in front of everyone. And as for Christ, Pilate will just be holding onto him there.*
IV.iv.28	NOTARY, LUCIO SESTILIO: I, Pontius Pilate, I am President here in the royal, honored *altepetl* of Jerusalem, by authority of my ruler Tiberius Caesar, Emperor, ruler everywhere in the world, unsurpassable. The names of the Consuls are Luciano, Marso Misorio, Bale Notalio. And from the kingdom of Judea, the governor's name is Quinto Fabia. He pertains to the kingdom of Jerusalem, and the ruler of Galilee is Herod. And the chief priests are Annas and Caiaphas, and the war captains' names are Quinto Cornelio and Sexto Robilo. I pass judgment on people there in the palace, in the great court. I pass judgment on and I condemn to death Jesus, whom the *macehualtin* call Christ. And I have seen all the proceedings and evidence. And Christ's home is over in Nazareth. He goes around stirring things up and contradicting the laws of Moses, and he also contradicts the great emperor Tiberius Caesar. And with my sentence I pass judgment on him and so I proclaim that he is to die. He will be made to stretch his arms on a cross. He will be attached to it with nails, as is done to those who are sinners, because he assembled, he gathered together, many people, rich people and poor people. And he does not want to stop stirring things up everywhere in Judea. They go around calling him the child of God and the king of Israel. And he threatens them, he tells them that the great *altepetl* of Jerusalem will fall into ruin, along with its supremely good temple. And he does not acknowledge the tribute that is to be given to Caesar. He dared to enter here into the *altepetl* of Jerusalem with palm fronds in his hand, and many tree branches were waved, as if he triumphed. And many *macehualtin* came to stand, and there he entered the supremely good place, the temple of Solomon. Therefore, I command first Leader, Centurion Quinto Cornelio, that they take Christ, that they put him on display in the said *altepetl* of Jerusalem. As to how he will be taken, he will go tied up and he will go wearing a circle of very painful thorns, and he will go wearing his clothes so that he will be recognized. And he will

IV.iv.28
(*cont.*)
go carrying on his own shoulder the crossed-wood device, the cross, on which he will be made to stretch his arms, so that it will be an example to every person, they who have bad deeds, so that no one will act like this. And two thieves, murderers, will go along with him, who have also been judged. And likewise I desire and I command with my sentence that when they have displayed him everywhere in the *altepetl* of Jerusalem, they will take this person in the manner that I stated above out of the *altepetl* of Jerusalem at the gate called Galiola, which now is called Antoniana. Thus, it will go being cried out, they will go announcing all his sins as they go set in order in my sentence. And they will take Jesus with the others over on top of Skull Hill, the place where justice is done to people, the place called Calvary, so that justice will be done to him there, as it is done to other scoundrels. There he will be made to stretch his arms. And his body will hang on the cross. And the others will have it done to them the same way. On the cross I will place his royal name in three languages, in Hebrew and Greek and Latin is how it will lie written, so that all will see and will say that this is Jesus of Nazareth, ruler of the Jews, so that all will understand it perfectly and will recognize him. This sentence was made in the year 2187 and the 25th day of the month of March. Tiberius was ruling. And I command that no one shall dare to dispute this justice as I have adjudicated it, as I have put it down, so that it can be executed with my words of judgment and the commands of the rulers, the Romans. And anyone who disputes my words of judgment, on them it will be made known that they dispute the kingdom of Rome. And they who became witnesses, in front of whom the sentence was made, are twelve, who came from the twelve lineages of Israel. It was made in front of two notaries, the first from the Hebrews, whose name is Matheo Bereto. And from the kingdom of Rome and the presidency that I have mentioned, his name is Lucio Sestilio.

IV.iv.29   *When Notary has read the sentence, Christ will fall down. They will drag him around. All the Jews will raise a clamor. They will cry out.*

IV.iv.30   JEWS: You have shown us favor, O ruler!

IV.iv.31   CENTURION: We are very grateful. You have shown us favor, O ruler, as you have passed judgment on Christ.

IV.iv.32   *Then they will put Christ in the jail. Then they will go inside.*

ACT V: THE *VIA CRUCIS*, CRUCIFIXION, AND DESCENT FROM THE CROSS.

Scene i: John fetches the women from Bethany.

V.i.1   *Saint John will come out. He will go crying out, he will go to Bethany.*

V.i.2   SAINT JOHN: Where will I find the royal noblewoman in order to tell her, to announce to her, that her beloved only child has been betrayed? They are causing him to suffer greatly. His precious face is no longer visible. And how will I have the courage to recount for her what is so heart-crushing? Given that her heart is very sad, she will weep indeed when I tell it.

V.i.3   *Saint John will go to the door.*

V.i.4   SAINT JOHN: Come open the door, O dear Magdalene.

V.i.5   *Magdalene, Martha, and Saint Mary will come out.*

V.i.6   SAINT JOHN: Oh, O my beloved mother, alas, O noblewoman, what's been done to my lord—it's all over.

V.i.7   *Saint John will swoon, with weeping.*

V.i.8   MAGDALENE: O my loving one, O my lord!

V.i.9   SAINT MARY: O my child, O my dear nephew, what of your teacher, my beloved child? Where did you go and leave my happiness? My heart knows well that something has happened to him, who used to love you especially greatly.

V.i.10   MAGDALENE: Don't worry, O beloved noblewoman. Be strong! It is by his own will that he is to die so that we will be saved, we people of the world, because of our burden of sin.

V.i.11   SAINT JOHN: O beloved noblewoman, alas, O my beloved mother, may you know that your beloved child, your consolation, your strength, your jewel, your heart, has fallen into the hands of the scoundrels, the Jews. It was the great scoundrel Judas who sold him, who betrayed him, who cast him into the hands of the Pharisees, the chief priests in Jerusalem. They paid Judas thirty pieces of silver for him.

V.i.12   SAINT MARY: O my children, O my daughters, your teacher has been sold. A price has been put on him. His price was thirty pieces. He is now in custody.

V.i.13   MAGDALENE: O how very tear-inducing, saddening, are the words that you say to us. Where did you go and leave our consoling happiness?

V.i.14   MARTHA: O how very heart-crushing, that such a thing is happening to our benefactor, our treasure. We ourselves will perish! It is only by our benefactor's help that we were living on earth. It is true now that everything our beloved teacher used to counsel us about has already happened to him. That is the return that is made for his marvelous deeds. It is not yet very long ago that the *altepetl* of Jerusalem used to revere him. Let us go to see him. Let us follow behind our beloved teacher. Let us weep for him. Where will we be able to see him? Tell us, O my child.

V.i.15   SAINT JOHN: O my beloved mother, may you know, since you all are asking me, how it happened. Our teacher and all of us spent Passover over on Mount Zion, in the home of a beloved friend of his. He fed, he gave refreshment to, his students there. And he spoke a great many words to us there, some very comforting, of our salvation, and some very afflicting, pity-inspiring. And when it was finished, then he took us over to the base of the mountain, to the prophet David's garden, called Gethsemane. He went there to pray to his beloved father, for your sake and for the sake of us sinners. He sweated with blood. His precious and revered blood ran right onto the ground, because of his fear. And when it was finished, he'd prayed to his beloved father, God, then Judas Iscariot came in, leading a great many Jewish soldiers who went fitted out for war, went prepared with metal [weapons]. The chief priests, the nobles in Jerusalem, sent them. With a kiss Judas placed him into his enemies' hands. They did not treat him with any respect. They went and tied his hands with ropes. They tied him around the neck with metal [chains], slapped his face, spit on him, and threw him down on the ground. He went tied up as they took him to Jerusalem. It was very saddening, the way they kept shoving him and kicking him, the way they went dragging him along. And therefore, I came quickly, I came to tell you, if you want to see your beloved child, let us go quickly. What I came to tell you, the saddening words, is that in sadness you will see your beloved child. When you see him, you'll no longer recognize him. His beloved face and eyes no longer look human. What do you think? Let's go! Please hurry over to Jerusalem. Maybe it is no longer possible for you to see him, for his death is fast approaching. Let's get running along, let's go!

V.i.16   *Saint Mary will kneel.*

V.i.17   SAINT MARY: Ah, O you utterly splendid one, you utterly merciful one, O compassionate one, I leave my beloved and revered child in your hands, to you. Do not make him suffer, for he is a humane and merciful person. Everyone loves him. O my lord, may my beloved child, Jesus, not die. He has done nothing bad at all. But if you want it, it is your will, I

V.i.17 (*cont.*)	implore you: let the people of the world be saved, but let it just be by some other thing that they are saved, for you are all-powerful. Don't let my child die. Save him from the hands of the sinners. Give him to me!
V.i.18	MAGDALENE: Oh, O my beloved ruler, my deity, my teacher, my benefactor, you have been arrested, you have been seized. And it is by your help alone that I live, as you showed me favor. By your help I obtained favor. And now you are going to leave me, you my beloved lord.
V.i.19	*Then Magdalene will embrace Mary.*
V.i.20	MAGDALENE: O beloved noblewoman, do not faint with weeping. Exert all your breath, your effort. Be strong, you my beloved child.
V.i.21	SAINT MARY: O my daughters, O my companions, do me this favor. Come with me to Jerusalem. Let us go quickly to see my beloved child. Let us go and die along with your teacher.
V.i.22	SAINT JOHN: Exert all your effort, O beloved noblewoman. You must come quickly if you want to see your beloved child. We are taking quite a long time. Take to your feet. Come and follow me, all of you.
V.i.23	MARTHA: O my beloved older sister,[45] O Magdalene, let's go with our beloved mother. You have seen that she is very discontented. Let's go follow her to Jerusalem.
V.i.24	*Then they will all go.*

Scene ii: The way to Calvary.

V.ii.1	*First Jew and Reuben will pass by. Saint Mary will question them on the road.*
V.ii.2	SAINT MARY: O my lords, have you by chance seen my beloved and revered child? Where have they taken him? Tell me.
V.ii.3	FIRST JEW: Who is your child? Declare to us what he is like.
V.ii.4	SAINT MARY: O my lords, I resemble my beloved child. Listen. He is very fair and like a roseate spoonbill. His face is surpassingly splendid.
V.ii.5	REUBEN: Maybe, after all, he is the one they brought out here in the streets. But he is no longer as you describe him. His hair just goes scattered in his eyes. His face is no longer visible. He is just going to perish, among others. And if he is your child, it is not for no reason that you go weeping, noblewoman.
V.ii.6	*They will bring Christ out. They will make him carry the cross on his shoulder. The two thieves will come tied up. The good thief will be tied up at Christ's right hand with a rope. And the bad thief will be tied up at his left hand. They will go along kicking Christ.*

V.ii.7 FLANQUINO: O our friends, quickly, take the red cloak off him. Dress him again in what he wore as he went around teaching people so that every person will see, all the scoundrels here in Jerusalem will take an example from him. And make him carry the cross on his shoulder, since judgment has been passed on him. *(To Christ:)* Come here. Hurry up. Take it off and you will be putting on your usual clothes, put on what you wore when you went around teaching people. And carry on your shoulder the cross on which you will be made to stretch your arms.

V.ii.8 CENTURION: Bring out the crossed-wood device, the cross. Perhaps they have prepared it by now. Quickly, we will make the bewilderer, Christ, carry it on his shoulder.

V.ii.9 MALCHUS: Don't delay us. Quickly, go grab the crossed-wood device, the cross.

V.ii.10 THIRD JEW: I'm going. I'm going to grab the crossed-wood device, the cross. Don't worry.

V.ii.11 *Third Jew will go. He will go to grab the cross. When he has grabbed it, he will lay it on the stage in front of Christ.*

V.ii.12 THIRD JEW: Here is the crossed-wood device, the cross. Make him carry it on his shoulder, according to how he was sentenced. We are to make him stretch his arms on it.

V.ii.13 CHRIST: O, you precious and chosen cross, how can it be that you are to be so fortunate, so favored, that I will be made to stretch my arms on you? You will be revered forever, and your royal name will be exalted. May you be praised, as you will become the weapon, the shield, of the sinners in the world. And come along, let me accompany you as we overcome the human horned owls. May the will of my beloved father, God, so be done.

V.ii.14 LEADER: Come here, you, town crier. Go and announce to people how judgment was passed on this person so that all will hear it, they of the water, they of the hill, the people of Jerusalem.

V.ii.15 *Trumpets will be played. Town Crier will cry out.*

V.ii.16 TOWN CRIER: Listen here, you of the water, you of the hill, to the justice.[46] President Pontius Pilate, governor here in Jerusalem on behalf of Emperor Tiberius Caesar, gives commands. This person whom they call Jesus of Nazareth, whose home is over in Galilee, because he bewilders people with a great many things here in the *altepetl* of Jerusalem, and he destroys the commands of Moses and the great ruler Emperor Tiberius, therefore today he has been sentenced to death. He will be made to

V.ii.16
(*cont.*) stretch his arms on wood so that every person will take an example from him, so that no one here in Jerusalem will do likewise.

V.ii.17 *Then they will take him to Calvary. Then his beloved mother, Saint Mary, will meet him, along with Magdalene, Martha, and Saint John. Saint Mary will weep. "O vos omnes [qui transitis per viam attendite et videte si est dolor sicut dolor meus]"⁴⁷ will be sung. First fall.*

V.ii.18 SAINT MARY: O my beloved child, O my love, O my sweetness, now you are going to leave me. I raised you with great love. Now you are just like this. You no longer can be seen. What of your precious face, how it used to shine on things, so splendid it was. It is as if you have sins that are destroying you. Let me die with you. Why, for what reason, is this happening to you, you who are my jade, my only child? Have compassion for me. Do me the favor of addressing me.

V.ii.19 *First Jew will kick Saint Mary.*

V.ii.20 FIRST JEW: What are you standing there saying? We'll destroy you here. Go over there. *(To Christ:)* Run along, get moving, O scoundrel.

V.ii.21 *Christ will turn around. He will see Saint Mary.*

V.ii.22 CHRIST: O my beloved mother, do not weep very much for my sake. Do not faint with sadness. It will come true, it will be done, as it lies written about me in the sacred book. Truly, everything will happen here in your presence, the torments that are assigned to me. You will suffer everything, O my beloved and revered mother.

V.ii.23 MALCHUS: *(To Mary:)* You don't want to listen. What on earth are you standing there saying?

V.ii.24 FLANQUINO: Just get moving, O scoundrel, O tough guy. You're really delaying us now. If you don't get moving, we'll annihilate you, we'll kill you.

V.ii.25 *Then Simon of Cyrene will meet the others on the road to Calvary. First Jew will go to look. He will go and grab him.*

V.ii.26 FIRST JEW: Come here, you, you passerby, you from Cyrene. Help this bewilderer here so that he will carry the crossed-wood device on which he is to be made to stretch his arms. He is already quite exhausted. He mustn't go and faint uselessly on the road. Go help him, and you carry the cross in your arms until it reaches Calvary. We will give you something for your weariness.

V.ii.27 SIMON OF CYRENE: Very well. Let it so be done. You are making the prophet greatly fatigued. Aren't you afflicting the one who used to be your teacher and who cured a great many of your sick people? Don't you

V.ii.27
(*cont.*)
know that his precious and revered power is very great inside heaven and everywhere in the world? What has he done, what did he do that you are punishing him for?

V.ii.28   SECOND JEW: What he's being punished for is none of your business. Just do the job we are giving you. Shut up.

V.ii.29   SIMON OF CYRENE: O my beloved and revered teacher, O Jesus Christ, it will be my good fortune, my reward, sinner that I am, that I will lend you a hand. No payment for me. I am not rugged. My strength is as nothing. You are great, you are valiant. In a great many ways you are supreme. Give me your royal power so that my weariness may then lend a hand, if it is your desire.

V.ii.30   CHRIST: Let it be, do help me, O my friend, so that we will overcome our enemies, the human horned owls.

V.ii.31   *Simon of Cyrene will help Christ. And the thieves will go following behind. And Veronica will come out. She will clean his face.*

V.ii.32   VERONICA: O my deity, O my ruler, how you go suffering pain is most extreme. You go bathed with your blood; you go soaked with your blood. Your precious face is no longer visible, which used to shine greatly. And now you are suffering very much on account of our sins. And now I beseech you, you my deity, you my ruler, before you die, leave me something, you my benefactor.

V.ii.33   CHRIST: O dear woman, you, Veronica, I have heard your tearful words. Bring the fine white cloak that is draped on your head. Clean my face with it. You will always remember me with it, and your sickness will be cured with it.

V.ii.34   *Then Veronica will kneel. She will clean Christ's face. It will be left as a sign.*

V.ii.35   VERONICA: Ah, you my beloved teacher, it seems it is true that you alone are the divine royal prince. Endure your torment, because of the sins in the world, since you are our lord, since that is why your beloved father, God, sent you here.

V.ii.36   *Saint Mary, Saint John, Martha, and Magdalene will bow down. Veronica will show them his face [imprinted on her cloak].*

V.ii.37   VERONICA: You beloved and utterly good noblewoman, you who are Saint Mary: please look at the precious and revered face of the beloved and revered fruit of your revered womb. How very heart-crushing it is, since by my hands, and by means of a marvel, it was copied onto the cloak. And exert all your breath, your effort. Be strong, you noblewoman, you maiden.

V.ii.38   *Saint Mary will kiss the face of Christ [on the cloth]. Veronica will show it to people everywhere. She will turn around in all directions.*

V.ii.39   VERONICA: With a great marvel my teacher's precious and revered face has been copied on the little cloak with which I cleaned his face. I do not deserve it, I do not merit it. Let every person marvel at the sacred marvel that my benefactor has made. Look here, how very tear-inducing, saddening, and heart-crushing is the precious visage of the ruler of the world, the beloved child of God the father. Let us thus be grateful for his compassion, since it is for our sake, for us people of the world, that everything is done to him. May you, my female friends, you daughters of Jerusalem, encourage him. Let all of us follow behind him, because of his precious suffering.

V.ii.40   LEADER: Go over there, O wretched little woman, so we don't destroy you here. The chief priests are angry. Hurl yourself down over there, get away from here!

V.ii.41   *Then they will hurl Christ down.*

V.ii.42   LEADER: Get up, O deceiver. What have you done? You can't walk anymore? Where did your rulership go? You went around saying you were a great ruler.

V.ii.43   *Christ will stand up. He will walk along a little bit. He will turn toward the women of Jerusalem. They will go weeping.*

V.ii.44   CHRIST: You daughters of Jerusalem, you dear women: do not weep for me. Do not spill your tears for me. Keep them. You'll spill them for your own sakes and for the sake of your children. For the time will come when you will say, "How very fortunate are the wombs that have not given birth to a child, the breasts that have not nursed a child." And at that time, you who are sterile, you who are childless, will say, "Come crumbling down upon us, you mountains! Come crumbling down upon us, you hills! Cover us!" Now your shady wood is still green. But when it has dried, that is when you will weep.

V.ii.45   LEADER: Just get walking, O little brave one, O scoundrel. Will we let you go even though you are crying out to the mountains? No way will you save yourself like that anymore.

V.ii.46   *Everyone will walk along. When Christ has reached Calvary, he will fall on the ground once again. Thus he will fall three times, like in the sacred words.*

Scene iii: The crucifixion.

V.iii.1   *They will make Christ sit down while they make holes in the cross. Some of them will make fun of him.*

V.iii.2   FOURTH JEW: Now we have reached Calvary, where we will kill him, where we will make him stretch his arms on the cross. Hurry up, O our friends. Some of you dig a hole where the cross is to stand. And some of you make hand holes in the cross.

V.iii.3   FLANQUINO: Take the cross down off him. Quick, get his clothes off him. And push him down on the cross, make him stretch his arms. Did all the nails come, with which we will attach his hands and his feet? What about the hammer we will need here?

V.iii.4   SECOND JEW: We brought everything here, whatever will be needed. Here are the nails and the hammer.

V.iii.5   MALCHUS: The cross is ready now. Lay him on it. Stretch him by the arms. With a nail each, attach his hands. Strike him quickly in the middle of the palms with the nails, and let us press the cups of his hands flat so that they'll reach to where the holes are in the crossed-wood device. And attach his feet with just one nail.

V.iii.6   *Then they will all surround Christ. All the Jews will be pounding things.*

V.iii.7   THIRD JEW: Good. Tighten the nails. Pound them with the hammer.

V.iii.8   LEADER: Quick, let's raise it up. It's already midday, and the onset of our festival is approaching. Let everyone quickly take an example from him so that no one who lives here in Jerusalem will do likewise.

V.iii.9   *They will raise Christ right up. All the Jews will beat their lips, will cry out. And the two thieves will be tied to wooden poles. The good thief will be on the right. And the bad thief will be on the left. They will raise them right up. They will be spread out at Christ's sides. The Jews will distribute his shirt among themselves. They will gamble for it.*

V.iii.10   REUBEN: Come on! Knock down God's temple and raise it up again in just three days! Save yourself! If it's true that you are the child of God, come down from the cross!

V.iii.11   SIMEON: He saved others. But he can't save himself. If it's true that he's the ruler of the people of Israel, let him come down from the cross so that we will believe.

V.iii.12   CHRIST: O my beloved father, I implore you, may you be so generous as to have compassion for my tormentors. They do not know what they have done. Pardon them.

V.iii.13   GESTAS: If it's true that you are Christ, the child of God, save yourself, and we who are punished here along with you, save us as well.

V.iii.14   DIMAS: What are you saying? Stop. Shut your mouth. Don't you fear God? We had judgment passed on us in just the same way. As for us, it is quite right that we are punished, since it is the payment for our sins, which are notorious. But he who is dying here, he seems to be without sin. It is just through false testimony that he is dying.

V.iii.15   *"Domine memento mei cum veneris in regnum tuum"*[48] *will be sung.*

V.iii.16   DIMAS: O our lord, O ruler, remember me when you go to your home in the place of happiness. Do not forget me.

V.iii.17   *"Amen dico tibi: Hodie mecum eris paradiso"*[49] *will be sung.*

V.iii.18   CHRIST: Truly I say to you, today you will rejoice with me over in Paradise,[50] in my royal home.

V.iii.19   SAINT MARY: It seems that it is over. Now you are leaving me, your mother. Let me go on ahead, you my beloved child.

V.iii.20   *She will weep.*

V.iii.21   CHRIST: O my beloved mother, I am not leaving you. Be strong.

V.iii.22   *"Ecce mater tuam. Ecce filius tui"*[51] *will be sung.*

V.iii.23   CHRIST: O noblewoman, here is your child. Look at him. And you, John, here is your beloved mother.

V.iii.24   SAINT JOHN: O my beloved teacher, I will carry out all your words. Be strong, exert all your effort!

V.iii.25   *Magdalene will go and kneel at the foot of the cross. She will embrace the cross.*

V.iii.26   MAGDALENE: O my lord, O my ruler, O beloved child of God, you sacred lamb, why, for what reason, have you left yourself in the hands of sinners, such that they dishonored your sacred body? It is because of our burden of sin. And now I beseech you, let me become your companion in death. Let me die with you, you my beloved teacher. It is by your favor, yours alone, that I live on earth.

V.iii.27   *"Eli, Eli, lamma sabacthani?"*[52] *will be sung.*

V.iii.28   CHRIST: O my deity, O my deity, you, Elijah, why have you forgotten me?

V.iii.29   REUBEN: Now he's calling to Elijah. Let's watch. Maybe he'll come to help him. Maybe he'll come to take him out of our hands.

V.iii.30   LEADER: Please just leave him alone, you all. Maybe Elijah will come and save him.

V.iii.31   *And Annas, Caiaphas, and Samuel will go on horseback. Notary will go to leave the signboard. It will be placed on top of the cross.*

V.iii.32   NOTARY: Here is the signboard that is to be stuck to the top of the cross. His name is stated there, Jesus of Nazareth, ruler of the Jews, in the three languages: Hebrew, Greek, and Latin.

V.iii.33   ANNAS: It's really funny that you are standing with your arms stretched on the cross, Christ. If it is true that you are a deity, where are all those you used to go around with? Let them come help you. Now we just believe you to be false. Now you are powerless. You are just a liar.

V.iii.34   *All the chief priests and Jews will read the signboard. They will point to it. They will say, "Jesus of Nazareth, ruler of the Jews." They will all say it in this way.*

V.iii.35   CAIAPHAS: Come here, you, Leader. Go tell the ruler Pontius Pilate that we all implore him, as it is quite shameful how he put "Jesus of Nazareth, ruler of the Jews." And we made him stretch his arms on the cross. May he change it to something else, what he put on the signboard.

V.iii.36   LEADER: May it so be done, O high priest. Let me go carry out your royal command.

V.iii.37   *[Leader will go to Pilate's home.]*

V.iii.38   LEADER: O ruler, the chief priests beseech you. They say, "Tell the ruler Pontius Pilate that we implore him to change it to something else, what he put on the signboard. Let him put something else."

V.iii.39   PILATE: Tell the chief priests that what I put on the signboard will be that way. What I put cannot be undone, as I have passed judgment.

V.iii.40   LEADER: May it so be done. Let me tell them that your word is thus, O ruler.

V.iii.41   *Leader will come back. He will go to give the orders to the rulers.*

V.iii.42   LEADER: The ruler Pontius Pilate says, "Tell the chief priests that I cannot change my words that I placed on the signboard."

V.iii.43   *"Sitio, sitio"[53] will be sung.*

V.iii.44   CHRIST: I am very thirsty. I am very thirsty.

V.iii.45   LEADER: Bring here that bitter water mixture that lies over there. Make him drink it, if he's thirsty.

V.iii.46   SECOND JEW: Here's what you're asking for. Drink it right up.

V.iii.47   *They will give him bitter water and vinegar to drink.*

V.iii.48   ANNAS: Quick, kill the two thieves who are spread out next to him. Break their shin bones.

V.iii.49   FOURTH JEW: May it so be done, O ruler. Let us kill the thieves.

V.iii.50   *Then they will kill the two thieves. They will break their shin bones.*

V.iii.51   CENTURION: And so that there's no way anything can be done to them, let's bury them, you all.

V.iii.52   *"Consummatum est"*[54] *will be sung.*

V.iii.53   CHRIST: It is over, it is finished. Everything that I came to earth to do has been done. Moreover, my torments have come to an end.

V.iii.54   *"In manos tuas domine commendo spiritum meum"*[55] *will be sung.*

V.iii.55   CHRIST: O my beloved father, in your hands I leave my heart, my soul. Come and take it, come and receive it with joy.

V.iii.56   *Christ will hang his head. Saint Mary will kneel.*

V.iii.57   SAINT MARY: What on earth are you about to do to my beloved child? With the help of God, do not gravely afflict him any longer. Wretched am I, for I am his mother. And you have killed my beloved child. Perhaps you thought you have some enmity with me. I will bury my beloved child, since he has died. (*She calls on the angels:*) O residents of heaven, those who, above the world, praise the sacred ruler, God, now you see and you know that nothing will reach, nothing will equal, my anguish. Tell me, what's to become of me? So I will bring my soul, my beloved and revered child, down from the cross. How will I bury him honorably somewhere? What shall I do? Help me with your strength, now in my anguish!

V.iii.58   *Two angels will flank the cross, and they will answer her.*

V.iii.59   ANGELS: O you beloved and revered royal noblewoman, may you be strong, may you exert all your effort! You will yet endure, you will yet see your beloved and revered child, our lord Jesus Christ. It won't be long until his torment is finished. He is all-powerful. Very great is his power, so that he will open eternal happiness, residence in heaven, for the sinners in the world, and he wants his established agreement to come true. And if not, would we not have quickly carried out your royal entreaty, such that we would have taken him away, we would have taken him down, our lord God, our ruler? But his will brings us to a halt. He will spill his precious blood. It is the help, the salvation, of the people of the earth, by which it will be evident how he loved them, how he saved them, how he planted things here with his blood, with his death. Moreover, if they will not love, if they will not honor, their salvation, thus it will be obvious that ultimately they will be punished in the place of the dead, in the place of suffering, forever.

V.iii.60   CENTURION: Move aside, wretched little woman. Nothing will happen to you here.

V.iii.61   *Then each of the Jews will try to pierce him. They will be unable to do it.*

V.iii.62   FIRST JEW: He really is the child of God. I have carried out my task well.

V.iii.63   SECOND JEW: There's still me. Bring [the lance] here. I'll carry out my task.

V.iii.64   *They will all say these words. Then they will call Longinus.*

V.iii.65   FIRST JEW: Come here, you, blind person, Longinus. Seize the metal [lance] well. Now give force to your hand. Pierce him in his side.

V.iii.66   *He will pierce him in his side. Then he will see. He will look up. He will kneel. The motet "O Domine Jesu Christe"⁵⁶ will be sung.*

V.iii.67   LONGINUS: O my lord, O my ruler, Jesus Christ, if I had known that it was you, my deity, you, my ruler, I would not have done what I did. If you'd given me my sight, I would not have done this. Wretched me, wretched blind me! Do not despise me! Pardon me, sinner that I am.

V.iii.68   CENTURION: I believe indeed that he truly is the child of God who has died today.

Scene iv: The descent from the cross.

V.iv.1   *Saint Mary will swoon, weeping.*

V.iv.2   SAINT MARY: My heaven, my sacred lamb, now the will of your beloved father, God, has been carried out. Now they have opened your precious side with a metal staff. All your precious blood has been spilled. So now I am dying, I your mother.

V.iv.3   SAINT JOHN: You Jews, why have you increased your depravity? Don't you see that my teacher has already died? What do you want? Will you kill his beloved mother along with him? Move aside. Let her be.

V.iv.4   SAINT MARY: O my daughters, are the Jews, the lordly rulers, not content that they have killed my beloved child? Here come a great many people. They just come raising up a cloud of earth and dust. Let them not come and do some torment to my beloved child. He is already a dear dead one.

V.iv.5   SAINT JOHN: Don't worry, O my beloved and revered mother. Those who are coming are Joseph, Nicodemus, and others beloved of our teacher.

V.iv.6   JOSEPH: O my beloved older brother, I am very worried now on account of our beloved savior, Jesus Christ. Here for our sake they made him stretch his arms on a crossed-wood device, on a cross, because of our sins, we people of the world. Now may it be done by order of God the father that we take our beloved savior down. Let us go. Let us go to see the ruler President Pontius Pilate. We will implore him that he give us his authorization so that it will be us who take down and bury our beloved savior.

V.iv.7   ARIMATHEA: O my beloved younger brother, may it so be done. Let us carry out your words. Let us go to see Pontius Pilate.

V.iv.8   *Joseph and Arimathea will go.*[57]

V.iv.9   SAINT JOHN: O you, you who are parents, with anguish, with pain, with weeping may your hearts consider what happened today to the soul of our beloved and revered mother, the noblewoman Saint Mary, for the sake of her beloved and revered child who is hanging here. Tell me, you, you man or you woman, if you have a child, an only child, whom you love very much, whom you brought up lovingly. And for the sake of other people they are flogged, they are tied to a stone column, they are tortured, they are dragged around by the hair, they are slapped in the face, they are spit at in the face, they are kicked, they have a frightful thorn circle beaten into their head. And afterward they have judgment passed on them such that they will die, they will suffer torment, they will be destroyed. What will you say, what will you do, you who are parents, as you see what will happen to your beloved only child? Will you be very faint with sadness, will you weep with anguish, will you cry out in fear? And look here at our beloved savior, Jesus, who is without sin. Just so does he love you. O people of earth, you do not weep. Let your tears flow forth. What are your hearts? Are they metal? You help Saint Mary with weeping. See that the sun, the moon, the stars are weeping together. The sky is sad. The residents of heaven are weeping, are sad. The house of the place of the dead has taken fright, has trembled. The graves have opened. The dead have revived, have come to look about on earth. It is very frightening, what has happened to the great *altepetl* of Jerusalem. And how the great temple in Jerusalem is upside down, the mountains, the crags, have split in half. The ground is broken open. They beat against each other, they weep for one another, they take fright because the ruler of the world is dying today. Christians, Christians, what are your hearts? You do not weep, you do not let your tears flow. Who are you, you wretched sinner who are there, who are enjoying yourself? Stop. Untie the ropes with

V.iv.9
(*cont.*)

which your soul goes about tied, with which the human horned owl tightly binds you (all). Cease, scorn your various sins that are attached to your soul. Look up, see your ruler, how just with his blood he is covered. For your sake he is lanced with metal, he had holes made in him. His royal hands were pierced with metal. His precious feet were pierced with metal. With a metal staff he had a hole made in his side. His royal head was enclosed with human horned owl thorns; so very frightful is the thorn circle, as if made of metal, as it is very strong. His left hand did not reach, the way the crossed-wood device had holes made in it. They bound him tightly with ropes. Then his precious bones, his precious and royal body, came apart. And so they stripped him, so they removed his shirt from him. Then they hauled his precious body about such that they reopened his wounds, such that he was dressed in blood, such that he was greatly tormented, such that he was drowning in [blood]. It is the salvation of your life forces, your souls, just because he so loves you, he wanted to die in torment. And so, weep with anguish, let your tears flow. Let your sadness reach inside you. Beseech him humbly so that he will have pity on you. Say to him, "O our lord, O Jesus Christ, when you enter your home, the place of delight, remember me there. Have pity on your humble subjects who are here on earth, those who came following you. Have compassion for them, remember them when you go to your royal home. And now, save them with your compassion so that they will remember you always and forever." And now, O my beloved and revered mother, be strong, exert all your effort, for they are taking your beloved child, they are going to bury him. Let us all follow behind him, let us go weeping, let us go to bury him. And you Christians, why did you leave the mother of God alone for not a little while? You will go helping her with your weeping. Go with her as she goes to bury her beloved child. All of you, follow our only beloved and revered mother. Her only child has destroyed her strength. Do not abandon her, for she is very faint with weeping, all alone. O my beloved and revered mother, since no one wants to go with you as you go to bury your beloved child, fortify yourself. Let us go, let us follow behind him, let us go weeping. And as for the people on earth, let them go about enjoying themselves, since they are without anguish.

V.iv.10   *Joseph and Arimathea will go to Pilate's home.*

V.iv.11   JOSEPH: Be joyful, you ruler, you, Pontius Pilate.

V.iv.12   PILATE: Come here. You (all) have endured fatigue. Do you need something?

V.iv.13   JOSEPH: You great ruler Pontius Pilate, we have come here before you. We implore you in regard to our beloved savior, Jesus Christ, so that you will give us your royal authorization. Let us take him down, and we will bury him. You already know that he used to love us well when he was living among us.

V.iv.14   PILATE: What are you saying? Don't give me a headache. Get out the door. Don't give me problems.

V.iv.15   *Then they will go in front of Christ once again. When they have arrived, they will kneel. Arimathea will speak.*

V.iv.16   ARIMATHEA: O my deity, O my ruler, for the sake of our being saved, here they have made you stretch your arms. Have mercy on us so that we will take you down.

V.iv.17   *When Arimathea has prayed, then he will get up again. He will speak.*

V.iv.18   ARIMATHEA: O my younger brother, let us go once again before the ruler Pontius Pilate. Maybe he will obey us, in respect to our humility.

V.iv.19   *Then they will go once again to Pilate's home. When they have arrived, then he will speak.*

V.iv.20   ARIMATHEA: You great ruler Pontius Pilate, we beseech you, bowing in reverence. Give us your royal authorization. May it be that we take down our beloved savior. We implore you, with humility.

V.iv.21   PILATE: You (all) are really giving me a headache because of your misguided belief. You give me a great many problems. I really don't know what to tell you now. But I say that you are a high official, Joseph. And this heart of mine knows well that if I do not obey you, I will thereby offend you. And so, go. Take Christ down, your teacher whom you take as a deity. I will not look at him, for he really frightens me. You're not to bring him in front of me. Go away. Leave me.

V.iv.22   ARIMATHEA: You have shown us favor, O ruler. Let us take our leave of you.

V.iv.23   *Then Joseph will go get a sheet. And Arimathea will go get myrrh with a crystal jar. They will go to Calvary. They will weep very much. They will kneel.*

V.iv.24   JOSEPH: O noblewoman, O our beloved mother, give us your beloved and revered authorization so that we may take down and bury our beloved teacher. It is our fortune, our favor, that we will take down the sacred lamb. And here is a fine white cloak with which his precious body will be wrapped. Do not worry, beloved noblewoman.

V.iv.25   ARIMATHEA: O noblewoman, O our beloved mother, exert all your effort so that we may take him down. Don't faint. For we have prepared a tomb so as to bury our lord Jesus Christ there. Here is a precious unguent that we will rub on him so that nothing will happen to your beloved child. You will see him just the way he is, beloved and revered noblewoman.

V.iv.26   SAINT MARY: O God's beloved ones, proceed, take down my beloved child. You have shown me favor. I beseech you, just be gentle, on my behalf. Do no harm to my jade, the child I raised, my strength.

V.iv.27   *Then Joseph and Arimathea will go up on a wooden ladder.*

V.iv.28   SAINT JOHN: And now remove from him his royal name.

V.iv.29   *They will remove the signboard from him.*

V.iv.30   SAINT JOHN: Give it to me; may his beloved mother see it. (*To Mary:*) O noblewoman, look at your beloved and revered child's royal name.

V.iv.31   SAINT JOHN: And now, remove from him the thorn circle. Let me give it to his beloved mother. Let it be very gently, O God's beloved ones. (*To Mary:*) Be strong, beloved noblewoman. Here is your beloved child's crown of thorns, which was laid on the head of my beloved teacher.

V.iv.32   SAINT JOHN: And now, remove the nails from his precious hands—let it be very gently—and his precious feet—let it be very carefully. You are not to do him any harm. Give them to me. Let his beloved mother see them. (*To Mary:*) Exert all your effort! Look at the nails with which your beloved child's precious feet were pierced with metal. Kiss them.

V.iv.33   SAINT JOHN: And now, very carefully remove [the ropes?] from him and take down my beloved savior. Let his beloved mother see him. (*To Mary:*) O noblewoman, with all your tears, look at your beloved and revered only child. And by the will of his beloved father, God, he has died.

V.iv.34   *Then Saint Mary will take her child in her arms. She will weep indeed.*

V.iv.35   SAINT MARY: O my beloved only child, O my jade, O my emerald, O child I raised, O beloved child of God, what harm have you done that your enemies the Jews have destroyed you in this way? It is because of our salvation and that of the people of the world.

V.iv.36   SAINT JOHN: O God's beloved ones, let us go to bury our beloved savior.

V.iv.37   *Then they will wrap him and go to bury him. The Marys will go following. Then the procession will begin. "Adoramus te Christe"[58] will be sung.*

Notes

INTRODUCTION

1. On clandestine religious practices and periodic "anti-idolatry" campaigns, see Tavárez 2011.

2. Two examples are Juan de la Cruz, leader of the Talking Cross religion and its Cruzob rebels in the so-called Caste War of Yucatan (Bricker 1981, 155), and Jacinto Uc (or Jacinto Canek), leader of a previous revolution in Yucatan, in 1761 (Patch 2002, 135, 146). Among the Central Mexican religious rebels discussed by Serge Gruzinski (1989), Antonio Pérez of Yautepec, investigated in 1761, engaged most deeply with the Passion of Christ, using images and Passion implements, but he did not claim to be Christ.

3. Speaking of the New Spain context more broadly, Hanks (2010, 21) characterizes the relationship between evangelizers and Indigenous people as one not of simple domination or resistance but a "volatile and sometimes baleful mix" of "love, hate, respect, and contempt" on both sides.

4. The concept of survivance comes from the Anishinaabe writer Gerald Vizenor. In his words, "Native survivance is an active sense of presence over absence, deracination, and oblivion; survivance is the continuance of stories, not a mere reaction, however pertinent . . . Survivance stories are renunciations of dominance, detractions, obtrusions, the unbearable sentiments of tragedy, and the legacy of victimry" (Vizenor 2008, 1).

5. On this process of embodiment and impersonation, see especially Bassett 2015. "Sacrifice" is not an Indigenous notion, so I do not refer to pre-Columbian executions or to Christ's staged death in the Passion plays as human sacrifices. On the use of terms related

to sacrifice and offering in early Nahuatl texts on the Passion, see Sánchez Aguilera 2015. On re-evaluating the conventional treatment of Mesoamerican ritual killing as human sacrifice, see Elizabeth Graham's work on this topic: Graham 2001, 40–42; in press; uc l.ac.uk/archaeology/research/directory/myth-human-sacrifice.

6. Many of these reports were published in Spanish in Ramos Smith et al. 1998. Their volume contains a wider array of documents relating to the regulation and suppression of various kinds of theater in New Spain.

7. This is the play at Princeton University.

8. Such was reportedly the fate of Huejotzingo's play. See discussion in chapter 1.

9. That is, if Nahuatl plays ended up in markets, like the Spanish one that instigated the Inquisition investigation (AGN, Inquisición vol. 1072, legajo 5, folio 196); see also Mosquera's (2005, 171–172) discussion of this marketplace transaction and its significance. On the marketing of religious goods in Mexico City, carried out especially by Indigenous women, see Truitt 2018, chapter 5.

10. AGN, Inquisición vol. 1072, legajo 5, f. 202r, 226v, 234v–243v.

11. Alberto Sánchez Rodríguez, personal communication, August 20, 2019.

12. Macuil Martínez has informed me that he is working with another such fragment (personal communication, November 17, 2022).

13. University of Pennsylvania Libraries, Berendt-Brinton Linguistic Collection, Ms. Coll. 700, Item 200, f. 1r; *La Passion de Nr̄o Sen̄or Jesu christo desde que se despidio su Magestad de su santissima Madre Juntamete con sus Apostoles luego que se despidio fue llebando sus dicipulos para la Ciudad de Jerusalen en donde le Recibieron i le Cantaron el osana filium dabid benedictus qui beni y nomine domine osana yn excelcis.*

14. *los que salen en la passion son estos* (1r).

15. I refer to these men as the authors of the Gospels for convenience and because people in colonial Mexico would have assumed that to be the case; in reality, of course, their production history is more complicated.

16. Princeton University Mesoamerican Manuscript no. 13, 1r; *Nican pehua in itlazohmahuizpasiontzin in totecuiyo Jesucristo inic omomiquilihtzinoh topampatica in titlahtlacoanimeh inic otechmomaquixtilihtzinoco. Nican ompehua cementerioh caltenco. Hualmoquixtiz Christo. Mochintin apóstoles tlayacanazqueh. Judíos achtopa calaquizqueh. Pehuaz in pasión.—Pasion domini nostri Jesu Christo secundum Mateo.—Hosana filium David Rex Israel.*

17. AGN, Inquisición vol. 1072, legajo 5, f. 224v.

18. AGN, Inquisición vol. 1072, legajo 5, f. 224v.

19. On colonial Nahua naming patterns and their status associations, including the usage of "don," see Lockhart 1992, 117–130.

20. According to a list of historical events in Mexicaltzingo on the Estado de México website (estadodemexico.com.mx/municipio/mexicaltzingo). Also mentioned is the fiftieth anniversary of his ordination, in 1943.

21. *Propiedad del Pbro Canuto Flores Tlalnepantla Es de Mx.* On the back of the cover is another note, possibly in his hand but too illegible to be helpful.

22. *Año de 1757. # Estos seis quadernos rimitio R. P. Cura Mintro. fray Miguel de Torres, y son de su jurisdiccion de Xonacatepec.* AGN Indiferente Virreynal, Clero regular y secular, exp. 040, caja 6610.

23. *Axcan Jueves 11 de septiembre de 1732; Nican pehua in pasión in ipantzinco omochiuh in totecuiyo Jesucristo inic omocalaquih in ipan altepetl Jerusalén ipan Domingoh de ramos. Nican mochi neztica, in ixquich tlaihiyohuiliztli ipantzinco omochiuh in totecuiyo Jesucristo inic otechmomaquixtililih in toyoliah in tanimah in cemanahuac titlacah* (f. 2r).

24. See images of the manuscript on the Passion plays website, passionplaysofeighteenth centurymexico.omeka.net/items/show/71.

25. The manuscript is numbered on each page, and I use these numbers rather than recto and verso numeration.

26. *Dominicah pasión de Ramos pehuaz.*

27. *Pasion Domini nustri Jesu Xpo Secudu Mathe = illu tenPure Dixit Jesus y tecipuli Suys.*

28. The orthography of the Tepalcingo play is idiosyncratic and distinct from those of the other two Jonacatepec scripts, which also differ from one another but not so strikingly.

29. In the Tlatlauhquitepec play, the letter "s" appears only in Spanish words, perhaps indicating an earlier date or regional variation. The spelling of *teo(tl)* as *theo(tl)* in this text (also common in the Penn play) may suggest a date around 1700 (Sell and Burkhart 2009, 126n1).

30. See, for example, Bright 1990.

CHAPTER 1: CONTROVERSIAL PASSIONS

1. In addition to Vetancurt's account cited later in this section, Palm Sunday as the performance time is attested by Francisco Larrea in his 1768 report for the Inquisition investigation (Archivo General de la Nación Inquisición vol. 1072, legajo 5, f. 224v) and by the title inscription on the Tepalcingo Passion play.

2. Osowski (2010, 171) discusses the importance of religious festivals to commerce for both Indigenous and non-Indigenous merchants.

3. AGN, Bienes Nacionales vol. 990 exp. 10 sin número; I thank Jonathan Truitt for sharing his transcription of the documents. Because the manuscript is in poor condition, Truitt was able to make only a rapid draft transcription, which did not include folio numbers. If possible, this document will be added to the digital Passion play project at some point. Truitt (2018, 107–108) and Osowski (2010, 182–184) discuss this case.

4. See especially Horcasitas 1974, 2004; Sell and Burkhart 2004, 2009; Burkhart 2011; Leeming 2022.

5. On Fernández's Passion works, see Valero Moreno 2003; his *Auto de la Pasión* can be viewed at cervantesvirtual.com/obra-visor/auto-de-la-pasion/html/e6828eb5-855e-49d0 -9572-e99e65eaa6ec_2.html. Some earlier records of Spanish Passion performances also may refer to descent plays: a 1425 expenditure for cloth for the "Marys of the Passion" in Toledo; a short play in Latin staged at the foot of the cross in Salamanca early in the fifteenth century (Stern 1996, 39–40, 120).

6. Mark Christensen is preparing for publication a nineteenth-century Maya text of this sort, in which a priest is the sole speaker (personal communication, August 10, 2022).

7. There may, of course, be extant Spanish plays that I am not aware of.

8. *el comulga con mucha devoción*.

9. Horcasitas 1974, 562; the historical chronicle in the Florentine Codex places the event in 1531 (Sahagún 1950–1982, bk. 8, 8), while the Nahua historian Chimalpahin places it in 1533 (quoted in Horcasitas).

10. Horcasitas 1974, 251, 335–336; Robert Haskett, personal communication, February 4, 2010; on this document, the *Códice municipal de Cuernavaca*, see Haskett 2005.

11. See also Sánchez Aguilera 2015; he is preparing an edition of this Passion narrative. Pilar Máynez (2004) also has a brief study of this Passion text.

12. Tribute records have also been found in at least two other such statues. Such reuse of these documents may have been a way of incorporating *altepetl* identity into the statue. See universia.net/mx/actualidad/orientacion-academica/encuentran-codice-novohispano -dentro-cristo-cana-833874.html and lainformacion.com/arte-cultura-y-espectaculos/exper tos-mexicanos-descubren-un-codice-indigena-en-un-cristo-en-andalucia_4ZWAs95hc 4ijKvL3gN1Hj2/.

13. *Pasión en lengua mexicana*, Rare 497.2011, P282. On "Christian copybooks" as an Indigenous-language manuscript genre, see Christensen 2016.

14. Bautista and the Nahua scholar Hernando de Ribas wrote a Nahuatl version of the Spanish Franciscan Diego de Estella's *Libro de las vanidades*, which was never published, and in 1604 Bautista published *Libro de la miseria y breuedad de la vida humana*, based on the Dominican Luis de Granada's *Libro de la oración y meditación* (Tavárez 2013, 231).

15. Some images of these murals can also be seen at mexicosmurals.blogspot.com/2017 /06/san-miguel-huejotzingo-church-murals.html.

16. As indicated at the end of the Princeton Passion; see chapter 2.

17. Schwaller (2021, 196) traces this community to the Huauchinango municipality in the Sierra de Puebla, where there was once a village called San Juan Chicahuastla. Hence "de San Juan" seems to be part of the place name, and Mateo gives only his baptismal name.

18. In 1991, Pope John Paul II introduced an alternative list containing only events that are attested in the Gospel accounts (usccb.org/prayers/scriptural-stations-cross).

19. *los Naturales no tienen mas entendimiento que los ojos*; Vetancurt 1971, pt. 4, 42.

20. *Scādale grād de representer la passion de notre Seigneur par personnages*, in Gentian Hervet's (1584) French translation. Vives lived outside of Spain for many years, so any plays he witnessed firsthand were probably performed elsewhere in Europe.

21. *laides & deshonnestes*.

22. Enders's (2008, 126) citation of a reprint of Roy (1904, 315n2) led me to this French translation of Vives's Latin.

23. Chimalpahin hints that similar sequences of images were carried in Holy Week processions in Mexico. Recounting the first time a particular image was carried from Tlatelolco to the cathedral, he says: "It was very marvelous how the whole passion of our lord God went lined up" (alternatively, "all the passions," with the word designating individual torments, or *tlaihiyohuiliztli*; *cencah mahuiztic inic tecpantiya mochi ipassiontzin totecuiyo Dios*; Lockhart, Schroeder, and Namala 2006, 247).

24. On this usage, see Lockhart 1992, 114–115.

25. Thus, where Jesus says "you *macehualtin*, you Jews" (I.vii.11), this could be read as semantic parallelism or as a reference to two different groups, depending on how people imagined the population of Jerusalem and its temporary identification with their own *altepetl*.

26. AGN, Bienes Nacionales vol. 990 exp. 10 sin número; Truitt 2018, 108; Osowski 2010, 183–184.

27. See Larkin 2010 and Viquiera Albán 1999 for more extensive discussions of the reforms.

28. These colonial categories remain: contemporary Nahuas are still taught in school to see mestizos as *gente de razón* whom they should emulate (de la Cruz de la Cruz 2020, 33).

29. AGN, Inquisición vol. 1072, legajo 5, ff. 195–303.

30. *los que llaman en los Pueblos gentes de razon tomaron ā su cargo representar la Passion, y traduciendola del idioma Mexicano en nuestro castellano la representan en algunos Pueblos con grave escandalo, irrision, y desprecio*; AGN, Inquisición vol. 1072, legajo 5, f. 195r.

31. In this I follow Daniel Mosquera, my collaborator in the digital publication project.

32. *una comedia cuio titulo es Passio Domni Nostri Jesu Xpti, y estar sin nombre de autor y tener cosas (a mi pareser) contra nuestra santa fe*; AGN, Inquisición vol. 1072, legajo 5, f. 196. The Xp here represents the Greek letters *chi* and *rho*, the first letters of "Christos." This abbreviation was very common, and Nahua scriptwriters used it constantly: *xpo* occurs far more often than *Christo* or *Cristo*.

33. The latter is the town now called Tenango del Aire. The Ozumba play was previously published, with an accompanying analysis, by Juan Leyva (2001).

34. *gravíssimos pecados, imponderables inconsequencias, irrisiones, vanas observaciones, irreverencias, supersticiones, y demas justas causas*; in Ramos Smith et al. 1998, 263.

35. In 2020 and 2021, during the COVID-19 pandemic, a closed performance streamed on television and the internet replaced the crowded outdoor event. Parts of the 2022 event were performed live.

36. Klenicki praises the Passion play performed at the Park Performing Arts Center in Union City, New Jersey (Ashe, Rock, and Klenicki 1996, 12). On the changes to the Oberammergau play, which include the removal of the blood curse, see Michael Paulson, "'It's My Tradition Too': A Town's Centuries-Old Passion Play Evolves," *New York Times*, August 24, 2022.

37. The volume edited by Marcia Kupfer (2008b) was inspired in part by the controversies over this film's anti-Semitism.

38. For example, the anti-Jewish book *Gamaliel* (see chapter 4) appears on book ownership registries for lawyers throughout Iberia at this time, and Laura Delbrugge (2020, 72) suggests it may have been used to justify the Great Expulsion.

39. As seen in the Nahuatl play *The Destruction of Jerusalem* (Burkhart 2010).

40. See, for example, Greenleaf 1961, 1969; Don 2010. Case files for Central Mexico are published in *Procesos de indios idólatras y hechiceros* (1912).

41. On the *escribanoh* role's emergence in the context of the early colonial Nahua *cabildoh*, see also Mundy 2020.

42. Some women learned to read, but comparatively few; given that public roles as notaries were held by men, female literacy is more difficult to see. For women as well as men, literacy was mainly the province of elites, including those who chose to become nuns once that path opened for Indigenous noblewomen. The first three convents for Indigenous women opened in 1724, 1737, and 1782, with literacy in Spanish a prerequisite for the profession (Truitt 2018, 90; Díaz 2010, 7–9). Mónica Díaz (2010) examines the writings of these Indigenous nuns.

43. I review a number of these testing situations in my chapter "Christian Doctrine" in Boone, Burkhart, and Tavárez 2017, 82–84. Caterina Pizzigoni (2003) discusses the archbishops' inspection tours. Taylor (1996, 240) cites a case in which a man was called upon to recite the Apostles' Creed to counter an accusation of idolatry. Hanks (2010, 270) is correct in labelling these testing situations "instruments of surveillance," but the bar was often set rather low.

44. This is the Passion-related verb *tlaihiyohuia* discussed in the introduction to this volume.

45. *topampa in omotlaihiyohuiltih itencopa in Poncio Pilato in itech cruz omahmazoaltiloc omomiquilih ihuan tococ*. This is my reading, consistent with sixteenth-century printed catechisms, of the pictorial text in the San Sebastián Atzaqualco catechism; Boone, Burkhart, and Tavárez 2017, 176. See also figure 5.1.

46. *Jesu Christo topampa motlaihiyohuiltih momiquilih in itech cruz ihuan tococ*; Boone, Burkhart, and Tavárez 2017, 210–211.

47. See my decipherment of the pictorial catechism from San Sebastián Atzaqualco, in Boone, Burkhart, and Tavárez 2017, 176, 210–211, 226–227.

48. Constantino Reyes-Valerio (1989, 10) estimates that their work, often based on imported European woodcuts, covered 200,000 to 300,000 or more square meters of wall surface. He lists events in the Passion with locations of mural painting depicting

the respective scenes (116). For excellent examples of such Passion paintings, see Richard Perry's images of murals at Epazoyucan, Tezontepec, and Huatlatlauhca: colonialmexico .blogspot.com/2015/04/epazoyucan-part-two-convento-and-its.html;colonialmexico.blogspot .com/2015/05/epazoyucan-part-three-sala-murals.html; mexicosmurals.blogspot.com/2019 /05/tezontepec-cloister-murals-part-2.html;mexicosmurals.blogspot.com/2019/06/huatlatlauca -convento-murals-2.html. See also my student intern Jack Curtin's collection of Passion-related colonial Mexican art on the project website, passionplaysofeighteenthcenturymexico .omeka.net/collections/show/6.

49. One particularly notable seventeenth-century example is the mural paintings at the Sanctuario de Jesús Nazareno in Atotonilco, near San Miguel de Allende, Guanajuato, painted over a thirty-year period mainly by the Indigenous artist Miguel Antonio Martínez de Pocasangre.

50. AGN, Inquisición vol. 1072, legajo 5, f. 227r.

51. *salga parecida a la passion original.*

52. Similarly, the classification of an image as "black," as in the case of the Christ of Chalma, does not mean that colonial-era devotees—whether themselves Black, Indigenous, or Spanish—viewed that image in terms of racial solidarity or otherness (Taylor 2016, 219–226).

53. AGN, Inquisición vol. 1072, legajo 5, f. 224r.

54. Lardizábal's reports are on folios 234v–243v of the Inquisition file, AGN, Inquisición vol. 1072, legajo 5. Leyva (2001, 17–20) and Mosquera (2005, 171–172, 185n7) also discuss the information he gathered.

55. *i que no lo acian por modo de irricion, ni huelga sino por Costumbre i debocion a la Pacion de Christo nr͂o Sôr*; AGN, Inquisición vol. 1072, legajo 5, f. 239v.

56. *ninguno de los representantes era de los que bulgarmente suelen llamar de rrazon, porque todos eran Yndios, aunque los mas de ellos Caciques i principales*; AGN, Inquisición vol. 1072, legajo 5, f. 239v. *Principales* would be nobles of lesser rank than *caciques*.

57. *de donde sacaron los Papeles*: AGN, Inquisición vol. 1072, legajo 5, f. 242r.

58. *i que se acabo Esto porque hauiendo muerto ahogado por su misma Ebriedad (como tiene dicho) Dⁿ Bernabel Bustamante que hiso el papel de Judas se intimidaron todo sus Compañeros, i no huuo lla de ellos, quien quisiera encargarse de este papel, y que esto, i no otra cosa dio motibo a que desde esse tiempo, huuiessen sesado las tales representaciones*; AGN, Inquisición vol. 1072, legajo 5, f. 239v.

59. Macuil Martínez (2016, 236) reproduces this list. It refers to Atentzinco and Chimalpan, constituent communities of Atlihuetzia. No date is provided for the text.

60. On this site, especially in regard to its use in processions, see also Schwaller 2021, 73–77.

61. The shrine of El Señor de Chalma, a bit to the east in the State of México, was (and remains) another important devotion centered on an image of the crucified Christ with a legend of miraculous origin. On these devotions, see also Taylor 2016.

CHAPTER 2: SETS, SIGHTS, SCRIBES, AND SOUNDS

1. The text says *tlatepechco*, which could refer to a leveled-off place on the ground or might be an error for *tlapechco* 'on the stage.'

2. All versions of the death warrant from L'Aquila (to be discussed in the section on literacy) specify through which of Jerusalem's gates Jesus is to be removed from the city. These names vary and appear to be fictional, but all say the spot was formerly called Antoniana. The Antonia fortress was built by Herod the Great and was the site of Pilate's praetorium. Departing through some kind of gate would be consistent with the death warrant, in the two plays that include it (Penn and Princeton).

3. In the *Gamaliel* Passion narrative (see chapter 4), Peter wields a large *cuchillo* (Delbrugge 2020, 112).

4. *Niman quimohuiquilizqueh teilpiloyan in Cristo. Hualneciz teixpan in teilpilcalli, tlachiuhtli inic mochi tlacatl quittaz otacatl, machiyotl.*

5. Being tied to a tree may have been perceived as a form of lockup or punishment. In contemporary Huastecan Nahua communities, a drunk or disorderly person may be tied to a tree, sometimes overnight (Abelardo de la Cruz de la Cruz, annotation on Amacuitlapilco Passion play, passionplaysofeighteenthcenturymexico.omeka.net/collections/show/7, 42n72).

6. *Nopiltzintzine ye tzonquiztihuitz. Itech inin tlahcuilolli mochi in iahcuallachihualiz. Omochiuh inin Probanzas ica miac testigostin.*

7. While *probanza* is an ordinary Spanish term for evidence or proof, *probanzas sumarias* is not so common. Searching online, I have found the phrase in three eighteenth-century Spanish books, two of them dealing with legal practices: Álvarez 1753, 311; Castillo de Bobadilla 1775, 428; and Villadiego Vascuñana y Montoya 1766, 157.

8. *In nehhuatl Poncio Pilato presidenteh in nican Jerusalen itencopa in notlahtocauh in Cesar su[perior?] Augusto. Ixquich nixpan oquiz in causas, in probanzas, in inneteilhuil, in intlahtlaniliz in Judiosmeh in quiteixpanhuihqueh in Jesus in itoca Cristo in oquihtohqueh inic tetlapololtihtinemi in nican Jerusalen. Auh ca oniquittac in ixquich in causas, in probanzas, in iteixpanhuiloca. Notencopa omecahuitecoc, otlaihiyohuiltiloc. Auh ahmo ic inyolloh opachiuh. Occeppa oquihtohqueh inic miquiz, inic miac tlacatl itech mixcuitiz. Ca cencah quimatatacah inic quimahmazohualtizqueh. Auh ca oniccelih in intlahtlaniliz. Auh immac oniccauh in yehhuantin. Ipan quichihuazqueh in quenin quinequiz in inyolloh. Omochiuh inin sentenciah nican ipan altepetl Jerusalen ipan metztli marzo itlamiyan* (cf. Tepalcingo's death sentence in Sell and Burkhart 2009, 234–235).

9. 1766 is the date on the Passion play from Tenango (275v).

10. Santos Otero (1956) cites a 1786 published version of Guerra's text. I do not have evidence of the L'Aquila text being incorporated into Iberian Passion plays (the Villasinta play's sentence is not related; Lozano Prieto 1985, 100). However, while a scribe reads Pilate's death sentence in all versions of the Oberammergau Passion play, Ferdinand Rosner (1974, 232), in

his 1750 revision, replaced a brief statement referring to the flagellation and Christ's innocence with a 259-word decree that specifies details of the crucifixion. This change may have
been influenced by the L'Aquila text, but Rosner did not follow that model closely.

11. *no consta en la sagrada historia*; AGN, Inquisición vol. 1072, legajo 5, 226r. Translations
of this document and the two Spanish-language death warrants can be viewed on the Passion play project website.

12. AGN, Inquisición vol. 1072, legajo 5, 217v, 251v, 273v, 292v.

13. *Textilo* is the passive form of *texti* 'to become flour, to be crumbled.' For more on the
death warrant and the Notary character, see Burkhart (in press).

14. Triumphal entry on a donkey, rather than a horse, indicated that a ruler came in peace
and not as a conqueror (MacArthur 2008, 17). For Nahuas at this time, riding while everyone else walked may have simply indicated Christ's higher status, while his foreknowledge of
the donkey's location demonstrated his omniscience and obedience to prophecy.

15. For example, in the murals at Epazoyucan, Hidalgo (commons.wikimedia.org/wiki
/File:Ecce_homo,_Epazoyucan,_Hidalgo.jpg), and the representations of Pilate in picto-
graphic catechisms, for example, figure 5.1; Boone, Burkhart, and Tavárez 2017, 176, 210.

16. AGN, Bienes Nacionales vol. 990 exp. 10 sin número. Horses may have been easier to
obtain outside of Mexico City.

17. In the Axochiapan play (26v) an angel is to cry out, but this is one of a number of stage
directions written in a distinctive hand that also inscribed other errors. García Garagarza
(2020, 466–467) discusses the use of whistles to imitate the sound of the barn owl.

18. Michael is also depicted in this context in pictorial catechisms (e.g., Boone, Burkhart,
and Tavárez 2017, 168; Basich de Canessi 1963, 11; Cortés Castellanos 1987, 254, 456).

19. *Ca izcatqui in caliz inic ticmititzinoz in chichicatl.*

20. Whether metaphorically interpreted as a "cup of wrath" or a "cup of suffering" (Brown
1994, vol. 1, 168–170).

21. *Ma ximochicauhtzinoh! Ma ixquich in motlahpaltzin! Ca tihuei, titiahcauh. Ca huei
chichinaquiliztli, tonehuiztli in ye toconmihiyohuiltiz.*

22. On angel and demon roles in Nahuatl theater, see Burkhart 2013.

23. *Auh in amehhuantzitzin, ma ximohuihtihuian, ma itlantzinco ximoyetztiyecan in
notlazohnantzin.*

24. In the literary tradition behind the Nahuatl play *The Destruction of Jerusalem*, this garment protects Pilate from harm until its removal causes his instant death (Sell and Burkhart
2009, 274–275; Burkhart 2010).

25. The plays name some fictional Jerusalemites after figures from the Hebrew Bible: Reuben, a son of Jacob; the prophet Samuel; Eleazar, a son of Aaron (Tepalcingo only).

26. In the *Gamaliel* Passion text of fifteenth- and sixteenth-century Iberia, a Reuben is a
member of the Sanhedrin rather than a porter (Delbrugge 2020, 91).

27. Judas's payment was "paltry," in Exodus 21:32 the price paid for an enslaved person gored by an ox (Gundry 2010, 115–116).

28. *Nopiltzintzine, ca in nehhuatl in nimacehualpol. Onotlahueliltic! Ca zan nimotolinih-tinemi. Ma amopaltzinco itlahtzin xinechmotlaocolilican; Ma ihui. Ca cualli. Cempohuallate-mantli in iztac teocuitlatl timitzmacazqueh; Nopiltzintzine, oanechmocnelilihqueh. In quenin anquimonequiltizqueh in ihcuac mochihuaz.*

29. Some Nahuatl texts have an anonymous *porteroh* facilitate Judas's entry: for example, the one from the Mexicaltzingo Cristo (Carrillo y Gariel 1949, vol. 2, 72) and the first Tulane Passion text (*Pasión en lengua mexicana* n.d., 19r).

30. A *real* is one eighth of a peso. There is no mention of silver.

31. Cuaderno 1, 205v; Ozumba, 247v; Tenango, 263r–263v; Amecameca, 279r–279v.

32. Explicit instructions on the number of falls are not always included, but judging by how many times lines are repeated, I find one fall in the Penn script (22r), two in Princeton (26v–27r) and Tepalcingo (71–72), and three in Amacuitlapilco (31r), Axochiapan (23r), and Tlatlatlauhquitepec (7v). Three of the Spanish plays include a fall; instructions for the soldiers to repeat their question three times in the Ozumba play suggest that they might get up and fall down each time, but *caen* 'they fall' is not repeated (248v).

33. The motif endured: according to Reyes García (1960, 79), Ichcatepec's "Jew" and "Pharisee" impersonators pretend to hunt (a statue of) Jesus in a mock forest. Three times a voice calls out, "Who are you looking for," and they answer, "Jesús Mazareno" [*sic*].

34. Chimalpahin expresses a similar interest in sweeping historical numbers. In his annals entry for 1608, he notes that it has been 6,361 years since the creation of the world, 4,165 since the great flood, 2,361 since the founding of Rome, 1,608 since Christ's birth and 1,576 since his death, 1,559 since the Mexica arrived at Aztlan, 1,538 since the destruction of Jerusalem, and on and on, working his way up to the present time (Lockhart, Schroeder, and Namala 2006, 116–145).

35. On the importance of music and song in these missions, see Mann 2010.

36. The *clarín* was a long, straight horn, while the cornets and trumpets were shortened by bending, like the modern versions (Mauleón Rodríguez 1995, 75n1).

37. One of Alva's grandmothers was a Nahua noblewoman of the Tetzcocan dynasty; his other grandparents were Spanish.

38. Truitt (2018, 101) found Nahua testators, including women, bequeathing harps and guitars in seventeenth-century Mexico Tenochtitlan.

39. *Ronca* refers to the sound of a rutting stag or of snoring. A *ronca*, or *sarronca*, can also be a percussion instrument: a traditional Portuguese instrument made of an animal skin stretched over a clay or wooden vessel (folclore.pt/os-membranofones/). I am grateful to Veronica Pacheco for this information and for the Salazar reference.

40. All of these are in the composite play, and the notes give the Bible verse and the location in Navarro.

41. A European precedent for this Latinized performance can be seen in the Catalan play from Cervera, where the third through seventh of these sayings (*paraules* in Catalan) are numbered accordingly and spoken only in Latin (Duran i Sanpere and Duran 1984, 121–122).

42. For this purpose, I use the Cantus Index database (cantusindex.org). Sources may have circulated in colonial Mexico with chants not registered on this site.

43. This is not the version adapted into Nahuatl by Vetancurt but a more elaborate one associated with Miguel Angel de Candia (John Frederick Schwaller, personal communication, June 23, 2020).

44. The text in Guatemala, named the Santa Eulalia codex, is described by Stevenson (1964, 346–349); the Princeton text is Garrett-Gates Mesoamerican Manuscripts, no. 258; dpul.princeton.edu/mssstreasures/catalog/b2774078k.

45. *Hosanna filio David benedictus qui venit in nomine domini rex Israel hosanna in excelsis* (cantusindex.org/id/003142).

46. In the uncorrected Latin, *S."tus Santos S"tus S."tus Dominos deus saba"th pleni s°t seli et 'ear gloria tua hosana yn eecxelsis.*

47. *Ante diem festum paschae sciens Jesus quia ejus hora venit ut transeat ex hoc mundo ad patrem et cena facta surrexit linteo praecinxit se misit aquam in pelvem coepit lavare pedes discipulorum venit ad Petrum dicit ei Simon non lavabis mihi pedes in aeternum respondit Jesus si non lavero tibi non habebis partem mecum domine non solum pedes tantum sed manus et caput* (cantusindex.org/id/001431).

48. Stevenson (1964, 346) identifies this setting of the hymn as the one by Juan de Urrede.

49. The text is: *O bone Jesu, miserere nostri nobis, quia tu creasti nos, tu redemisti nos sanguine tuo pretiosissimo* 'O good Jesus, have mercy upon us, for thou hast created us, thou hast redeemed us by thy most precious blood' (Latin and English from cpdl.org/wiki /index.php/O_bone_Jesu,_miserere_nobis).

50. Marrow 1979, 65; cantusindex.org/id/004095. It is also the Bible text for a Last Supper sermon by fray Alonso de Escalona (*Sermones en mexicano* n.d., 207r).

51. On this man, see Villella 2012; Burkhart 2016.

52. The term denotes a person of Spanish ancestry born in the colony.

53. *The Merchant, How to Live on Earth, The Life of Don Sebastián*, and *The Three Kings* are in Sell and Burkhart 2004; the Guadalupan plays are in Sell, Burkhart, and Poole 2006; *The Animal Prophet* is in Sell, Burkhart, and Wright 2008; and *The Star Sign* and *The Destruction of Jerusalem* are in Sell and Burkhart 2009.

54. AGN, Bienes Nacionales vol. 990 exp. 10 sin número; see introduction to this volume.

CHAPTER 3: SADNESS AND SOLIDARITY

1. In the latter category is the version in the *Gamaliel*, one of the assorted devotional texts that comprise this miscellany's third book (Delbrugge 2020, 186–190).

2. *Lucero de Nuestra Salvación*.

3. Nahua fathers today defy the "macho" stereotype applied to non-Indigenous Mexican men. They are very involved with their children and are not domineering toward them (Taggart and Sandstrom 2011; Alan R. Sandstrom, personal communication, February 5, 2021).

4. For English translations of Bible verses, I use the Revised Standard version, familiar to me from my upbringing in the Moravian Church. Readers can consult Catholic or other Protestant Bibles for alternative phrasings.

5. On this tradition and its presence in a Nahuatl narrative about Judas, see Olko 2017.

6. Verb subjects are ambiguous throughout Judas's statement. In the first two sentences the subject may be Jesus or Magdalene. If it is Magdalene, the verbs in the third sentence may be second-person, referring to Jesus.

7. *Auh in ihcuac in oquittac in yehhuatl in Judas niman cencah cualan. Quihtoh, "Tleica in iuh quichihua? Zan oquinenpoloh. Intla ticnamacani[h] ahmo cencah miac ticcuizquia[h] in teocuitlatl inic tiquintlaocolizquia[h] in motoliniah." In iuh quihtoh in Judas in ichtecapol. Ca ahmo nelli in quihtoh. Ca intla yehhuatl quinamacani[h] ahmo mochi in quintlaocolizquia[h] in motoliniah. Zan quiyelloz* (transcription and translation of this string are uncertain) *cequichtequizquia* (I read *cequi* as the object of *ichtequi*; alternatively, read *cequi quichtequizquia*) (25v). Brackets around glottal stops indicate verbs that may be second-person singular, referring to Jesus, or first-person plural.

8. *In yehhuatl in Judas cencah omoxicoh. Ca in yehhuatl inic neci ca cencah tlaelehuiani in Judas, auh cencah moxicoani, auh cencah ichtequini. Auh yeh ica oquimonamaquilih in totecuiyo inic cencah in quitlazohtla in teocuitlatl* [26r].

9. *Ma ximopachoh. Ma mocpac nicteca in tlazohtli pahatl*.

10. *Nican catqui in tlazohpahatl mocpac nictecaz*.

11. *Tleipampa in oquinec in onenpoliuh in cencah cualli tlazohpahatl? Nomati zan ticnequi netequipacholli ic tinechmacaznequi. Auh ca tel tiquixtlahuaz in ipatiuh. Intlacamo, macamo notoca niJudas Iscatiote*.

12. In John 12:5, the amount is 300 *denarii*, a year's full-time wage for a manual laborer (Gundry 2010, 417).

13. Some translations of the Bible omit this passage or mark it as questionable, as it does not occur in the earliest manuscripts of this Gospel (before AD 400) (Keith n.d.).

14. *Ca tinotlazohtzin timochihuaz* (Axochiapan 6r; Tepalcingo 13).

15. The Yucatec Maya were particularly assertive in accusing priests of sexual abuse; see Chuchiak 2007.

16. McNamer refers to texts in which John returns the women to Magdalene's house and shuts them inside; in the Nahuatl plays, he calls or knocks at the door when he comes to get them.

17. This role of women in ensuring continuity across points of rupture has an analog in Aztec dynastic history, as analyzed by Susan D. Gillespie (1989). Legitimate rule passed from one noble lineage to another through female nodes, whether these women ruled in their own right or were the daughters and wives of successive male rulers at critical points of transition.

18. An earlier Nahuatl example is in the Passion narrative "De la passion de noestro señor ie. xº" (n.d., 209v).

19. Or Cleopas/Cleophas, Saint Joseph's brother according to a tradition reflected in Lope de Vega Carpio's play *The Mother of the Best*, adapted into Nahuatl by Bartolomé de Alva around 1640 (in Sell, Burkhart, and Wright 2008).

20. Sometimes Nahuas included the Spanish plural suffix *-s* and appended their own *-meh*, as here; alternatively, they could omit the *-s*, as just seen in *Mariameh*.

21. The Villasinta Passion play has Mary, Mary Salome, Mary Jacobe, and Mary Magdalene accompany John back to Jerusalem. Mary is the only one of these characters who has a speaking part in the play (Lozano Prieto 1985, 102).

22. In Cuaderno 1 (218v), John tells the women of Christ's woeful appearance as he is carrying the cross and then accompanies them to see him, but he makes no analogous recap here or in the other Spanish-language plays.

23. The narrative was part of the collection of texts published under the title *Gamaliel*, a central character in its opening text (see chapter 4).

24. Other variations continued to circulate. In the *Gamaliel*'s Passion narrative, Christ is already nailed to the cross but still on the ground when Veronica arrives. Mary wipes Christ's face with Veronica's headcloth, and Veronica's leprosy is suddenly healed (Delbrugge 2020, 120).

25. On these conflicting stories, see MacGregor 2000, 90–93; Wilson 1991.

26. Veil of Veronica, https://www.newworldencyclopedia.org/entry/Veil_of_Veronica; http://catedraldejaen.org/santo-rostro/; Wilson 1991, 101–102.

27. My translation of *6 ynic chiquaSeCa netlaquaquetzaliztli EstaÇiÔn Nauhpohualli tla yhuan matlactli OCe ycxineanaliztli omonenemilititia yn toteotzin niCan Cani OtliCa oquimonamiquilico yn totemaquixticatzin yn mahuiztlaCatzintli ytocatzin Veronica yn quac oquimotili huel Çenca Opoposaahauh huel otlitlileuh oxoxohuixi yn itlasoxayaCatzin ôyeyez tien yn ixtelolotzxin nimân ôquimoquixitilitihuetzi yn iztaCanahuac yn tilmatzintli yniquimixpopohuiliz yntonehuilizxayaCAtzin AUh CenCa huey tlamahuisoltican omochiuh ynic yexCanpa cuell pachiuhtiCa yn tilmatli OmoyexCâCopintzino yn yn itlasoxayaCatzin yn totemaquixtiCatzin* (Schwaller 2021, 123n52; orthography as in original).

28. "Encuentro de Cristo y la Verónica Camino al Calvario," eighteenth century, Guanajuato. ARCA: Arte Colonial, artecolonialamericano.az.uniandes.edu.co:8080/artworks/3926.

29. As the scenes are not entirely compatible, the composite translation leaves out some content.

30. These are the Amacuitlapilco/Axochiapan variant (50v, 39r) and Princeton (44r).

31. Colonial pictorials typically show Indigenous men wearing knotted cloaks over their Spanish-style tunics and trousers, while women's traditional blouses (*huipilli*) and skirts sufficed to mark them as Indigenous. However, women in *tilmahtli* can be seen in, for example, the Florentine Codex. In don Lucas Mateo's 1714 pictorial catechism from Tizayuca, Jesus, God, and male saints wear *tilmahtli* while Mary and female saints wear *huipilli* (Burkhart 2016). The diminutive *tilmahtzintli* is an appropriate adaptation of the term to a woman's head covering or shawl.

32. *in itlazohtlachiyaliztzin in cemanahuac tlahtoani; ca oncan motlacanexitia in itlazohx-ayacatzin ihuan itlazohnacayotzin.*

33. This memento motif may derive from Europe. For example, in a late fourteenth-century version, Veronica is on her way to ask a painter to paint Christ's face on her head-cloth when she meets Christ himself on his way to Calvary (Matthaeis 2018).

34. The green wood or tree is interpreted as representing the current time of peace, the dry wood the upcoming time of war (Gundry 2010, 339).

35. The verb here is *ilpia*, not the *mecati* that references sexual relationships specifically; *Ac tehhuatl in nican tetzalan ticcac in titlahtlacoani? Ma xictoma in tliltic mecatl moquechtlan ca inic otimolpih.* In the morality play *Don Rafael*, the title character's sin is represented by a black rope around his neck, which later turns into a snake (Sell and Burkhart 2009, 354–355, 362–363).

36. *O notecuiyo, notlahtohcatzin, notlazohtemaquixticatzin, in ye ixquich cahuitl ca cencah tinechmotlazohtiliaya [ihuan in occequintin t?]ichpochhuan Jerusalén.* "Daughters" is pluralized, so she is not speaking only of herself.

37. *Ma xicmoyolehuacan in annocihuaicniuhtzitzinhuan in amipilhuan Jerusalén. Ma timochintin in tictotepotztoquilican in ica in itlazohtlaihiyohuiliztzin.*

38. *Auh in amehhuantin in antetlatzontequilianimeh, ca cencah miac inic ic amoca cayahuah in ichpochhuan Jerusalén.*

39. *Cihuapille, izcatqui in moconetzin.*

40. *Cihuatzintli, ca izcatqui in moconetzin. Ma xicmittilih. Auh in tehhuatl in tiJuan, ca izcatqui in monantzin.*

41. *O in tinotlazohconetzin, in tehhuatl in ca ye tinechmocahuilia in nimonantzin; Notlazohnantzine, ca ahmo nimitznocahuilia. Ma ximochicauhtzinoh; Notlazohtemachticatzine, nican mohuetzticah in motlazohnantzin.*

42. In addition, the later annotator of the Amacuitlapilco play changed Joseph's name to Nicodemus in one of his speeches (55v), its sole occurrence in the manuscript.

43. Sandro Sticca (1970, 150) notes that the scene of the entombment, with Joseph of Arimathea and Nicodemus and including Joseph's dialogue with Pilate, was popular in medieval Passion plays.

44. For another version, see the mural painting at Epazoyucan, Hidalgo, in which Mary cradles her son's body, accompanied by John and three other women. In the rear stand figures representing Joseph of Arimathea and Nicodemus, while a ladder still leans against the cross. It can be viewed at mexicosmurals.blogspot.com/2018/03/the-epazoyucan-murals-two-lamentations.html.

45. *Auh ma ic ximochoquizellelahxiltican, ma ximixayopatzcacan. Ma amihtic ahci in amotlaocoyaliz.*

46. *Niman pehuaz tlayahualoloz.*

47. *Cuix ahmo no titlamachtil in nican oquihualhuicaqueh?*

CHAPTER 4: THURSDAY AT GAMALIEL'S

1. *Auh in yeuantin hierusalem tlaca cenca pahpaque in cecexiuhtica inic quiquixtiaya pasqua ylhuitl in iuh axcan teuantin ticquixtia pasqua.* Orthography from original manuscript. This sixteenth-century *sermonario* is the subject of a collaborative research project led by Berenice Alcántara Rojas, and I thank her for sharing her translation of this and other sermons in advance of publication on sermonesenmexicano.unam.mx/.

2. He has this title and no name in the Penn play's list of dramatis personae (1r).

3. The name may come from the alternative source Tepalcingo's scriptwriter used for the scenes of the Jewish council and Judas's visits there.

4. Information from jewishencyclopedia.com/articles/6494-gamaliel-i; britannica.com /biography/Gamaliel-I;newadvent.org/cathen/06374b.htm;catholicsaints.info/saint-gamaliel/; and https://orthodoxwiki.org/Gamaliel#Finding_of_the_relics_of_the_Righteous_St. _Gamaliel.

5. Joseph and Nicodemus also assert that Jesus is the Messiah, while Caiaphas insists he is not the awaited Messiah (II.i.2, 21, 23).

6. This shift occurs in six of sixteen cases in Princeton and in all instances in Amacuitlapilco, Axochiapan, and Penn.

7. catholicherald.co.uk/pope-benedict%E2%80%88xvi-the-last%E2%80%88supper/. The theological reasoning here is that Jesus himself took the place of the sacrificed lamb.

8. Tenango (259v) simply mentions the lamb; Cuaderno 1 (206v) and the Amecameca play (282r) have a lamb of *bizcocho*; the Ozumba play (246v) specifies *pan*, in an excised stage direction.

9. Again, I draw on Berenice Alcántara Rojas's transcription and translation.

10. *in yehhuatl in ompa chaneh niman ixpantzinco quimotequilih in ichcaconetl tlatlehuatzalli in oncan onotiuh quetzalitztli in caxitl cencah tlazohtli. Auh in yehhuatl in totecuiyo niman conmanilih, niman quimotzahtzayanilih. Auh niman quimonahuatilih in apostolomeh mochintin quicuazqueh in iuhca in nahuatilli.*

11. Cuaderno 1, 205v; Tenango, 257v; Amecameca, 279v.

12. Ozumba, 246r, 247r.

13. AGN, Inquisición vol. 1072, legajo 5, f. 226r; *sentado a la mesa el representante de Christo con los que hacen papeles de los doce Apostoles toma el pan, lo bendita, y consagra con palabras vulgares del idioma castellano, o mexicô, y lo distribuie entre los doce, despues toma el caliz del vino, lo bendice, consagra en el mismo método, y les dice que beban de el todos: que ciertamente es vn hecho lleno de errores, y por consiguiente intolerable entre catholicos.* Transcriptions from Larrea's report are based on a pdf file of the original, but I fill in some text obscured at the verso pages' margins using the modernized transcription in Ramos Smith et al. 1998, 313–315.

14. AGN, Inquisición vol. 1072, legajo 5, f. 226r; *Y también es de advertir, que al tiempo de representar la consagración de las especies de pan y vino, cantan el hymno* Pange lingua *traducido a lengua vulgar, y como en el vltimo verso convida la Yglesia a la adoracion del divissimo* [sic] *con estas palabras* tantum ergo sacramentum veneremus cernui *se hincan de rodillas, y adoran asi el pan y vino que consagro, o quiso consagrar el representante de Christo, o cuia consagracion está puramente representada: si este no es error gravissimo, que error avra en el mundo.*

15. AGN, Inquisición vol. 1072, legajo 5, f. 225v.

16. AGN, Inquisición vol. 1072, legajo 5, f. 226v; *no oi palabras de consagración; y aunque las hubiera oído, no las hubiera entendido, solamente vi que el representante de Christo, y podia ser vivo exemplo de paciencia, humildad, y mansedumbre, bendixo el pan y el vino, y los distribuio entre los de la mesa: pero ninguno se hinco de rodillas, ni adoro, ni se canto hymno alguno.*

17. AGN, Inquisición vol. 1072, legajo 5, f. 226v; *Yo que indignamente represento la persona de nro señor Jesu Christo os hago saber que en la noche de la cena vltima tomó en sus santas manos el pan lo bendijo, y consagró en el mismo modo que los sacerdotes lo practican en el altar, y lo repartio entre sus discípulos, como yo hago ahora con vosotros: y para el vino diga y haga lo mismo mutatis mutandis.*

18. AGN, Inquisición vol. 1072, legajo. 5, f. 226v; *pues sera lastima que por vn error que cometen con innocencia y sin malicia, se les prohíba la representacion, que les puede ser mui util para la doctrina, para la fee, y para las buenas costumbres.*

19. This location is identified as part of the parish of Yecapixtla, in what is now the state of Morelos. It is not the Nochistlán in Zacatecas.

20. AGN, Inquisición vol. 1072, legajo 5, ff. 199r, 230r, 232r, 234r; *la gravísima circunstancaia de que quando se hace la cena simula este que consagra alza una hostia y se hincan todos a adorarla.*

21. AGN, Inquisición vol. 1072, legajo 5, f. 239r–239v; *y que tampoco es cierto que todo el Auditorio se yncava á Adorar la Ostia que se simulava consagrar; porque solo lo hacían los que hacían papel en la Representacion.*

22. Cuaderno 1, 208v; Ozumba, 247v; Tenango, 262r.

23. The "white" designation could derive from observations of the Mass or from literary usage. Sánchez Aguilera (2015, 289–290) discusses an early colonal text about communion

in which the host is called *ce tepitzin tlaxcalcanatzintli, huel iztac* 'a small thin (honored) tortilla, quite white.'

24. *Ma xicmottilican inin tlaxcaltzintli. Ca huel yehhuatl in notlazohnacayotzin. Auh in axcan, ma xicmocuilican, ma xicmocelilican.*

25. Seventeenth-century Jesuits in the northern missions, until they finally grew their own, had to import wheat over great distances and would forgo celebrating Mass when they had none (Hackett 1923–1937, vol. 3, 11, 95, 145; Trigg 2004, 241).

26. Amacuitlapilco's stage directions do use the word *pantzin* 'little breads' (18v); the terms were to some extent interchangeable. However, the consistency with which the dialogue in all plays uses *tlaxcalli* 'tortilla(s)' suggests that the maize products were presented onstage. Even if not, the word invokes that everyday foodstuff.

27. *Notlazohpilhuane, ma xicmottilican inin vinoh niconi. Ca yehhuatl in notlazohezzotzin nonoquihuiz. Ma xicmocelilican.*

28. The wording is distinct from the passage in Matthew that can be seen at the bottom of figure 4.1. See cantusindex.org/search?t=hoc+est+corpus+meum+quod+pro+vobi& cid=&genre=All&ghisp=All.

29. *Auh in axcan ca machiyotl, octacatl, namechtlalilitiuh, inic mochipa iuhqui anquichi-huazqueh in iuh axcan anquittazqueh. Ca namechnocahuililitiuh in nonacayotzin, in nez-zotzin in ixiptlahtzin. In ye axcan nicnoteochihuiliz inin tlaxcaltzintli ihuan in vinohtzin. Ca ipan nahci in nehhuatl. In nican amotlantzinco nihuetztiyez. Cemihcac nixiptlahtzin mochihuaz.*

30. *In iuh oquicuaqueh in ichcaconetl niman zan macuilli in tlaxcaltzintli. Niman ipan quimihtalhuih in teotlahtolli. Quimihtalhuilih, "Inin yehhuatl nonacayotzin. Ammochintin xicmocualtican."*

31. *Xocomecatl* 'sour-plum vine' referred to multiple species of wild grapevine native to Mexico; its fruit is used today in various culinary and medicinal concoctions—some of them fermented—and a shampoo is made from the leaves (Cruz-Castillo, Franco-Mora, and Famiani 2009). Nahuas extended the term to cultivated grapes when they and wine were introduced. I am reading *xocomecatzintli* as *xocomecatl* plus *atl* 'water'; the diminutive/honorific *-tzintli* was often added to *atl* (as in I.viii.19).

32. I thank Abelardo de la Cruz de la Cruz for reviewing my analysis of the different phrasings for the tortilla and wine transformation. He commented that in contemporary Huastecan Nahuatl, the phrase *ipan ahci* can be used to denote similarity or resemblance (Abelardo de la Cruz de la Cruz, personal communication, September 7, 2021).

33. *Ca ic chicahuaz in amotlaneltoquiliz. Ca miaquintin impan noquihuiz. Ic polihuiz in intlahtlacol.*

34. In clandestine contexts, Christ could be identified directly as a deification of maize. The Nahua religious leader Antonio Pérez, investigated by the Audiencia of Mexico in 1761, recounted the following narrative during his testimony: "Christ's soul was corn. When they

buried him, a shoot was born from the heart of Christ. As soon as that stalk bore a green ear of corn, it yielded also the heart of Jesus Christ, which then changed into a ripe ear, and it is in corn that the soul of Jesus is found" (Gruzinski 1989, 142).

35. *Nopilhuane, inin tlaxcaltzintli in nonacayotzin. Zan ic tlapachihui tlaxcaltzintli. Ca yehhuatl inic amopampatica cruztitech nimahmazohualticaz. Ma xicmocualtican, nopilhuane.* The script has *tlapachhui* (in the next passage as well); I assume, as Barry Sell and I did when we published this play in 2009, that this should be read *tlapachihui.*

36. Alexis Wimmer's online dictionary defines *tlapachihui* as *se couvrir, se remplir* 'to cover oneself, to fill up' (sites.estvideo.net/malinal/nahuatl.page.html); Molina (1992, pt. 2, 130v) has related forms.

37. *Notlazohpilhuane, inin vinoh in nezzotzin. Zan ic tlapachihui in vinoh, ca yehhuatl inic amopampatica in cruztitech nonoquihuiz in ipampa ic chicahuac yez yancuic nemiliztli. Ma xicmitican, xiquixcahuican, nopilhuane.*

38. *Quimotlapaniliz ihtec ce teocuitlaplatoh inic mochintin quimotlaceliltiliz cecenyaca in apostoles.*

39. *Ximomahcehuitzinocan xicmocualtican inin tlaxcaltzintli onicnoteochihuilih. Ipan ehua in nonacayotzin.*

40. The full line reads: *Xicmitican in vinoh onicnoteochihuilih. Ipan pohuiz in notlazohez-zotzin. Cencah ic chicahuaz in amotlaneltoquiliz ihuan in ixquichtin tlalticpac tlacah ic chipa-huaz in inyoliya in imanimah.*

41. Judas does address Jesus as "Rabbi" in the Garden of Gethsemane, in Penn (21v) and Tlatlauhquitepec (7v), following Matthew 26:49 (III.ii.10). This is likely retained from the model play.

42. "One of his disciples, whom Jesus loved," understood as the purported author of this Gospel.

43. *Auh in yehhatl in San Juan niman ichtaca inacaztlan quimotlahtlanilih in totecuiyo, quimolhuilih, "Totecuiyoe, ma mopaltzinco xinechmolhuilih, ac yehhuatl in temac mitzmotla-xiliz?" Auh in yehhuatl in totecuiyo niman quimolhuilih, "Notlazohpiltzine, ic tiquixmatiz nicmacaz tlacualli moltica nicpaltiliz." Auh niman conmocuilih in tlaxcalli moltica quimo-paltililih. Niman conmomaquilih in Judas.*

44. *Auh in ihcuac conmomaquilih in tlaxcalli, niman ihcuac ihtec calac in tlacatecolotl.*

45. *in momatqueh ahzo itlah quichihuatiuh in tlacualli, anozo quintlaocoliz in motoliniah.*

46. The foot-washing scene was not often painted in sixteenth-century murals, but Richard Perry has an image of the scene at Huejotzingo: mexicosmurals.blogspot.com/2017/06/san-miguel-huejotzingo-sala-murals.html.

47. John's speech at the end of the Princeton play, discussed in chapter 3 (see V.iv.9), is even longer, but this seems to be a later addition—not part of the model play—and possibly based on a sermon or contemplative narrative.

CHAPTER 5: VIOLENCE AND ANGER

1. In John 2:19–22, this scene is where Jesus says he could build a new temple in three days, alluding to the upcoming resurrection of his own body. Though every play highlights this assertion in the witnesses' hearsay evidence about Jesus's misdeeds (III.iv.14, III.viii.4, IV.i.18), none of the three plays includes it here.

2. Tlatlauhquitepec begins at a later point in the story.

3. *Auh inin Malco meuhtehuaz quimixtlatzinilitiuh huel iuhqui.*

4. He seems to have disqualified himself from ritual execution in a major festival by whining and weeping over his fate, and his suicide atoned for that dishonor; see Allen (2015, 493–495), who classifies weeping in such an instance as "bad tears," and Johansson (2014, 91–92). Johansson's study provides an extensive discussion of suicide in pre-Columbian Mexico.

5. Sousa assumes that this fall was fatal; however, the *Anales* does not explicitly say that, and Chimalpahin Quauhtlehuanitzin (1997, vol. 2, 42–43) records don Luis's death as occurring in December 1565. Hence, the effects of his fall are uncertain.

6. The historical Herod Archelaus died several decades before Rome's AD 70 invasion.

7. *Niman yaz cuauhtitech. Mopilotiuh in Judas ica ce mecatl.*

8. *Ichpochtli*, the word for a girl or an unmarried young woman, was used throughout Nahuatl Christian literature as the nearest analog to "virgin" and thus was ubiquitously associated with Mary.

9. "Son of man" would have to be rendered something like *inpil oquichtin* 'child of men' (contradicting his divine paternity), *ipil tlacayotl* 'child of humanity,' or *ipil oquichyotl* 'child of manliness.'

10. The plays are *The Three Kings* (Sell and Burkhart 2004, 118–145) and *The Star Sign* (as titled by Barry Sell and me in Sell and Burkhart 2009, 74–125; Burkhart, de la Cruz, and Sullivan 2017). On the parallels between Herod and Moteuczoma, see Burkhart 2008; Brown and Terukina Yamauchi 2017. On the scapegoating of Moteuczoma, see Gillespie (2008) on "blaming Moteuczoma" and Restall (2018, 46–50) on "Montezuma the Coward"; Dufendach (2019) reads the Florentine Codex accounts of Moteuczoma's reactions to the Spanish in terms of debilitating fright rather than cowardice.

11. Molina's dictionary (1992, pt. 2, 83r, 132v) defines *tlapoloa* as *perder el juizio y desatinarse* and *tetlapololtia* as *desatinar a otro.*

12. *tener enojo con otro y aborreciemiēto*; *indignación; enojo o furia del que esta ayrado y lleno de saña.*

13. In other literature, an early example of this usage for the devil occurs in fray Alonso de Escalona's sermon for the second Sunday in Lent (*Sermones en mexicano* n.d., 173r); again, I thank Berenice Alcántara Rojas for the use of her transcription and translation. A later example is in the 1714 play about Saint Helen (Sell and Burkhart 2009, 292–293).

14. See passionplaysofeighteenthcenturymexico.omeka.net/items/show/73, 9n9.

15. *es grandisimo echisero que tiene pacto con los Demonios.*

16. Reyes García (1960, 85) documents a more recent manifestation of this fear. During his fieldwork in Ixcatepec, a jeep with federal soldiers arrived in the town on Holy Saturday. The priest, panicked at the sight of "Pharisee" enactors bearing their hand-carved wooden lances, had called a nearby military detachment.

17. AGN, Ramo Inquisición vol. 1072, legajo 5, f. 198r. The death warrant from Ameca-meca does not include any version of the preamble.

18. This Simeon is a fictional character not to be confused with the elderly Simeon who recognizes the infant Christ as the savior in Luke 2:25–35, mentioned at I.viii.14.

19. *Todos: Su sangre caiga sobre nosotros, y sobre nuestros hijos.* Cuaderno 1, 217v; Tenango, 273v; Amecameca, 292v. Only the play from Ozumba lacks the line.

20. Tlatlauhquitepec cuts off shortly before this.

21. This may be another indication that the Princeton scriptwriter had occasional recourse to an alternative script that diverged in some ways from the others.

22. *auh ca tehhuantin ye tocontomamaltiah* (Tepalcingo, 106); *in ye tocontomamaltiah* (Princeton, 39v).

23. In many Mexican communities, the effigy burned on Holy Saturday is identified as Judas. In Chamula, performers run over burning thatch to effect a similar decontamination (Bricker 1973, 125).

24. *Auh ahmo zan quimomecaxihxipehuilizqueh, ca huel quimotzahtzayanilizqueh in icuitlapantzin, in icelticanacayotzin, huitztlacotica, tepozmecatica . . . iuhquin ezameyalli, iuhquin ezatezcatl.*

25. On *altepetl*-level crime and punishment, see Sousa 2017.

26. Hanks (2010, 84), for example, notes that local Maya leaders sometimes refused to carry out punishments they were ordered to inflict and told their subjects that the friars did not have the authority to punish them.

27. *Ma nictlatzacuiltih inic amoyolloh pachihuiz. Nicmecahuitequiz inic aocmo occeppa teiztlacahuiz, tetlapololtiz. Xihualhuian in annotiahcahuan. Xiquilpican tetlaquetzaltitech. Xicmecahuitequican. Yeceh ahtle niquittilia itlahtlacol inic miquiztlatzontequililoz.*

28. *Ahnicnonotzaz. Nicmecahuitequiz. Huel iez quizaz, huel tzahtzayaniz in inacayo, inic aocmo ceppa itlah ic tetlapololtiz.*

29. *Sentencia de azotes: In Jesus Nazarenoh ahcualtlachihuani, yeh ica ic teilhuilo ipampa in toteopixcatlahtohcahuan inic ahmo quimocacanequi* [read *quimotlacamatinequi?*] *in itenahuatiltzin in Moisés, xictlatohtomican ihuan xiquilpican temimiltitech cencah chicahuac. Xicmecahuitequican ica huitztlahcotl. Ma iuh neltiloz. Presidenteh Poncio Pilato.*

30. *Auh niman quimohuiquilizqueh teilpiloyan, ompa quimohuitequilizqueh. Niman quihualmoquixtilizqueh.*

31. *Quimopetlahuilizqueh. Quimolpilizqueh itech cuahuitl. Intla ye omocencauhqueh, quimotlalilizqueh ipan tetzontli. Quimixquemilhuizqueh. Intla ye omocencauhqueh, quimoquentiliz chichiltic capotilloh.*

32. *Zan oquimohuitequilizqueh. Mohuetzitiz tlalpan.*

33. *Huel teixpan tlapechco quimopehpetlahuilizqueh in Cristo. Tlahtic quimopiyaliz in maxtlatl. Huel neciz. Teixpan quimolpilizqueh tetlaquetzaltitech. Niman quimopehualtilizqueh. Quimohuitequilizqueh. Mochintin mopahpatlazqueh in Judiosmeh. Inic neltiz inic otlatzontec Poncio Pilato.*

34. Dibble and Anderson identify this plant as cardoon, a thistle, citing Santamaría (1959, 641); he, however, equates the Nahuatl term with the prickly-leaved *Bromelia pinguin*.

35. The same plant appears in other Nahuatl Passion texts, for example, León 1611, 34r. The name may be explained by its use as a protection against sorcerers (Sahagún 1950–1983, bk. 4, 45), *tlacatecolotl* 'human horned owl' having been a type of sorcerer before the word was adopted to refer to demons. In a Passion context, the demon association makes the thorns seem threatening rather than protective (cf. Burkhart 1996, 225–226).

36. Another Mexican example is a woodcut published in both fray Melchor de Vargas's Spanish-Nahuatl-Otomi *doctrina* (1576, 18v) and fray Pedro de Feria's Zapotec *doctrina* (1567, 33r), the latter with an adjoining woodcut of the flagellation (John Carter Brown Library, viewable on archive.org).

37. *Ma ximopaquiltihtiye! Izcatqui in cuayahualolli inic timitztotlapalhuilizqueh tintlatocauh in Judiostin; Ca nican cah in motlahtohcacoronah. Ma ximopahpaquiltihtiye, tlahtoanie; Ma ximopaquiltihtiye in tintlatocauh Judiosmeh.*

38. *Totlahtohcatzine, ca nican catqui in motlahtohcacoronahtzin. Ma xoconmaquitzinoh. Ma timitztaquiltilican. Ca huel mahuiztic inic tlachihchihualli, inic tlazohtli teocuitlatl icpac xochitl ochihualoc. (Quimaquiltilizqueh coronah.) Xictehtehuican, tocnihuaneh. Ma huel popolaqui in itlahtohcatzontecon in tlahueliloc.*

39. *ihuan icpac onmantiyaz huitzyahualli, yehhuatl in huel tecocoh huiztli.*

40. *Nican cah in motlahtohcacoronah, huitzyahualli. Xictennamiqui. Cencah mahuitztic, tlazohtli. Axcan mocpac tictlalizqueh. Huel pohpolaquiz itech in motzonteco. Ximopachoh. Xinechpalehuiquih, tiahcahuaneh. Tictlalilizqueh in itlahtohcacoronah in teixcuepani.*

41. See File:Ecce homo, Epazoyucan, Hidalgo.jpg–Wikimedia Commons.

42. This entailed tying the person's hands behind their back and then suspending them by the wrists, resulting in dislocation of the shoulders.

43. *In iopochcopamatzin in amo in ahcic inic tlacohcoyonilih in cuauhnepanolli. Mecatica oquitititzqueh. Ca niman omomahmacauh in itlazohomiyotzin, in itlazohtlahtohcaoquichnacayotzin.*

44. There was execution by arrows, of a localized embodiment of Xipe Totec, but this was distinct from the hammering of nails directly into hands and feet. However, the nails used in the crucifixion were sometimes called metal arrows (*tepozmitl*), suggesting some sense of similarity to arrows.

45. There is no reliable evidence that Indigenous Mesoamericans ever practiced crucifixion outside of staged Passions, despite reports to the contrary that some twentieth-century historians and anthropologists accepted as factual or at least likely. The most notorious case involves the notion that Mayas in Yucatan were, at least for some years just prior to 1562, tying or nailing male and female children to crosses before cutting out their hearts. The Franciscan friar Diego de Landa ordered witnesses to be tortured to elicit these stories; like people accused of witchcraft in Early Modern Europe, they learned to tell the sort of story their torturers insisted on eliciting. In this case, as Alejandro Enriquez attests, the story has its roots not in Maya practices but in the false stories of Jewish ritual murder of Christian children, which could, as in the widely repeated story of the Santo Niño de la Guardia from 1491, include the motifs of crucifixion and heart removal. Fray Francisco de Toral, who arrived in Yucatan in 1562 as its first bishop, rejected all of these confessions as false. See Enriquez 2018; also Tedlock 1993. Similarly, the alleged crucifixion of a boy named Domingo Gomes Checheb on Good Friday in 1868 by Maya insurgents in Chamula, Chiapas, has been discredited as anti-Indigenous propaganda (Rus 1983, 157–159).

46. Or, consistent with my usage in this project, "crossed-wood device" (*cuauhnepanolli*).

47. On the introduction of shirts, pants, and other male-gendered European garments to Nahua men, see Olko 2014, 335–337.

48. Joseph of Arimathea's quest to gain Pilate's permission to bury Jesus is similarly urgent: if not buried by sundown, the body would have had to be left on the cross until after the Sabbath (Gundry 2010, 218).

49. The 1856 Passion play from Villasinta, León, includes an additional motif from the legend: some of Christ's blood falls onto Longinus's face, so it is the blood that cures his eyes (Sticca 1970, 159). However, this play rationalizes the blind man's ability to aim a spear by having an accompanying Pharisee position the point against Christ's chest. Additional Villasinta stage effects include everyone but Longinus falling on the ground when Christ dies, a ray of light illuminating the site of the wound, and Longinus casting the lance away and raising his hands to his eyes as he begs for pardon (Lozano Prieto 1985, 107–108). The *Gamaliel*'s Passion text also has a Jew position the sword for Longinus, who touches his eyes after Christ's blood flows down the lance (Delbrugge 2020, 122).

50. *Ca huel nitlaneltoca ca huel nelli ca yehhuatzin in Dios ipiltzin in axcan omomiquilih.*

51. *Inin ca melahuac in dios in ipiltzin in ipampa ca quitlahtlani in intlapohpolhuiloca in nican quitlaihiyohuiltiah.* My placement of the line at V.iii.68, after the lancing, is arbitrary; as I include Centurion's rudeness to Mary at V.iii.60, his change of heart needed to come later.

52. These songs are translated in full in Burkhart 1996, 270–278.

53. Gluckman (1955) provides a classic study of rites of reversal. Scott (1990) revises the structural-functionalist view that ritualized inversions simply strengthen or renew the dominant order, finding that inversions provide opportunities for critique and the emergence of new forms of resistance.

THE NAHUATL PASSION PLAY: A COMPOSITE TRANSLATION

1. The word "all" in parentheses indicates the use of second-person plural, where this is not obvious from the context.

2. The verb *ana* refers more broadly to acts of seizing, grabbing, or capture. Where it refers to Jesus being taken into custody, I use "arrest."

3. Jesus meets this blind person on the way to Jericho, not Jerusalem, in Luke 18:35–43.

4. The reference is to Zechariah 9:9.

5. The place name is given first in Spanish and then Nahuatlized.

6. A formulaic statement of welcome.

7. From Spanish *testamento*.

8. Mount Sinai has been confused with Mount Zion.

9. The angels (or choir) chant the *Sanctus* from the Mass here, from Isaiah 6:3 and 1 Corinthians 34:6–7. The Latin reads: "Holy Holy Holy. Lord God of hosts. Heaven and earth are full of your glory. Hosanna in the highest."

10. Adam and Eve.

11. *Tlacatecolotl*, the term for a type of sorceror adapted to refer to demons or the devil.

12. An allusion to John 8:59, though this passage precedes the account of Holy Week: "So they took up stones to throw at him; but Jesus hid himself, and went out of the temple."

13. "Not during the feast, lest there be a tumult among the people." Navarro 1604, iv; Matthew 26:5.

14. As Judas in the Gospels is paid in silver, I use this throughout. The word *teocuitlatl* can mean either gold or silver.

15. "You know that after two days the Passover is coming, and the Son of man will be delivered up to be crucified"; Navarro 1604, iv; Matthew 26:2.

16. A formulaic greeting.

17. Or "esteemed."

18. "Now as they were eating, Jesus took bread, blessed and broke it, and gave it to his disciples"; Navarro 1604, 5v; Matthew 26:26. This is also a liturgical antiphon (cantusindex.org/id/001781).

19. A hymn attributed to Saint Thomas Aquinas. The first lines read: *Pange lingua gloriosi corporis mysterium sanguinisque pretiosi quem in mundi pretium fructus ventris generosi rex effudit gentium* ("Of the glorious Body telling, O my tongue, its mysteries sing, And the Blood, all price excelling, Which the world's eternal King, In a noble womb once dwelling Shed for the world's ransoming") (chantcd.com/lyrics/glorious_body.htm; see this site for complete lyrics to this and "Tantum ergo").

20. The "Tantum ergo" is the last two stanzas of "Pange lingua gloriosi." The lines refer to adoration of the Eucharist and praise of the Trinity.

21. The dialogue here would continue with the remaining apostles.

22. "The Lord Jesus, after He had supped with his disciples, washed their feet and said to them: 'Do you know what I, your Lord and Master, have done for you? I have given you an example that you also may do likewise'"; antiphon sung at the foot-washing ceremony (cantusindex.org/id/002413); English translation from soundcloud.com/gregorian-cantor/maundy3.

23. "O Lord, do you wash my feet? Jesus answered and said to him, if I do not wash your feet you will have no part in me." Antiphon sung at the foot-washing ceremony (cantusindex.org/id/002393), from John 13:6–8. This is from the Tlatlauhquitepec Passion. The Penn Passion calls instead for the antiphon *Mandatum novum do vobis ut dilitatis invicem sicut dilexi vos dicit dominus*, from John 13:34 ("A new commandment I give to you, that you love one another even as I have loved you, said the Lord"; cantusindex.org/id/003239d).

24. That is, the devil.

25. He has worn himself out.

26. "What will you give me if I deliver him to you?"; Navarro 1604, 3r–3v; Matthew 26:15.

27. In some scripts, Samuel says "maybe he will be satisfied."

28. "My soul is very sorrowful, even unto death; remain here, and watch with me"; Navarro 1604, 8r; Matthew 26:38. The passage is also a liturgical antiphon (cantusindex.org/id/005187).

29. From Matthew 26:49.

30. Or sword.

31. Spanish *información*.

32. The witnesses are generally called *testigos*, from Spanish, but this is occasionally paired with *tlaneltilianimeh* 'those who testify to things.'

33. "He has uttered blasphemy: why do we still need witnesses? You have heard his blasphemy. What is your judgment?"; Matthew 26:65–66; Navarro 1604, 13v–14r.

34. "And Peter remembered the saying of Jesus: 'Before the cock crows, you will deny me three times.' And he went out and wept bitterly"; Matthew 26:75; Navarro 1604, 15v. The line is also a liturgical antiphon (cantusindex.org/id/004578).

35. That is, God's child. Judas's use of this respectful diphrase expresses his newly recovered reverence for Jesus.

36. *probanzah*, from Spanish.

37. *mojusticiah*, from Spanish.

38. "Have mercy on me, God"; phrase in several Psalms and, with *miserere* repeated at the end, antiphon verse for the foot-washing ceremony (cantusindex.org/id/001780zb).

39. Whistles or trumpets, perhaps.

40. "Here is the man," Pilate's statement in John 19:5. Liturgical source uncertain; Navarro's *Passio secundum Joannem* has *Ecce, rex vester* 'here is your king' (Navarro 1604, 84r), which is chanted further on (IV.iv.19), at the point corresponding to this line in John.

41. "Here is the man"; John 19:5.

42. "Away with him, away with him"; John 19:15.

43. "Here is your king." Navarro's *Passio secundum Joannem* may be the source here (Navarro 1604, 84r).

44. Spanish *causas*.

45. At I.viii.18, Magdalene addressed Martha as her older sister (*nopihtzin*) from Tepalcingo (24). Here, from Tlatlauhquitepec (10r), Martha addresses Magdalene with a different term for older sister (*notlazohhueliuhtzin*). The contradiction does not occur within a single play.

46. *justiciah*, from Spanish.

47. "All you who pass by on the road, look and see if there is any sorrow like my sorrow." Antiphon, from Lamentations 1:12, used on Holy Saturday (cantusindex.org/id/004095) and also arranged as a motet by, among others, the Spanish Renaissance composer Tomás Luis de Victoria (cpdl.org/wiki/index.php/O_vos_omnes_(voci_impari)_(Tom%C3%A1s_Luis_de_Victoria).

48. "O Lord, remember me when you come into your kingly power"; Luke 23:42; Navarro 1604, 70v.

49. "Truly, I say to you, today you will be with me in paradise"; Luke 23:43; Navarro 1604, 70v.

50. Latin *Paradiso*, from Luke 23:43.

51. "Behold your mother. Behold your son"; John 19:26–27; Navarro 1604, 86v–87r.

52. "My God, my God, why have you forsaken me?"; Matthew 27:46; Navarro 1604, 23v.

53. "I thirst"; John 19:28; Navarro 1604, 87r.

54. "It is finished"; John 19:30; Navarro 1604, 87v.

55. "Into your hands, O Lord, I commend my spirit"; Luke 23:4; Navarro 1604, 74r.

56. The full text of this Renaissance motet is: *O Domine Jesu Christe, adoro te in cruce vulneratum, felle et aceto potatum: deprecor te, ut tua vulnera morsque tua sit vita mea* ("O lord Jesus Christ, I worship you, wounded on the cross, with gall and vinegar to drink. I beseech you, that your wounds and your death may be my life") (cpdl.org/wiki/index.php/O_Domine_Jesu_Christe,_adoro_te_in_cruce_vulneratum; my translation with assistance from Stafford Poole, C.M).

57. Their scene continues at V.iv.10. John's speech here is an alternative ending.

58. *Adoramus te Christe, et benedicimus tibi quia per crucem tuam redemisti mundum* ("We adore you, Christ, and bless you, because by means of your cross you redeemed the world"); antiphon sung for the feast of the Holy Cross (cantusindex.org/id/001287; my translation).

References

Allen, Heather J. 2015. "'Llorar Amargamente': Economies of Weeping in the Spanish Empire." *Colonial Latin American Review* 24 (4): 479–504.

Alvarado Tezozomoc, Hernando. 1975. *Crónica mexicana . . . precedida del códice Ramírez.* Edited by Manuel Orozco y Berra. Mexico City: Editorial Porrúa.

Álvarez, Diego. 1753. *Memorial ilustre de los famosos hijos del real, grave, y religioso convento de Santa María de Jesús.* Ávila: Doña María García Briones, Impresora de la Universidad.

Andrews, J. Richard. 1975. *Introduction to Classical Nahuatl.* Austin: University of Texas Press.

Anunciación, Domingo de la. 1565. *Doctrina christiana breve y compendiosa por via de dialogo entre un maestro y un discipulo.* Mexico City: Pedro Ocharte.

Anunciación, Juan de la. 1575. *Doctrina christiana muy cumplida, donde se contiene la exposicion de todo lo necessario para doctrinar a los indios, y administralles los sanctos sacramentos.* Mexico City: Pedro Balli.

Anunciación, Juan de la. 1577. *Sermonario en lengua mexicana.* Mexico City: Antonio Ricardo.

Ashe, Kevin, Jay Rock, and Leon Klenicki. 1996. "A Dialogue on Passion Plays and Judaism." In *Passion Plays and Judaism*, ed. Leon Klenicki, 3–12. New York: Anti-Defamation League.

Basich de Canessi, Zita, ed. 1963. *Un catecismo del siglo XVI.* Mexico City: Editorial Offset.

https://doi.org/10.5876/9781646424511.c008

Bassett, Molly. 2014. "The Pre-Racial Saint? Ma(r)king Aztec God-Bodies." In *Sainthood and Race: Marked Flesh, Holy Flesh*, ed. Molly Bassett and Vincent Lloyd, 199–215. New York: Routledge.

Bassett, Molly. 2015. *The Fate of Earthly Things: Aztec Gods and God-Bodies*. Austin: University of Texas Press.

Bautista Viseo, Juan. 1600. *Huehuetlahtolli*. Mexico City: Melchor Ocharte.

Baustita Viseo, Juan. 1606. *A Iesu Christo S. N. ofrece este sermonario en lengua mexicano*. Mexico City: Diego López Dávalos.

Berdan Frances F., and Patricia Rieff Anawalt, eds. 1992. *Codex Mendoza*. 4 vols. Berkekey: University of California Press.

Berliner, Rudolf. 2003. "Das Urteil des Pilatus." In *Rudolf Berliner (1886–1967): "The Freedom of Medieval Art" und andere Studie zum christlichen Bild*, ed. Robert Suckale, 43–59. Berlin: Lukas Verlag.

Beskow, Per. 1983. *Strange Tales about Jesus: A Survey of Unfamiliar Gospels*. Philadelphia: Fortress Press.

Bestul, Thomas. 1996. *Texts of the Passion: Latin Devotional Literature and Medieval Society*. Philadelphia: University of Pennsylvania Press.

Bierhorst, John, trans. and ed. 1998. *History and Mythology of the Aztecs: The Codex Chimalpopoca*. Tucson: University of Arizona Press.

Bishops' Committee for Ecumenical and Interreligious Affairs, National Conference of Catholic Bishops. 1988. *Criteria for the Evaluation of Dramatizations of the Passion*. Washington, DC: US Catholic Conference. Reprinted in Leon Klenicki, ed. 1996. *Passion Plays and Judaism*, 21–38. New York: Anti-Defamation League.

Blecua, Alberto. 1988. "Sobre la autoría del *Auto de la Pasión*." In *Homenaje a Eugenio Asensio*, ed. Luisa López Grigera and Augustín Redondo, 79–112. Madrid: Gredos.

Bogdanow, Fanni. 2009. "The Relationship of the Portuguese *Josep Abarimatia* to the Extant French MSS. of the *Estoire del Saint Graal*." *Zeitschrift für romanische Philologie* 76 (5–6): 343–375.

Boone, Elizabeth Hill, Louise M. Burkhart, and David Tavárez. 2017. *Painted Words: Nahua Catholicism, Politics, and Memory in the Atzaqualco Pictorial Catechism*. Washington, DC: Dumbarton Oaks Research Library and Collection.

Bricker, Victoria Reiffler. 1973. *Ritual Humor in Highland Chiapas*. Austin: University of Texas Press.

Bricker, Victoria Reiffler. 1981. *The Indian Christ, the Indian King: The Historical Substrate of Maya Myth and Ritual*. Austin: University of Texas Press.

Bright, William. 1990. "'With One Lip, with Two Lips': Parallelism in Nahuatl." *Language* 66 (3): 437–452.

Brown, Katherine L., and Jorge L. Terukina Yamauchi. 2017. "Paradojas performativas: *La adoración de los Reyes* o *exemplum.*" *Estudios de cultura náhuatl* 54: 207–254.

Brown, Raymond E. 1994. *The Death of the Messiah: From Gethsemane to the Grave.* 2 vols. New York: Doubleday.

Brylak, Agnieszka. 2019. "Hurtling off a Precipice, Falling into a River: A Nahuatl Metaphor and the Christian Concept of Sin." *Ethnohistory* 66 (3): 489–513.

Brylak, Agnieszka. 2021. "Buffoons and Sorcerers: Witchcraft, Entertainment, and Evil Professions in Colonial Sources on Pre-Hispanic Nahuas." *Colonial Latin American Review* 30 (3): 342–360.

Burkhart, Louise M. 1988. "The Solar Christ in Nahuatl Doctrinal Texts of Early Colonial Mexico." *Ethnohistory* 35 (3): 234–256.

Burkhart, Louise M. 1989. *The Slippery Earth: Nahua-Christian Moral Dialogue in Sixteenth-Century Mexico.* Tucson: University of Arizona Press.

Burkhart, Louise M. 1996. *Holy Wednesday: A Nahua Drama from Early Colonial Mexico.* Philadelphia: University of Pennsylvania Press.

Burkhart, Louise M. 1998. "Pious Performances: Christian Pageantry and Native Identity in Early Colonial Mexico." In *Native Traditions in the Postconquest World*, ed. Elizabeth H. Boone and Tom Cummins, 361–381. Washington, DC: Dumbarton Oaks Research Library and Collection.

Burkhart, Louise M. 2000. "The Native Translator as Critic: A Nahua Playwright's Interpretive Practice." In *Possible Pasts: Becoming Colonial in Early America*, ed. Robert Blair St. George, 73–87. Ithaca, NY: Cornell University Press.

Burkhart, Louise M. 2001. *Before Guadalupe: The Virgin Mary in Early Colonial Nahuatl Literature.* Albany: Institute for Mesoamerican Studies, University at Albany, State University of New York.

Burkhart, Louise M. 2008. "Meeting the Enemy: Moteuczoma and Cortés, Herod and the Magi." In *Invasion and Transformation: Interdisciplinary Perspectives on the Conquest of Mexico*, ed. Rebecca P. Brienen and Margaret A. Jackson, 11–23. Boulder: University Press of Colorado.

Burkhart, Louise M. 2009. "Pageantry, Passion, and Punishment: Eighteenth-Century Nahuatl Community Theater." In *Nahuatl Theater*, Volume 4: *Nahua Christianity in Performance*, edited by Barry D. Sell and Louise M. Burkhart, 3–50. Norman: University of Oklahoma Press.

Burkhart, Louise M. 2010. "The Destruction of Jerusalem as Colonial Nahuatl Historical Drama." In *The Conquest All over Again: Nahuas and Zapotecs Thinking, Writing, and Painting Spanish Colonialism*, ed. Susan Schroeder, 74–100. Brighton, UK: Sussex Academic Press.

Burkhart, Louise M. 2013. "Satan Is My Nickname: Demonic and Angelic Interventions in Colonial Nahuatl Theatre." In *Angels, Demons, and the New World*, ed. Fernando Cervantes and Andrew Redden, 101–125. Cambridge, UK: Cambridge University Press.

Burkhart, Louise M. 2014. "The 'Little Doctrine' and Indigenous Catechesis in New Spain." *Hispanic American Historical Review* 94 (2): 167–206.

Burkhart, Louise M. 2016. "2014 Presidential Address: Christian Salvation as Ethno-Ethnohistory: Two Views from 1714." *Ethnohistory* 63 (2): 215–235.

Burkhart, Louise M. In press. "Nahua Notaries of Jerusalem: Lucio Sestilio and His Partners in Crime." In *Nahua Studies: Past and Present*, ed. Galen Brokaw and Pablo García Loaeza. Denver: University Press of Colorado.

Burkhart, Louise M., ed. 2011. *Aztecs on Stage: Religious Theater in Colonial Mexico*. Translated by Louise M. Burkhart, Barry D. Sell, and Stafford Poole. Norman: University of Oklahoma Press.

Burkhart, Louise M., Abelardo de la Cruz, and John Sullivan. 2017. *In Citlalmachiyotl/The Star Sign: A Colonial Nahua Drama of the Three Kings*. Warsaw: University of Warsaw, Facultad de Artes Liberales.

Burns, Kathryn. 2010. *Into the Archive: Writing and Power in Colonial Peru*. Durham, NC: Duke University Press.

Bynum, Caroline Walker. 1988. *Holy Feast and Holy Fast: The Religious Significance of Food to Medieval Women*. Berkeley: University of California Press.

Campbell, Stephen J. 2008. "The Conflicted Representation of Judaism in Italian Renaissance Images of Christ's Life and Passion." In *The Passion Story: From Visual Representation to Social Drama*, edited by Marcia Kupfer, 67–90. University Park: Pennsylvania State University Press.

Carreño, Elvia. n.d. "Diego López Dávalos y la tipografía mexicana en el siglo XVI." Mexico City: Apoyo al Desarrollo de Archivos y Bibliotecas de México. adabi.org.mx /content/servicios/libro/articulos/diego.jsfx. Accessed January 6, 2022.

Carrillo y Gariel, Abelardo. 1949. *El Cristo de Mexicaltzingo: Técnica de las esculturas en caña*. 2 vols. Mexico City: Instituto Nacional de Antropología e Historia and Secretaría de Educación Pública.

Cartas de Indias. 1970. Facsimile of 1877 Madrid edition. Edited by Edmundo Aviña Levy. 2 vols. Guadalajara, Mexico.

Castillo de Bobadilla, Jerónimo. 1775. *Política para corregidores, y señores de vasallos, en tiempo de paz, y de guerra*. Vol. 1. Madrid: Imprenta Real de la Gazeta.

Chimalpahin Quauhtlehuanitzin, Domingo de San Antón Muñon. 1965. *Relaciones originales de Chalco Amaquemecan*. Translated and edited by Silvia Rendón. Mexico City: Fondo de Cultura Económica.

Chimalpahin Quauhtlehuanitzin, Domingo de San Antón Muñon. 1997. *Codex Chimalpahin*. Translated and edited by Susan Schroeder and Arthur J. O. Anderson. 2 vols. Norman: University of Oklahoma Press.

Christensen, Mark Z. 2013. *Nahua and Maya Catholicisms: Texts and Religion in Colonial Central Mexico and Yucatan*. Stanford and Berkeley, CA: Stanford University Press and Academy of American Franciscan History.

Christensen, Mark Z. 2016. *The Teabo Manuscript: Maya Christian Copybooks, Chilam Balams, and Native Text Production in Yucatán*. Austin: University of Texas Press.

Christenson, Allen J. 2016. *The Burden of the Ancients: Maya Ceremonies of World Renewal from the Pre-Columbian Period to the Present*. Austin: University of Texas Press.

Christian, William A., Jr. 1981. *Local Religion in Sixteenth-Century Spain*. Princeton, NJ: Princeton University Press.

Chuchiak, John F., IV. 2007. "The Sins of the Fathers: Franciscan Friars, Parish Priests, and the Sexual Conquest of the Yucatec Maya, 1545–1808." *Ethnohistory* 54 (1): 69–127.

Clendinnen, Inga. 1990. "Ways to the Sacred: Reconstructing 'Religion' in Sixteenth Century Mexico." *History and Anthropology* 5 (1): 105–141.

Concilio III provincial mexicano: *celebrado en Mexico en el año de 1585*. 1870. Edited by Mariano Galván Rivera. Barcelona: M. Miro and D. Barsa.

Conrad, Geoffrey W., and Arthur A. Demarest. 1984. *Religion and Empire: The Dynamics of Aztec and Inca Expansionism*. Cambridge, UK: Cambridge University Press.

Cortés Castellanos, Justino. 1987. *El catecismo en pictogramas de Fr. Pedro de Gante*. Madrid: Fundación Universitaria Española.

Cruz-Castillo, J. G., Omar Franco-Mora, and Franco Famiani. 2009. "Presence and Uses of Wild Grapevine (*Vitis* spp.) in the Central Region of Veracruz in Mexico." *Journal International des Sciences de la Vigne et du Vin* 43 (2): 77–81.

Davis, Mark Evan. 2013. "'The Evangelical Prophecies over Jerusalem Have Been Fulfilled': Joachim of Fiore, the Jews, Fray Diego de Landa, and the Maya." *Journal of Iberian Medieval Studies* 51 (1): 86–103.

de la Cruz de la Cruz, Abelardo. 2020. "Migración, lenguaje y formación indígena: continuidad cultural entre los nahuas residentes en el Estado de Zacatecas (1990–2020)." Unpublished paper.

"De la passion de noestro señor ie. xᵒ." n.d. In *Miscelánea sagrada*. Biblioteca Nacional de México, Mexico City, Fondo Reservado, MS. 1477, 201r–220v.

Delbrugge, Laura, ed. and trans. 2020. *A Scholarly Edition of the Gamaliel (Valencia: Juan Jofre, 1525)*. Leiden: Brill.

Díaz, Mónica. 2010. *Indigenous Writings from the Convent: Negotiating Ethnic Autonomy in Colonial Mexico*. Tucson: University of Arizona Press.

Díaz Balsera, Viviana. 2008. "Celebrating the Rise of a New Sun: The Tlaxcalans Conquer Jerusalem in 1539." *Estudios de cultura náhuatl* 39: 311–330.

Dierksmeier, Laura. 2020. *Charity for and by the Poor: Franciscan and Indigenous Confraternities in Mexico, 1527–1700*. Norman, OK, and Berkeley, CA: University of Oklahoma Press and Academy of American Franciscan History.

Don, Patricia Lopes. 2010. *Bonfires of Culture: Franciscans, Indigenous Leaders, and the Inquisition in Early Mexico, 1524–1540*. Norman: University of Oklahoma Press.

Driscoll, J. F. 1912. "Salome." In *The Catholic Encyclopedia*. New York: Robert Appleton. newadvent.org/cathen/13403a.htm. Accessed March 19, 2020.

Dufendach, Rebecca. 2019. " 'As if His Heart Died': A Reinterpretation of Moteuczoma's Cowardice in the Conquest History of the Florentine Codex." *Ethnohistory* 66 (4): 623–645.

Durán, Diego. 1994. *The History of the Indies of New Spain*. Translated and edited by Doris Heyden. Norman: University of Oklahoma Press.

Duran i Sanpere, Agustí, and Eulàlia Duran, eds. 1984. *La Passió de Cervera: Misteri del segle XVI*. Barcelona: Curial Edicions Catalanes.

Earle, Rebecca. 2010. " 'If You Eat Their Food . . .': Diets and Bodies in Early Colonial Spanish America." *American Historical Review* 115 (3): 688–713.

Enders, Jody. 2008. "*Coups de Théâtre* and the Passion for Vengeance." In *The Passion Story: From Visual Representation to Social Drama*, edited by Marcia Kupfer, 121–130. University Park: Pennsylvania State University Press.

Enriquez, Alejandro. 2018. "The Exuberant Imagination: Blood Libel and the Myth of Maya Ritual Murder in the 1562 Sotuta Confessions." *Journal of Medieval Iberian Studies* 10 (2): 276–294.

Farmer, David Hugh. 1992. *The Oxford Dictionary of Saints*. New York: Oxford University Press.

Feria, Pedro de. 1576. *Doctrina christiana en lengua castellana y çapoteca*. Mexico City: Pedro Ocharte.

Ferrer Gimeno, María Rosario. 2011. "De entre los libros prohibidos: *Gamaliel*." *eHumanista* 17: 271–285.

Fischer, Eugene J. 1996. "Prologue." In *Passion Plays and Judaism*, ed. Leon Klenicki, 1–2. New York: Anti-Defamation League.

Ford, Alvin E. 1993. *La Vengeance de Nostre-Seigneur: The Old and Middle French Prose Versions*. Toronto: Pontifical Institute of Mediaeval Studies.

Fulton, Rachel. 2003. *From Judgment to Passion*. New York: Columbia University Press.

García Garagarza, León. 2020. "The Tecolotl and the Chiquatli: Omens of Death and Transspecies Dialogues in the Aztec World." *Ethnohistory* 67 (3): 455–479.

García Pimentel, Luis, ed. 1897. *Descripción del arzobispado de México hecha en 1570 y otros documentos*. Mexico City: José Joaquín Terrazas e Hijas.

Gell, Alfred. 1998. *Art and Agency: An Anthropological Theory*. Oxford: Clarendon.

Gillespie, Susan D. 1989. *The Aztec Kings: The Construction of Rulership in Mexica History*. Tucson: University of Arizona Press.

Gillespie, Susan D. 2008. "Blaming Moteuczoma: Anthropomorphizing the Spanish Conquest." In *Invasion and Transformation: Interdisciplinary Perspectives on the Conquest of Mexico*, ed. Rebecca P. Brienen and Margaret A. Jackson, 25–55. Boulder: University Press of Colorado.

Gluckman, Max. 1955. *Custom and Conflict in Africa*. Glencoe, IL: Free Press.

Gossen, Gary. 1974. *Chamulas in the World of the Sun: Time and Space in a Maya Oral Tradition*. Cambridge, MA: Harvard University Press.

Gossen, Gary. 1998. *Telling Maya Tales: Tzotzil Identities in Modern Mexico*. New York: Routledge.

Graham, Elizabeth. 2001. *Maya Christians and Their Churches in Sixteenth-Century Belize*. Gainesville: University Press of Florida.

Graham, Elizabeth. In press. "What's Wrong with 'Human Sacrifice?'" In *Maya Religion and History: Proceedings of the 22nd European Maya Conference, Malmö, Sweden, December 11–16, 2017*, ed. Harri Juhani Kettunen, Bodil Liljefors Persson, and Christophe Helmke. *Acta Mesoamericana* 31. Munich: Anton Saurwein.

Greenleaf, Richard E. 1961. *Zumárraga and the Mexican Inquisition, 1536–1543*. Washington, DC: Academy of American Franciscan History.

Greenleaf, Richard E. 1969. *The Mexican Inquisition of the Sixteenth Century*. Albuquerque: University of New Mexico Press.

Gropp, Arthur E. 1933. *Manuscripts in the Department of Middle American Research*. New Orleans: Department of Middle American Research, Tulane University.

Gruzinski, Serge. 1989. *Man-gods in the Mexican Highlands*. Translated by Eileen Corrigan. Stanford, CA: Stanford University Press.

Guerra, Domingo Valentín. n.d. *Libro de varias noticias y apuntaciones que dexó escritas, en latín, español, francés e ytaliano, Domingo Valentín Guerra, obispo de Segovia*. Biblioteca Nacional de España, Biblioteca Digital Hispánica. bdh-rd.bne.es/viewer.vm?id=0000145015&page=1. Accessed April 29, 2020.

Gundry, Robert H. 2010. *Commentary on the New Testament: Verse-by-Verse Explanations with a Literal Translation*. Peabody, MA: Hendrickson.

Hackett, Charles, ed. 1923–1937. *Historical Documents Relating to New Mexico, Nueva Vizcaya, and Approaches Thereto, to 1773, Collected by Adolph F. A. Bandelier and Fanny R. Bandelier*. 3 vols. Washington, DC: Carnegie Institute.

Hanks, William F. 2010. *Converting Words: Maya in the Age of the Cross*. Berkeley: University of California Press.

Haskett, Robert. 1991. *Indigenous Rulers: An Ethnohistory of Town Government in Colonial Cuernavaca*. Albuquerque: University of New Mexico Press.

Haskett, Robert. 2005. *Visions of Paradise: Primordial Titles and Mesoamerican History in Cuernavaca*. Norman: University of Oklahoma Press.

Hervet, Gentian, trans. and ed. 1584. *Sainct Augustin: De la Cité de Dieu . . . illustrée des commentaires de Jean Loys Vives*. Paris: Michel Sonnius.

Hook, David. 2000. *The Destruction of Jerusalem: Catalan and Castilian Texts*. London: Kings College London.

Horcasitas, Fernando. 1974. *Teatro náhuatl: Épocas novohispana y moderna*. Mexico City: Universidad Nacional Autónoma de México.

Horcasitas, Fernando. 2004. *Teatro náhuatl II: Selección y estudio crítico de los materiales inéditas de Fernando Horcasitas*. Edited by María Sten, Óscar Armando García, Ricardo García-Arteaga, and Alejandro Ortiz Bulle-Goyri; translations revised by Librado Silva Galeana. Mexico City: Universidad Autónoma Nacional de México.

Hourihane, Colum. 2009. *Pontius Pilate, Anti-Semitism, and the Passion in Medieval Art*. Princeton, NJ: Princeton University Press.

Hughes, Jennifer Scheper. 2010. *Biography of a Mexican Crucifix: Lived Religion and Local Faith from the Conquest to the Present*. New York: Oxford University Press.

James, Montague Rhodes. 1924. *The Apocryphal New Testament*. Oxford: Clarendon.

Johannson K., Patrick. 2014. "*Nenomamictiliztli*: El suicidio en el mundo náhuatl prehispánico." *Estudios de cultura náhuatl* 47: 53–119.

Karttunen, Frances. 1983. *An Analytical Dictionary of Nahuatl*. Austin: University of Texas Press.

Karttunen, Frances, and James Lockhart. 1976. *Nahuatl in the Middle Years: Language Contact Phenomena in Texts of the Colonial Period*. Berkeley: University of California Press.

Karttunen, Frances, and James Lockhart, eds. and trans. 1987. *The Art of Nahuatl Speech: The Bancroft Dialogues*. Los Angeles: UCLA Latin American Center.

Keith, Chris. n.d. "Manuscript History and John 8:1–11." bibleodyssey.org/en/passages /related-articles/Manuscript%20History%20and%20John. Accessed March 26, 2020.

Kellogg, Susan. 1995. *Law and the Transformation of Aztec Culture, 1500–1700*. Norman: University of Oklahoma Press.

Kellogg, Susan. 1997. "From Parallel and Equivalent to Separate but Unequal: Tenochca Mexica Women, 1500–1700." In *Indian Women of Early Mexico*, ed. Susan Schroeder, Stephanie Wood, and Robert Haskett, 123–143. Norman: University of Oklahoma Press.

Klein, Cecilia. 2001. "None of the Above: Gender Ambiguity in Nahua Ideology." In *Gender in Pre-Hispanic America*, ed. Cecilia Klein, 183–239. Washington, DC: Dumbarton Oaks Research Library and Collection.

Klenicki, Leon, ed. 1996. *Passion Plays and Judaism*. New York: Anti-Defamation League.

Kubler, George. 1982. *Arquitectura mexicana del siglo XVI*. Translated by Roberto de la Torre and Graciela de Garay. Mexico City: Fondo de Cultura Económica.

Kupfer, Marcia. 2008a. "Introduction." In *The Passion Story: From Visual Representation to Social Drama*, edited by Marcia Kupfer, 1–19. University Park: Pennsylvania State University Press.

Kupfer, Marcia, ed. 2008b. *The Passion Story: From Visual Representation to Social Drama*. University Park: Pennsylvania State University Press.

Kurylak, Ewa. 1991. *Veronica and Her Cloth: History, Symbolism, and Structure of a "True" Image*. Cambridge, MA: Basil Blackwell.

Larkin, Brian. 2004. "Liturgy, Devotion, and Religious Reform in Eighteenth-Century Mexico City." *The Americas* 60 (4): 493–518.

Larkin, Brian. 2010. *The Very Nature of God: Baroque Catholicism and Religious Reform in Bourbon Mexico City*. Albuquerque: University of New Mexico Press.

Laso de la Vega, Luis. 1649. *Huey tlamahuiçoltica omonexiti in ilhuicac tlatocacihuapilli Santa Maria totlaçonantzin Guadalupe in nican huey altepetzin Mexico itocayocan Tepeyacac*. Mexico City: Juan Ruiz.

Leeming, Ben. 2022. *Aztec Antichrist: Performing the Apocalypse in Early Colonial Mexico*. Louisville, CO, and Albany, NY: University Press of Colorado and Institute for Mesoamerican Studies.

León, Martín de. 1611. *Camino del cielo en lengua mexicana*. Mexico City: Diego López Dávalos.

León-Portilla, Miguel, ed. 1994. *Cantares mexicanos*. Facsimile edition of the manuscript in the Fondo Reservado, Biblioteca Nacional de México. Mexico City: Universidad Nacional Autónoma de México.

Leyva, Juan. 2001. *La Pasión de Ozumba: El teatro religioso en el siglo XVIII novohispano*. Mexico City: Universidad Nacional Autónoma de México.

Livingston, Michael, ed. 2004. *Siege of Jerusalem*. Kalamazoo, MI: Medieval Institute Publications.

Lockhart, James. 1991. *Nahuas and Spaniards: Postconquest Central Mexican History and Philology*. Stanford and Los Angeles: Stanford University Press and UCLA Latin American Publications.

Lockhart, James. 1992. *The Nahuas after the Conquest: A Social and Cultural History of the Indians of Central Mexico, Sixteenth through Eighteenth Centuries*. Stanford, CA: Stanford University Press.

Lockhart, James, Susan Schroeder, and Doris Namala, trans. and eds. 2006. *Annals of His Time: Don Domingo de San Antón Muñón Chimalpahin Quauhtlehuanitzin*. Stanford, CA: Stanford University Press.

López Hernández, Miriam. 2017. "*In tetl, in cuahuitl*: Los sistemas jurídicos nahuas prehispánicos ante el adulterio." *Relaciones: Estudios de historia y sociedad* 38 (149): 193–227.

Lozano Prieto, Victor, ed. 1985. *Autos sacramentales y folklore religioso de León*. León, Spain: Editorial Celarayn.

MacArthur, John. 2008. *The MacArthur New Testament Commentary: John 12–21*. Chicago: Moody.

MacGregor, Neil, with Erika Langmuir. 2000. *Seeing Salvation: Images of Christ in Art*. New Haven, CT: Yale University Press.

Macuil Martínez, Raul. 2016. "La Pasión de Atlihuetzia en lengua nauatl, siglos XVII y XVIII." *Indiana* 33 (1): 223–249.

Macuil Martínez, Raul, trans. and ed. 2010. *La pasión de Tlatlauhquitepec: obra de teatro Tlaxcalteca en náhuatl del siglo XVI*. Tlaxcala, Mexico: Gobierno del Estado de Tlaxcala, Instituto Tlaxcalteca de la Cultura.

Madajczak, Julia. 2017. "Toward a Deconstruction of the Notion of Nahua 'Confession.'" In *Words and Worlds Turned Around: Indigenous Christianities in Colonial Latin America*, ed. David Tavárez, 63–81. Boulder: University Press of Colorado.

Mann, Kristin Dutcher. 2010. *The Power of Song: Music and Dance in the Mission Communities of Northern New Spain, 1590–1810*. Stanford, CA: Stanford University Press.

Marín-Guadarrama, Nadia. 2012. "Childrearing in the Discourse of Friars and Nahuas in Colonial Mexico." PhD dissertation, Department of Anthropology, University at Albany, State University of New York.

Marrow, James H. 1979. *Passion Iconography in Northern European Art of the Middle Ages and Early Renaissance: A Study of the Transformation of Sacred Metaphor into Descriptive Narrative*. Kortrijk, Belgium: Van Ghemmert.

Marrow, James H. 2008. "Inventing the Passion in the Late Middle Ages." In *The Passion Story: From Visual Representation to Social Drama*, edited by Marcia Kupfer, 23–52. University Park: Pennsylvania State University Press.

Massip, Jesús-Francesc. 1987. "Les primeres dramatitzacions de la Passió en llengua catalana." *D'Art* 13: 253–268.

Matthaeis, Nicoletta de. 2018. "Las santas imágenes aquerópitas (2) La Verónica: ¿pero cuántas hay?—(segunda parte) 'La Santa Faz' y el 'Santo Rostro.'" reliquiosamente.com /2018/08/26/las-santas-imagenes-aqueropitas-2-la-veronica-pero-cuantas-hay-segunda -parte-la-santa-faz-y-el-santo-rostro. Accessed March 20, 2020.

Mauleón Rodríguez, Gustavo. 1995. *Música en el Virreinato de la Nueva España (Recopiliación y notas, siglos XVI y XVII)*. Puebla, Mexico: Universidad Iberamericano Golfo Central.

Máynez, Pilar. 2004. "Un texto en náhuatl sobre la pasión de Cristo." *Estudios de cultura náhuatl* 35: 261–270.

McNamer, Sarah. 2009. "The Origins of the *Meditationes vitae Christi*." *Speculum* 84 (4): 905–955.

McNamer, Sarah. 2010. *Affective Meditation and the Invention of Medieval Compassion*. Philadelphia: University of Pennsylvania Press.

McNamer, Sarah, ed. and trans. 2018. *Meditations on the Life of Christ: The Short Italian Text*. Notre Dame, IN: University of Notre Dame Press.

Mendieta, Gerónimo de. 1980. *Historia eclesiástica indiana*. Edited by Joaquín García Icazbalceta. Mexico City: Editorial Porrúa.

Molina, Alonso de. 1678. *Doctrina christiana, y cathecismo, en lengua mexicana*. Mexico City: Viuda de Bernardo Calderón.

Molina, Alonso de. 1992. *Vocabulario en lengua castellana y mexicana y mexicana y castellana*. Facsimile of 1571 edition. Edited by Miguel León-Portilla. Mexico City: Editorial Porrúa.

Molina, Juan de, ed. and trans. 1536. *Gamaliel: Nuevamente traducido en lengua castellano*. Seville: Dominico de Robertis.

Mosquera, Daniel O. 2005. "Consecrated Transactions: Of Marketplaces, Passion Plays, and Other Nahua-Christian Devotions." *Journal of Latin American Cultural Studies* 14: 171–193.

Motolinia (Toribio de Benavente). 1979. *Historia de los indios de la Nueva España*. Edited by Edmundo O'Gorman. Mexico City: Editorial Porrúa.

Mundy, Barbara E. 2020. "The Emergence of Alphabetic Writing: Tlahcuiloh and Escribano in Sixteenth-Century Mexico." *The Americas* 77 (3): 361–407.

Muñoz Camargo, Diego. 1966. *Historia de Tlaxcala*. Edited by Alfredo Chavero. Facsimile of 1892 edition. Edited by Edmundo Aviña Levy. Mexico City: Secretaria de Fomento.

Nash, June. 1968. "The Passion Play in Maya Indian Communities." *Comparative Studies in Society and History* 10 (3): 318–327.

Navarro, Juan. 1604. *Liber in quo quatuor passiones Christi Domini continentur: octo Lamentationes, oratioq, Hieremie Prophete*. Mexico City: Diego López Dávalos.

Olko, Justyna. 2014. *Insignia of Rank in the Nahua World: From the Fifteenth to the Seventeenth Century*. Boulder: University Press of Colorado.

Olko, Justyna. 2017. "The Nahua Story of Judas: Indigenous Agency and Loci of Meaning." In *Words and Worlds Turned Around: Indigenous Christianities in Colonial Latin America*, ed. David Tavárez, 151–171. Boulder: University Press of Colorado.

Olko, Justyna, and Julia Madajczak. 2019. "An Animating Principle in Confrontation with Christianity? De(re)constructing the Nahua 'Soul.'" *Ancient Mesoamerca* 30 (1): 75–88.

Olko, Justyna, and John Sullivan. 2014. "Toward a Comprehensive Model for Nahuatl Language Research and Revitalization." *Proceedings of the Annual Meeting of the Berkeley Linguistics Society* 40: 369–397.

Osowski, Edward. 2008. "Passion Miracles and Indigenous Historical Memory in New Spain." *Hispanic American Historical Review* 88 (4): 607–638.

Osowski, Edward. 2010. *Indigenous Miracles: Nahua Authority in Colonial Mexico*. Tucson: University of Arizona Press.

Pardo, Osvaldo. 2006. "How to Punish Indians: Law and Cultural Change in Early Colonial Mexico." *Comparative Studies in Society and History* 48 (1): 79–109.

Paredes, Ignacio de. 1758. *Catecismo mexicano*. Mexico City: Bibliotheca Mexicana.

Pasión en lengua mexicana. n.d. Manuscript in the Latin American Library, 497.2100, P282, Tulane University, New Orleans, LA.

Paso y Troncoso, Francisco del. 1902. "La comedia de los Reyes." In *Biblioteca Náuatl*, vol. I. Florence: Salvador Landi.

"Passio domini nr̄i Jesu Christi." 1617. In *Sermones y ejemplos*, 323–353. MS. 1480, Biblioteca Nacional de México, Mexico City, Fondo Reservado.

Patch, Robert W. 2002. *Maya Revolt and Revolution in the Eighteenth Century*. Armonk, NY: M. E. Sharpe.

Peck, George T. 1980. *The Fool of God: Jacopone da Todi*. Tuscaloosa: University of Alabama Press.

Pérez de Ribas, Andrés. 1645. *Historia de los triumphos de nuestra santa fee . . . conseguidos por los soldados de la milicia de la Compañia de Iesus*. Madrid: Alonso de Paredes.

Pérez-Prieto, Miguel Ángel, ed. 1997. *Teatro medieval*, vol. 2: *Castilla*. Barcelona: Crítica.

Pietsch, Karl, ed. 1924. *Spanish Grail Fragments: El libro de Josep Abarimatia, La estoria de Merlin, Lançarote*, vol 1: *Texts*. Chicago: University of Chicago Press.

Pizzigoni, Caterina. 2003. "Amid Idealisation and Practice: Archbishops, Local Clergy, and Nahuas in the Toluca Valley, 1712–1765." *Swedish Missiological Themes* 91 (2): 249–273.

Pizzigoni, Caterina. 2012. *The Life Within: Local Indigenous Society in the Toluca Valley, 1650–1800*. Stanford, CA: Stanford University Press.

Pizzigoni, Caterina, and Camilla Townsend. 2021. *Indigenous Life after the Conquest: The de la Cruz Family Papers of Colonial Mexico*. University Park: Pennsylvania State University Press.

Procesos de indios idólatras y hechiceros. 1912. Publicaciones del Archivo General de la Nación, vol. 3. Mexico City: Guerrero Hermanos.

Psalterium Ant[i]phonarium Sanctorale, cum Psalmis et Hymnis. 1584. Mexico City: Pedro Ocharte.

Ramos Smith, Maya, Tito Vasconcelos, Luis Armando Lamadrid, and Xabier Lizárraga Cruchaga, eds. 1998. *Censura y teatro novohispano (1539–1822): Ensayos y antología de documentos.* Mexico City: Consejo Nacional para la Cultura y las Artes, Instituto Nacional de Bellas Artes, Centro Nacional de Investigación e Información Teatral Rodolfo Usigli, and Escenología, AC.

Read, Kay Almere. 2005. "Productive Tears: Weeping Speech, Water, and the Underworld in the Mexica Tradition." In *Holy Tears: Weeping in the Religious Imagination,* ed. Kimberley Christine Patton and John Stratton Hawley, 5–66. Princeton, NJ: Princeton University Press.

Restall, Matthew. 2018. *When Montezuma Met Cortés: The True Story of the Meeting That Changed History.* New York: HarperCollins.

Reyes García, Luis. 1960. *Pasión y muerte del cristo sol (carnaval y cuaresma en Ichcatepec).* Xalapa, Mexico: Universidad Veracruzana.

Reyes García, Luis, trans. and ed. 2001. *¿Cómo te confundes? ¿Acaso no somos conquistados? Anales de Juan Bautista.* Mexico City: Centro de Investigaciones y Estudios Superiores en Antropología Social and Biblioteca Lorenzo Boturini, Insigne y Nacional Basílica de Guadalupe.

Reyes-Valerio, Constantino. 1960. *Tepalcingo.* Mexico City: Instituto Nacional de Antropología e Historia.

Reyes-Valerio, Constantino. 1989. *El pintor de conventos: Los murales del siglo XVI en la Nueva España.* Mexico City: Instituto Nacional de Antropología e Historia.

Richie, Annette McLeod. 2011. "Confraternity and Community: Negotiating Ethnicity, Gender, and Place in Colonial Tecamachalco, Mexico." PhD dissertation, Department of Anthropology, University at Albany, State University of New York.

Robinson, Cynthia. 2013. *Imagining the Passion in a Multiconfessional Castile: The Virgin, Christ, Devotions, and Images in the Fourteenth and Fifteenth Centuries.* University Park: Pennsylvania State University Press.

Romeu i Figueras, Josep. 1967. "Els textos dramatics sobre el davallement de la creu a Catalunya, i el fragment inédit d'Ulldecona." *Estudis romànics* 11: 103–132.

Rosner, Ferdinand. 1974. *Passio Nova: Das Oberammergauer Passionsspiel von 1750.* Edited by P. Stephan Schaller. Bern: Herbert Lang.

Roten, Johann G. n.d. "Holy Kindred." In *All about Mary.* udayton.edu/imri/mary/h/holy -kindred.php. Accessed March 19, 2020.

Roy, Emile. 1904. "Le mystère de la Passion en France du XIVe au XVIe siècle." *Revue Bourguignonne* 14 (3–4).

Rubin, Miri. 2008. "The Passion of Mary: The Virgin and the Jews in Medieval Culture." In *The Passion Story: From Visual Representation to Social Drama*, edited by Marcia Kupfer, 53–66. University Park: Pennsylvania State University Press.

Rubin, Miri. 2009. *Mother of God: A History of the Virgin Mary*. New Haven, CT: Yale University Press.

Rus, Jan. 1983. "Whose Caste War? Indians, Ladinos, and the 'Caste War' of 1869." In *Spaniards and Indians in Southeastern Mesoamerica: Essays on the History of Ethnic Relations*, ed. Murdo Macleod and Robert Wasserstrom, 127–168. Lincoln: University of Nebraska Press.

Sahagún, Bernardino de. 1583. *Psalmodia christiana, y sermonario de los sanctos del año*. Mexico City: Pedro Ocharte.

Sahagún, Bernardino de. 1950–1982. *Florentine Codex, General History of the Things of New Spain*. Edited and translated by Charles E. Dibble and Arthur J. O. Anderson. 12 vols. Santa Fe, NM, and Salt Lake City: School of American Research and University of Utah Press.

Sahagún, Bernardino de. 1986. *Coloquios y doctrina cristiana*. Edited and translated by Miguel León-Portilla. Mexico City: Universidad Nacional Autónoma de México and Fundación de Investigaciones Sociales.

Salazar, Adolfo. 1951. "Sobre algunos instrumentos de música mencionados por Cervantes." *Nueva revista de filología hispánica* 5 (1): 71–77.

Sánchez Aguilera, Mario. 2015. "En torno a las voces y los conceptos de la muerte ritual en cuatro manuscritos nahuas sobre la Pasión de Cristo." *Estudios de cultura náhuatl* 50: 261–295.

Santamaría, Francisco J. 1959. *Diccionario de mejicanismos*. Mexico City: Editorial Porrúa.

Santos Otero, Aurelio de. 1956. *Los evangelios apócrifos*. Madrid: La Editorial Católica.

Schechner, Richard. 1985. *Between Theater and Anthropology*. Foreword by Victor Turner. Philadelphia: University of Pennsylvania Press.

Schwaller, John Frederick. 2017. "Fr. Agustín de Vetancurt: The 'Via Crucis en Mexicano.'" *The Americas* 14 (2): 119–137.

Schwaller, John Frederick. 2021. *The Stations of the Cross in Colonial Mexico: The Via crucis en mexicano of Fray Augustin de Vetancurt*. Norman, OK, and Berkeley, CA: University of Oklahoma Press and Academy of American Franciscan History.

Scott, James D. 1990. *Domination and the Arts of Resistance: Hidden Transcripts*. New Haven, CT: Yale University Press.

Sell, Barry D., trans. and ed. 2002. *Nahua Confraternities in Early Colonial Mexico: The 1552 Nahuatl Ordinances of Fray Alonso de Molina, OFM*. Berkeley: Academy of American Franciscan History.

Sell, Barry D., and Louise M. Burkhart, eds. 2004. *Nahuatl Theater*, Volume 1: *Death and Life in Colonial Nahua Mexico*. Norman: University of Oklahoma Press.

Sell, Barry D., and Louise M. Burkhart, eds. 2009. *Nahuatl Theater*, Volume 4: *Nahua Christianity in Performance*. Norman: University of Oklahoma Press.

Sell, Barry D., Louise M. Burkhart, and Stafford Poole, trans. and eds. 2006. *Nahuatl Theater*, Volume 2: *Our Lady of Guadalupe*. Norman: University of Oklahoma Press.

Sell, Barry D., Louise M. Burkhart, and Elizabeth R. Wright, eds. 2008. *Nahuatl Theater*, Volume 3: *Spanish Golden Age Drama in Mexican Translation*. Norman: University of Oklahoma Press.

Sell, Barry D., and Susan Kellogg. 1997. "We Want to Give Them Laws: Royal Ordinances in a Mid-Sixteenth-Century Nahuatl Text." *Estudios de cultura náhuatl* 27: 325–367.

Sermones en mexicano. n.d. Biblioteca Nacional de México, Mexico City, Fondo Reservado, MS. 1482.

Shergold, N. D. 1967. *A History of the Spanish Stage: From Medieval Times until the End of the Seventeenth Century*. New York: Oxford University Press.

Silva Cruz, Ignacio. 2001. "De cómo el nieto desobedeció a su abuelo y por ello fue arrastrado al infierno." *Boletín del Archivo General de la Nación, Nueva Época* 1: 9–40.

Sousa, Lisa. 2017. *The Woman Who Turned into a Jaguar, and Other Narratives of Native Women in Archives of Colonial Mexico*. Stanford, CA: Stanford University Press.

Sousa, Lisa, Stafford Poole, C.M., and James Lockhart, trans. and eds. 1998. *The Story of Guadalupe: Luis Laso de la Vega's* Huey tlamahuiçoltica *of 1649*. UCLA Nahuatl Studies Series no. 5. Stanford and Los Angeles: Stanford University Press and UCLA Latin American Center Publications.

Stern, Charlotte. 1996. *The Medieval Theater in Castile*. Binghamton: Center for Medieval and Early Renaissance Studies, State University of New York at Binghamton.

Stevenson, Robert. 1964. "European Music in 16th-Century Guatemala." *Musical Quarterly* 50 (3): 341–352.

Sticca, Sandro. 1970. *The Latin Passion Play: Its Origins and Development*. Albany: State University of New York Press.

Stoler, Ann Laura. 2010. *Along the Archival Grain: Epistemic Anxieties and Colonial Common Sense*. Princeton, NJ: Princeton University Press.

Surtz, Ronald E. 1992. *Teatro castellano de la edad media*. Madrid: Taurus.

Sutcliffe, Edmund F. 1949. "An Apocryphal Form of Pilate's Verdict." *Catholic Biblical Quarterly* 9 (4): 436–441.

Taggart, James M. 1983. *Nahuat Myth and Social Structure*. Austin: University of Texas Press.

Taggart, James M. 1997. *The Bear and His Sons: Masculinity in Spanish and Mexican Folktales*. Austin: University of Texas Press.

Taggart, James M., and Alan R. Sandstrom. 2011. "Commentary: The Nahua Father and the Legacy of Oscar Lewis." *Nahua Newsletter* 50: 16–29.

Tavárez, David. 2011. *The Invisible War: Indigenous Devotions, Discipline, and Dissent in Colonial Mexico*. Stanford, CA: Stanford University Press.

Tavárez, David. 2013. "Nahua Intellectuals, Franciscan Scholars, and the 'Devotio Moderna' in Colonial Mexico." *The Americas* 70 (2): 203–235.

Taylor, William B. 1979. *Drinking, Homicide, and Rebellion in Colonial Mexican Villages*. Stanford, CA: Stanford University Press.

Taylor, William B. 1987. "The Virgin of Guadalupe in New Spain: An Inquiry into the Social History of Marian Devotion." *American Ethnologist* 14 (1): 9–33.

Taylor, William B. 1996. *Magistrates of the Sacred: Priests and Parishioners in Eighteenth-Century Mexico*. Stanford, CA: Stanford University Press.

Taylor, William B. 2005. "Two Shrines of the Cristo Renovado: Religion and Peasant Politics in Late Colonial Mexico." *American Historical Review* 110 (4): 945–974.

Taylor, William B. 2010. *Shrines and Miraculous Images: Religious Life in Mexico before the Reforma*. Albuquerque: University of New Mexico Press.

Taylor, William B. 2016. *Theater of a Thousand Wonders: A History of Miraculous Images and Shrines in New Spain*. New York: Cambridge University Press.

Tedlock, Dennis. 1993. "Torture in the Archives: Mayans Meet Europeans." *American Anthropologist* 95 (1): 139–152.

Torroja Menéndez, Carmen, and María Rivas Palá. 1977. *Teatro en Toledo en el siglo XV: "Auto de la Pasión" de Alonso del Campo*. Madrid: Anejos del Boletín de la Real Academia Española.

Tovar, Juan de. n.d. *Historia de la benida de los yndios*. Manuscript at the John Carter Brown Library, Brown University, Providence, RI. World Digital Library, wdl.org/en/item/6759. Accessed May 19, 2021.

Trexler, Richard C. 2003. *Reliving Golgotha: The Passion Play of Iztapalapa*. Cambridge, MA: Harvard University Press.

Trigg, Heather. 2004. "Food Choice and Social Identity in Early Colonial New Mexico." *Journal of the Southwest* 46 (2): 223–252.

Trinidad Basurto, J. 1901. *El arzobispado de México*. Mexico City: El Tiempo.

Truitt, Jonathan. 2018. *Sustaining the Divine in Mexico Tenochtitlan: Nahuas and Catholicism 1523–1700*. Norman: University of Oklahoma Press.

Valero Moreno, Juan Miguel. 2003. "La Pasión según Lucas Fernández." *La corónica: A Journal of Medieval Hispanic Languages, Literatures, and Cultures* 31 (2): 177–216.

Vargas, Melchor de. 1576. *Doctrina christiana muy vtil, y necessara en Castellano, Mexicano y Otomi*. Mexico City: Pedro Balli.

Vetancurt, Agustín de. 1971. *Teatro mexicano, Crónica de la Provincia del Santo Evangelio de México, Menologio francisano*. Facsimile of 1698 edition. Mexico City: Editorial Porrúa.

Villadiego Vascuñana y Montoya, Alonso. 1766. *Instrucción política y practica judicial conforme al estilo de los consejos, audiencias, y tribunales de corte, y otros ordinarios del reyno*. Madrid: Antonio Marín.

Villella, Peter. 2012. "Indian Lords, Hispanic Gentlemen: The Salazars of Colonial Tlaxcala." *The Americas* 69 (1): 1–36.

Viquiera Albán, Juan Pedro. 1999. *Propriety and Permissiveness in Bourbon Mexico*. Translated by Sonya Lipsett-Rivera and Sergio Rivera Ayala. Wilmington, DE: Scholarly Resources, Inc.

Vizenor, Gerald. 2008. "Aesthetics of Survivance." In *Survivance: Narratives of Native Presence*, ed. Gerald Vizenor, 1–23. Lincoln: University of Nebraska Press.

Warner, Marina. 1976. *Alone of All Her Sex: The Myth and the Cult of the Virgin Mary*. New York: Alfred A. Knopf.

Webster, Susan Verdi. 1997a. "Art, Ritual, and Confraternities in Sixteenth-Century New Spain: Penitential Imagery at the Monastery of San Miguel, Huejotzingo." *Anales del Instituto de Investigaciones Estéticas* 19 (70): 5–43.

Webster, Susan Verdi. 1997b. "The Descent from the Cross in Sixteenth-Century New Spain." *Early Drama, Art, and Music Review* 19 (2): 69–85.

Webster, Susan Verdi. 1998. *Art and Ritual in Golden-Age Spain: Sevillian Confraternities and the Processional Sculpture of Holy Week*. Princeton, NJ: Princeton University Press.

Wilson, Ian. 1991. *Holy Faces, Secret Places*. New York: Doubleday.

Yepes, Rodrigo de. 1583. *Tractado y descripcion breue y cõpendiosa dela tierra sancta de Palestina*. Madrid: Juan Yñiguez de Lequerica.

Index

Page numbers followed by *f* indicate figures. Page numbers followed by *n* indicate endnotes.

Calderón de la Barca, Pedro, 75

Calvary: 43*f*; staging of, 54, 66, 169–70; women at, 103–6, 111. *See also* crucifixion

Camacho Villavicencio, fray Miguel: criticizes expense of plays, 66, 84; on drunkenness of actors, 29, 184; on laughter at plays, 30; sees plays as acceptable in past but no longer, 34, 182; on reverence for Christ actor, bread, and blood, 29, 45, 113; on women as actors, 29, 45

Campbell, R. Joe, 6

Campo, Alonso de. *See* Toledo, Passion play from

Cana, 147

Cantares mexicanos, 24

Carnival, 34, 158

Carochi, Horacio, 25

Carrillo y Gariel, Abelardo, 25

catechism: Michael in, 67; Passion in, 40, 45, 60, 182; pictorial, 40, 161*f*, 168*f*, 270*n45*, 270*n47*, 273*n18*, 278*n31*; set to music, 74; teaching of, 39, 162, 180

Cauli, Giovanni da, 85–86

cemeteries: confraternity events in, 13; Passion plays performed in, 12–13, 46, 51, 82, 182–83

censorship, 5, 26, 136

centurion: in Atlihuetzia document, 47; in contemporary festivals, 158; in death warrant, 64, 157; in Holy Week processions, 156; in Matthew, 174; as play character, 60, 105, 115, 117, 156, 173, 176

Cervantes, Miguel de, 75

Cervera, Passion play from: Christ's last words in, 275*n41*; dating of, 22; death sentence in, 62, 63; Gamaliel in, 123; lacks Last Supper scene, 120; Reuben in, 71; Veronica in, 108

Chalco, 4, 33, 48

chalice, 67–68, 70, 127

Chalma, 271*n52*, 271*n61*

Chamula, 158, 284*n23*, 286*n45*

Chapa de Mota, 13

Chapultepec, 149

Charles V, Emperor, 106

children, in plays, 52, 79, 81

Chimalpahin Quauhtlehuanitzin, don Domingo de San Antón Muñon: on alleged uprising by Black people, 31; on autos-da-fé, 36; on destruction of Jerusalem, 37; on early Passion play, 23; on Franciscan mission to New Mexico: 74; on processions, 27, 31, 269*n23*

Chimalpopoca, 149

choirmasters, 13, 45, 76–86, 181

Christensen, Mark Z., 25–27, 138, 268*n6*

Christenson, Allen J., 171–72

Christian, William A., 36

Cipac, don Luis Santa María, 149, 283*n5*

Clendinnen, Inga, 180

cloaks (*tilmahtli*): donkey saddled with, 65; Caiaphas tears his, 151; Christ dressed in, 71, 138, 167; Christ's shroud as, 114; gender of, 278*n31*; Pilate wears Christ's, 172; Veronica's veil as, 109–11. *See also* costumes

Codex Mendoza, 98, 149

Colloquios y doctrina christiana, 67

Colloquy of How the Fortunate Saint Helen Found the Precious and Revered Wooden Cross (Nahuatl play), 75, 81, 84, 156, 172, 283*n13*

column, 68, 87, 159, 160, 161*f*, 163–64

Commandments, Ten, 40

communion, 23, 121, 129, 130–31, 280*n23*

compassion, 19, 71, 95, 102, 110, 116, 138; in European devotions, 86; Nahua concept of, 90–91

confession, 40, 67, 153, 154, 162

confraternities: donations to, 183; in Huejotzingo murals, 27, 108, 160; of Jesús Nazareno, 41; majordomos in, 72; meet in cemeteries, 13; in Seville, 27; sponsor plays, 23, 182; women in, 45

Conquest of Jerusalem, The (Tlaxcalan performance), 66–67

consecration, of bread and wine, 9, 127–28, 131. *See also* communion; host

Constantine, Emperor, 75, 81, 105

conversos, 35, 36

Corpus Christi, 79, 132

costumes, 20, 43–44, 156, 179; of Christ, 71, 138, 159, 164–65, 167, 172; of Gamaliel, 65–66; of Magdalene, 184. *See also* cloaks

Coyoacan, 23

cross: Christ falls with, 73; Christ removed from, 115, 116*f*; Christ's words on, 78; in early colonial art, 41, 42*f*, 43*f*; in crucifixion enactment, 169, 170, 172; investiture with, 159; miraculous, in Tlayacapan, 48; as play prop, 67–68, 69, 87, 96; recovered by Helen, in Nahuatl play, 172; in rosary, 40–41; Spanish and Nahuatl terms for, 17; in Stations of the Cross, 28. *See also* crucifix; crucifixion

www.ingramcontent.com/pod-product-compliance
Lightning Source LLC
Chambersburg PA
CBHW070610030426
42337CB00020B/3742